THE ARMY AFTER NEXT

THE ARMY AFTER NEXT

The First Postindustrial Army

Thomas K. Adams

PRAEGER SECURITY INTERNATIONAL

Westport, Connecticut · London

Library of Congress Cataloging-in-Publication Data

Adams, Thomas K.
    The Army after next : the first postindustrial army / Thomas K. Adams.
p. cm.
    Includes bibliographical references and index.
    ISBN 0–275–98107–X (alk. paper)
1. United States. Army—Reorganization—History—21st century. 2. United States. Army—
Reorganization—History—20th century. 3. United States—Military policy. 4. Military doctrine—
United States—History—20th century. 5. Military doctrine—United States—History—21st century. I.
Title.
UA25.A67 2006
355.30973—dc22   2006021062

British Library Cataloguing in Publication Data is available.

Library of Congress Catalog Card Number: 2006021062
ISBN: 0–275–98107–X

First published in 2006

Praeger Security International, 88 Post Road West, Westport, CT 06881
An imprint of Greenwood Publishing Group, Inc.
www.praeger.com

Printed in the United States of America

The paper used in this book complies with the
Permanent Paper Standard issued by the National
Information Standards Organization (Z39.48-1984).

10 9 8 7 6 5 4 3 2 1

CONTENTS

It will be enough for me, however, if these words of mine are judged useful by those who want to understand clearly the events that happened in the past and which, human nature being what it is, will at some time or other and in much the same ways, be repeated in the future.

—Thucydides, *History of the Peloponnesian War*

CHAPTER 1

INTRODUCTION

The Army has no wish to scrap its previous experience in favor of unproven doctrine, or in order to accommodate enthusiastic theorists having little or no responsibility for the consequences of following the courses of action they advocate. While the Army is adapting itself readily to the employment of new weapons and new techniques, nothing currently available or foreseeable in war reduces the essentiality of mobile, powerful ground forces, the only forces which can seize the enemy's land and the people living thereon, and exercise control of both thereafter.[1]
—General Matthew B. Ridgeway, Chief of Staff, Army, June 27, 1955

In that admirably concise statement, General Ridgeway captured the enduring attitude of the U.S. Army toward change, technology, and the service's role in the national defense. The most important element is probably the last phrase of the last sentence. The Army has always seen itself as the decisive warfighting component because only the Army can seize and hold ground and thereby control its inhabitants. Other services are valuable adjuncts, but without the Army their efforts are at best transient and temporary.[2]

This set of beliefs was seriously challenged during the later part of the twentieth and early part of the twenty-first centuries. Military theorists and others began to believe that new technologies were generating a "revolution in military affairs" (RMA). Everyone agreed that RMA capabilities have profound implications, but there was little consensus on their exact nature, interrelationship, or ultimate outcome. Nevertheless, by the late 1990s RMA concepts had become the central element in the U.S. armed forces' vision of future warfare. Along with the related notions of netwar, cyberwar and information war, it set the terms for discussing future warfare and military requirements.[3]

At the same time, it was believed that the United States was in a "strategic pause," a decade or more when no serious enemies or large-scale conflicts were expected. It was an ideal time to reduce conventional forces in favor of experiments to "leap ahead" with RMA technologies.

In theory, the RMA's new technologies combined with new doctrine and organization could be employed to shock and stun an adversary with precision air power in such a way that its will and capability were shattered without the need for large-scale ground combat. Beginning in 2001, President George W. Bush and his Secretary of Defense Donald H. Rumsfeld set out to transform the U.S. armed forces by adopting RMA concepts and capabilities. President Bush promised to "redefine war on our terms" and "to move beyond marginal improvements—to replace existing programs with new technologies and strategies. To use this window of opportunity to skip a generation of technology."[4] This was to be accomplished through a set of programs collectively referred to as military transformation or just "transformation."

Military transformation was officially defined as "the set of activities by which DOD [Department of Defense] attempts to harness the revolution in military affairs to make fundamental changes in technology, operational concepts and doctrine, and organizational structure."[5] For Rumsfeld and those around him this meant a truly integrated joint force led by air power and leaving the Army with a distinctly lesser role.

> The basic notion behind military transformation is that information technologies allow you to substitute information for mass. If you buy into that, the whole force structure changes. But the vision of all this is totally dependent on information technologies and the network. If that part of the equation breaks down, what you have are small, less capable battle platforms that are more vulnerable.[6]

In other words, it was a wonderful idea if it worked and a disaster if it did not.

All of this works to the advantage of the U.S. Air Force (USAF), the Army's principal competitor for the central position in American military strategy. According to David Ochmanek of the RAND Corporation, a strident air power advocate, "The division of labor between ground and air has shifted." Because of advanced warplanes and precision bombing, "the enemy's army should be largely destroyed before we get on the ground."[7] As the world's leading exponent of the high-tech approach, the USAF was quick to embrace transformation as key to the dominance of air power. Under the slogan "Global Power, Global Reach," airmen argued that worldwide responsiveness and firepower are best provided by aircraft.[8]

The beguiling vision of quick, precise, and relatively bloodless war from the air has been greatly appealing to politicians. Unlike the slow litany of deaths from Iraq, air power promises to deliver destructive power from a safe distance with missiles or bombs. Rather than a series of bloody tactical battles, it offers to strike directly at the political and military centers of enemy power.[9] Since the First World War, air forces have chafed at the use of their resources to support land and sea forces. Now they can almost see their dream coming true. Billy Mitchell and Giulio Douhet's heady vision of air armadas supplanting old-fashioned land and sea forces seems almost within reach.

While candidate Bush was promising to redefine war, the U.S. Army was already in its own Army Transformation program and had been since 1999. It was a massive, costly effort to reinvent itself. Instead of ponderous armored formations with hundreds of thousands of soldiers supported by tens of thousands of vehicles, its units would become much smaller and deadlier, light and agile, capable of rapid deployment across intercontinental distances. This book is a narrative account of Army Transformation, the attempt to create a postindustrial army, the greatest change in American military structure since the Civil War.

The highlight of the RMA was information processing, so the core capability of Army Transformation was to be a network of automated information systems— computer. Land forces would fight as "networked systems" and "distributed formations." In this new warfare formations would be flexible—battlefields fluid and ill-defined. Using newly developed sensors and a dense computer-enabled communications network, the new kind of army would understand all the relevant information about the battlefield. Its units would have a "common operational picture," a complete near real-time picture of the friendly and enemy situation. It would find and avoid enemy formations while destroying them from a distance with high-precision artillery.[10]

The short-term exemplar for these changes was the Stryker armored vehicle fielded in 2003, an attempt to replace heavy, tracked armored vehicles with a single class of multivariant ones. Stryker and its variants were to spearhead the movement from an Army organized around the tank and the armored personnel carrier to one that uses fast, light wheeled vehicles, replacing armor with new technology that provides protection through advanced materials and better information. The end product of this high-tech approach would be a radically reorganized force based on a highly speculative Future Combat System, usually referred to simply as FCS. The organization that FCS enabled is called the Future Force.[11]

As originally conceived and endlessly briefed, the Future Force program was an incredibly ambitious effort to replace 70 ton M1 tanks and 35 ton Bradley fighting vehicles with the Future Combat System, an amalgam of about 18 separate high-tech elements. The Future Force would be mounted on 15 to 18 ton vehicles that could perform all the functions of the M1, the Bradley, and conventional artillery with greater lethality and no loss of survivability. As planned, the Future Force would be organized for rapid deployment, the ability to drop a brigade anywhere in the world, fully supplied and ready to fight, in 36 hours followed by the full division (2 more brigades, plus) within five days. Five more divisions would arrive within 30 days.[12] It was remarkable ambition, and nobody had any real idea how to do it.

Like most large, successful institutions, the U.S. Army does not welcome change, especially not radical change; but transformation of some kind is inevitable—the Army will transform whether it wants to or not. There is no choice, given the pressure of new technologies, new enemies, and political realities. However, inevitability does not imply simplicity, nor does it guarantee that correct choices will be made.

There is no easy path to radical change. The collision between ambition and reality has produced results quite different from the ones envisioned.

Events were further complicated by the fact that Army Transformation takes place within the larger vision endorsed by President Bush and championed by Defense Secretary Rumsfeld. There is a collision between visions. The Army still regarded itself as the central element in a transformed defense establishment, supported by the other services. As interpreted by Army officers, the Defense Department leadership saw the Army primarily as a bill payer, to be stripped in order to free up funds for transition initiatives that would primarily benefit the Navy and the Air Force.

But suddenly the decade of relative peace evaporated in the Al-Qaeda terrorist attacks of September 11, 2001. The American sanctuary was breached, and its armed forces no longer had the luxury of a "strategic pause" to absorb RMA concepts and technologies.[13]

The Bush administration responded with a national grand strategy to attack terrorism around the world while undermining and eliminating the regimes, principally in the Middle East, that allowed or supported terrorist organizations. It was at heart a scheme for political reformation, the creation of democracies where none had existed. But much of the method was to be military. Transformation would allow America's great but still finite military structure to take on indefinite, globe-girdling responsibilities.

The defeat of the Taliban in Afghanistan was widely hailed as a successful example of transformed warfare: a relatively small number of elite Army Special Forces and CIA operators working with local forces to guide air delivered precision munitions against the enemy. But for the airmen, the key lesson was the use of air power.[14]

The spring and summer of 2003 brought a serious bump in the road to the Future Force. The spectacular early success of the Iraq War turned into a grinding occupation that lasted much longer than transformation optimists had predicted. In Afghanistan the Taliban refused to accept defeat and go away. Instead, they pursued a persistent low-level guerrilla war. In order to accommodate these unforeseen realities, the service created the so-called Modular Army, a plan to stretch the overcommitted force by reorganizing as brigade-based task forces rather than conventional divisions. These "Units of Action" would fight the war while the service continued toward the Future Force.[15]

Far-reaching change creates new opportunities and often exacerbates existing frictions. Despite the Department of Defense (DoD) emphasis on "jointness" and interservice cooperation, the push for transformation has done nothing to quell old rivalries. President Bush and Secretary Rumsfeld focused on air forces, delivering precision guided munitions (e.g., "smart bombs") on targets developed through automated systems and applications of information technology. The mainstay of the ground forces—sustained, heavy armored combat with tanks, artillery and the like—was dismissed as "old think."[16]

But events seemed to support the Army view in the wake of the Iraq War. A basically conventional but "information enabled" armored U.S. ground force convincingly trounced a much larger (poorly led, poorly equipped) army and captured the country's capital in the astonishing time of 21 days. The immediate postwar period was even more salient for the ground forces. The drawn-out struggle toward reconstruction had still less dependence on USAF-style air power and was chiefly an affair of small units and patrols, depending heavily on armored vehicles, including the Stryker, often supported by armed helicopters. The war in Afghanistan was conducted by old-fashioned infantry. Air power was a big help, but no solution.

It was frustrating to Army leaders when Pentagon analysts trumpeted the war as a victory for the new information-enabled way of fighting while diminishing the indispensable role played by heavy armored forces and downplaying the number of soldiers required. Under the urging of Secretary Rumsfeld, the conflicts in Afghanistan and Iraq were touted as demonstrations of transformation—light, agile, "networked" military operations with a premium on technology and a minimum number of personnel on the ground.[17]

The Air Force believes Afghanistan (and to a lesser degree Iraq) prove that air power can provide a quicker, cleaner, and cheaper victory with fewer casualties than ground forces.[18] Furthermore, it is argued, wars of sustained high-intensity ground combat (the Army's specialty) do not happen any more. Indeed, one of the promises of the RMA was that there would be no more sustained war. The extended "postwar" fighting in both Afghanistan and Iraq show what happens when the enemy does not agree with this assessment.

Ground warfare advocates point to these as the kind of unsatisfactory outcomes to be expected in "air centric" warfare.[19] In this view air power was unarguably important, but "obsolete" industrial age infantry and armored formations carried the brunt of the battle. Then insurgents insisted on prolonging the fight. Afghanistan and Iraq demonstrated the effectiveness of the new technologies on the ground and in the air, but warfare is not primarily a technology demonstration. The philosophy of transformation sees warfare as a purely military business. The objective is to attack and destroy military forces and their command and control arrangements. As described by Fredrick W. Kagan:

> The advocates of a "new American way of war," Secretary of Defense Donald Rumsfeld and President Bush chief among them, have attempted to simplify war into a targeting drill. They see the enemy as a target set and believe that when all or most of the targets have been hit, he will inevitably surrender and American goals will be achieved.[20]

But war is a matter of will, not merely capability.

Asymmetric Warfare

Predictions are hard to make, especially about the future.

—Yogi Berra

The opposite set of beliefs about future warfare is often capsulated as the "asymmetric approach," closely related to the ideas of unconventional warfare (although that term has a different meaning in U.S. doctrine), terrorism, and insurgency. Sometimes referred to as the *counterrevolution* in military affairs, its central concept is that Western (especially American) methods of warfare can be sidestepped often enough to blunt their potency. In short, this approach concerns "all forms of conflict where the other side refuses to stand up and fight fair."[21] Except for the campaigns against Iraq in 1990–1991 and 2003, the U.S. military has not been involved in conventional war since Korea. The attempt to force conventional warfare on an unwilling enemy in Afghanistan and Iraq illustrates the difference.

Groups using the asymmetric approach are seldom organized as regular military forces. Too often, they function outside any nation's control, operate across national boundaries, lack rigid structures, and employ methods of stealth to attack nonmilitary "soft" targets. Terrorists are the best-known practitioners of this form of warfare. An obvious example is the loosely confederated Al-Qaeda network led by Usama bin Laden.[22] The insurgents in Iraq are another too well-known example.

According to military analyst William Lind,

> The more successful terrorists appear to operate on broad mission orders that carry down to the level of the individual terrorist. The "battlefield" is highly dispersed and includes the whole of the enemy's society. The terrorist lives almost completely off the land and the enemy. Terrorism is very much a matter of maneuver: The terrorist's firepower is small, and where and when he applies it is critical.[23]

Worse yet, these conflicts seem to occur in out-of-the-way places like Afghanistan, Somalia, Rwanda, East Timor, Haiti, and Kosovo, often with little direct bearing on the national interests of the United States. This makes them difficult to reach, objectives are often unclear, operations there are confusing, and they produce mostly ambiguous outcomes. For adherents of the asymmetric approach, all the attention and funding granted to high-tech, military technical methods is at best misdirected and at worst actively dangerous. After witnessing the initial campaign in Iraq (2003), no enemy wants to go toe-to-toe with conventional U.S. forces. For this reason, advocates of asymmetry believe that other-than-war conflicts will continue to be the most common form of military involvement for the advanced countries.

The anti-Taliban and Al-Qaeda campaigns in Afghanistan and the postwar fighting in Iraq have shown the weakness of a high-tech military. Countering asymmetric warfare may include high-tech methods but emphasizes soldiers on the ground, local solutions, cultural awareness, and psychological operations. Success is gradual, incremental, and often visible only in hindsight. Furthermore, there is seldom robust public support for such missions. This is not welcome news in the conventional Army.

The primary military practitioners of asymmetric warfare in the West have been the special operations forces (SOF). In the United States, special operations forces are elements drawn from all the services under the umbrella of the U.S. Special Operations Command in Tampa, Florida. As described by the U.S. DoD, they specialize in conflicts below the threshold of war, such as terrorism, insurgency, hostage rescue, sabotage, and "situations requiring regional orientation and cultural and political sensitivity, including military-to-military contacts and noncombatant missions like humanitarian assistance, security assistance, and peacekeeping operations."[24] During their ascendance in the Vietnam War, they often managed to combine military, political, and informational elements to create a unique capability in their ability to work with foreign civilians and local militaries.

But these quasi-political missions were often derided as "social work" and lost favor both within the SOF community and the larger DoD. During transformation, attention was drawn to the potential offered by SOF (especially Army Special Forces) and air-delivered precision guided munitions (PGMs). Using their commando skills, small special operations elements can be rapidly positioned to guide PGMs with pinpoint accuracy. It was a winning combination in Afghanistan and heralded as a new American way of war. But those methods had little application to the bitter postwar insurgencies in Iraq and Afghanistan.

Background to Transformation

Unfortunately, the questions related to transformation are not decided entirely on their abstract merits. Powerful vested interests are involved in these debates. Each military service has a huge investment in equipment and personnel as well as their traditional roles to protect.

Behind the services are the industrial firms, contractors, and subcontractors in the highly lucrative business of producing the tools for war. So far, these firms have managed to have it both ways—the companies that manufacture the accoutrements of armored land warfare continue to supply the conventional Army, while the Future Force program provides a multibillion dollar cash cow in research and development. All manner of technology firms, researchers, and producers from material sciences to software have seized the opportunity to sell and often oversell the potential of their products. About 23 different companies, each with its own legion of subcontractors, are engaged in building and tying together the incredibly complex "system of systems" that will be the Future Combat System.

In order to make this all work, another new generation of systems is required. None of them are cheap. The orbiting Enhanced Imaging System (EIS) is an example. According to published reports, EIS is designed to help provide high fidelity radar and photo images as part of "information dominance." The EIS reportedly has the ability to dwell, or "hang," for a longer period over an area of interest and can transmit its collected data more quickly. This kind of capability is vital to the planned Future Force and the rest of DoD transformation. But each satellite costs a reported $1.5 billion, not including the Lockheed Martin–built Titan 4B launch vehicle or the ground-based equipment to receive and process the information EIS provides.[25]

The prospect of a new, highly networked Army means that the whole tradition of armored land warfare and the industries that supply it are fighting for their lives. In this fight, partisans of traditional armored war face two problems as illustrated above. First of all, the early twenty-first century seems to hold few enemies worth the attention of these high-tech, high intensity forces. It is also true that, unlike air power, all the paraphernalia of high intensity land warfare must be transported to war by sea and air over a period of months. Worse yet, they require extensive support including an "iron mountain" of fuel and spare parts to keep them in action.[26]

In order to resolve these concerns, the Army focused on rapid deployability as a critical capability. Nearly all of the changes under the rubric of Army Transformation are intended to enhance rapid deployment across strategic distances. Allegedly, ground forces that cannot do this will become strategically irrelevant, replaced by the "global power, global reach" of air power.[27]

The Stryker Brigade Combat Teams, built around the thin-skinned Stryker light armored vehicle, supposedly exemplify these improvements. These brigades were intended to lead the technological leap to a Future Force based on the advanced FCS. But what makes FCS unique is that the component systems (e.g., vehicles, mobile guns, robots, reconnaissance drones, etc.) will be connected by a very fast, secure computer network enabling them to function as a single distributed system. If it works as planned, the multimission Future Force will provide networked command, control, communication, and computer functionalities; robotic systems; precision fires; sensor platforms; air defense; and Reconnaissance Surveillance Target Acquisition (RSTA) capabilities.[28]

An FCS Brigade is conceived as a sort of virtual unit, a distributed system that combines the functions of infantry, tanks, artillery, and reconnaissance in a web or grid of systems. Hundreds of platforms, both manned and unmanned, will spread across hundreds or perhaps thousands of meters. Separate gun- or missile-carrying robotic vehicles ("platforms") will move independently of the command vehicle. Using sensors mounted in small unmanned aerial vehicles and reconnaissance robots to direct coordinated fires, this approach seeks to mass "effects" rather than units.

The dates for all of this are very slippery and depend on a shifting configuration of funding, political will, military interest, and technological development. Delays slowed the preparation of the first two Stryker Brigades, and they were judged not ready for the initial phase of the Iraq conflict. Army leaders originally hoped at least one of the futuristic FCS-based units could be operational by 2008. Now it seems more likely that a modest version might be ready about a decade later.[29]

Ironically, the kind of advances sought for FCS might end the style of warfare they are intended to fight. Wide area surveillance combined with the proliferation of precision munitions and small antitank guided missiles may make it impossible to build armored vehicles that can survive the high-tech battlefield. The Stryker Brigade Combat Teams, like FCS, seek to end run the problem by fielding units that use superior "battlefield awareness" to make preemptive attacks while avoiding being targeted themselves. Protection is abandoned in favor of speed and stealth, ending the reign of traditional armored warfare. Information is armor. Once again, the enemy failed to cooperate with this vision. Lacking futuristic weapons, Iraqi insurgents equipped only with small arms, conventional explosives, and rocket-propelled grenades continued to extract a heavy cost from the U.S. and coalition forces long after the end of "major combat operations." The Strykers were forced to abandon their rapid-deployment rationale and add heavier armor and special slat screens for protection.

To survive, FCS requires near-perfect information to avoid timely detection by the enemy while still having almost complete knowledge of the battlefield situation. It seems very unlikely that any force, no matter how well-equipped will have such complete information that an enemy can consistently be defeated before it ever comes within direct fire range. But this is what is intended. It is a highly dangerous way to do business. If it fails to occur and occur consistently, the smaller, lightly armored FCS units will almost certainly be overcome by "obsolete" industrial age enemies.

The doctrine clash between the Army and the Air Force becomes even more important in this connection. There is more at stake than an interservice food fight. The Army's planning for the Future Force is predicated on the assumption that the Navy and Air Force will be willing to invest in new ships and planes to carry the Army. For purposes of rapid deployment, the U.S. Air Force becomes the linchpin. The Air Force is understandably less interested in its role as the Army's taxi service.[30]

Since the Army, and for that matter the entire Department of Defense, is obsessed with naming and renaming things, transformation programs have undergone a number of name changes; for example, the Future Force program was originally called the "Objective Force." Infantry Fighting Vehicles are renamed Interim Fighting Vehicles and then Stryker Vehicles. The reasons for these changes are seldom obvious and often confusing. In order to present a clearer narrative, many of these title changes have been simplified or eliminated. To include and thoroughly explain all, or even most, of them would require a much larger book with a matching glossary and thesaurus.

For simplicity's sake, the first adaptation, grafting information processing systems on the existing industrial-era Army is captured as "Force XXI." The second, to reorganize the existing fighting structures of the Army is called the "Modular Army" program. The third and most ambitious, the plan to create a wholly new kind of fighting force and new methods of combat is the "Future Force" program. If the organization produced by the Modular Army initiative is the next Army, then the one resulting from the Future Force program is the Army after Next. Remarkably, all of these things are supposedly happening at once.

Despite problems, the United States Army is currently well ahead of other militaries in its effort to adopt present and expected technological advances. But this change is likely to be far less rapid than originally hoped and planned. It seems reasonable to believe that it will require decades from the time those new formations first emerge until the last of the industrial age Army disappears. This timeline is based on the U.S. Army's own planning with allowances made by the author for expected funding difficulties and the inevitable failure of some technologies to emerge on schedule. Like everything else about transformation, it should not be taken as guaranteed.

> *It must be considered that there is nothing more difficult to carry out, nor more doubtful of success, nor more dangerous to handle, than to initiate a new order of things.*
>   —Niccolo Machiavelli, *The Prince*

CHAPTER 2

THE ROOTS OF THE REVOLUTION

A satisfactory theory of war never conflicts with reality.

—Karl von Clausewitz

The Context of Change

The concept of transformation begins with the fact that possession of unique and advanced military technology is an important part of the American military's self-image. But so is an attachment to tried and tested methods and organizations. Thus, during the 1990s the U.S. Army and the other services steadily made changes to incorporate new technologies, but those changes were superimposed on existing doctrine and structures. Furthermore, as Andrew Bracevitch observed, their concept of warfare continued to resemble "World War II in the fancy dress of high-technology."[1]

The first indication of radical, concrete change came on October 12, 1999, at the annual meeting of the Association of the United States Army. These meetings are normally staid, even boring, gatherings of military leaders and defense contractors. But this one was rocked when General Eric K. Shinseki announced that he was going to transform the entire Army as soon as possible. Gradual improvements were inadequate. New advances would make current ground forces not merely obsolete but irrelevant. Through a process of rapid, radical change, the Army would become lighter, more lethal, and less dependent on elaborate logistics. There would be no more lip service given to the promise of "leap-ahead" technologies. Under an umbrella program called "Army Transformation" the service would "leverage" (i.e., take advantage of) information technologies, improvements in battlefield sensors, robotics, new materials, and other innovations in doctrine, organization, and equipment to create a wholly new form of ground combat force called the "Objective Force" and have it in place by 2012. In the words of one of those present, Shinseki's speech "was a mind-blower." If there had not been a military revolution before, there was one now.

But, great changes do not spring full-blown into existence. The Chief's announcement had its roots in the West's faith in progress and the strong technological bias of Western militaries.

Welcome to the Revolution

Historian Michael Roberts coined the term "military revolution" in 1955.[2] But the contemporary idea began with Soviet Army Marshall N. V. Ogarkov and his notion of a "military technical revolution." During the 1970s and early 1980s, Ogarkov's studies led him to believe that the most advanced industrial nations (the United States, Japan, and those in Western Europe) were on the verge of a military-technical revolution that would transform conventional warfare.

His logic and his powers of persuasion must have been considerable because he managed to convince the notably hidebound Soviet Army to accept his vision. Future war would be dynamic, high tempo, and high intensity with land and air operations encompassing vast areas and extending into outer space. The key to victory was information, the ability to understand this complex and deadly combat. This meant mastering the processing, sorting, and analyzing of intelligence products from high-tech collection systems and managing command and control to provide some order in battle's chaos. It was a very technical view of warfare that put a premium on technological integration, professionalism, and effective training.[3]

One of those most impressed by all this was Andrew W. Marshall, the scholarly looking director of an obscure Pentagon group called the Office of Net Assessment (ONA). He recognized the importance of Ogarkov's work and became one of its most ardent students. ONA found a number of possible revolutions in past military technologies. The adoption of effective firearms was an obvious one, and most analysts agreed that the mating of the industrial revolution to warfare c. 1850–1914 and the rise of maneuver warfare after World War I also qualified.[4]

More importantly, they saw that true revolutions were more than technical developments—armies could not merely improve their performance. A revolution meant that they had to significantly alter the way they did business. The idea of a mere military-technical revolution seemed too limiting, and the broader concept of a revolution in military affairs (RMA) evolved. Marshall defined an RMA as having three components:

1. Technological innovation.
2. Operational concept (or doctrine).
3. Organizational adaptation.[5]

The last two points are important since new technologies are of marginal benefit if not utilized correctly. The key to utilization is organization and doctrine. An operational concept can grow out of historical concepts or emerge in response to specific challenges. These include not only purely military challenges, but geographic, economic, cultural, political, and demographic dilemmas as well. Although doctrinal issues are often contentious, serious changes in military organization (as opposed to tinkering around the edges) are even more so. Militaries are notoriously committed to tradition and can be counted on to resist radical change. Contemporary armies grew out of World War II and made no fundamental changes for nearly 60 years. They preferred incremental shifts in the mix of force types and command and control, incorporating new technologies as they developed. Up through the early 1990s, there was little recognition of a need to do things differently.

Technological developments outpaced doctrine and organizational adaptation because so many more creative energies and dollars are engaged in the former. Technologies are "real." They are visible and material and, at least in theory, subject to empirical testing. Operational concepts and organizational changes are "fuzzy," are subject to endless debate, and attract fewer dollars. Military theorists tended to take considerably less notice of revolutions that were social, intellectual, and organizational, but not technical.[6] For example, American military theorists often credit Napoleon as the first to effectively harness industrialization and mass armies. Less attention is paid to the way Napoleon took advantage of the new mass armies to yield a revolution in command. Even less attention is paid to the importance of the new revolutionary ideologies in bonding and motivating Napoleon's armies.[7]

The RMA was an intriguing idea and set off an avalanche of articles, papers, and conferences. All were aimed at developing the notion, identifying these revolutions, and determining their consequences, but tended to be a bit vague when it came to concrete applications.[8] The RMA also spawned a jargon of its own featuring terms such as "systems of systems," "information dominance," and "asymmetric warfare." In most uses, however, the concept was little more than a metaphor for rapid change.

Despite the jargon, the RMA vision of the future could be explained fairly simply: New information technology created major advances in military capabilities, e.g., precision munitions, remote battlefield sensors, spy satellites, and so forth. More importantly, all these systems could be networked together and coordinated by a central command. This idea of networking was the central concept of the RMA. This was the system of systems and the source of information dominance. The owners of the network would know more and be able to react faster and more effectively than any enemy. The networking of sensors with computer analysis and long-range precision strike capabilities would revolutionize warfare. As phrased by Nicolas Lemann, "Maybe there would be no battlefield, no 'closing with the enemy'—just people at terminals launching missiles."[9]

One follower of Marshall's theories was Donald H. Rumsfeld, the U.S. Secretary of Defense (SecDef) (1975–1977) under President Gerald R. Ford. Rumsfeld was an early convert to the RMA concept, a set of ideas he would carry forward when he returned to the SecDef job almost 25 years later.[10]

Finding the Right Way to Fight: Doctrine for Ground Combat

All great armies of the world rest their land combat power upon the tank...[Soviet doctrine] emphasizes heavy concentrations of armor.
                                    —1976 Version FM 100-5, *Operations*, p. 2-2

While Ogarkov and Marshall were contemplating technologies on the horizon, most of the world's armies (and all the major armies in the west) were operating on some variety of maneuver warfare doctrine, as demonstrated by the German "blitzkrieg" in World War II. Ground combat prior to World War I had been primarily an infantry affair supported by artillery and cavalry. But the fruits of the industrial revolution (including armored vehicles, the machine gun, aircraft, and wireless communications) were widely applied in the war and heralded enormous changes. Numerous countries including Russia, Great Britain, Germany, the United States, and France experimented with mechanized forces after World War I. During the 1920s and 1930s military writers began to speculate on the use of faster, more reliable armored vehicles and airplanes coordinated by radio to conduct operations in depth. These ideas, as developed by Heinz Guderian in Germany, were put into spectacular practice by the Wermacht against Poland and France.

In the American Army, the direct result was the U.S. 1943 model armored divisions that George S. Patton led so successfully against Germany, using variations on Guderian's own methods. World War II in Europe became the dominant element in the Army's self-image because, in the worlds of Carl Builder, "nothing the Army has done since...can compare to who it was or what it did from June 1944 to May 1945."[11] The methods and organization that made it all possible became the "right" way to fight.[12]

Unfortunately the real world seldom accommodates itself to doctrine, and the Army's next two major engagements offered little scope for sweeping armored battles. In Korea (1950–1953) and Vietnam (1965–1975) not the enemy, the terrain, nor the political circumstances of the war were suitable for the fighting the "right" way. In the wake of Vietnam, General Creighton Abrams, the last U.S. commander there, became Army Chief of Staff (1972–1974) and set about regenerating the Army. For some analysts, the military-technical approach to war (material supremacy, battlefield agility, and massive firepower) had been applied in Vietnam and failed miserably. But, however bitter the outcome, the war failed to shake the Army's fundamental faith in mechanized warfare and military technology. General Abrams turned his back on the Vietnam experience and returned to the post-World War II doctrines of sustained heavy combat as the primary focus of the Army. Messy engagements like Vietnam were an aberration, and there was little patience for those who said otherwise.

Over the following years and several conflicts the specter of something-other-than-conventional war rose up over and over, but the Army and, for that matter, the entire U.S. defense establishment, resolutely avoided making them an important part of its doctrine. A confusing multitude of terms were coined to describe these involvements: small wars, guerrilla wars, irregular wars, unconventional wars, three-block wars, insurgencies and counterinsurgencies, constabulary operations, stability operations, stability and reconstruction operations, postconflict operations, small-scale contingencies, stability and support operations, wars of the third kind, fourth generation warfare, peacekeeping, or peacemaking, or peace enforcement, Chapter VI or VII (of the UN charter) operations, military operations other than war, and low-intensity conflict, among others.[13] None lent much clarity and at best were considered lesser included cases of conventional warfare. But Vietnam and subsequent engagements did provide one enduring lesson that would condition the next generation of soldiers and politicians: casualty aversion. Long wars would generate unacceptable numbers of casualties and create widespread public opposition. Successful wars had to be short wars with minimal casualties.

The October War

The U.S. Army was still withdrawing from Vietnam when an event occurred that seemed to vindicate the military-technical approach. On October 7, 1973—Yom Kippur, the Jewish Holy Day of Atonement—the Egyptian Army stormed across the Suez Canal in a sophisticated combined arms attack that caught the Israelis by surprise and threw them back across the Sinai Peninsula. Syria and Iraq joined the assault. Despite initial setbacks, the Israel Defense Forces quickly took the offensive, drove back across the Canal, and were in the act of surrounding the Egyptian Third Army when a cease-fire ended the war.[14] This conflict seemed like a perfect template for America's expected confrontation with the Soviets in Europe. The Israelis had used primarily U.S. equipment to fight a short, sharp, high casualty war against an enemy superior in numbers, attacking by surprise, equipped by the Soviet Union, and employing Soviet tactics. Lessons learned from the Israelis in 1973 were influential in the U.S. Army's thinking, training, and equipping throughout the Cold War. The war highlighted the importance of new technologies including tactical anti-aircraft and antitank guided missiles, sophisticated fire-control systems, and vastly improved tank gunnery. It also served as a welcome antidote to the Army's Vietnam-era concentration on infantry-airmobile warfare at the expense of other forces.

This lesson was welcome in the American Army, where the central focus was purely on military technique, the use of weapons, the maneuver of forces, and the like. Odd as this might seem to soldiers of earlier eras, when political and military knowledge were inextricably bound up together, it was a typical attitude in all the U.S. armed forces. American soldiers ardently believed in the advantages conferred by technology and sought technological solutions. "Soft" solutions, those using tools like unconventional warfare, propaganda, and quasi-political methods, were scorned.

For U.S. military analysts, the October War showed that aggressive ground combat doctrine overcame superior numbers by using attack aircraft and armored vehicles, specifically tanks, to maneuver deep into enemy rear echelons. The Israeli example was also welcome because it followed the model set by Hienz Guderian in

1938—air power as highly mobile artillery able to follow fast-moving ground forces. The focus remained clearly on land power and the tank.

The Rise of the Active Defense

The traditional military description for the Israeli operations in October 1973 would probably be "strategic defense" accomplished by "tactical offense." In other words, the overall purpose was defensive; the protection of the national borders. But the means was through aggressive offensive action at the local level. The U.S. Army coined the term "active defense" to describe this type of activity. General William E. DePuy, commander of the Training and Doctrine Command (TRADOC), made it his challenge to devise post-Vietnam doctrine. In so doing, he solidified active defense conducted by heavy armored forces as the Army's central methodology.

General DePuy personally wrote much of the 1976 edition of 100-5, *Operations*, the Army's basic how-to-fight manual. To DePuy, the post-Vietnam Army, riddled with doubts about its ability to wage a modern war, required something stronger than the usual simple set of guiding principles. It needed the prescriptive formula of the active defense. The Army of the 1970s was receptive to these ideas, not only because of the humiliation of Vietnam, but because they coincided with very basic beliefs about how success was achieved in war. Large numbers of officers believed passionately in the importance of heavy mechanized forces. The most senior of these, including DePuy, were veterans of World War II where they had experienced decisive combat that contrasted vividly with the stalemate of Korea and the morass of Vietnam.

In July 1976, the Army published the new *Operations* manual, marking the doctrinal exit from Vietnam and a refocus on mechanized warfare. Its message was that Army leaders had been right all along and their faith in the tank was not misplaced. One of those leaders was General Donn A. Starry, commander of the Army's armored warfare school at Fort Knox and DePuy's successor at TRADOC while the latter prepared to become Army Chief of Staff. With "tank generals" as chief of staff and chief of doctrine, the active defense strategy was expanded to include simultaneous offensive operations over the full breadth and depth of the battlefield. Active defense became enshrined as Airland Battle Doctrine, the newest incarnation of maneuver warfare, in the 1982 version of FM 100-5.

This was a clear articulation of fundamentals that American generals had understood and practiced since World War II.[15] Perhaps most attractive of all, AirLand Battle saw ground combat as the only truly decisive form of warfare and, accordingly, made the Army the centerpiece of American military policy. Needless to say, the other military services did not agree with this analysis. But, for the Army, the principal instrument of AirLand Battle was the Army-led combined arms team, fully integrating the capabilities of all land, sea, and air combat systems, rapidly shifting by fire, and maneuvering to concentrate decisive combat power at the proper time and place on the battlefield.[16] In the 1980s the U.S. Army began to practice that art at a huge National Training Center training area at Fort Irwin, California, an area larger than Rhode Island. Whole armored brigades honed AirLand Battle tactics in the California desert against a simulated Soviet force equipped with Warsaw Pact weapons and vehicles.

AirLand Battle was a highly technological approach to warfare. It depended on sophisticated sensors and surveillance systems to locate deep targets and enemy battlefield forces, rapid communications, and automated data processing to compile information and control forces and weapons systems (including tactical nuclear weapons) with the range and accuracy for "deep battle," strikes against targets at ranges of more than 100 kilometers. The arrival of new developments in long-range artillery and missiles was expected to allow the Army to extend its striking range well beyond anything it had ever been.

AirLand Battle also endorsed the comfortable and well-understood division structure directly descended from the 1943 model armored division. However, to better support its new doctrine, in 1982 the Army began to modernize these units, adding more artillery and armored vehicles under what it called the "Division '86" concept. Armored divisions (those consisting principally of tanks) received even more tanks while infantry divisions received more tanks and armored personnel carriers to become mechanized infantry, essentially identical to armored divisions except in the mix of forces. The number of personnel in each such division rose to about 15,000. This left a very uniform fighting force and an extremely heavy one. To deploy a Division '86 division outside the continental United States could take up to two months for initial elements and up to four months for all the supporting elements to arrive.[17] It reduced strategic mobility to a glacial pace, prompting one cynic to remark that the Army was building the finest irrelevant force in the world.

The cure for this problem was "forward presence." Heavy armor lacked strategic mobility, but it did not matter because large Army forces were already present in the two places they were expected to be needed, Germany and South Korea. In addition, large stockpiles of equipment were created in Europe, containing the arms and material for additional armored units. All that was needed was to add the troops who were far easier to ship across an ocean. Finally, since the attention of U.S. and allied intelligence assets was firmly fixed on the USSR, it was felt that there would be sufficient strategic warning to begin the necessary troop movements well before any hostilities could begin.

This was all fine and widely accepted, at least among Army planners. But there was still the nagging problem of "out of area contingencies" meaning conflicts outside Europe, in the Middle East, for example. How would the United States respond to that sort of contingency? It was a legitimate worry, and it gave rise to the Light Infantry Divisions (LID). These were smaller (10,000 men) organizations that could be moved from the United States to, say, Saudi Arabia entirely by air in a few days. But speed was purchased by removing nearly all of the heavy equipment from these units, including tanks, artillery, armored personnel carriers, aircraft, and most of the trucks. Once on the ground, the LID was not very mobile and did not have very much to fight with beyond small arms and mortars. Accordingly, the "light" division began to gain weight as transport and support units were added. These elements would make the LID more effective but at the cost of mobility and increased logistic support. Rapid deployability and combat effectiveness seemed to be mutually exclusive concepts.

Naturally, AirLand Battle Doctrine had its detractors. Within the Army it was objected that the force configured to support that doctrine was too uniform and unsuited for anything other than a major theater war. The other services were apprehensive about any doctrine that made them servants of the Army. This was awkward since the deep strikes the doctrine called for were to be conducted by the Air Force (AF), a relationship that the Army preferred to call "a strong partnership." AirLand Battle was advertised as joint doctrine, but to the Air Force, it sounded more like an Army scheme to control AF assets.

Nevertheless, AirLand Battle doctrine, epitomized by FM 100-5/1986, was probably the high point of industrial age warfare. The service did begin a project called AirLand Battle–Future to explore new force designs, but it was a halfhearted effort and nothing came of it. Having achieved perfection, the Army saw no reason to tinker with its doctrine. In 1988 the Chief of Staff of the Army was moved to say, "Airland Battle describes how we will fight now and into the foreseeable future."

The year 1988 also saw a quiet harbinger of the future, the AN/PSN-8 "Manpack," the first portable Global Positioning System (GPS) receiver designed for soldiers in the field. It was big and cumbersome, cost $40,000, weighed about 17 pounds, and tended to eat batteries. But it could be carried by a single soldier, was easy to use, and provided very accurate and reliable positioning within several meters. The PSN-8 was heralded as a practical application of the electronic revolution, and the Army determined it might eventually need as many as 900 of the units. Within four years the demand for GPS devices had increased to almost 75,000.[18]

The Role of Air Power

Despite grumbling, the Air Force was remarkably acquiescent to its role under AirLand Battle. New Army tactical missile systems that could strike as deep as 165 km created some friction. Also, some aspects of command arrangements were an issue since the airmen traditionally regarded everything beyond artillery range as theirs.[19] But the air service had been in something of a doctrinal muddle since the end of the Vietnam War. As the mission of strategic nuclear attack lost importance with the waning Soviet threat, the air service lost focus among a welter of lesser tasks. According to a 1989 internal White Paper produced by Headquarters USAF, "The Air Force has lost a sense of its own identity and of the unique contributions airpower makes to warfighting. Fragmentation thus permeates our internal planning and consequently the way we present ourselves to others."[20]

Within the Air Force and its supporters a strong cadre of true believers held with great fervor that air power was the decisive military arm. In the tradition of Hugh Trenchard and Billy Mitchell, they saw air power as the natural replacement for the ground and sea services. This had become apparent with the publication of a

National Defense University thesis by Air Force Colonel John Warden. Called "The Air Campaign," the work was ostensibly a review of the logic of military goals and objectives and how to reconcile the operational and strategic levels of war.

However, the interesting part for proponents of air power was the underlying theme of air dominance. Although carefully caveated with ritual obeisance to "joint-ness," it was, in fact, an air power manifesto, and chapter titles like "War Can be Won from the Air" left little doubt about it. Warden's ideas and those of other air-men began to coalesce as a new vision of warfare to replace the prevailing view that the Air Force's principal job was to support the Army. This spirit was manifested in a 1990 Air Force White Paper that coined the slogan "Global Reach—Global Power" and stressed the independent role of air power. [21]

Asymmetric Warfare and the Anti-Soviet War in Afghanistan

America's most recent and serious bout with an asymmetric opponent had it roots in a faraway conflict that seemed to have no connection with the arcane issues of U.S. Army doctrine. In 1979, the Soviet Union invaded Afghanistan to support a totter-ing pro-Soviet government. American military special operators were initially impressed with the use of Russian *Spetznaz* (special forces) but the war turned into a long, messy, and brutal struggle between Soviet troops, their Afghan supporters, and the opposing Muslim fighters called *mujahideen* or *jihadis,* both meaning "holy warriors." Militarily, there did not seem much to learn from another messy insur-gency in a remote corner of the world. The American government protested by boy-cotting the 1980 Moscow Olympic Games, but that was about the end of it.

Then, under the administration of President Ronald Reagan, the United States began active (but still minimal) support to the Muslim insurgency. With covert aid from the United States, Saudi Arabia, and others, resistance fighters in Afghanistan developed a worldwide recruitment and support network. Assisted by the clandestine services of anti-Soviet nations, especially Pakistan, this network equipped, trained, and funded thousands of the most radical mujahideen.[22] After almost ten years of costly and fruitless struggle, the USSR finally gave up the fight in 1989. It was counted as an important victory for the free world, but, since the Soviet Union was then in its death throes, attention quickly turned elsewhere.

Afghanistan slid toward chaos as rival warlords, local militias, religious factions, and bandit chiefs fought for control of various slices of the country. But some of the hardened mujahideen veterans rejected this Muslim against Muslim conflict and sought new venues for what they saw as a wider struggle against anti-Islamic forces.[23]

Around 1990, the world intelligence community began to turn up indications that the Afghan network was still in operation under the control of one Usama bin Laden, a young Saudi millionaire. Now he seemed to be re-forming the Islamist network as a loose international terrorist organization known by the Arabic word "al-Qaeda," lit-erally, "the base." [24] The Afghan mujahideen were among the first recruits.

Also known variously as the Islamic Army for the Liberation of the Holy Places, the World Islamic Front for Jihad Against Jews and Crusaders, and the Islamic Salvation Foundation, bin Laden's network helped finance, recruit, transport, and train Islamic extremists to fight what they considered anti-Islamic forces around the world. This was interesting and perhaps troubling, but the soldiers, politicians, and intelligence officers of the West had other, more urgent concerns.

Operation Desert Storm, the Gulf War of 1990–1991

On August 1, 1990, Iraqi dictator Saddam Hussein made the single worst military calculation of the late twentieth century. His limited patience exhausted by a long simmering dispute over drilling rights at adjacent oil fields, he sent his armored divisions crashing into neighboring Kuwait while threatening Saudi Arabia. On August 6 the United Nations Security Council imposed comprehensive economic sanctions against Iraq. Operating under a United Nations mandate, the United States and its European allies began to assemble a formidable coalition that included even Arab states in a united effort to oust the Iraqis from Kuwait. Meanwhile, Hussein's modern T-72 tanks stood on the Arabian border with a clear road to the ports and airfields at Dhahran and nothing to oppose them except Saudi militia.[25] A credible opposing force needed to be in place quickly, within 24 to 36 hours. America's heavy tank divisions would be ideal, but it would be a month before they could even begin to arrive. Even the LIDs were too slow, so the only units with that capability, the lightly armed 82nd Airborne Division and a USMC Expeditionary Force, were rushed to the Middle East.

The problem of strategic mobility, long wished away, had arrived with a vengeance. The Marines and paratroops could do little more than dig in and hold on until the heavy forces arrived. In the words of one 82nd soldier, "we would have been no more than a speed bump for the Iraqis." Fortunately, the Iraqi tankers displayed neither competence nor a will to fight, and the lightly armed Americans only needed to wait while Hussein dithered.

The first few M1 Abrams tanks did not arrive in Saudi ports until August 31, almost three weeks behind the Marines and paratroopers. The first armored unit was not ready for combat until mid-October. While Coalition forces began the months-long process of actually reaching the scene, analysts filled the popular media with dire predictions. They warned that the veteran Iraqi Army, heavily equipped with modern tanks and artillery and battle hardened after a seven year war with Iran, would become an "Iraqi meat grinder." Whole divisions would be destroyed, and friendly casualties would number in the tens of thousands. But after a month-long air campaign and a ground war of less than five days, the carnage among Iraqi units was so great that U.S. President George Bush stopped the war. Thousands of Iraqi soldiers had died, but the total number of combat deaths for Coalition forces amounted to less than 50. The predominantly American and British Coalition had inflicted a decisive military defeat in a shorter time, with fewer friendly casualties, than anyone had believed possible.

Largely unmentioned, but not unnoticed, was the annoying fact that it had taken the Coalition, including the United States, six months to get to the war. In the last analysis Hussein's unfathomable failure to take the initiative had made the victory possible.

Although it could never replace World War II in the affections of the Army officer corps, Desert Storm quickly became the favorite war of military theoreticians. While the victory was gratifying, the important point for military analysts was the use of advanced technology, especially precision weapons, long-range air power, and information systems. The long awaited "military-technical revolution" had finally arrived.

Two minutes behind the B-2s came eight B-1B Lancers from the 7th Wing at Dyess AFB, Texas, also launched from Anderson AFB and refuelled from KC-10As at Diego Garcia. Their targets were two battalions of troops in barracks adjacent to Bushehr airport. Each unloaded twelve AGM-154 Joint Standoff Weapons (JSOWs) from their weapons bays. Following a two-minute gliding flight, the ninety-six JSOWs, guided by onboard GPS receivers, unloaded their payloads of BLU-97/B Combined Effects Munitions (CEMs). They blanketed over a hundred acres of troop billeting and vehicle-parking areas with thousands of CEMs, and the effects were horrific. The two minutes since the bombs from the B-2 strike had given the troops time to throw on their boots, grab weapons, and rush outside to be shredded into hamburger by exploding cluster munitions.[26]

For the America's soldiers, victory was especially sweet. Desert Storm was the anti-Vietnam of American wars. Where the Vietnam War was long, costly, indecisive, and finally ended in defeat, Desert Storm was a quick, decisive victory at minimal cost. Never mind that it was a unique event, or rather a confluence of unique events—extraordinary military and political ineptitude on the part of Iraq combined with extraordinarily favorable political, technical, climatic, and geographical conditions for the Coalition. Unlike the North Vietnamese, Saddam Hussein set his armies directly against the strengths of the American-led Coalition. He presented the United States Army and its Coalition allies with exactly the war they had been preparing to fight for 40 years, on terrain ideally suited for the purpose. Given that opportunity, the Army fought magnificently. No one denied these facts; indeed, a small group of critics pointed them out endlessly. But the real attention was elsewhere—on the technology involved and the role of air power.

For the most part it seemed to be a war of machines, in particular missiles and airplanes. The record of a new generation of precision guided munitions (PGMs) was especially impressive. In the six-week air war, the Coalition air forces dropped more than double the number of laser-guided bombs used during the nine months of Operation Linebacker II in Vietnam, with more effect and far fewer losses.

After the war, an Iraqi general reflected on his experience under precision bombardment:

During the Iran war, my tank was my friend because I could sleep in it and know I was safe...During this war my tank became my enemy...none of my troops would get near a tank at night because they just kept blowing up.[27]

In large part because of PGMs, the Coalition air strikes were remarkably effective and avoided much "collateral damage" (incidental or unintended destruction). The Air Force was quick to showcase this with videos of F-117 stealth fighters firing precision munitions while the Navy provided shots of its submarines and battleships launching cruise missiles. The ground campaign had been very brief, and the world press corps (virtually none of whom had the least idea what they were seeing) focused on the long air campaign that led up to the ground assault. Space-based assets provided intelligence and communications while unmanned aerial vehicles (UAVs) conducted reconnaissance and surveillance. The Coalition enjoyed such good control of the battlefield that the mere presence of their forces kept the Iraqis from using their own radars. Iraqis were known to simply abandon their equipment on the approach of Coalition units. In one memorable incident, a group of Iraqi soldiers actually surrendered to a UAV.

Some problems also arose during the conflict. Lack of strategic air and sea transport for one. Numerous observers commented on the fact that few enemies were likely to wait quietly for six months while opposition forces flowed in unmolested. Precision weapons were in short supply, and there was an urgent demand for better coordination among all the services. Special operations and intelligence needed to be better integrated into the war plan. Many (or most) of the euphoric reports of PGM success turned out to be exaggerated or sometimes just plain wrong. Weapons put to the test for the first time displayed significant shortcomings, like laser-guided bombs that tended not to work in bad weather.

Despite the Coalition victory, Saddam Hussein remained in power. But then, the announced purpose of the war had been to eject his military from Kuwait, and that had been achieved. At the end of hostilities Saddam was forced to sign a number of agreements under UN Security Council Resolution 687, renouncing weapons of mass destruction while submitting to United Nations inspection. He also agreed to a "no-fly" zone covering much of northern and southern Iraq where his air force would not be allowed. No one really expected the notorious despot to keep his word, and the agreements were well short of a surrender. For this reason, the United Nations did not lift the sanctions imposed before the start of the war, keeping them as leverage to press for Iraqi disarmament.

Even if the outcome was not totally satisfactory, the war seemed to promise a uniquely favorable military future for America. As the world leader in the application of military technologies—and one of the few nations able to apply them on a large scale—the United States could expect to dominate any major future battlefield as decisively as it had the sands of Iraq.

Intelligence Operations

Ogarkov and Marshall had been adamant about the importance of information in modern war. Operation Desert Storm took a great step forward in making strategic information resources available at the tactical level. This was critical to later developments because information, accurate, complete, timely, and available from the highest to the lowest levels, is the cornerstone of the Future Force concept. Without this kind of data the concepts of early engagement and distributed formations simply will not work. Elaborate automated information processing systems feed on this kind of data, and without it the network will starve. Furthermore, raw data (e.g., sensor input) are of limited value. Data need to be analyzed. Analyzed information is called "intelligence."

Prior to the desert war the tactical intelligence needed by a theater commander (such as commander U.S. Central Command, aka CENTCOM) came almost entirely from his own resources. National-level intelligence was used for national strategic purposes; it informed policy decisions and even military planning and procurement, but as far as the warfighting commander was concerned the data arrived either too late or not at all. It might as well have been nonexistent. But that changed in Desert Storm—the U.S. Army Intelligence and Security Command (INSCOM) delivered 13 satellite downlink terminals to provide "reach-back," funneling national level data and analysis from the United States to CENTCOM tactical commanders. INSCOM was the Army's "echelons above corps" organization that brought together national assets (e.g., satellites) and the service's intelligence resources at the highest level. It began to bridge the gap to put national level assets at the service of tactical commanders. Corps commanders could receive national intelligence, and in a few specific, critical sectors timely intelligence was passed down to lower echelons. In at least one instance an opposing enemy unit was targeted down to the platoon level.[28]

The commander of the 24th Infantry Division reported that the intelligence was so accurate that in the battle for Basara he was able to hold his forces out of range and destroy Iraqi artillery based on imagery received from across the Atlantic Ocean. It was a real world example of what the revolution in military affairs (RMA) hoped to accomplish on a larger scale. The system was not perfect. Spread out among corps commanders and ten committed divisions, it could support only the most urgent requirements. Maps of Iraqi doctrinal force disposition were relayed by satellite to Saudi Arabia, but then distributed by courier. Many commanders received little or no timely support. Some received none. And there were serious bandwidth problems—in some cases downloading a complex photo product could take up to an hour. Still, it was a huge improvement and a promise of better to come.[29]

Air Power Seizes the Revolution

For true believers in the USAF, Desert Storm symbolized "the domination of air power and a new paradigm of warfare" presaging "a fundamental shift in the way many wars will be conducted and the need for a new way of thinking about military operations."[30]

There was some validity in the belief that Desert Storm was a new kind of war, but the differences were more of degree than kind. Some new technologies had a prominent role (such as precision guided munitions), but it was not a revolution. Desert Storm was fought by the doctrines of AirLand Battle, a direct descendent of Guderian's blitzkrieg, enhanced by major improvements in firepower, mobility, command

and control, logistics, and reconnaissance. The mostly British-American Coalition had the good fortune to apply its doctrine against a relatively static defender on ideal terrain, and the results were awesome. But even though the great improvement in air power effectiveness made a wider range of targets possible, the types of targets were the same as during WWII, Korea, and Vietnam. This air success was also made possible in large part because the Coalition had a surfeit of air power available (President Bush had ordered a near doubling of air strength on November 8).

Furthermore, some of the most prominent high-tech systems such as the Army Patriot antimissile batteries turned out not to have performed nearly as well as first thought.[31] Moreover, of the 88,500 tons of bombs dropped, only 6,520 tons—7.4 percent—were precision guided ordnance, according to official Pentagon figures. Most of the weapons used were conventional bombs and artillery. But overall the high-tech weapons (stealth aircraft, laser guided bombs, cruise missiles, etc.) proved uniquely effective and might be considered at least a military technical revolution. Nevertheless, to many commentators it looked like the real thing, an actual revolution in warfare, or, rather, a revolution in military affairs.[32]

Then-Secretary of Defense Richard Cheney believed so. He stated in the official Gulf War after-action report, that the war "demonstrated dramatically the new possibilities of what has been called the 'military-technological revolution in warfare.'"[33] He also handed kudos to the Coalition air forces, "The air campaign was decisive," later adding that Iraq could not fight back "because the air war turned out to be absolutely devastating."[34]

A study of the war conducted by the Center for Strategic and International Studies was equally enthusiastic. It contained an entire chapter entitled "The Revolution in Warfare" that was almost rhapsodic as it contemplated a future of automated battle management systems, space platforms, and unmanned aerial vehicles.

> In sum, the nature of warfare is changing. Although the revolution in warfare is still underway, its outlines have become clear. The effects of technology—in precision guided weapons, in stealthy delivery systems, in advanced sensor and targeting systems, in battle management platforms—is transforming and in fact already has demonstrably transformed the way in which armed forces conduct their operations.[35]

Air power enthusiasts, led by the U.S. Air Force, were certain that the revolution was at hand and were quick to trumpet the role air power played in the war. The Battle of Khafji was offered as an example of air power halting an armored advance in a major theater war. Iraq had launched its only offensive of the Gulf War, moving armored units against the lightly defended town of Khafji, just across the border in Saudi Arabia. Their intent was to lure Coalition forces into a ground battle. What they got was flight after flight of Coalition warplanes that hammered the oncoming tanks, turned them, and harried them relentlessly during their retreat. One tank brigade, caught in the open, was practically destroyed from the air. The success at Khafji became the seed of what was later called "halt-phase" strategy, the idea that air power alone could halt an aggressor until friendly ground forces arrived.

Among the most enthusiastic celebrants was General Merrill A. McPeak, the U.S. Air Force chief of staff. Although he was careful to show respect for "jointness" ("all the services made a very important contribution"), he also emphasized that the story of the war "is largely a story about airpower, a success story for U.S. and Coalition air forces. This is the first time in history that a field army has been defeated by airpower."[36]

McPeak was pleased and impressed with the performance of PGMs in the war, but he also understood their shortcomings, especially their high cost and their inability to function in bad weather. Accordingly, he dashed off a handwritten memo to the Air Force weapons development team, "We need all-weather precision-guided munitions." And they needed to be cheap, to avoid the quick exhaustion of inventory experienced in Iraq.[37]

The U.S. Air Force celebrated its victory with a White Paper called "Reaching Globally, Reaching Powerfully: The United States Air Force in the Gulf War." "The Coalition's victory," it said, "came from the wise and appropriate application of air power. Air power found, fixed, fought, and finished the Iraqi military." The paper added modestly that "The Gulf War illustrated that the precision of modern air attack has revolutionized warfare." In sum, air power had handed the ground forces a walkover.[38]

Finally, it concluded with a gratuitous slap at the Army. Air Force doctrine, it opined, "did not constitute a dusting-off of some doctrinal notions salvaged from the height of the Cold War, or an attempt to rework aging strategic visions to a rapidly changing world. Rather, it constituted a thoughtful, reasoned approach to the use of military force and presence in the post-Cold War period."

Post-Desert Storm

Ultimately, AirLand Battle and the Army that created it barely survived its success. The slow motion collapse of the Soviet Union more or less coincided with the Gulf War, and the world looked like a different place afterwards. Surveying the scene, Chairman of the Joint Chiefs General Colin Powell remarked, "I'm running out of demons. I'm down to Kim Il Sung and Castro." Soon after, an article in *Aerospace Daily*, a leading defense industry newsletter, recalled Powell's remarks and predicted: "Pentagon Budget Headed for $150 Billion—Half Current Level—By 1996." In the absence of any clear threat, policy makers saw the opportunity to trim military spending and demobilize large portions of the standing force.

Doctrine at the Crossroads

Given the atmosphere of strategic ambiguity and the "easy" victory in the Gulf War, the services were hard pressed to defend their Cold War–era structure. In the Army, doctrine writers, planners, and strategists struggled with the so-called New World Order. Whom and where might the Army have to fight and how should it be done?

The responses fell into two camps. The conventional wisdom was that Desert Storm was the model for future warfare. This kind of decisive operation meant deploy rapidly, decisively defeat the enemy force, and return quickly to base. What happened in the conflict area after that was someone else's problem. Given the realities of shrinking budgets and force structure, this camp advocated an Army composed of lighter but more effective forces capable of rapid deployment.[39]

The second and far smaller camp answered that the Army seldom fought that kind of war. Since Korea it had been doing something other than conventional warfighting. The something was poorly defined and had a host of names, including asymmetric operations, low intensity conflict, military operations other than war, peace operations, stability and support operations, or nation building, among others. It required a very different set of capabilities from those required for decisive operations. Furthermore, objectives in these missions were often unclear, and operations tended to be confusing and produce mostly ambiguous outcomes. It was messy, indecisive, and roundly loathed among senior officers. These missions were seen as aberrations and not useful predictors of future warfare.[40]

The Army's first response was a not-very-starling concept called AirLand Operations, a revised version of AirLand Battle that emphasized joint operations but left the Army as the centerpiece of combat, supported and aided by the other branches.

It was widely accepted that there were no more peer competitors and, in the oft-heard phrase, the United States was "the sole remaining superpower." Nevertheless, American military doctrine continued to focus on large-scale conventional warfare. Army doctrine still emphasized sustained ground combat using armored forces, that service's strong suit. Very little attention was paid to terrorism and even less to insurgency. The military role in counterterrorism was seen as occurring in two parts, small scale action by special operations units and deterrence against state sponsors of terrorism. The United States retaliated with air power against Libya in 1986 for a terrorist attack and against Iraq in 1993 for an alleged plan to assassinate former president George H. W. Bush. This kind of limited, low-risk retaliation was considered an effective form of deterrence against acts of terrorism. It was also inexpensive both in dollars and personnel required. This fit nicely with the overall pattern of force reductions.

A reduction had been underway in 1990 when the Gulf War interrupted it. So it was no surprise when President Bush announced a military drawdown in his 1992 State of the Union Address. On Bush's orders, Chairman of the Joint Chiefs General Colin Powell created a "Base Force" plan to steeply reduce the U.S. military—the Army from 16 to 12 active divisions; the Navy from 530 ships and 15 Carrier Battle Groups to 450 and 12, respectively; and the Air Force from 22 to 15 active fighter wing equivalents.[41]

Naturally, the prospect of a severe drawdown encouraged the perpetual conflict among the services as each became ever more desperate to preserve and, if possible, expand its share of the defense pie. Competition over the respective roles of ground and air power became intense to the point of bitterness in some quarters. This newest iteration of the long-term doctrinal struggle over air power was serious enough to cause the Army and Air Force to create an annual series of "Army-Air Force War-fighter Talks" to "identify and resolve" the "tough issues." Unfortunately, resolving the tough issues required some agreement on interpretations of the Gulf War. From the Army viewpoint there were several caveats about the high-tech Air Force performance. Infrared, electro-optical, and laser systems were all seriously degraded by weather, dust, and smoke. Even high-resolution radars on aircraft such as the F-15E had difficulty distinguishing tanks from trucks at tactical distances. There was no air threat since the enemy air force was absent and the USAF's advanced munitions did not have to deal with even basic Iraqi countermeasures.[42] Despite great efforts, allied air power and "information dominance" did not help find Iraq's mobile Scud missile launchers or its chemical and biological capabilities.[43]

Undaunted, some in the Air Force began to argue that air power alone, enabled with precision munitions, could counter an aggressive enemy long before ground forces could even reach the theater of operations. Khafji showed that the quick, effective use of strike aircraft and missiles could blunt and even turn back an invading army.

The Army was more inclined to be satisfied with what it had. After the victory in the Gulf War and the collapse of the Soviet threat, the Army slowed its exploration of radical changes in doctrine and force design. Operating on the axiom "if it ain't broke don't fix it," Army Chief of Staff General Carl E. Vuono concluded that there was no need to change for the sake of change. "Future modifications...would be disciplined and incremental, closely tied to the Army's operational doctrine," a business as usual approach.[44]

Vuono's successor, General Gordon Sullivan, was somewhat less inclined toward the status quo. Although no fan of radical change, he endorsed the idea of "digitizing" Army divisions by adding automated information systems. Digitization became the phrase of the day, and the bureaucracy responded, as it normally does, by creating more bureaucracy—in this case two Digitization Special Task Forces followed by a new Army Digitization Office. The Army Science Board was ordered to develop recommendations to guide the integration of the range of new technologies. Based on these recommendations, General Sullivan gave his official blessing in early 1994 to "Force XXI," a program designed to, in his word "transform" the Army for the twenty-first century. In so far as possible, this was to be accomplished without major structural changes.[45]

Training Matters

The emphasis of military planners was on the possibilities of new technology and doctrine to employ it. But technology without soldiers was useless. Some analysts, notably Elliot Cohen, argued that the planners were too focused on high-tech without adequately considering the operators. In the words of the Major General Barry MacCaffrey, 24th Infantry Division commander during the first Gulf war:

Equipment didn't win this thing. If we had used the Iraqi equipment we still would have prevailed. It was the training of our officers and men that made it happen.

Seen this way, the real RMA was a revolution in training, and it had already occurred—back in the 1980s or even slightly earlier. The key to victory in the Gulf was not merely advanced technology but the skillful exploitation of modern military technology by highly trained soldiers; in fact, the argument went on, the American training revolution of the 1970s was the real revolution in military affairs. In the aftermath of Vietnam, "the Army began a revolution in training and leader development that touched every aspect of the way the Army prepared for war." Leaders were determined to create training conditions that approximated actual battle conditions as closely as possible. If you "lost" there, you learned better how to win in combat.[46] The application of new technologies (especially information technology) made it possible to create sophisticated training areas such as the National Training Center at Fort Irwin, California. At Fort Knox, Kentucky, would-be tank crewmen could train by driving their simulated vehicles across a computer-generated battlefield, interacting with the enemy and with each other. When coupled with careful recruitment and retention policies, the result was a new class of armed forces.[47]

This view held that technology is important, but no more so than the high level of training now achieved by military organizations. Only militaries that can draw on a technologically advanced population and that can afford to give soldiers constant and realistic (hence extremely expensive) training can fully exploit the possibilities of contemporary weapons. The difference between American and other armed forces was not merely technological but also due to important changes in personnel policies and training methods. In the past American soldiers spent much of their time on routine housekeeping chores like peeling potatoes or "busy work" like painting rocks. Their military skill training was only episodic and often highly stylized. Beginning in the late 1970s, they spent most of their time soldiering.

Viewed in this light, the triumph of the Gulf War was not the result of innovations that created new forms of warfare. Instead, the victory resulted from a very long-standing trend, the increasing gap between skilled and unskilled organizations in the face of changing technology. Marine Corps units fought the Iraqis with obsolescent M60 tanks instead of the Army's state-of-the-art M1s but scored the same decisive kill ratios. The difference was one of training, not technology.

After the first Gulf War, the leader of an armored cavalry unit was "asked how his troop had been able to do so well in their first time in combat, he [Captain Sartiano] answered that this hadn't been their first time; he and others in his troop had been in combat before—at the National Training Center."[48] It remained to be seen how this kind of tactical training might apply to the digitizing Army.

A New World Dawns

After the collapse of the Soviet Bloc, the belief arose, especially in America, that the world was moving towards global acceptance of democracy and free markets to the general benefit of all. If this was so, then the obvious national strategic goal was to promote this process. The major impediments to the prospect of worldwide peace and prosperity were identified as rogue or "backlash" states, those that refused to accept the inevitability of democracy and free-market economies and encouraged various internal conflicts (sectarian, irredentist, or ethnic). The day after Iraq invaded Kuwait, President Bush made it clear that regional conflicts would become a focus of U.S. policy. Speaking in Colorado, the President stated that the demise of the Soviet Union meant that the U.S. military would be "increasingly shaped by the needs of regional contingencies."[49] By 1993, it was pretty much agreed in U.S. national policy circles that regional instability was the most important threat to American security. The Secretary of Defense, Richard Cheney, underlined this in his final Report to the President and Congress when he observed that "the focus of the new [security] strategy is on meeting regional threats and challenges and on shaping the international security environment in ways that help to preclude the rise of hostile, non-democratic powers aspiring to regional hegemony."[50]

President William J. Clinton entered office in 1993 with the reputation of one who disliked military means. His election platform pledged that his primary attention would be on domestic issues and especially the economy. As a candidate in 1992, Clinton chastised the Republican candidate, George H.W. Bush for failing to enunciate a "new American purpose." But when the Clinton administration finally annunciated its vision of "democratic enlargement," it hardly lived up to the standard of a new purpose: "The successor to a doctrine of containment must be a strategy of enlargement—enlargement of the world's free community of market democracies."[51] Noted Yale political scientist Gaddis Smith called it "banality on stilts," but the notion of expanding the community of free-market democracies emerged as the central tenet of the Clinton administration's foreign policy.[52]

The enlargement was to be accomplished principally by engagement, meaning the use of diplomatic and economic tools of influence. In military strategic terms, this meant an increased emphasis on secondary functions, including reassurance, coercion, punishment, and conflict management (or "stability operations"). New functions were added as well, counterproliferation and "environment shaping"—the use of military power in peacetime to help channel world events down paths favorable to U.S. interests.

Given these priorities, the new security establishment, Secretary of Defense Les Aspin (who later resigned and was replaced by William Perry and then William Cohen), Chairman of the Joint Chiefs John Shalikashvili, and National Security Adviser Anthony Lake, accepted the "rouge state" analysis. The primary states covered under this definition were Iraq, Libya, Syria, and North Korea, all seen as potential sources of serious regional conflict. The fact that this meant a significant expansion of America's international goals went almost unremarked.[53] Instead of a defined enemy occupying a particular area and possessing a specific set of capabilities, the last remaining superpower faced a world full of annoying, ambiguous conflicts whose exact relation to U.S. national interests was not always clear.

But, aside from adopting the language of "democratic enlargement," few basic changes were made in existing policy and doctrine. Indeed, the Clinton Defense

Department did not issue its own national security strategy until two years later in 1995.[54]

In any case, the role of the U.S. military was to deter or defeat the identified national security threats, in large part through humanitarian assistance and peace-keeping missions. These were principally Army missions, but that service considered them of marginal interest. There was some debate over a possible "peacekeeping" division, but the officer corps strongly supported the existing structure and no important changes were made to accommodate these missions.

However, a sort of modus operandi did emerge for the use of military force. As analyzed by Cohen and Andrew Bacevich, it amounted to a form of remote, chiefly unilateral, intervention conducted on the cheap. It was a sort of skeletonized version of future warfare as predicted by RMA advocates. Since most of the places requiring U.S. intervention were third or fourth rate powers without advanced military technology (especially modern air defenses) American cruise missiles and air delivered PGMs could be launched against them from safe altitudes and distances. Military interventions would be quick and clean. High-tech, high precision ordnance could pressure the enemy leadership by striking key economic and military targets without excessive civilian casualties or great danger to Americans, neatly avoiding political repercussions either internationally or nationally. Some degree of international sanction might be required for legitimacy, but the United States would clearly be the dominant partner and conduct hostilities largely on its own terms.[55]

It was a comfortable, low-risk method that required substantially fewer forces than Soviet-era policy. The Clinton administration continued the rapid post-Cold War reduction begun under his predecessor. The Bottom Up Review (BUR) of 1993 pared an already shrinking military. The BUR cut Navy ships from 450 to about 320, reduced Air Force active and reserve fighter wings to 20, cut Army divisions from 12 to 10, and lowered the number of active-duty troops from 1.7 million to 1.4 million. These reductions were justified as able to support the established "two-war" concept as the basis for U.S. military planning. But how could the United States intervene overseas, at unpredictable times and places quickly and effectively, while still reducing the size of the U.S. military? The answer was to increase the capability of intervention forces through technology. An increased emphasis on air power and increased lethality for Army equipment were supposed to result in a smaller, more deployable, and more effective force.

Contemplating these reductions, the USAF concluded that, with upgrades, its existing bomber fleet would be adequate for decades and that its development money would be better spent on fighters. No new bomber would be fielded until the mid-2030s or beyond. It was a solution that pleased two important fighter-oriented constituencies, the USAF's own Combat Air Command and the aerospace industry, especially Lockheed Martin and Boeing, primary competitors for the F-22, the next generation fighter. The F-22 survived, but the planned buy was cut by a third. Two other programs, the Multi-Role Fighter and the Advanced Strike program, were killed as unaffordable. In their place, the Department of Defense initiated the Joint Advanced Strike Technology program to encourage development of an affordable next-generation strike aircraft for all four U.S. armed services. After review, it was later renamed the Joint Strike Fighter program.

More Troubles with Saddam Hussein

Despite the victory in 1991, Iraq remained a problem. Throughout its tenure, the Clinton administration engaged in endless wrangles with Saddam Hussein, who evidently delighted in finding ways to harass and annoy the United States.

In June 1993 the U.S. Navy fired Tomahawk missiles against the headquarters building of the Iraqi Intelligence Service (IIS) in Baghdad in response to evidence of a plot to assassinate former President Bush. The target was the command and control complex housing the IIS, the strike timed for 2:00 AM local time to minimize the risk to innocent civilians. Six buildings were targeted by 25 Tomahawk LAM-C missiles but only 23 were launched successfully. Of the 23, 16 missiles hit the target. Three others struck their programmed aim points, but those points were incorrect because of a mission planning software error. As a result, all three impacted in a residential area, killing 9 civilians and wounding 12. Four missiles were unaccounted for and presumably landed in the ocean or desert.[56]

Defense Secretary Aspin described the attack as a "wake up call" for Saddam Hussein. The operation demonstrated the U.S. ability to strike targets at will with little risk to American forces and may even have damaged the Iraqi intelligence capability. This commended a policy of using low-risk remote attacks in response to various provocations. It also demonstrated that despite all the post-Desert Storm hype, the systems were well short of perfection.

Two months later Congress issued a report on the U.S. military performance during the 1991 Gulf War. The report concluded that the U.S. Central Command had greatly exaggerated damage done to Iraqi military equipment, such as tanks and naval vessels, by air strikes.

Back in Iraq, Hussein and his military had never been notably cooperative with the UN weapons inspectors and interfered continuously with their work. In 1998 Hussein was sufficiently emboldened to order the teams out of the country. Furthermore, almost daily, Iraqi air defense radars "lit up" U.S. and British planes enforcing the no-fly zones. The planes were often tracked by air defenses and occasionally fired on. The United States and Britain would then retaliate by attacking the offending installations. The only result was an endless series of provocations and retaliations.

Grasping at Change

Proclaiming a revolution is one thing—actually producing it is another. For its part, the Army certainly was willing to believe in the Desert Storm RMA. It became the official Army view that a Revolution in Military Affairs had resulted from "dramatic developments" in weapons technology and information systems as "epitomized" in Desert Storm.[57] This did not mean that they were ceding pride of place to the Air Force. But now they were the ones in a doctrinal muddle. Lacking a

defined enemy and given the reduction in forces and the shift in strategy, Army doctrine writers were apparently still unsure of what to make of it all. In the absence of a
specific, well-defined enemy, how should they apply the new technology? How
should they organize, equip, and train military forces? Iraq had been heavily armed
in the Gulf War but with technology that was a generation behind, few indigenous
resources, and no allies. Its value as an example of future adversaries was very limited.

General Powell, still chairman of the Joint Chiefs, had assembled the Joint Staff
after the Gulf War and told them he wanted a new doctrine that would encompass
air, land, sea, and space forces and go beyond AirLand Battle to produce truly joint
campaigns. His objective was to begin the process of instilling a joint perspective of
warfare in the armed forces. What he received was a fierce display of service parochialism. The six-month drafting process for the publication was marked by a deep
desire by each service to preserve its own culture while making strenuous attempts
to promote the idea of separate ground, sea, and air campaigns. U.S. JCS Joint Publication Number 1, *Joint Warfare of the U.S. Armed Forces,* came out on schedule, but
the interservice fighting was nothing compared to the bloodletting that accompanied
the creation of the next manual, Joint Publication Number 3-0, *Doctrine for Joint
Operations.* The infighting became so intense that Powell ordered the Joint Staff to
undertake an intensive, high level effort to find common ground on key issues, the
chief one being the role of air power.

The 1993 BUR of U.S. National Military Strategy remarked in its report that,
"The likelihood that US military forces will be called upon to defend US interests
in a lethal environment is high, but the time and place are difficult to predict." That
was certainly true but not very helpful.

The BUR raised several issues including the idea of a "halt phase" credited to Secretary of Defense Les Aspin. This was Khafji writ large. The basic idea was that the
first phase of U.S. combat operations would typically be to halt a moving enemy
and that success in this phase was probably essential to further operations. The problem was that any such contingency was likely to occur in some distant location where
the United States did not have enough forces to do the job. According to *Air Force*
magazine, "That requirement had airpower written all over it."[58] This was a godsend
to air power proponents since the concept of the halt phase went a fair distance
toward making air attack the primary feature of a campaign. The Army was much
less enthusiastic for two reasons. First, because the logical consequence of such an
emphasis on air power for warfighting was a significant reduction in the Army's
active force structure. Second, the idea of an air dominated halt phase meant that
there would inevitably be fewer aerial resources available to support what they considered to be the inevitable ground battle. The idea was not mature yet, but it continued to bubble in air power doctrine circles for the next few years.

Army doctrine writers, like theoreticians, were certain that something new was
happening, but the doctrine they produced was not very revolutionary. As noted earlier, the 1993 edition of 100-5 seemed to suffer from ambivalence, dropping the
term AirLand Battle and introducing the idea of "full dimensional dominance,"
meaning that the Army was expected to be able to dominate the entire spectrum of

conflict from benign humanitarian assistance missions to a full-scale war of national survival. The result was a more generalized doctrine that avoided the name of Air-land Battle but still relied on its concepts of massive firepower and technological advantage as the keys to victory. To the surprise of absolutely no one, it looked very much like AirLand Battle II, an improved version of the same old thing.[59] It was the product of a cautious, resource-rich, technologically based military culture that relied on material superiority and the direct approach.

The Air Force, on the other hand, was pressing targeting concepts that would "decapitate" the enemy military (and perhaps civil) command structure, making the success of any ground action a forgone conclusion. In part this was due to Colonel John Warden's work in planning the air strategy during the desert war. As far as Warden and the other airmen were concerned, Desert Storm was the vindication of their long discredited belief that strategic air power could prevail with only marginal assistance from ground forces.[60] At the extreme, some air power enthusiasts were willing to state that not only could air power substitute for ground power, but in some cases for naval forces as well.[61] The buzzword was now "force projection" instead of "forward presence," and force projection was an Air Force specialty. According to one USAF general, "Who could deny that the relative importance of land, sea and airpower has shifted heavily in the favor of airpower in the recent past?" Given the Army's gradual withdrawal from its forward bases around the world, it was now the Air Force alone that had the ability to strike quickly anywhere in the world while the Army was still trying to get its tanks to the nearest port. For these partisans, Desert Storm had finally validated the long-held theories of Mitchell, Giulio Douhet, and Alexander de Seversky that air forces would supplant land and sea forces as the decisive instrument of military victory.[62]

CHAPTER 3

THE INFORMATION ARMY

Uncertainty is a dominating characteristic of the landscape. Most striking is the fact that we do not even know who or what will constitute the most serious future threat.
—Paul Davis, RAND Corp.[1]

General Gordon Sullivan continued as Army Chief of Staff under the Clinton administration, and his Force XXI process also continued in its deliberate way. The Army was in its period of slow, almost leisurely transition into the digital world. Sullivan saw no particular urgency, so his approach was very conservative and based on the idea that the Army should move in a deliberate manner to "conduct experiments to find out what works. Then we will redesign operational concepts and units to optimize the military capabilities." The organization that it yielded was to be called "Army XXI."

Army XXI

Operating from the premise that Desert Storm was the model of future war, Army XXI was to be "capabilities-based" rather than threat-based because there was no urgent external danger to focus on. The service's way of coping with this uncertainty was to emphasize emerging technologies that could provide leverage on a variety of future battlefields. Most notably, this meant information technology linking sensors and combat elements with sophisticated computers, enabling units to share situational awareness, and allowing commanders to make rapid, accurate tactical decisions. The Army XXI process would move toward this ideal by enhancing the "digitizing" process, meaning it would provide more information-age equipment to selected units and conduct a series of computer exercises and live "warfighting" experiments. The results would be evaluated and modifications made in the technology and the units' organization, doctrine, tactics, and techniques. This process was to continue until the optimum systems and force structure were developed.[2]

> Digitizing the battlefield is the application of technologies to acquire, exchange, and employ timely digital information throughout the battlespace, tailored to the needs of each decider (commander), shooter, and supporter. Digitization allows each soldier to maintain a clear and accurate vision of the common battlespace necessary to support planning and execution.
>
> —Army Digitization Master Plan[3]

After some debate it was decided that a hybrid heavy division design was the best option for experiments on force modernization. This was called the Force XXI heavy division, and it aimed to make armored and mechanized formations more deployable and agile while increasing combat power through information dominance. Modifications included increased fire support, expanded reconnaissance and intelligence capabilities, greater consolidation of logistics support functions, and additional infantry. Enhanced deployability and battlefield agility were achieved in part by the simple expedient of reducing the number of personnel. The division was to be cut from 18,069 troops to 15,719.[4] The fact it was conceptually little more than the 1943 armored division with better telephones was not allowed to dampen the general enthusiasm.

Forging New Doctrine

High-tech systems are of little benefit without some clear idea of how they should be employed—this is the realm of doctrine, the establishment of guiding principles, and their application.

In June 1993 the Army had produced its doctrine for the new world in the form of a newly rewritten FM 100-5, its basic how-to-fight manual. The Army would be expected to exert "full dimensional dominance," meaning being able to deter or win conflict at every level of the spectrum. Oddly for an operational manual, it stressed the strategic level of war and provided very little in the way of tactical advice. It also tried to deal with the problem of strategic ambiguity by describing a spectrum of conflict with disaster relief at the lowest level, counterinsurgency and counterterrorism slightly above, limited conventional war in the middle, and large-scale nuclear/conventional war at the high end. The manual recognized that things were changing but failed to provide much specificity in how to deal with it.[5] However, this use of the term "dominance" was appealing, and it was shortly applied to all sorts of things.

For the first time, the manual defined "operations other than war," the stuff at the low end of the spectrum, as important, but things like unconventional warfare and insurgency were largely ignored by everyone except a few Special Forces diehards tucked away at Fort Bragg. During the 1980s U.S. military doctrine and especially Army doctrine had folded most forms of other-than-conventional war into something called low intensity conflict. Insurgency and counterinsurgency were safely pigeonholed, and terrorism was ignored. The lack of appeal was easy to understand—unlike conventional operations, few troops were involved, the operating tempo was much reduced, less big-ticket equipment was required, and the scope of operations involved more quasi-political and informational activities. The role of air power was often reduced to no more than transport and surveillance.[6]

This sort of thing was considered the province of special operations, and the U.S. special operations capability had been greatly revived since its nadir in the 1970s. But it was seen as useful to the degree that it supported conventional "big Army" missions, or at least removed the need to worry about something other than conventional war. Let the special operations forces (SOF) take care of all those messy, marginal conflicts. For their part, important elements of the SOF community were also uninterested in that kind of politically charged conflict. Instead, they preferred to focus on "direct action," the commando, gunfighting part of special operations. Like rapid deployment, various forms of low-intensity conflict were wished away.

The year 1993 might be regarded as the dawn of digital warfighting. In September of that year a single platoon of four M1A2 tanks equipped with the Inter-Vehicular Information System, a developmental battlefield computer system, was tested at the National Training Center. "The system was fragile, hard to use, and the racket produced by the constant warble of the carrier wave was almost unbearable," but for the first time it allowed the tankers to "see" each other and to coordinate and pass information instantly. It was primitive, fragile, and slow, but this kind of "digital battle command" hinted at real possibilities.[7] In April 1994 an experiment called Desert Hammer VI tested a brigade-size version, but again with mixed results.

Meanwhile the 2nd Armored Division at Fort Hood [later redesignated the 4th Infantry Division (Mechanized)] was tapped to be the Experimental Force for Force XII. It soon became obvious that waiting for fully functioning digitization would have meant a delay until the next century. The concepts espoused may have been sound projections of existing capabilities, but expecting the technical architecture to be built quickly was expecting too much. Instead of full digitization, it was decided to begin by equipping a combat brigade with an "appliqué" system (a prototype set of hardware and software providing common computer links) based largely on existing commercial systems.[8] The 1st Brigade of the 2nd Armored was designated as Task Force XXI, the first unit to fully equip itself with "Information Age" equipment and technology and train as an information-based force. These were important technical advances but, as per FM 100-5, they were still employed in conventional force-on-force doctrine based on AirLand Battle.

Operation Deliberate Force

The ink was barely dry on the new FM when something happened that seemed to prove that the Gulf War was no fluke. The role of air forces really had changed. The warring factions in former Yugoslavia had been in sporadic conflict since 1992 and had shown a fine disregard for UN mandates. Increased factional fighting and attacks on UN "safe areas" during 1994 and 1995 culminated with a Bosnian Serb Army shelling of the Sarajevo market place on August 28, 1995, killing 38 civilians. NATO responded with Operation Deliberate Force, a bombing campaign against Serb forces that lasted from August 29 until September 14 when the warring factions agreed to cease operations and return to the UN brokered Framework Agreement.[9]

Although some artillery was employed, no other ground forces participated, and the NATO combatants were almost exclusively air forces. Over 11 days NATO aircraft conducted a carefully restrained campaign, dropping 1026 bombs, including 708 precision munitions against 338 targets. In contrast to the Gulf War, most of the munitions NATO employed were precision ones. Publicly available facts indicate that American forces employed laser-guided, electro-optical, or infrared-guided weapons and 13 Tomahawk Land Attack cruise missiles. Spanish, French, and British strike aircraft added 86 laser-guided bombs to the total.[10] American airmen dropped only 12 "dumb" bombs. The USAF lost no opportunity to highlight these figures.

A total of 293 aircraft flew 3,515 sorties from 15 European locations and three aircraft carriers. At least 700 of these sorties targeted command and control, supporting lines of communication, direct and essential targets, field forces, and integrated air defenses. A total of 67 percent of such targets engaged were destroyed, 14 percent experienced moderate to severe damage, 16 percent experienced light damage, and only 3 percent were judged to have experienced no damage. Most targeting was accomplished by JSTARS, U-2 aircraft, unmanned aerial vehicles, and reconnaissance satellites. An amazing performance when measured against any previous standard for accuracy in air bombardment.[11]

NATO losses were two French airmen apparently executed by Serb forces after their Mirage fighter was shot down by a man-portable surface-to-air missile. The operation was dominated by air power and, as viewed by the USAF, "air and space superiority was a driving and decisive factor in achieving peace." Airmen hailed it as the major influence in bringing Serbs to the bargaining table and enabling the November 1995 Dayton Peace Accords to halt the fighting.[12] It was not exactly an exclusive air campaign, but the role of non–air forces was negligible. The performance of PGMs received a great deal of attention, especially the introduction of the JDAM (pronounced jay-dam), short for Joint Direct Attack Munitions. Where previous PGMs were expensive, special purpose designs, the JDAM is a strap-on kit by Boeing that turns ordinary gravity bombs into precision guided munitions for the relatively modest price of $18,000–$20,000 each. For close-support missions, ground personnel relay target data to a strike aircraft overhead. The satellite-based global positioning system (GPS) guides the bomb to the target. Almost any warplane can launch a JDAM up to 15 miles from the target in any weather and strike within 10 feet of the intended spot.

The fact that the Yugoslavs had proven adept at deceiving both PGMs and their human overseers was less widely routed. It seemed almost churlish to point out that a fair amount of ordnance had been expended against dummy vehicles built mostly from plastic garbage bags and wood frames. The more sophisticated versions featured tin cans of fuel oil and sand that burned to create an infrared signature. It was also found that big splashes of black paint looked like bomb damage to U.S. reconnaissance assets, causing the operators to evaluate undamaged buildings, bridges, and runways as "destroyed."

The gloomy mood at the Department of the Army was not helped at all when former Assistant Secretary of State Richard Holbrooke evaluated the Yugoslav campaign on national television:

> One of the great things that people should have learned from this is that there are times when air power—not backed up by ground troops—can make a difference. That's something that our European allies didn't all agree with. Americans were in doubt on it. It made a difference.[13]

Almost casually, Holbrooke was implying that the traditional notion of massing a large ground force to confront an opponent on a field of battle was archaic.

The USAF certainly agreed and in 1997 produced its "strategic vision" document—*Global Engagement: A Vision for the 21st Century Air Force*. Although making the usual references to "the joint warfighting team," *Global Engagement* drove home the point that "what distinguishes the Air Force from the other Services—and provides unique leverage for combatant commanders—is our responsiveness and global perspective made possible by the air and space mediums in which we operate." The document went on to stress that "the unique capabilities offered by Air Force core competencies have often made the Air Force the instrument of choice in operations around the world." At least from the USAF perspective it looked as if the Army's role in any future war could be reduced to providing a band for the surrender ceremonies.

Airmen did not miss the opportunity to promote the crown jewel of future air power, the F-22, "the next-generation air superiority fighter."[14] "...[T]he F-22 [will be] the world's premier air superiority fighter, and its design will also make it a formidable air-to-ground weapon system. We expect the first F-22 unit to be operational in early FY 2005. Between 1999 and 2013, 438 operational F-22s will be produced to fill a planned four combat wings."[15]

Another observer, Harlan Ullman, a former Navy officer at the National Defense University, was less impressed with the performance of either air or ground forces in the war. There should, he believed, be a more effective way to apply the new technologies. Together with his colleague James P. Wade and others, he began to think through the problem.

The Army After Next

By now the Army leadership agreed that something had to be done or they might really end up as the finest irrelevant force in the world. In February 1996, the latest Army Chief of Staff, General Dennis J. Reimer, ordered the Army's Training and Doctrine Command to start work on a hypothetical "Army After Next." "The mission of the AAN Project is to conduct broad studies of warfare out to the year 2025 to assist senior leaders in developing a vision of future Army requirements. The project examined a wide range of areas including the future strategic setting and force projection concepts." In short, the idea was to gain some idea of what came after the Next Army, the digitized but conventional Force XXI. The 30-year point of focus for the AAN project was meant to help military planners and technologists think past Force XXI to more novel approaches.[16]

Building the Digital Force

While AAN was gathering steam, the digitizing process continued. The Department of Defense implemented the worldwide Secure Internet Protocol Router Network, instantly dubbed SIPRNet. In effect, SIPRNet was a military version of the civilian World Wide Web that allowed rapid, secure communications between units and services. It was enormously successful and quickly became an essential part of Department of Defense (DoD) operations. Over the decade of the 1990s SIPRNet spread throughout the entire defense establishment with tentacles reaching into other agencies. Now there was a virtual "joint community," a forum for discussion and a system for e-mail, chat rooms, and easy dissemination of operational information. It also lent credibility to the whole concept of digitization. It also provided a glimpse of future problems as users scrambled to fence off particular parts of the system.

However useful, SIPRNet was still a deskbound utility based on civilian systems. Adapting digital systems for combat was another matter. During the first seven months of 1996, the 4th ID's 1st Brigade (the Force XXI test-bed) was transformed and manipulated by various experts, specialists, contractors, and consultants. Two complex processes occurred: (1) building fundamental tactical skills, and (2) integrating the immature Tactical Internet (TI) into combat training. The last was vitally important because the TI was the glue to hold the information system together. The unit was closely scrutinized by the Army leadership and subject to stresses placed on no other brigade.[17]

The TI consisted of a radio network comprising the Enhanced Position Location Reporting System (a GPS variant) and the Single Channel Ground and Airborne Radio System. The data needed for battlefield situational awareness and command and control decisions would be available through this Tactical Internet to commanders at all levels of the Army's Battle Command System. The TI showed great promise but provided less than optimum help. It was fragile and complex, and the doctrine for its use ranged from vague to nonexistent. Commanders were left to figure out how to integrate it into tactics and soldiers how to maintain it, exploit its advantages, and accommodate its disadvantages. Still, it was astonishing that any system was produced that quickly, no matter how fragile.

The equipment's potential was obvious, but there was a great difference between potential and actual performance. The immaturity of the new technology affected all areas. It gave low-level units only a marginal ability to conduct digital operations, and development was slow. The percentage of tactical vehicles displayed on appliqué computer screens did not increase. However, this low percentage filled the screens with blue icons, making it appear that the TI had improved greatly. But, even lackluster TI performance was useful to a higher headquarters. Fragile technology was issued to uncertain soldiers, and they suffered the consequences. But, as the soldiers gained experience and the technicians improved the systems, a standard of "just-good-enough" developed. Rather than looking for the promised "complete operational picture," the soldiers learned to expect hints of truth and to build their estimates from there. Although the TI reported intermittently or incompletely, "it gave them more concrete facts than they had previously imagined receiving."[18]

Al-Qaeda—An Asymmetric Threat

By the mid-1990s bin Laden was well-known to the world's intelligence community, but so far Al-Qaeda appeared to be nothing more than a regional threat, one more collection of violent extremists in an area of the world that seemed to generate new ones almost continuously: dangerous certainly, but nothing unique.

In the meantime, the Saudi dissident did not seem cowed by the possibility of infinite watch-style missile attacks. Instead, he presented them as evidence of American cowardice and ineffectiveness. According to the terrorist leader, such attacks showed only that the United States (and Saudi Arabia) "bear the greatest enmity towards the Islamic world." "America," he claimed, was engaged in a "fierce Judeo-Christian campaign against the Muslim world, the likes of which has never been seen before," a "campaign against the Muslim world in its entirety, aiming to get rid of Islam itself." By then bin Laden had become sufficiently notorious that the Saudi government withdrew his citizenship, cancelled his passport, and froze his assets.[19]

In early 1995, a long-time terrorist leader named Ramzi Yousef was captured in Pakistan in connection with the 1993 attempt to topple New York's World Trade Center while releasing a cloud of poisonous cyanide gas. Yousef's capture produced a surprise. According to Pakistani authorities, he was closely linked to Usama bin Laden and the Al-Qaeda network.[20]

Bin Laden's name was certainly on the radar now, and it turned up among all sorts of violent Muslim movements in places like Chechnya, Bosnia, Yemen, Egypt, Sudan, Saudi Arabia, and even the Philippines. Then, in late 1996, a group of hard-line Islamic fundamentalists called the Taliban took control of much of Afghanistan. Their leader, Mullah Omar, welcomed bin Laden and Al-Qaeda, giving them use of some local facilities. Now bin Laden had something new, a territorial base where he could receive supplies and create training camps, transit points, even laboratories. He wasted no time in doing so.

The tall Saudi clearly had money, influence, experience as a fighter, respect as a leader, and a radical Islamist agenda. In case there was any doubt, he made his purpose clear in an August 1996 "Declaration of jihad" (holy war) from Afghanistan entitled, "Message from Usama bin Laden to his Muslim Brothers in the Whole World and Especially in the Arabian Peninsula: Declaration of Jihad Against the Americans Occupying the Land of the Two Holy Mosques; Expel the Heretics from the Arabian Peninsula."[21]

Some U.S. and foreign intelligence analysts continued to doubt his importance, but in 1996 the CIA decided to create a station devoted to "Osama bin Laden," the first time that the agency devoted a station solely to a single person.[22] By 1997, the Saudi had moved much of his operation to Afghanistan and the bin Laden unit at CIA developed a plan to capture him there and return him to the United States for trial. The Agency consulted with the Special Operations Command, who were dubious but did not actively oppose the plan as long as it involved only CIA assets. Nevertheless, the capture attempt was finally abandoned on the grounds that the risk of civilian casualties was too high.[23]

Exercises and Experiments: Building an Information Army

Meanwhile, things did not go so well for the information revolution in the demanding environment of California's Mojave Desert. In March 1997, more than 6,000 soldiers participated in the Task Force (TF) XXI AWE (Advanced Warfighting Experiment) at the Army's National Training Center (NTC). This was the first attempt to actually field a Force XXI style digitized organization with technologies properly integrated to attain significant increases in lethality, operational tempo, and survivability. TF XXI was provided with an improved version of the Tactical Internet for its wireless network of more than 1,000 computers, routers, and radios mated to tactical platforms (vehicles and dismounted soldiers).

If all went as planned, the result would be "dominant situational awareness," for leaders down to at least brigade level, providing near real time information on the friendly situation: current unit positions and their tactical/logistical status. Furthermore, the TI would enable a continuous flow of information on enemy locations and analysis of probable enemy intent. Because of this "information dominance," units would know more than the enemy and be able to act on this information significantly faster. They would be inside the enemy decision loop.

Unfortunately, the experiments did not go as well as hoped. The concept of appliqué systems, simply adding off-the-shelf information systems to existing equipment, did not provide the anticipated dividends. Standard military radios, for example, did not integrate well with the new systems. The TF's systems lacked the capacity for heavy digital traffic, making the information flow much slower than required, the computers tended to break down under constant use in desert conditions, leaders distrusted the information, and too often soldiers relied on the digital readouts and displays rather than simply looking around. In fact, the digitized force performed somewhat worse than typical conventional units. One important unexpected lesson did surface, however. A young, computer-savvy Signal Corps major used his terminal to relay a blow-by-blow account of the exercise's troubles to his friends at the Signal Corps Center in Fort Monmouth. These messages quickly leaked into the Internet where they were widely circulated among not only soldiers but military buffs and interested spectators of all kinds. The information revolution was harder to control than the Army thought.

As described by then-Major Thomas D. Morgan, a participant:

These high tech gadgets were designed by digital wizards who know little or nothing about combat and by defense contractors who are overprotective of their business secrets.

Those advanced devices did not integrate well with other systems being fielded, were not durable, were hard to operate and resulted in serious fratricide problems.

In other words, the holy grail of the common operational picture was still out of reach, and the digital force ended up shooting at itself.

Nevertheless, the TF XXI AWE was considered at least a qualified success. The Army believed that new, untested equipment and the limited time available to train in its use led to the lackluster results. After all, what was tested was really a system of systems, a very difficult matter to get right on the first try. Another part of the problem was that all of the equipment remained fragile and some was still in the prototype stage. Technology problems received the most attention, especially the appliqué systems and the Tactical Internet. But these were only two of the more than 75 systems tested, each with its own set of problems

Seven months later, the 4th Division conducted a much more closely guarded exercise called the Division Advanced Warfighting Experiment (DAWE) at Fort Hood. Rather than a field exercise, the DAWE was a "constructive simulation" with approximately 3,000 soldiers to evaluate the new Division design by exercising new digital operations centers (called Digital TOCs, for Tactical Operations Centers). Digital battlefield command capabilities were explored along with future operational concepts and combat service support designs, as well as the vulnerabilities of digital technologies on the battlefield. This augmented network supported multicasting applications, video teleconferencing, and high-bandwidth data transfers, as well as previously used network applications. The network architecture was 8 to 48 times faster than the net developed for TF XXI, but still exhibited growing pains. Even the habitually optimistic language of military briefings described the systems as "immature."

Despite reservations, the experiments yielded enough results to move ahead with plans to digitize the remainder of the 4th Division by the year 2000, employing an intranet/Internet backbone similar to the system tested in the Task Force XXI AWE. It was also decided to field a digitized corps (III Corps) in 2004.

Joint Vision 2010

At the doctrinal level, the Army staff pondered the results of the digitizing exercises and decided they had been right all along. When the Joint Staff offered their concept of warfighting for the twenty-first century, the Army contribution was an emphasis on digitizing the battlefield. The resulting publication, *Joint Vision 2010* analyzed American goals and interests in a world that included a wider range of threats than the twentieth century because of various new combinations of technologies and adversaries (both old and new). The pamphlet went on to offer the by now familiar "full spectrum dominance" as the key characteristic of future U.S. forces.[24] As before, this meant that the U.S. armed forces are expected to dominate in all forms of conflict from very low-level contingencies to full-scale war. This was to be achieved through "network centric warfare" that would fuse multiservice intelligence, operational, and logistic data to deliver "information superiority" and enable U.S. forces to anticipate, forestall, and outmaneuver the enemy. "Full spectrum dominance" was pretty much identical to the "full dimensional dominance" promulgated in the Army's 1993 *Operations* manual, FM 100-5.

Full Spectrum Dominance

Joint Vision 2010 constituted the official version of the future and the services quickly fell into line, each producing its own version and each stressing interservice cooperation ("jointness") while portraying itself as the dominant force and first among equals.

Full spectrum dominance was a very ambitious goal, but the Army expected to achieve it through a variety of means, all ultimately based on information superiority. Four elements were identified that added up to full spectrum dominance: dominant maneuver, precision engagement, full dimensional protection, and focused logistics. First was dominant maneuver—the application of information, firepower, and mobility to position friendly forces for best advantage. At the same time, these forces would employ the now-familiar litany of precision engagement—sensors and reconnaissance systems would locate enemy units, objectives, or targets, assign the appropriate weapons, assess the results, and reengage when required. While all this was happening, the friendly units would benefit from full dimensional protection—control of the area of operations to ensure that enemy forces were unable to interfere with maneuver and engagement. Finally, maneuver, engagement, and protection would be enabled by vastly improved logistics. Info-tech combined with new transport technologies would be able to react quickly to changing situations, track and shift assets even while en route, and deliver tailored logistics packages directly to the units in action.[25]

The Army used its version of *Joint Vision 2010, Army Vision 2010,* to argue for its own relevance, including a lengthy argument for the existence of ground forces, that began by noting:

> With the end of the Cold War, a prominent theory arose that there would no longer be a need for large land forces, that power projection and national military strategy could primarily be carried out through precision strikes using technologically advanced air and naval forces. This "standoff" approach would reduce the level of US involvement and commitment and thus the requirement for large land forces. Reality proved that theory to be invalid.

Army Vision 2010 then went on to point out that the Army had conducted 25 "significant" deployments since 1990. None of these involved conventional warfighting, but that was not allowed to interfere with the vision of "decisive operations." *Army Vision* also served notice that the ground forces could play the technology card as well as any service arm. Naturally, this called for another reorganization. The announcement was met by a chorus of criticism claiming that all this amounted to was a reduction in strength and a minor upgrade of the long-standing Cold War formations.[26]

The Air Force Version

By now the Army's expansion into the digital age began to create profound unease among Air Force planners. Writing for the USAF's Project 2025 program, Dr. Grant T. Hammond submitted a paper provocatively titled, "Paths to Extinction: US Air Force 2025," arguing the Army (and to a lesser extent the Navy) was gradually taking over Air Force functions. He characterized Army information dominance as "the exploitation of other people's sensors and platforms." He and others were concerned by Army future concepts such as long-range and long-endurance organic unmanned aerial vehicles with multiple missions, a better-protected GPS, and a set of transatmospheric vehicles called Hopper, Skipper, and Jumper. As interpreted by Hammond, "These indicate not only the intent but a search for capabilities to allow the US Army to undertake current US Air Force roles and missions." Project 2025 issued its "Final Report" outlining a number of possible futures, none of which featured a central role for land forces.[27]

The year 1996 turned out to be a seminal year for doctrine. That summer General Ronald Fogleman, new Chief of Staff of the U.S. Air Force, became the first service chief to officially disapprove a combatant commander's fundamental strategy. At issue was a Central Command plan for the defense of Kuwait and Saudi Arabia against any future Iraqi attack. Fogleman contended that the plan applied air power inappropriately, which would result in unacceptable casualties, loss of territory and resources, and an excessively long war. The general advised his staff that he was increasingly concerned about what he called the "ground-centric" use of air power in joint operations plans. Accordingly, he directed the Air Staff to develop a strategic analysis that was "air-dominant rather than land-centric."[28]

General Fogleman got his air-dominant strategy, prominently featuring the "halt phase" concept. Using the example of Desert Storm, Fogelman's planners pointed to the long, slow ground force buildup that preceded the war. It was very unlikely, they argued, that any adversary would be as generous. Instead, air power could be rapidly applied to stop a large-scale armored invasion. The basic idea was that precision air and missile strikes launched from as far away as the United States could halt an enemy attack and prevent it from seizing critical objectives until ground forces could arrive. For the airmen it was obvious that the speed and range of air power, bolstered by advances in aircraft, weapons, and targeting technology, made the halt phase concept feasible. Better yet, relying on such a philosophy for major regional conflicts would require a large investment in future aerospace force structure. As appealing as this might be to air power advocates, it became anathema to the Army.

About the same time Fogleman offered that a "new American way of war" was making it possible to break free of "brute force" attrition campaigns and move toward "a concept that leverages our sophisticated military capabilities to achieve U.S. objectives by applying what I would like to refer to as an asymmetric strategy."[29] In November, Fogleman and Secretary of the Air Force Sheila E. Widnall published their own "vision" statement "Global Engagement: A Vision for the 21st

Century Air Force," a document that emphasized the worldwide capabilities of the force and predicted a greater emphasis on space operations in years ahead.

Reporters asked the general about an assertion in *Army Vision 2010* that land power makes permanent "the otherwise transitory advantages achieved by air and naval forces." He replied that "those who say only ground forces can be decisive" in conflicts of the future "are clearly wrong."[30]

Meanwhile, the Air Force, eager to capitalize on its perceived advantage after Operation Deliberate Force, was explaining to anyone who would listen that, "In the first quarter of the 21st century you will be able to find, fix or track, and target —in near real-time—anything of consequence that moves upon or is located on the face of the Earth" with aircraft.[31] Army partisans responded that this might be true for the most obvious targets such as tanks or aircraft carriers (provided they can be distinguished from similar friendly or civilian objects). But it is unlikely to be true, particularly at standoff distances, for small arms, for forces in cities, for enemy soldiers interspersed among a background population or in heavy forests or jungles, for mortars and antitank and antiaircraft missiles hidden in trucks or caves, and for properly secured weapons of mass destruction.[32] Only 2 of the estimated 60 mortars that fired on friendly troops in Mogadishu during the U.S. operation there in 1992–1994 were spotted and targeted quickly enough to be destroyed.[33]

Rapid Dominance/Shock and Awe

The year 1996 was not only seminal for Air Force doctrine. Along with the Army After Next initiative and the Halt Phase debate, there were continuing attempts to interpret the Desert Storm campaign in the light of the revolution in military affairs (RMA). The Joint Chiefs of Staff, for example, produced drafts for a new JCS Pub 3.0 and the U.S. Army contributed its 525-5 Pamphlet to the discussion, but neither seemed wholly satisfactory. Both advised the reader to exploit operational rapidity and simultaneity but failed to provide concrete suggestions or a larger concept. The ideas of Shock and Awe and Rapid Dominance would fill that need.

Harlan Ullman and James Wade of the National Defense University introduced these concepts in a slim volume titled *Shock and Awe: Achieving Rapid Dominance.* Ullman, Wade, and their coauthors called for military operations with "sufficiently intimidating and compelling factors to force or otherwise convince an adversary to accept our will." More importantly, they provided at least a glimpse of an organizing principle for the RMA.

The modern roots of Shock and Awe as a military method stretched back to the early 1990s, when military commanders and analysts began to think about "how to get out of this attrition warfare, force on force," by changing the "will and perceptions [to] shape the enemy's behavior without necessarily destroying all of his forces."[34]

According to Ullman, "The Japanese quit [in World War II], because they couldn't appreciate that one bomb could do what 500 planes did in a night. That was shock. Now, can you take that level of shock and apply it with conventional weapons? We thought you could."[35]

In this analysis, Desert Storm succeeded less because of advanced technology than because of the particular way it was applied. The secret lay in the series of rapid, simultaneous attacks designed to apply decisive force against key targets. To be truly effective, the aim should be stun and then rapidly defeat the enemy through a series of carefully orchestrated, simultaneous strikes against many military and enemy government targets across a wide battle space. The resulting paralysis of the enemy's will and ability was described as *Shock and Awe*.[36]

Shock and Awe and Rapid Dominance were important because they gave focus to the RMA and the technologies associated with it, especially those that resulted in "dominant battlefield awareness." According to proponents, it was not merely a better way to do the old business. It was a new application for the new technologies.[37]

> Rapid Dominance is aimed at influencing the will, perception, and understanding of an adversary rather than simply destroying military capability, this focus must cause us to consider the broadest spectrum of behavior, ours and theirs, and across all aspects of war including intelligence, training, education, doctrine, industrial capacity, and how we organize and manage defense.[38]

As described by the authors, Shock and Awe neutralize an adversary's ability to command, to provide logistics, to organize society, and to function. It included the ability to control, regulate, and deny the adversary information, intelligence, and understanding of what is and what is not happening.[39] In their opinion, a military organized for Rapid Dominance, using Shock and Awe as a method, could win a major regional contingency such as Desert Storm far more quickly and cheaply with far fewer personnel. In addition, according to Ullman and coauthors, a force structure optimized for Rapid Dominance will have a more effective capacity to deal with grey areas such as Operations Other Than War.

Although Ullman and his coauthors were careful to specify that Rapid Dominance/Shock and Awe was a *joint* concept, the emphasis was clearly on air forces. "Shock and Awe" offered a way to wield U.S. firepower and win a war without large troop deployments like Desert Shield and Desert Storm. This did not make it welcome in Army circles.

The Quadrennial Defense Review and Other Threats

Although it would make for a simpler narrative, the services and the Secretary of Defense (SecDef) are not the sole arbiters of military issues. Congress also has a vote. When Rumsfeld returned to the Pentagon after 24 years, he told one interviewer that he was shocked at the increase in congressional "nitpicking and micromanaging." "The number of congressional staffers [concerned with defense issues] had doubled from something like 8,000 to something like 16,000." Those staffers demanded hundreds of reports on all manner of topics, many of no obvious value. The SecDef made his disdain plain, which, combined with his self-assured style, led to an often sour relationship with the legislative branch.[40]

For its part the Air Force was still pushing hard for an air dominated "halt phase," and advancing it in a series of studies and articles. By 1997 the idea had matured as an emerging concept and was something like quasi-doctrine. It was attractive to Congressional policy makers because it offered a way to cope with the possibility of two simultaneous major theater wars. If ground forces were committed to one war, air strikes would hold off enemy advances in a different contingency with a minimal number of troops until additional ground forces were either shifted or mobilized from the reserves. Fewer troops meant fewer casualties. It also nested nicely with the ideas of Rapid Dominance and Shock and Awe. In the airmen's view, given free rein, the arriving ground forces would have little to do but mop up after the air campaign.

With Congress peering over their collective shoulders, the individual armed services and the Department of Defense slogged through one study after another, trying to understand the future role of the military and how forces should be structured to meet it. There had been the 1991 Base Force Review, the Bottom Up Review in 1993, the 1995 Commission on Roles and Missions study, a Mobility Requirements Update study the same year, *Joint Vision 2010* in 1996, then came the Deep Attack Weapons Mix Study followed by the Joint Strategy Review, and then in 1997 the first Quadrennial Defense Review (QDR).

The QDR is a congressionally mandated Defense Department self-study and for that reason is often viewed with skepticism. For critics, this kind of navel-gazing rarely produced anything important. However, for the services, the 1997 QDR was an important battleground in the unending war for budget share that was the lifeblood of the armed forces. It would set the terms of debate for the next four years.

In some respects the 1997 QDR bore out the skeptics. The final document doubted the rise of a peer competitor before 2015 but hedged its bets. To help decide near-term policy, the Review relied on simulations of war in 2014 against what might be called a "half-way peer"—a regional great power with armed forces significantly larger and more capable than those of Iraq, Iran, or North Korea.

Congress wanted the review to be a fundamental appraisal of the way national defense was to be conducted. But the first report was, for the most part, a status quo document that basically accepted the various service versions of their own futures. One critic later termed it "a crass vindication of bureaucratic and armed service business-as-usual; and a surrealistic assertion that the United States could still fight and win two (more or less) simultaneous major wars, presumably in Korea and the Persian Gulf."[41] The so-called "two war" strategy was really a way of determining required force size, not a strategy at all. The truth was that by 1997 the United States military structure would barely support one major overseas conflict, let alone two.

Importantly for the Air Force, the QDR did endorse the concept of the halt phase. The report did not merely reaffirm the national strategy of being able to fight and win two nearly simultaneous major regional conflicts, now referred to as major theater wars (MTWs). It described the two-MTW requirement as the defining capability of a superpower. More to the point, it identified the halt phase as the critical aspect of the two-MTW strategy, requiring the capability to rapidly halt an enemy advance while other U.S. and allied forces are en route to the conflict. The review said that halting an enemy force rapidly, short of its objective, might avoid a bloody ground campaign to regain captured territory.[42]

On the other hand, it also recommended moderate force reductions that worried the airmen. A cut of 26,900 USAF military personnel was recommended against cuts of 15,000 for the Army and 18,000 for the Navy. The U.S. Marine Corps cut was placed at only 1,800 active duty military slots. The report also recommended slowdowns in a few major equipment purchases and sought to reduce planned purchases under some major USAF programs—the F-22 fighter, the B-2 Stealth Bomber and the airborne Joint Surveillance Target Attack Radar Systems.

The F-22 Raptor was a particularly sensitive issue for the USAF. This was their next generation air superiority fighter, stealthy and highly maneuverable with advanced integrated avionics, and aerodynamic performance allowing supersonic cruise without an afterburner. It was the single most important item on the Air Force wish list but acquiring it had become a painful process. The Raptor had been in development since the 1980s and only now was in flight testing. Originally, it was planned to acquire over 900 of the planes, a number then reduced to 648 (total cost $86.6 billion). But after the Bottom Up Review, that number was dropped to 442 at an estimated cost of $71.6 billion. Now the QDR recommended another reduction, this time to 339 aircraft. Critics argued that the Raptor was another Cold War leftover, designed to penetrate a Soviet air space that no longer existed, besides it was already over budget and behind schedule. To the airmen it looked as if their most important program was being nibbled to death.[43]

On the whole the report seemed to be more or less good news for the ground forces. It endorsed Army "digitization" and suggested accelerating the Force XXI "Digital Army" effort by two years. Nevertheless, the Army was sufficiently threatened to circulate the following as part of the official guidance for answering media queries about the Army reaction to the QDR:

> Why an Army: (1) The Army, as a relevant supporter of the national military strategy provides boots on the ground any time/any place needed...(2) We have the world's best Army, a full spectrum force, trained and ready for victory. The Army is a total force of quality soldiers...equipped with the most modern weapons and equipment the country can provide...We are changing to meet the challenges of today, tomorrow and the 21st century. (3) The Army must be prepared to project its capabilities rapidly and effectively in support of the national military strategy. (4) Land forces provide the nation the full range of options for shaping the world environment. (5) The Army is transitioning from an industrial to an information age Army. The Army of the future will be a knowledge and capabilities-based, power projection Army, capable of land force dominance across the continuum of 21st century joint military operations. (6) The Army's ability to use information to dominate future battles will give the United States a new key to victory, for years if not generations to come. (7) The Army has shifted its intellectual and physical focus from a predominately forward deployed force to a United States based force

projection Army...The imperative for a smaller, better, high-tempo Army is to maintain and even increase its capabilities through modernization.[44]

This had the slightly desperate air of most recent Army pronouncements but worse was on the way.

First of all, the Air Force reacted to its perceived slights by formally unveiling the "Halt Phase Strategy/Doctrine." The halt concept was gradually progressing to other areas of DoD planning and programming. National documents including the National Security Strategy, the National Military Strategy, and the Defense Planning Guidance adopted the requirement to rapidly halt an invasion in two nearly simultaneous MTWs. The President's National Security Strategy in 1997 stressed the need for rapid success in the halt phase. Using words almost identical to the QDR final report, it stated: "The United States must maintain this ability to ensure that we can seize the initiative, minimize territory lost before an invasion is halted, and ensure the integrity of our war fighting coalitions." By stopping the enemy quickly, the United States and its allies could then take the initiative against a debilitated opponent. The National Security Strategy also noted that such a capability would deter potential aggressors who might take advantage of a situation where the United States was also heavily involved in an MTW or a smaller-scale contingency in another part of the world.[45] How it would apply to terrorists, insurgents, or other such threats was not specified.

For many in Congress the QDR smacked too strongly of business-as-usual and not what they had in mind. Consequently, it chartered the National Defense Panel, a blue-ribbon commission, to review the QDR. While the other studies had recommended little in the way of fundamental change, the Panel report was different.[46]

In December of 1997 the National Defense Panel (NDP) issued, *Transforming Defense: National Security in the 21st Century.* The report began by criticizing the QDR as weak in that it "views Major Theater Warfare as a traditional force-on-force challenge," an assumption that "inhibits the transformation of the American military to fully exploit our advantages as well as the vulnerabilities of potential opponents." It warned the Pentagon not to get too comfortable with the current force structure; it may not be "optimal" as new technologies become available, which in turn "may permit us to be successful with smaller but far more lethal and effective forces."

According to the report, nothing less than a "transformation" of the U.S. military was needed to meet emerging threats. However, the NDP's findings were disquietingly vague about exactly what the threat was and what the transformed force should look like. It offered little in the way of a clearly defined end state strategy and failed to deliver on Congress's request for alternative force structures. The panel also thought that DoD could make do with less expenditure on forces because the United States could afford to accept more risk in the near term. The NDP called for diverting $5 billion to $10 billion a year from existing accounts—which paid for current forces and their immediate successors—in order to give more to new "initiatives in intelligence, space, urban warfare, Joint experimentation, and information operations."[47]

Another of its findings was that future opponents were less likely to confront the United States directly than to seek to disable the underlying structures that enable military operations. Forward bases and forward-deployed forces would likely be challenged and coalition partners coerced. Critical nodes that enable communications, transportation, deployment, and other means of power projection would be primary targets.[48]

The NDP might lack specificity as to structures, strategy, and end states, but it could be specific when it wanted to. The Army was chastised for its inability to deploy rapidly and its decision to pursue a new main battle tank when it should be developing a new "very light" armored vehicle "half the weight" of the M1 Abrams. The Army, it said, should move toward lighter weight and more lethality in all of its platforms and go to smaller units. It should seek to acquire a lighter combat vehicle in the 30- to 35-ton range and a hypervelocity gun. The Army generally should become "more expeditionary" with "fast, shock-exploiting forces." Finally, the NDP produced a template of critical capabilities—"mobility, stealth, speed, increased range, precision strike," and a "small logistics footprint"—that it believed would be important between 2010 and 2020. These might all be good qualities, but as usual there were few hints on how they could be realized.

The Army was not happy with the report but managed to accept it without too much unpleasantness, as well as without directly promising to actually do anything about it. The Air Force was not pleased since the report failed to point out how admirably that service fitted the NDP "critical capabilities" list. Additionally, NDP spokesmen were at pains to say they did not endorse the B-2 bomber, which supposedly exemplified those capabilities, or a follow-on, such as a B-3. Worse yet, it recommended that two of the USAF's priority programs be reduced or eliminated—the F-22 fighter and the Joint Strike Fighter, both programs that had been endorsed by the QDR.[49] The Air Force found further unhappiness in the fact that the report excluded any mention of the halt phase. There were dark (and public) accusations that the omission was largely due to behind-the-scenes work by the Army, which was allegedly opposed to giving air power (obviously pivotal to the halt phase) too prominent a role.

One lasting result of the NDP was the enshrinement of the term "transformation," meaning to capitalize on the new RMA technologies to produce "fundamental changes in military capabilities accompanied by changes in doctrine, operational concepts and organizational structure."[50] From that time forward, any service initiative hoping to receive serious consideration had to be clearly labeled as part of transformation.

The Leap Ahead and the Army after Next

The QDR's endorsement of the Army digitization program was cold comfort in the light of the NDP report and continuing modernization problems. The service was not slow to react. In February 1998, General Dennis Reimer, Sullivan's successor as the Army Chief of Staff, announced that beginning in fiscal year (FY) 1999 the service would shed the "traditional incremental approach" and reject marginal changes for a "leap ahead" approach. Force XXI would still be the vehicle for change—"knowledge and capabilities based, threats-adaptive force organized around information and information technologies." But, the QDR had mandated change and the contemplative approach of the Army After Next lacked urgency. No one was sure what that really meant; after all, AAN was a concept and a process, not an actual organization. But it would be the basis for a real world organization and, if no one knew exactly what it looked like, it would assuredly be very different from the conventional ground force of 1998. AAN concepts (e.g., lightweight vehicles, modular brigades) remained imbedded in the Army's idea of the future, but more than anything it was a statement of faith and, still, no one had a firm idea of how it would be implemented.[51]

In the real world, things were equally uncertain. The spotty record of the digitization effort was highlighted in July 1999 when a General Accounting Office (GAO) report stated that the Army had so far failed to produce convincing evidence that its $20 billion plan to field advanced information systems would make its forces more effective on the battlefield. The report, unpromisingly titled "Battlefield Automation: Performance Uncertainties are Likely When the Army Fields its First Digitized Division," found that the results of past field evaluations of the Army's digitization effort "have been inconclusive" and showed "no significant increase" in the ability of soldiers armed with information systems to carry out battle operations.

The report also revealed that the Army was planning to field the linchpin command and control system of its digitization effort, known as Force XXI Battle Command Brigade and Below, before it had fully tested and evaluated the system's capabilities and interoperability. This would result in Army units receiving systems that had not been proven to work and that personnel had not been trained to use.

"This means that if current procurement plans proceed, the Army will have obligated $128.5 million [through fiscal year 2001] to purchase and install about two-thirds of the systems needed for the first digitized corps without conclusive determinations," according to the report. The GAO also criticized the Army's plan to fully digitize the Fourth Infantry Division by December 2000, the III Corps by the end of fiscal year 2004, and the remaining divisions between 2010 and 2012. Changes and delays in the program made this a "highly risky" acquisition strategy, according to the report.

Martin Libicki, a defense analyst with RAND Corp., commented that there are many ways of looking at the Army's digitization plans; but since results of experiments have been mediocre, "It could be that [digitization of the battlefield] is a much more profound [change] than the Army understands," Libicki said. "Or, we may be asking too much from command and control [technologies]." According to Libicki, although the Army was spending a lot on digitization, the negative GAO report, mediocre test results, and the uncertain nature of the future military threat made it a questionable investment.[52]

Division XXI

Continuing the momentum established by Sullivan, the Army under General Reimer began to reengineer its heavy combat division to incorporate the new technologies in the "Force XXI" division, also referred to as Division XXI, or sometimes the Limited Conversion Division. Still, the outward appearance of the new heavy division was quite similar to its predecessors. It had three maneuver brigades (one armor and two mechanized infantry), division artillery, and a division support command. Each armor brigade had two armor battalions and one mechanized infantry battalion, and each mechanized infantry brigade had two mechanized infantry battalions and one armor battalion. It would have been immediately recognizable to General Patton.

Once again, the trade-off for new technology, enhanced deployability, and battlefield agility was size. The Force XXI line battalions were reduced to three companies (versus the previous four-company structure) with a total of 45 "enhanced combat platforms" (M1A2 Abrams tanks or M2A3 Bradley fighting vehicles) in each battalion—down from 58 armored vehicles in the previous heavy battalions. Platoons continued to have four combat vehicles, and mechanized infantry platoons were be structured on the basis of three nine-soldier squads. At the same time the battalion's assigned area of operations was expended by 50 percent. Supposedly, "the new [digital] systems' enhanced capabilities, coupled with improved [situational understanding], would make these smaller battalions more effective." They were expected to be more agile, more mobile, and more deployable, while exercising more decisive dominant maneuver.[53]

While the Force XXI division was to be smaller, it was intended to dominate a dramatically larger battlespace, 140 percent larger than the area previously assigned to a heavy division. The Force XXI heavy division was projected to have the capabilities to cover a battlespace of 120 kilometers by 200 kilometers (a 120-kilometer frontage with a 200-kilometer depth) because its elements could be more dispersed through the use of advanced command and control systems. In addition, its intelligence systems would see farther, and its fire support would reach farther. As newer systems under development entered service (c. 2005), the Force XXI division's battlespace was expected to expand even further.[54]

The Army intended to structure battles of the future on purpose and timing, with a reduced emphasis on geometric boundaries, employing a balanced combination of precision fire and precision maneuver to produce overwhelming combat effects on exactly the right spot at exactly the right time. The Force XXI division was expected to fight four or five battles simultaneously and then be able to recover from and continue or reenter fights quickly.

The reorganization significantly affected the division support command, which was to be restructured and equipped to provide battalion/forward support company direct support of line units and to use the most modern capabilities to change from a supply-based system to a delivery-based system.

The result was intended to be a "modular" unit that could operate both as an independent unit and in joint task forces. This unit was to have a tactical "footprint" about a third smaller than a heavy division, thanks in part to logistics advancements that kept it supplied, reducing its need for an integral logistics "train." The 1st Cavalry Division was scheduled for conversion to the new heavy division structure by 2003, and III Corps headquarters was to be digitized by 2005 to command the new divisions. Other Army divisions were to follow as funding dictated.

In June 1998 the Army announced the beginning of the scheduled strength reductions under the Division XXI plan. Some divisions (the Limited Conversion Divisions) were to complete only limited conversion to the new design before they received digital systems. The 1st ID (M) (–) in Germany began such a limited conversion in FY 1999. The rest of the Army's mechanized divisions, except the 2nd Infantry Division in Korea, were scheduled for limited conversions in FY 2001. The Army National Guard mechanized forces began conversion to the limited Division XXI design in FY 2000.[55]

Critics, including Frank Finelli, a retired Army officer and force planner, were unimpressed: "I think the Army has missed an opportunity to transform its force structure and gain some efficiencies." Finelli, who served as a planner on the Pentagon's Joint Staff and then as an assistant to Senator Dan Coats (R-IN), chairman of the Armed Services subcommittee on ground forces, observed that "in reality, the adjustments are minor and reinforce the critique that the new force is nothing more than incorporating new technologies into the same organizational structures and using existing operational concepts."[56] The technology might be there, but organization and doctrine were still lagging.

The changes did little to solve the problem of strategic mobility. The "new" formations were still too slow and too heavy. This was a regrettable fact, but unavoidable. The Defense Science Board had commissioned a task force to investigate strategic mobility in 1996, and the Congressional Budget Office had studied it in 1997. Along the way a host of think tanks, contractors, consultants, and private commentators had contributed assessments. Since these studies varied widely in assumptions, methods, objectives, and even terminology, reconciling their conclusions was impossible.

By now it was commonplace for critics to complain that the Army's modernization process looked more like a technology shopping spree than a revolution. Army officials even considered a much smaller division, ceding more independence to subordinate brigades, similar to a plan outlined by Army Colonel Douglas Macgregor in his controversial 1997 book, *Breaking the Phalanx*. Macgregor's idea was a modular Army composed of brigade-sized combined-arms units that would be much smaller than conventional divisions, but larger and more capable than conventional brigades. Information systems at all levels would help tie together these basic "building blocks" into larger, mission-tailored task forces. The information-enabled units would also facilitate close cooperation with other services and other nations. These units, Macgregor believed, would not only be readily adaptable and rapidly deployable, but also "joint" (multiservice) and "combined" (multinational) from the bottom up. Despite considerable favorable publicity, the Army decided that McGregor's proposal would be too vulnerable and unworkable.[57]

General William W. Hartzog, commanding general of the U.S. Army Training and Doctrine Command, was concerned that new structures would be ineffective without new doctrine. The general announced that a rewritten Field Manual 100-5, *Operations,* was expected to be in the hands of soldiers by the end of 1998, but the manual became enmeshed in doctrinal disputes and failed to materialize on schedule. Most of the issues were petty and often excessively bureaucratic, but they dragged on endlessly.

When 1998 arrived, the Army and Air Force were still engaged in the lengthy struggle over their respective roles, motivated by the Army's fear and the airmen's desire that the Air Force would emerge as the decisive instrument of warfare (as air power partisans argued that it already had). The squabbling became acrimonious enough that Generals Dennis J. Riemer, Army chief of staff, and Ronald R. Fogleman, Air Force chief of staff, jointly penned an article called "Joint Warfare and the Army Air Force Team." Seeking at least overtly to pour oil on the roiling waters, the two chiefs acknowledged that "cooperation does not imply that we have identical views on all issues" and that "relations between the Army and the Air Force became strained as each tried to incorporate lessons learned in the Gulf." The article also cited "the heritage of teamwork and mutual respect between the two services" and the "great strides" made in "many areas of inter-service cooperation" as the basis for resolving their differences. They also made specific reference to Joint Publication Number 3, *Joint Operations,* as the source of authoritative guidance for senior commanders.[58] This point became interesting in the light of subsequent events. Any soothing effect all this might have had was short-lived.

CHAPTER 4

VISION AND TRANSFORMATION

The assumption of unilateral advantage seems to be a common fallacy afflicting those who fantasize about the uses of future technology in warfare.[1]

—Mark Gubrund

It is probably fair to say that the revised, urgent Shinseki version of transformation had two proximate causes. One is the drubbing administered by the 1997 report of the National Defense Panel. The other is the odd little 87-day war waged by the United States and its NATO allies against the regime of President Slobodan Milosevic, leader of what remained of the former Yugoslavia.

Kosovo

Reality delivered another nasty surprise in the spring and summer of 1998 when large-scale fighting broke out between Serbs and ethnic Albanians in the Serbian-controlled province of Kosovo in former Yugoslavia. Early the next year Milosevic decided to solve the problem with a campaign of "ethnic cleansing"—forcibly expelling the Kosovo Albanians.

Milosevic's intentions, of course, had nothing to do with doctrinal squabbles among the American armed forces. What he wanted was to stamp out a guerrilla independence movement, and his method was a brutal police, military, and paramilitary offensive. Angered by the wanton destruction and fearing further destabilization in the already shaken Balkans, the United States and its NATO allies brokered an on-and-off cease-fire followed by weeks of fruitless negotiation until Milosevic escalated the crisis with another large-scale offensive in Kosovo.

Once again the United States was faced with a crisis in an awkward place. The ideal intervention force would have been U.S. Army heavy armored units, but the closest ones were in Germany, and getting them to Kosovo would take weeks. Army planners considered sending the elite 82nd Airborne Division that could drop into Kosovo within days. However, the paratroopers lacked the firepower to stand up to Yugoslav armor. In other words, heavy forces were too slow and light infantry lacked the firepower. And the Army had nothing in between. Furthermore, NATO political leaders believed a show of force would quickly make Milosevic call off the paramilitaries and army troops carrying out the ethnic cleansing.

On March 24 NATO began Operation Allied Force (OAF). The Serbian leadership was insufficiently impressed, believing that the air strikes would be no more than "demonstrations," deliberately limited pinpricks lasting a few days. They may have also doubted NATO's political will to carry out an extended campaign. In any case, the initial results were horrible. Milosevic's forces responded to the cautious air war with a rampage, massacring hordes of refugees. A senior Joint Staff official phoned General Wesley Clark, commander of Operation Allied Force, with a question from the White House: When would they hit the Yugoslav troops and tanks?[2] The discussion of ground forces was revived, but NATO commanders still showed no enthusiasm for the prospect and U.S. President William Clinton publicly ruled out the possibility.

As a result, the various NATO air forces not only had center stage, but also virtually the entire show. Despite a slow start caused by bad weather, by early June NATO pilots were bombing targets from one end of Serbia to the other. NATO allies as well as U.S. Navy and Marine aviators participated, but the U.S. Air Force carried out most of the missions, putting their entire inventory on display. Advanced aircraft, including the F-117 stealth fighter, penetrated heavily defended areas to strike critical command and control targets with precision guided munitions (PGMs). The Joint Surveillance Target Attack Radar Systems (JSTARS) targeting aircraft searched for tactical targets. Venerable B-52 bombers flew from England with cruise missiles and gravity bombs, while B-1s attacked with precision bombs and cluster munitions. B-2 stealth bombers dropped satellite-guided bombs. Data from U-2 spy planes were bounced off satellites to the United States then back to the theater in finished form in 10 minutes.

Flying from the U.S.-controlled air base at Tuzla, in northeastern Bosnia, Predator unmanned aerial vehicles (UAVs) ranged over Yugoslavia, looking for targets and recording bomb damage. Images from sensors on the Predators were coupled with national satellite data to generate targets for F-16 strikes. Only two of the UAVs were lost to enemy fire, and a third crashed due to a fuel system fault on a final approach to Tuzla. The remains of the shot down Predators were collected by the Yugoslavs and put on display in their air force museum in Belgrade.[3]

Flying at night at or above 15,000 feet while avoiding unnecessary risks inevitably led to mistakes, including the bombing of two refugee convoys on the same day. New tactics were implemented with pilots flying lower to identify targets better but at greater risk. Three NATO fighter-bombers were hit by ground fire, and an American F-16 was shot down by Yugoslav antiaircraft fire.[4]

Targeting quickly became a serious problem. The primary tactical surveillance system, the airborne JSTARS, was really designed to detect moving targets, and the Serbs were not providing many. The other high-tech efforts had similar difficulty in finding worthwhile military objects. The Serbs had adopted the simple expedient of hiding their heavy armor and artillery while scattering numerous cheap decoys in the open to absorb the allied effort. NATO air target lists were expanded carefully to include more fixed targets that could be located on the ground, including some infrastructure such as bridges.

Since the object was to coerce Milosevic (who was, in effect, the Yugoslav government) and not punish the civil population, widespread bombing of infrastructure such as hydrodams and nonmilitary industries was largely ruled out. That left military targets and, after the initial attacks on command and control and air defense sites, these proved elusive. The tempo of the attacks grew, but Milosevic remained unmoved, forcing NATO to expand the campaign. The target list was extended again, this time into so-called sustainment targets, in other words, civil infrastructure—petroleum, lines of communication, and electrical grids.[5]

Eventually, the unwelcome subject of committing ground forces rose up again. Both military and civilian critics complained that NATO had failed to heed a basic lesson from history—no war had ever been won through air power alone. Then with a swiftness that caught many by surprise, Belgrade relented. Milosevic and the Kosovo guerrillas finally agreed, and at dawn on June 12, British, French, and American peace-keepers entered Kosovo with a "cooperating" force of Russian troops. On June 20, NATO declared the air war officially ended and began to settle down for a long-haul peace-keeping mission.

On paper, the numbers are remarkable: NATO dropped 20,000 bombs and 99.6 percent of them reportedly found their targets. NATO pilots flew some 35,000 sorties with a loss of two planes and no pilots (both were quickly rescued). Not a single allied solider, sailor, airman, or Marine died in combat.[6] The war also provided a tragic lesson in PGM accuracy when a U.S. missile strike landed at the programmed coordinates for a Serb "strategic target." The location, however, was that of the Chinese Embassy, not the strategic target believed to be there.[7] It was later claimed that NATO bombs also struck a hospital, killing four and, in a separate allied attack, damaged the Swedish Embassy. There were apparently at least 16 such incidents, including inadvertent attacks on another hospital and on civilian neighborhoods. Although exact figures are impossible to determine, the civilian death toll probably ranged somewhere between about 2,000 and 5,000.[8]

The operation also surfaced some other unglamorous questions about the future of military networking, especially networking on the vast scale anticipated by transformation theorists. The first issue was limited bandwidth. Simply put, the greater the volume of information to be transmitted, the more bandwidth required to move it—more bandwidth allows faster transmission of information.[9]

Although Allied Force was almost entirely an air operation, communications systems supporting combat operations remained saturated throughout the conflict. In large part this was because it was the first conflict to make extensive use of video teleconferencing and video transmissions from UAVs in addition to the other uses normally expected. Kosovo air operations alone soaked up more than twice the bandwidth used to support all the forces in Operation Desert Storm. To provide the required data throughput, the Pentagon bought over $20 million worth of commercial bandwidth during the 87-day conflict.[10]

Related to the problem of bandwidth was that of frequency availability. To speak of limited room for transmissions would strike many people as absurd. But, in fact, there is only so much of the radio-frequency spectrum that is usable. It is also true that only a limited portion of that is suitable for long distance, high volume data transmission. During OAF, frequency coordinators had the monumental challenge of deconflicting 44,000 frequencies.[11]

> During OAF, the European Command (EUCOM) operated no more than two Predators simultaneously from Bosnia. Each needed 6 Mbps to support video dissemination within the theater and the United States, a requirement that severely stressed the Defense Information Systems Network architecture and necessitated preemption of lower-priority channels while the UAVs were in flight. Maintaining a quality link remained problematic throughout the campaign. In addition to Predator, two Hunter UAVs flew from Macedonia, and each one required an additional 6 Mbps of bandwidth. When both Predator and Hunter moved from reconnaissance to targeting roles, communicators scrambled to increase the reliability of the Very Small Aperture Terminal (VSAT), a satellite communications system that handles data, voice, and video signals. Even with only a few UAVs operating in Kosovo, communications systems were stressed to the point that operational trade-offs were required and some activities had to be delayed or cancelled.[12]
>
> —Brigadier General Charles E. Croom, USAF

Despite the troublesome details, some analysts were ready to proclaim that air power had scored its first clear, solo triumph in history. Others were quick to note that the air campaign had failed abjectly in attaining the war's key goal—protecting ethnic Albanians from Serbian violence. Many commentators also failed to mention the contribution of the Kosovo Liberation Army that helped make Belgrade's control of the province untenable. Still others maintained that Russia's sudden abandonment of the Serb cause was the critical factor. According to Milosevic and the Serb leadership, it was not precision strikes that caused them to capitulate. Instead, it was the prospect of a World War II–style NATO bombing campaign that would raze their cities and slaughter the population.[13]

Some observers held that air power had been effective, but not in "plinking tanks" (attacking tactical forces) or bombing military command and control sites. Instead, it was the attacks on civilian infrastructure that finally succeeded by making the Serb populace suffer, thereby threatening Milosevic's hold on power and finally coercing compliance.[14]

According to William Odom, a retired Army lieutenant general: "This war didn't do anything to vindicate air power. It didn't stop the ethnic cleansing, and it didn't remove Milosevic."[15] Perhaps the most remarkable thing about the Kosovo campaign is not that air power beat Milosevic (if it did), but that it managed to do so *despite* a consistently risk averse senior leadership, a divided U.S. Congress, an indifferent U.S. public, a fractious NATO, and a committed and determined opponent with a high threshold of pain.[16]

It was also mentioned that the whole idea of an exclusive air campaign was a gross violation of the most basic U.S. military doctrine. U.S. JCS Joint Publication Number 1, *Joint Warfare of the US Armed Forces,* and Number 3, *Doctrine for Joint Operations,* both called for joint campaigns, using the advantages of a supporting maneuver to strike an enemy with land, sea, air, and space forces. Air power, like the other services, was placed in the context of a joint campaign, not presented as a separate entity.

But among air officers and partisans of air power the critiques were seen as no more than sour grapes. The hard-won acknowledgement that air power was equal to land or sea power and could even be the leading effort in a campaign seemed like small potatoes next to the prospect of the *exclusive* air campaign. Kosovo proved what they had contended since Desert Storm. Giulio Douhet's 80-year-old prediction (lovingly preserved by the U.S. Air Force) finally seemed to come true—"The army and navy would remain part of an 'indivisible whole' of the three armed services but would no longer be a significant factor in successfully resolving a war."[17] Air forces were now the decisive military arm, and ground and naval forces were required only to add color. According to Merrill McPeak, the now-retired general who ran the Air Force during the Gulf War (USAF Chief of Staff 1990–1994), "this air victory was about as pure as they come. Once you get the air defenses suppressed, you can just fly over and puke out JDAMS [precision guided bombs]. You can't beat the economics."[18]

A *New York Times* editorial agreed, claiming that NATO's "sustained bombing has been more effective than many critics allowed..."

The *Washington Post's* Stephen Rosenfeld wrote: "They said Bill Clinton was wrong to rely on air power alone to win the war, and—assuming the details are mastered—they were wrong....This time around, anyway, he showed he was right. His weighing of means and ends finally clicked."

Predictably, the Air Force rushed to advertise its dominant role in the campaign. According to a USAF press release, "Allied Force—this year's aerospace power-dominated operation that forced the Serbian army to withdraw from Kosovo—provided further proof of air power's capabilities to carry out the policies of the National Command Authorities."[19]

As Stephen Biddle put it:

If the costs were low enough, the public would accept the police work needed to maintain order in the provinces and allow Washington to advance longer-term US goals of political and economic openness around the world. US military involvements should thus be limited to air power, any action should be cloaked in multinational coalitions to lend legitimacy and spread responsibility, and public scrutiny should be limited through careful control of information.[20]

General McPeak was naturally among the chief cheerleaders, asserting that not only was air power responsible for a stunning success, but those who doubted it were timorous, deluded, or motivated by service parochialism.[21]

Unnoticed among the celebration and consternation surrounding the apparent triumph of air power was another and perhaps more significant harbinger. A network of computer hackers established by Serbia drew on computer experts in Europe and North America to attack NATO and allied government's Web sites and computer networks. The effect was insignificant, but it was still worrying.[22]

The Army's Credibility at Stake

The apparent strength of the allied air performance greatly encouraged those who believed that the day of ground forces, especially heavy armor, was almost over. Even the popular press celebrated the triumph of the air forces with headlines like "Winner: Air Power, Loser: The Army."[23] For the Army, the implication was clear: the use of ground forces was to be avoided. The entire affair was made even more bitter by the appearance that the service was not only irrelevant but incompetent.

At issue was a request from Army General Clark, commander of Operation Allied Force, who had asked for two dozen of the U.S. Army's Apache attack helicopters a few days after bombing started on March 24. The Army had spent $15 billion over two decades to make the Apache the most lethal and least vulnerable attack helicopter in the world. When it became apparent that the jets were not hitting enough of Serbia's armored equipment, the Apache seemed to be the solution.

Air Force General Joseph W. Ralston, the vice chief of the Joint Chiefs of Staff, was immediately dubious as were the other service chiefs. Clark's plan to rely on drones, radar, and satellites to find targets was too vague and unconventional. Ralston believed a stepped-up air campaign was more likely to cause Milosevic to relent. After much wrangling, Secretary of Defense William S. Cohen and General Hugh Shelton, Chairman of the Joint Chiefs, finally recommended approval, and on April 3 Clinton signed the order sending the Apaches to Albania.

The deployment was anything but rapid as thousands of soldiers arrived to prepare for, support, and guard the helicopters. To construct a protected base for Task Force Hawk (the helicopter task force) the Army brought in 10,300 pieces of equipment on 550 C-17 flights. Thirty-seven Black Hawk and Chinook helicopters went along as logistic support. In all, the Army sent 6,200 troops and 26,000 tons of equipment to Tirana, at a cost of $480 million, to support and protect the 24 Apaches.

It took three weeks before the last Apaches arrived from Germany, only to announce that they would not be ready for action for at least another two weeks. Shortly afterwards, two helicopters crashed during training flights in Albania, one crash killing two fliers. Interservice friction also reared its ugly head. According to one report, the Army and Air Force did not work well together: "There was friction....Individuals in both services neither understand nor appreciate the capabilities of one another." Sixty percent of all rehearsals were canceled because the supporting Air Force aircraft were not available, because they were either engaged in operations or grounded by weather. The helicopters never did see action. Sending the task force back to their base in Germany took 30 trains, 20 ships, and 81 C-17 flights.

All in all, it was a miserable performance followed by a great deal of finger-pointing. The Army blamed logistic problems but Senator John McCain (R-AZ) replied that the hesitation had "nothing to do with logistics. It's inexcusable bureaucratic practice within the Pentagon."[24] Still others claimed it resulted from fear of casualties and that the Army or the White House was inhibited by the multitude of small shoulder-fired antiaircraft missiles said to be held by the Serb forces.[25]

Under the front-page headline "Army's Apache Helicopter Rendered Impotent in Kosovo," the *Washington Post* opined, "the vaunted helicopters came to symbolize everything wrong with the Army as it enters the 21st century: its inability to move quickly; its resistance to change; its obsession with casualties; its post-Cold War identity crisis."[26]

Reportedly, General Hugh Shelton, Chairman of the Joint Chiefs and an Army officer, was both angered and embarrassed. The slow deployment of the helicopters created a perception that the Army could not get its forces to the war and that the Pentagon was afraid to use them once they got there. Despite decades of claims about its rapid deployment forces, the Army could not move even a relatively small fighting force quickly into place. This is not to suggest that the Task Force Hawk debacle was the sole or even principal impetus for Army Transformation. The Army had been wrestling with the problem of deployability vs. capability for years. But Task Force Hawk and its deployment issues brought the problem into sharp focus and gave it a very public immediacy that had been missing.

As the twentieth century ended, "the Army suffered a swirling mix of initiatives, lessons, bureaucratic dynamics policy and fiscal challenges and a myriad of realized and unrealized opportunities."[27]

Bin Laden Again

Usama bin Laden made no secret of his intention to challenge the United States both directly and indirectly. He reiterated his hostile intentions with a *fatwa,* a call to the faithful, issued in the name of Islam, to attack "Jews and Crusaders." The fatwa was published in the newspaper *Al-Quds Al-Arabi* and widely reprinted throughout the Arab world. In it bin Laden called on Muslims to kill Americans—including civilians—anywhere in the world.[28] But radical Islam is fond of bombastic threats, and this could have been just one more.

Then early on the morning of Saturday, August 7, 1998, truck bombs exploded within five minutes of each other at the U.S. Embassy buildings in Nairobi, Kenya, and Dar Es Salaam, Tanzania. When rescuers cleared away the rubble, at least

220 persons were dead or missing, perhaps as many as 4,000 were injured. Publicly, the attacks were blamed on unnamed terrorists, "shadowy" individuals who have shown "contempt for human life and the rule of law."[29]

By November, Usama bin Laden was officially a suspect in the case and a classified U.S. Justice Department report stated categorically that "the bombings were carried out by members and associates of Usama Bin Ladin's organization."[30]

The embassy bombings led to what was probably the most feckless use of high-tech weaponry to date. On August 20, 1998, President Bill Clinton announced on national television that the United States had struck at "one of the most active terrorist bases in the world...operated by groups affiliated with Osama bin Laden" and, second "a chemical weapons-related facility in Sudan" both described as part of the "terrorists' base of operation and infrastructure." The attacks, he said, were in retaliation for the Africa embassy bombings and "because we have compelling information that they were planning additional terrorist attacks against our citizens."[31]

At the President's order, U.S. Navy ships in the Persian Gulf fired Tomahawk cruise missiles against an Al-Qaeda training facility at Zahwar Kil in Afghanistan. At about the same time, Navy warships steaming in the Red Sea launched Tomahawks that heavily damaged the El Shifa Pharmaceutical Industries factory in Khartoum, Sudan. The training camp at Zahwar Kil consisted chiefly of caves, dirt roads, and adobe-like buildings and had apparently been evacuated.[32]

The immediate result was a series of denunciations from Afghanistan, which claimed more than 20 civilian casualties, and Sudan, which angrily denied the facility had any connection with chemical weapons and also claimed civilian deaths. For its part, the United States replied that the facility had ties to bin Laden and produced chemicals that can be used to make VX nerve gas. Pakistan also expressed its anger over the violation of its airspace and a few apparently defective cruise missiles that struck its soil, including at least one that apparently landed intact.[33] The Pakistani military, starved by decade-long U.S. sanctions against high-tech transfers, regarded it as a gift of American missile technology and immediately seized it for study.

The overall military effect was nil, and any intention to frighten bin Laden or the Taliban was apparently unfulfilled. For a number of observers it confirmed that America was impotent against the terrorist threat.

Al-Ahram, the Egyptian news weekly did point out one important effect of the attack:

> Until now, [bin-Laden] was an obscure figure stalked by undercover agents and known to a handful of experts and journalists. Now he is a world famous adversary of the sole superpower. His lean figure, restlessly shifting as he holds a wireless phone in each hand, is imprinted in a billion memories. His message is suddenly reaching out to millions, especially in the Middle East where resentment over US policies has risen high in the last eight years. If he is recruiting, Mr Bin Laden's pool of volunteers has certainly become bigger.[34]

Reuters news agency reported in April 1999 that soldiers of the U.S. Special Operations Command ("U.S. commandos") were operating along the Afghan-Pakistani border in hopes of finding and capturing the terrorist leader.[35] In June, Usama bin Muhammad bin Ladin joined the FBI's ten most wanted list. In July, the U.S. government formally placed sanctions against the Taliban, restricting airline landing rights, freezing bank accounts, and prohibiting investment in any undertaking owned or controlled by the Taliban.

The United Nations Security Council voted to place sanctions on the Taliban government of Afghanistan if bin Laden was not handed over to the United States for trial. The UN demanded that bin Laden's training camps must be closed, the threats and operational activity must cease, and the terrorist leader must answer for his crimes. The Taliban failed to comply and decried the effect the sanctions would have on the Afghan people. On November 15, the sanctions were imposed, with little apparent effect.[36]

By now the bin Laden organization was believed to operate at least a dozen camps in Afghanistan, providing training in arms, explosives, and logistics to Islamic terrorists from Chechnya to the Philippines. The largest camp, Tora Bora ("black dust"), was a fortified encampment between two ridges in the White Mountains. The complex included several buildings and a large tunnel network heated by electric power from mountain runoff water. Another location, bin Ladin's "Abu Khabab" camp, reportedly focused on chemicals, poisons, and other toxins.[37]

Wanting bin Laden was one thing, but getting him was something else. Despite the formidable intelligence resources of the United States and its allies, finding his exact location in advance was proving impossible. Bin Laden and his associates enjoyed the protection of the fundamentalist Islamic government, but even so, there had apparently been at least one failed attack on his life. For this reason, the Al-Qaeda leader surrounded himself with bodyguards and stayed on the move. Systems that could track an armored division or a carrier battle group were not up to the task of finding a small group of individuals.

Back at the Doctrine Wars

None of the foregoing seemed to be on the minds of the Department of Defense (DoD) Joint Staff in 1999 when they began drafting another revision of their capstone manual—Joint Publication (JP) 3-0, *Doctrine for Joint Operations*. Strategic doctrine, especially the determination of roles and missions, had always been a battleground between the services, but until the late 1980s most of the arguments were around the margins. But after the massive force reductions and budget cuts of the late 1980s and the 1990s, the services were in something close to panic. Writing doctrine went from an academic exercise to a life or death struggle. It became very important because it dictated roles and missions in a time of uncertainty, confusion, and shrinking budgets.

Initially, there seemed no need for Air Force officers to press hard on the subject of halt operations. They were confident that their case would be made for them since the representatives of the warfighting CINCs[38] presented war plans that already include a halt approach—primarily using aircraft and missiles—at the outset of major hostilities. References to a halt phase in the 1997 Quadrennial Defense Review

(QDR) and the National Military Strategy had already helped the Air Force argue for a stronger operational role and a meatier budget for weapons platforms.[39]

Meanwhile, the DoD commissioned a parallel revision in joint doctrine. The April 2000 Defense Planning Guidance tasked U.S. Joint Forces Command to develop "...new joint warfighting concepts and capabilities that will improve the ability of future joint force commanders (JFCs) to rapidly and decisively conduct particularly challenging and important operational missions, such as...coercing an adversary to undertake certain actions or deny the adversary the ability to coerce or attack its neighbors...."[40]

By February 2001 the Joint Staff was ready to cautiously circulate a closely held "final coordination" version of JP 3-0, including what might seem like a brief and innocuous mention of a "rapid halt phase." "A possible halt phase," the draft went on, "is necessary when decisive combat operations are required to terminate aggression and achieve US objectives." Further wording allowed for the use of other than air forces in the halt phase, and it was a small part of the 200-page manual.[41]

A year earlier the Air Force had triumphed in a lengthy doctrine fight over the joint manual on counter-air operations. At least as interpreted by the airmen, that manual, Joint Publication 3-01, went a long way toward giving the air commander in a given theater of war a great deal of independence, freeing him from the demands of the other services. Although it might seem like a small matter, some air officials considered it the service's "greatest political achievement of the past decade...In the view of some in the Air Force leadership, the publication provides the first and best opportunity to establish a primary role for airpower in joint doctrine."[42]

This was all too much for the Army, and when the Joint Staff proposed the halt-phase wording in February, the Army was swift to object, threatening to nonconcur with the draft. The Air Force responded that it would likewise withhold approval unless the halt phase wording stayed in. If "halt" were missing from the newly revised overarching doctrine publication, it would support the Army claim that ground forces play a unique and irreplaceable role in stopping an aggressor. The airmen feared that the ground forces would then try to divert aerospace funding to their own services. "What they can't win in real life, they try to win in doctrine," said one air power supporter in reference to Army officials.[43]

To add to the confusion, draft copies of the Joint Forces Command response to the Defense Planning Guidance endorsed "Rapid Decisive Operations." It defined the Air Force role in joint operations as, in part, to "rapidly gain aerospace superiority; halt the adversary short of its objective, gain battlespace access for follow-on joint forces."[44] This triggered another interservice wrangle.

At the same time the Defense Department was drafting another important document, the Joint Strategy Review (JSR). An appraisal of how to approach future threats, the JSR was meant to serve as part of the analytical foundation for the 2001 Quadrennial Defense Review. Moreover, it is one of the principal documents leading to changes in the National Military Strategy. According to published reports, the draft JSR had already been in circulation for months when Air Force leaders made an issue of the halt phase and demanded that it be included.

The argument finally rose to the level of General Shelton, the Chairman of the Joint Chiefs of Staff, who personally ordered that the halt-phase language be excised from the JSR, at least for the time being. Creating JP 3-01 had been a seven-year struggle, and it seems reasonable that the chairman wanted to forestall a similar battle over JP 3-0. Officials close to the chairman explained that Shelton thought it inappropriate to release the Joint Strategy Review before the services had sorted out their disagreements over the halt approach in JP 3-0, which was on a separate track for completion. The whole business was embarrassing for both services, but the stakes were too high for an easy compromise.[45]

Rapid Dominance and Shock and Awe

Everything is staked on a short, decisive war.
          —National Security Strategy of the United States, 1997[46]

By now Andrew Marshall had gained the status of guru of the military revolution. However, even the master himself still admitted he was unsure of exactly what that meant. Networked "information warfare," he said, was still a vague concept:

> a topic whose complexities and lack of consensus, at present, easily match its importance. Information advances will affect more than just how we fight wars. The nature and purpose of war itself may change. How wars start, how they end, their length, and the nature of the participants may change as shifts in the relative power of states and nonstate entities occur. In the face of the uncertainties of the future, and the disagreements of the present, I can only suggest caution and humility in predicting the future.[47]

Humility is not the usual theme in doctrinal struggles, and it was not much in evidence outside Mr. Marshall's office.

The concept of Rapid Dominance Operations, accomplished by Shock and Awe, gained popularity during the 1990s as an organizing concept for the information-driven revolution in military affairs. Building on this, Rapid Decisive Operations (RDO) had been proposed as doctrine in 2000. Much of the discussion focused on the use of precision munitions and the importance of massing "effects" rather than forces, "supplementing attrition-based, hard-kill techniques with a broader range of effects that will help break an adversary's will."[48] This gave rise to the idea of Effects Based Operations (EBO). This latter concept sought to implement RDO by analyzing an adversary as a system of systems that can be paralyzed by well-placed strikes against critical nodes. Rapidly advancing forces would paralyze an adversary with the psychological stress of facing an unstoppable force. It was a welcome notion among transformation advocates because it aimed at enabling a military response using smaller, lighter forces to strike with precision munitions in order to dominate an enemy and bring the conflict to a rapid and decisive close.[49] But not everyone was convinced that the concept was very different from the strategies that airmen had advocated for decades.[50] Cynics objected that Rapid Defensive Operations amounted to no more than a more elaborate restatement of Rapid Dominance and Effects Based Operations meant anything the user wanted it to. Nevertheless, former (and future) Defense Secretary Donald Rumsfeld was one of four former defense chiefs to sign a letter to the Clinton administration spelling out the strategy.

Among the unimpressed was Robert Pape, an air war specialist at the University of Chicago. The large-scale display of firepower aka RDO by means of Shock and Awe "is what air forces have been doing since World War I—that is always the plan... This is the 'same old,'" Pape objected. "We want to believe it is something new, because we want to believe we are always bigger and better. But this isn't it."[51]

Pape had long taken the position that strategic air power consistently failed to live up to its billing. He advocated instead that air power should focus on destroying enemy military forces at the tactical and operational levels, thereby denying an adversary the means to achieve its military and political objectives. Shock and awe may have key weaknesses as a strategy, he warned. "The big continuity, that I think is unfortunate, is that the center of our strategy is leadership decapitation." As seen by Pape, that strategy was an important part of the 1991 Desert Storm air campaign and the 1998 Operation Desert Fox, but "failed" each time. Pape estimated that the likely ratio of air power to ground force for any new conflict—if Kosovo was a standard with 100 percent reliance on air, and the 1991 Gulf War a 50-50 mix—at a dangerous 80-to-20.[52]

In the U.S. DoD, it was agreed that military forces that could harness the new technologies and concepts would gain a considerable advantage over those who did not. At a minimum, there was the by now well established consensus that standoff precision strikes; advanced command, control, and intelligence; and information systems were major advances in the tools available to soldiers. The most important of these was the leap forward in information processing made possible by advances in automated (computer-based) systems. This change made the others possible. Since Desert Storm there had been orders-of-magnitude improvements in information processing capabilities. For example, the system used by Gulf War commanders to transmit messages could move 2400 bits of information per second. In the year 2000, the commercially developed and operated Global Broadcast System was able to transmit 23 million bits per second into Bosnia. A message that took more than an hour to send in 1991 could be sent in less than a second.[53] Unfortunately, the way it turned out was that more, longer messages were sent, clogging the system and creating confusion. A solution was neatly turned back into a problem.

Meanwhile, the American Joint Chiefs of Staff reconsidered their 1996 *Joint Vision* concept of warfighting for the twenty-first century and concluded once again they had been right all along. In June 2000 they celebrated this discovery in *Joint Vision 2020,* a document built on and reendorsing the concepts set forth in the 1996 version, *Joint Vision 2010.* Like *JV 2010, Joint Vision 2020* asserted that power projection, with limited overseas presence, would remain the fundamental strategic concept for U.S. military operations. It reiterated *JV 2010's* contention that military forces could gain a decisive advantage through "information dominance," the ability to process information faster than an opponent and to have nearly complete situational awareness on the battlefield. The key here is the creation of a system of systems that allows information to be processed quickly and shared on the battlefield at all levels of command.[54] It also reiterated the concept of "full spectrum dominance" as the key characteristic of future U.S. forces.[55] Although perhaps useful for public relations purposes, it contributed very little that was new.

Rapid Decisive Operations built on the concepts outlined in *JV 2010/2020*: full spectrum dominance, dominant maneuver, precision engagement, focused logistics, and full-dimensional protection. Effects Based Operations seemed to offer a way to actually carry out the concept of Rapid Decisive Operations. At least it sounded like the missing doctrine piece for the employment transformed forces.

The language of EBO was eagerly adopted by airmen who saw the emphasis on precision operations as playing to their strongest capabilities and welcomed it as "change in the nature of warfare."[56] EBO as a concept quickly eclipsed Rapid Dominance and Rapid Decisive Operations as the preferred operating concept and "effects based" terminology quickly proliferated throughout the literature. Its advocates argued that it provided a "holistic" approach previously missing. Allegedly previous methods of warfare were wrongheaded in that they stressed attack on military targets for the sake of short-term results. EBO claimed to consider the full range of possible effects and take advantage not only of military power but to use all the instruments of national power to achieve those effects. It looked at the larger picture and attempted to determine the desired policy objective. From that, military operations could be crafted that would achieve those policy objectives in a more efficient and effective manner.[57] Furthermore, it asserted, EBO linked the elements of national power (diplomacy, information, military, and economic) at the strategic, operational, and tactical levels.[58] Like RDO, EBO focused on enemy will and perceptions. Information superiority was the key enabler. According to DoD, "RDO is predicated on effects based operations." Almost as an afterthought it added, "RDO is not designed for long-term commitment to solve enduring problems.[59]

Critics responded that EBO was taking the military out of the war business and into areas that were really not their provenance and certainly not under their control. Nevertheless, both the Army and the Air Force adopted the terminology with the Army claiming that it had always done EBO and had formalized the concept (but not the name) as part of AirLand Battle as early as 1982.[60] The Army's claim was interesting since what it really meant was that effects based operations were no more than an idealized form of the way war had been conducted throughout the modern era.

For its part, the Air Force continued to capitalize on its apparent advantage with new basic doctrine that institutionalized the service's concept of itself as the decisive instrument and preferred means of warfare. Recognizing that national command authorities were extremely leery of casualties, the doctrine made the point over and over that warfare from the air was the least likely to produce an unacceptable flow of body bags back to the United States. Theories also began to circulate suggesting that considerable savings could be realized if the Army was cut back severely and most of the surviving heavy forces placed in the reserve. There they would be cheaper to maintain and could always be called up in the unlikely event they were ever needed.

None of this was accidental. The timing was predicated on the approach of the second QDR in 2001, a review that was expected to determine the future course of national defense policy. The Air Force was already hard at work on an analysis of its performance in the 1997 QDR and set out specifically to counter what one colonel termed, "the momentum of outdated US warfighting concepts."[61]

General Shinseki's Vision

By now it should be apparent that General Eric Shinseki announced his Army Transformation initiative in a climate of criticism. Senator Ted Stevens (R-AK), Chairman of the Defense Appropriations Subcommittee (as well as the full committee), had been vocal in his discontent as had DoD officials. In a speech delivered a month before Shinseki's announcement, Deputy Defense Secretary John Hamre pointedly said, "if the Army holds onto nostalgic versions of its grand past, it is going to atrophy and die...[The Army] cannot simply be what it was, and think that it is going to be relevant for this new, complex world that is emerging."[62]

Certainly General Shinseki had these and other critics in mind, but he was also mindful of the 1997 National Defense Panel (NDP) and the prospect of the 2001 QDR when he named his modernization initiative the Transformation program, an apparent echo of the 1997 NDP's demand for a "transformation" of national defense. Further, his list of the Army's problems was very close to the list produced in the 1997 NDP. But it was certainly with the upcoming Quadrennial Review in mind that he called for an immediate upgrade of current forces to provide an interim capability. He would begin at once with the formation of two experimental brigade-size formations at Fort Lewis, Washington:[63]

> We intend to transform the Army...into a standard design with internetted C4ISR packages that allow us to put a combat capable brigade anywhere in the world in 96 hours...We will begin immediately to form initial brigades using existing equipment. As medium vehicles become available, we will begin the transformation to interim brigades.[64]

It was the same old story—in order to remain relevant, the Army had to be able to deploy rapidly, sustain a high operating tempo, and defeat an opponent quickly with minimum losses. It must then rapidly reposition, refocus, and execute subsequent missions against an adversary. This was a difficult proposition, no matter how it was viewed. As explained in the general's *Army Vision Statement* for 2000, Transformation would look like this:

> The change would proceed along three major paths, the Legacy Force and the Interim Force, culminating with the Objective Force, which would be the final form of the Army.[65]

Objective Force

The critical transformation path led to the Objective Force, the postindustrial Army with the characteristics and capabilities needed to be relevant; e.g., the deployability to place a combat ready brigade anywhere in the world in 96 hours, a division in 120 hours, followed by up to five divisions (a corps) in 30 days. It would be built around a yet-to-be-defined Future Combat System (FCS). The Objective Force would eventually include the entire Army.

Legacy Force

At the same time, portions of the Army would retain their present (year 2000) form. This was the Legacy Force—its lifetime extended by continuing the Force XXI modernization programs, such as the insertion of digital technologies. It would continue to be equipped with existing major weapons systems including the M1 Abrams tank, M2 Bradley fighting vehicle, and Black Hawk helicopter. This was the force that would go to war should someone miscalculate anytime in the next 15 years or so.

Interim Force

Bridging the gap in capabilities between 2000 and the Objective Force was the Interim Force, beginning with the initial Brigade Combat Teams formed at Fort Lewis, Washington. These initial brigades were to validate an organizational and operational model for the Interim Force. Based on this validated structure, the Interim Force would be fielded with current, off-the-shelf technology. The Interim Armored Vehicle, for example, would be some modification of an existing vehicle and used to equip Interim Force units until the Army was ready to begin fielding the Objective Force.

Transformation was no small feat since the Army as an institution strongly favored continuity over change. The U.S. Army's basic divisional structure of three brigades per division and three battalions per brigade grew out of the Spanish-American War in 1898. This flexible structure accommodated numerous changes in technology and persisted until 1955 when the Army undertook a disastrous experiment with the pentomic division. This initiative sought to replace the division's three brigades with five independent "battle groups," each somewhat larger than a battalion. The change proved unworkable and the Army returned to its basic concept of the three-brigade division as its central fighting organization.

Under the latest transformation, the Army not only had to sell the concept of radical transformation, it had to gain and sustain the support of military and civilian leaders as well as the Congress over a period of 30 years in the face of competing national security priorities and domestic concerns. To gain this support, something more concrete was needed than the vague generalities of the *Joint Vision Statement.* Accordingly, the Chief of Staff produced the *Army Transformation Campaign Plan,* a more complete statement of goals and objectives required to get to the Objective Force. The campaign plan tried to discuss defined transformation goals, set milestones for achieving them, and assign lines of responsibilities for each aspect of the plan.

As outlined, two Interim Brigade Combat Teams (IBCT) would be formed at Fort Lewis as quickly as possible. These forces, along with four to six more Interim brigades added later, would compose the Interim Force. According to plan, the brigades were to be organized, trained, and equipped around new light-armored wheeled vehicles ("interim armored vehicles") that were significantly more transportable than existing tanks and armored vehicles. This vehicle would be produced in ten variants. The most important were the infantry carrier, a command vehicle, and a mobile gun system. The mobile gun was especially critical since it was to substitute for both tanks and conventional artillery. Without it, the Interim Brigade's firepower was largely reduced to rifles and machine guns.

The brigade was to achieve its initial operating capability in 2001, and all Interim Force brigades were to be formed and equipped by about 2008. These units would provide an advanced operating capacity in case of need, but also serve as test and development platforms for Objective Force doctrine and equipment.

Beginning in 2008 and continuing beyond 2030, the entire Army [less special operations forces (SOF)] would transition to the Objective Force based in part on lessons learned from the Interim Brigades. During this period, all Army forces, including the Interim Force, would transform into new organizational structures called "Units of Action" operating under new warfighting doctrine. The key and overriding element, however, was the network. Without the network, the entire concept of the Objective Force fell apart.

Testing New Forces

If the depth and breadth of General Shinseki's initiative were unusual, so were the means he chose to achieve it. The creation of test formations like the experimental brigade combat team is infrequent in Army history because budgets seldom allow the luxury of separate experimental units. The brigade experiment ordered by Shinseki was the latest in a fairly sparse history of experimental units in the U.S. Army beginning with the nineteenth century attempt to create a U.S. Camel Corps and later bicycle mounted infantry. Neither was successful, and both survive today only in memory as quaint curiosities. During the twentieth century the Army fielded five experimental units with varying success. The Experimental Mechanized Force was created between 1928 and 1931 and, more recently, four other test units: the 11th Air Assault Division (Test), 1963–1965; the 1st Cavalry Division (TRICAP), 1971–1974; the 9th Infantry Division (High Technology Test Bed), 1980–1990; and the 7th Infantry Division (Light), 1983–1986.[66]

The test themes were remarkably consistent in all the examples (including the Camel Corps). Like Shinseki's new experimental brigades, they all sought better mobility, lethality, and deployability while issues such as logistic support and training requirements received less attention.[67] It was also noticeable that all of them were essentially tactical concepts. It was not always clear how these schemes would fit some larger concept of warfighting.

In all these cases, support by the Army's senior leadership was essential for an experiment's success. This included involvement of the Army Chief of Staff, which the IBCT and the transformation initiative certainly had. They were widely identified as the Chief's personal programs. But all the successful examples featured not only involvement by the Army Staff, but also its support. This was critical if the transformation was to survive Shinseki's term as Chief of Staff, but it was by no means guaranteed. Significant elements in the Army, especially in the Armor and Artillery branches, strongly disagreed with all or part of the new initiative. Perhaps for this reason, the general set a very ambitious schedule, incredibly ambitious by ordinary peacetime standards. Where the Light Infantry Division experiment had taken three years, the first Interim brigades were to begin fielding by September 2000 and successfully complete the final Capstone Exercise by March 2001. IOC (or Initial Operational Capability in military jargon) was planned for April 1, 2001. Probably the choice of April Fool's Day had nothing to do with it, but it was a deadline the brigades would miss by years.

None of this was well received by traditionalists in the Army or turf-conscious officials in the other services. First of all, there was considerable doubt that any wheeled vehicle could replace a tank. Also, tankers and artillerymen were worried by transformation's apparent intent to erase the distinction between their services by using generic fire support platforms to perform both functions, inadequately in the view of the traditionalists. Army missile men and aviators were also troubled by the Interim Force's planned dependence on fire support from Air Force, Navy, and coalition assets.[68]

The Air Force Association was quick to criticize the Army plan, asserting that "transformation cannot take place without a shift in service roles from the current emphasis on surface warfare to aero-space warfare." Stephen P. Aubin, the Director of Policy and Communications for the Association, made a pitch for the halt phase concept and also the by now routine charge that the Army was stuck in the past, "focused on the idea of closing with the enemy—be it with heavy or lighter forces—even if the enemy might be destroyed from the air or sea before the Army arrives."[69]

The Commandant of the Marine Corps warned both the Army and the Air Force against any attempt to trespass on the role of "expeditionary force." "There is no way," he said, "that the entire armed forces of the United States can fit into the tip of the spear."[70]

Air Mechanization Appears

A competing proposal for the IBCTs emerged in 2000 with the publication of *Air-Mech-Strike: Asymmetric Maneuver Warfare for the 21st Century*. Written by an all-star cast of former general officers and doctrine experts, the air mechanization concept was aimed directly at the Shinseki Transformation version of the future army. As usual with such innovations it was not entirely new—similar ideas had been floating around—but this was the first large, organized presentation of the concept. The term "air mechanization" was quickly shortened to "air-mech" and the concept was strongly advocated by those who thought Shinseki had the right idea but the wrong emphasis.[71]

The basic notion of air-mech was quite simple. For decades military helicopters had been moving vehicles and artillery around behind the battlefield. In Desert Storm the 101st Airborne Division (Air Assault) had staged a helicopter assault 170 miles inside Iraq to seize Highway 8 and positions on the Euphrates River to cut off the escape route of the Iraqi Army. The Army's UH-60 and CH-47 helicopters could lift trucks and artillery, and special operations choppers delivered light trucks in enemy rear areas. It seemed reasonable that, if armored vehicles could be made lighter and helicopters just a bit stronger, the same methods could deliver an armored task force deep in the enemy's rear—not lightly armed paratroopers, Toyotas, or HMMWVs, but tracked armored fighting vehicles. Until the Future Force managed to provide the promised lighter armored vehicles, existing M-113s and the M8 Armored Gun System would be air landed by Air Force C-130s.[72] It was an engaging innovation, and one general compared it to the introduction of the forward pass to football.

It had several qualities that were attractive. For one thing, Air-Mech came down squarely on the track side of the tracks vs. wheels question. For another, it advocated an updated M113A3 as the primary personnel carrier and the M-8 (essentially a light tank) as an armored gun system. Both vehicles were in existence and the type approved for production; plus the 113 was a primary competitor for the role of Interim Armored Vehicle, so research and development costs were nil. At 11 to 15 tons these vehicles were not helicopter transportable. But they fit aboard a C-130 and were light enough and small enough to meet the requirements of the proposed Interim Brigade Combat Teams and would serve until the development of the Objective Force.

Air mechanization was greeted as a competitor to the Shinseki version of Army Transformation and thus did not receive a warm welcome in the Pentagon. But its advocates were vocal, and the concept was more appealing in some circles than the futuristic plans for the Objective Force.

Legacy and Transformation

As noted earlier, Shinseki and his staff saw Transformation as occurring in three major phases: the Initial phase, the Interim Capability phase, and the Objective Force phase. Recognizing that the Army would need to retain its fighting ability, the transformation included parallel developments. One track led to the Interim Force, typified by the IBCTs, but another, simultaneous track led to the Force XXI modernization of the existing industrial-age units. These Force XXI "legacy" forces (the current light and heavy divisions and brigades) would continue as they were with improvements while the Interim Force was being developed and fielded, then, around 2012, the two types will unite as a medium weight force, combining the capabilities of both light and heavy units. Conversion to this Interim Force design would continue until science and technology provided a FCS with the desired Objective Force characteristics.[73]

The Initial phase began with the announcement of the Vision in October 1999. During this phase, the Army fielded Initial Brigade Combat Teams to validate an organizational and operational model for Interim Brigades and generate insights for further transformation of the force. Also in this first phase, the Army was to revise its key concepts, doctrine, and strategic plans—its conceptual framework—to address full spectrum operations in a complex environment that included other services, agencies, and nations.

Once the Army was prepared to proceed beyond Initial Brigade Combat Teams and begin transformation of additional units to the Interim Force design, the second phase was to begin. Before this occurred, the validation of the model for the Interim Force had to be complete. Although the transformation of units to the Interim Force design was expected to speed up in this phase, recapitalization and some new equipment fielding would be necessary to sustain the capability of the legacy forces and likely to raise the troubling question of money. How would it be paid for?

The Objective Force phase would begin when technology allowed the fielding of the FCS, the system of systems that will achieve the desired force characteristics. At this point, the legacy forces will begin their transformation to the new design. The Interim Force would require recapitalization in this phase in order to complete the transformation of the entire Army into the Objective Force. But the Army is more than tactical units.

The service also planned to begin the transformation of the Institutional Army (the recruitment, training, administration, and support base in the United States) in the first phase. This transformation was to address the systems, organizations, and processes by which the Institutional Army supported training, leader development, infrastructure, management, sustainment, combat and material development, and well-being.

Implementing the Army's Vision also required significant change in the way personnel were handled. This began with careful analysis of Army personnel requirements to support the new distribution of personnel and identify any mismatch between requirements and congressionally mandated end strength. The problem was that, despite reshuffling of personnel to fill combat units, the Army (and the other services) simply did not have enough people. More effective recruiting was the solution. But, despite a spate of optimistic announcements, a new advertising agency, and relentless comments of the "glass is half full, not half empty" variety, this proved hard to do. For several years all the U.S. armed services, except for the comparatively small Marine Corps, were unable to meet their recruiting goals despite a slow, continual, and dangerous lowering of requirements.

Transformation was a risky scheme because it depended so heavily on money and technology that did not exist and could not be guaranteed. As a practical matter, the transformation plan was really conditions-based, meaning that the pace of the transformation could not be preordained. At every step, the decision to progress to the next stage will depend on the determination that all necessary preconditions have been met.

Whether preparing for deployment or building organizations for tomorrow, the personnel problem alone did not allow regular Army forces of any scale to fight without significant support from the reserve components, the Army Reserve and National Guard. This fact had driven the integration of active and reserve forces to a degree never seen before.

This had real significance aside from confirming that the active Army structure bordered on inadequacy for its primary purpose of fighting major wars. Meanwhile, the notion that the Guard and Reserve were a solution to either manpower or deployment problems received a setback when a General Accounting Office report judged their capacity for rapid mobilization was "highly uncertain."[74]

The Objective Force and the FCS

Within a theater of operations, Army forces must be able to reposition rapidly to create and exploit advantage. The Army must reduce the size of its systems to attain the desired level of strategic and intra-theater deployability.[75]

The Objective Force would reduce or even eliminate the distinctions between light and heavy units, creating organizations that are prepared to transition from disaster relief to low-intensity contingencies to high-intensity warfighting without pause.[76] The centerpiece of this effort was the FCS scheduled to replace the heavy, tracked armored vehicles (e.g., the M1 tank and the M2 personnel carrier) by 2012. The FCS would be a network of several vehicles based on the common FCV (future combat vehicle) platform. A system of UAVs and possibly robot scouts on the ground would gather targeting data, then transfer it to a gun carrying variant of the FCV, perhaps eventually an unmanned, robotic gun or missile launcher. Human soldiers would occupy another variant of the FCV, somewhere behind the front lines, to oversee operations. The design of such a system was still uncertain, but the Army hoped the FCS would be three times as effective as the current Army with just one-third the sustainment.

As explained by the Army's Posture Statement for Fiscal Year 2001, the Objective Force was specifically designed to meet the precepts expressed in the Joint Vision. It was intended to meet the Joint Vision ideal of a full dominance force through dominant maneuver made possible by netted command, control, communications, computer intelligence, surveillance, and enhanced reconnaissance (C4ISR) capabilities.

The Objective Force would be capable of precision engagement because of weapons systems capable of accurate, long-range fires and the ability to employ joint fires to enhance their lethality. Better connectivity with national and joint assets, along with improvements to organic C4ISR and weapons systems, would enhance the Force's ability to conduct and support precision engagement.

The Objective Force would support full dimensional protection by greatly reducing the vulnerability associated with deployment and maneuver. Objective Force survivability, a product of integrated information technology, increased weapons systems' effectiveness, and the increased dispersion of Army systems, would also contribute to full dimensional protection.

As planned, the Objective Force went a long way toward reducing and simplifying the logistic burden imposed by heavy armored forces. Lighter, common-chassis systems, more accurate fires, and increased connectivity with joint capabilities were to reduce fuel, ammunition, and maintenance requirements. These improvements in sustainability were expected to reduce the demand on joint lift assets, contributing to more rapid logistical response and distribution for all services. Combined with the ongoing integration of information technology to better manage logistics supply and demand, the Objective Force would benefit from the precise application of logistics described in the Joint Vision.

In May 2000, the Army and the Defense Advanced Research Projects Agency selected four contractors to provide prototypes for the FCS. Contractor teams were required to submit two design concepts, each concept to provide the deployability, agility, versatility, lethality, survivability, and sustainability required for the Objective Force. The first concept was for a network-centric, distributed force with a manned command and control element/personnel carrier, a robotic direct-fire system, a robotic nonline of sight system, and an all-weather robotic sensor system, coupled with other layered sensors. The second concept would be the team's own design approach for a system of systems. If all went as planned, the Army would make a decision on engineering and manufacturing development in fiscal year 2006, with the first system fielding in 2012.[77]

Force XXI

The Parallel Army

None of the foregoing would be achieved by abandoning the Force XXI initiatives. The "Force XXI process" would keep legacy forces viable and relevant until the Objective Force came into being. This process would improve the capabilities of current forces, while integrating technologies to make it possible for the legacy forces to operate in concert with the Interim Force until transformation was complete.

The process of integrating information technologies into both combat and support systems—the broad effort referred to as digitization—was well under way. The Army had spent a great deal of money and effort on the Force XXI units, incorporating information technologies to provide near real-time situational awareness. At a minimum, increased effectiveness would reduce the number of combat vehicles in the division, which in turn improves the deployability of the unit. A parallel effort to enhance light force capabilities through application of information technologies was also underway. By 2012, the entire Army would have digitized and upgraded but still retain some Force XXI heavy forces as a hedge against contingencies. The radically altered Objective Force would follow—a new type of military force, not a typical industrial age army upgraded with add-on technology. It would be a true twenty-first century "information age" force, the Army After Next.

Continuing the Force XXI process would not only sustain the capabilities of current forces but also minimize the operating and replacement costs for aging equipment. This would not be cheap and would probably involve some adjustment of the Division XXI design to include selected fielding of already-programmed systems with essential capabilities, and recapitalization of existing systems. But it looked workable.[78]

The 4th ID (M) (–) at Fort Hood, Texas, became the Army's first Division XXI style digitized division in 2000. Key features of this new design included a reduction in the number of tanks and infantry fighting vehicles mentioned earlier while adding a reconnaissance troop in each ground maneuver brigade and a battalion of multiple launch rocket systems to each division. As planned, the new design would reduce each divisions' strategic lift requirement by 11 percent. Not huge differences but still worthwhile.

Because of practical difficulties (procurement, training, costs of installation), some divisions would have to be satisfied with a limited conversion to the new design before they received digital systems. The changes in the operational forces were the most visible part of Transformation; however, the simultaneous transformation of the Institutional Army, along with the preservation of the Legacy Force, was all part of what was increasingly looking like a very expensive strategy.

Money Versus Risk

Thanks to a series of defense funding cuts over the years, the Army's modernization funds were very limited. Its entire investment budget for the year added up to about five weeks' worth of sales at WalMart. This meant risks had to be taken no matter how it implemented the new technologies, and that in turn meant more hard decisions.

One example was the provisional plan to shut down the U.S.'s main tank production facility in Lima, Ohio, at the end of the 2000–2005 defense spending cycle. That plan sprang from the realization that the Army could not afford to continue major upgrades of the M1 Abrams while funding development of a next-generation armored vehicle. The problem was that the Army was not confident that it would know enough about the future maturity of leap-ahead technologies to make an informed decision on shutdown by 2003 or 2005. The FCS was little more than a list of adjectives on viewgraphs. If those adjectives proved unattainable or mutually exclusive or inappropriate circa 2025, then early shutdown of Abrams' production would be a colossal blunder, especially if major new threats to U.S. land power emerged in the intervening period.[79]

Special Operations

Conspicuously missing from most of the debate about military futures was the role of special operations forces. General Shinseki's vision was about the transformation of the conventional Army, especially armored forces. Except for the occasional *pro forma* mention, it had very little to say about the special operations units of the

Army except that Ranger, airborne, and special operations formations would continue as before. This was not too surprising since the Army's SOF had been the stepchildren of DoD since their inception in World War II. There has always been a slight distaste for elites and highly specialized units in the American military, in particular those lacking a technological base. Established to meet various special needs over the years, various SOF elements had been alternately created and abolished.

These were usually small, commando, intelligence gathering and raiding units employed on exceptionally difficult or dangerous missions and those requiring specialized or highly developed skills. The largest formations were the Army Special Forces Groups, each the equivalent of a brigade but about one-third the size of a conventional Army brigade. Some, such as the Army's Ranger units, were actually elite light infantry, performing mostly standard functions but at an extraordinarily high proficiency under the most difficult circumstances. Other SOF elements included Civil Affairs and Psychological Operations units, also small and generally underappreciated.

During the 1990s the Army SOF community and the SOF community in general held numerous meetings, conferences, and debates about SOF doctrine and the proper role for special operations forces in the future. None of these resulted in any firm conclusions.

The U.S. Special Operations Command (USSOCOM, often shortened to SOCOM) had its own budget authority and oversaw and coordinated special operations training, doctrine, equipment, and specialized support. The services retained control of their SOF units and provide routine support such as pay. SOCOM was organized in 1987 at McDill Air Force Base in Tampa despite the loud and vigorous objections of the various services (especially the Navy). It was created as a supporting command, meaning it provides personnel (provided in turn by the individual services), equipment, and support functions to the various regional combatant commanders, who direct their missions. Each of the regional commanders owns a small Theater Special Operations command to plan and execute missions. As a supporting command, SOCOM had almost no operational authority and only on the rarest of occasions did it carry out operations. National-level special operations were the province of small, highly elite special mission units (notably the Army's Delta Force and the Navy's SEAL Team Six) and were under the control of the highly secret Joint Special Operations Command at Fort Bragg and Pope Air Force Base.

Although the Army, Navy, and Air Force all fielded elite special operations units beginning in the 1960s, the largest number was in the Army. By 1990, that service included a grab bag of about 30,000 SOF soldiers, active and reserve, all grouped under the U.S. Army Special Operations Command. These included Special Forces (Green Berets), three revived Ranger battalions, a Special Operations Aviation Regiment, the storied Delta Force (national counterterrorist force), a Psychological Operations Group, and a Civil Affairs organization, as well as various smaller, highly specialized elements.

The Navy included about 6,000 special operators. Most were either SEAL (SEa, Air, Land) Team commandos or Special Boat Unit sailors. The Air Force had about 10,000 special operations personnel and 130 aircraft (mostly helicopters, C-130 transports, and AC -130 gunships) assigned to the Air Force Special Operations Command.

The Goldwater-Nichols reforms helped. After the debacle of the Iran hostage rescue attempt in 1980 and several stumbles in Grenada (1983), SOF had performed well on both routine and important missions and produced a credible record during the invasion of Panama (1989).

The SOF community, and especially the Army special operators, at first saw Gulf War I as an opportunity to prove their worth. But things did not work out that way, and SOF were sometimes treated as more of a hindrance than a help. General Norman Schwarzkopf, the Coalition Commander, had no fondness for the special operators and was planning a thoroughly conventional, by-the-numbers campaign based on heavy armored forces—the Army specialty.[80]

As a result, SOF had a useful role in the war but remained essentially marginal players. The exception was the hunt for Scud surface-to-surface missile launchers inside Iraq. The Iraqis had modified Soviet-model Scud missiles for longer range, further degrading its already lamentable accuracy. They were of no real military importance, but as terror weapons they could have real political importance. On January 18, 1991, Iraq Scuds began to fall on cities in Saudi Arabia and, very significantly, on Israel, a nonbelligerent.[81]

Attacks on Israel were intended to bring Tel Aviv into the war, making it politically impossible for the Arab members to remain in the alliance. At the same time, Tel Aviv could hardly be expected to stand idly by while Iraqi missiles continued to fall.

Fighter planes were the obvious answer, especially the advanced F-15Es of the USAF guided by overhead surveillance from satellites and spy planes. It was a made-to-order mission for an "information-dominant" force engaged in rapid dominance operations. But life is seldom so easy. The MAZ-543 launchers were extremely mobile, capable of setting up, firing, and escaping less than ten minutes later, well before fighter planes could respond. When not set up for firing they looked rather like ordinary semitrailer trucks. Despite priority use of national assets, the launchers proved elusive.

The solution was to use special operations units equipped with advanced helicopters and specialized tools including newly introduced Global Positioning System navigation equipment. USSOCOM created a Joint Special Operations Task Force (JSOTF) consisting of Delta operators, Army Special Forces, Britain's elite Special Air Service, and the Air Force's 20th Special Operations Squadron. Its sole and specific mission was to find and kill Scuds.[82] It was hoped that the introduction of America's primer commandos would satisfy the increasingly restive Israelis. Some teams stayed in the desert as long as three weeks, guiding strikes on an expanded list of targets, including communications sites, convoys, and command posts.[83]

The JSOTF was successful in locating worthwhile targets, but much less so in finding the elusive Scuds. Nevertheless, in the end, the basic purpose of the hunt was accomplished—it kept Israel out of the war and in all probability saved the Coalition by so doing. This is the kind of strategic level, political outcome that might be expected from national command assets. It did much to raise the reputation of special operations forces among strategic planners both inside and outside the Defense Department.[84]

CHAPTER 5

AN ARMY TRANSFORMED

Transformation is not just a new idea...it's a big idea.
—Paul J. Hoeper, Army Chief of Acquisition[1]

Too Slow to Run and Too Fat to Fight[2]

Eric Shinseki's transformation initiative was no spur-of-the-moment proposal. It was a carefully thought-out program that reflected some of the most progressive thinking in the U.S. Army. In a nutshell, the problem was this: the Army could not get to the war in time to do anyone any good. U.S. heavy armored units are unsurpassed for intense, direct fire battles. But these same units are too heavy for rapid deployment and, once deployed, are difficult and expensive to sustain.[3]

Some of the Army's premier systems, including the M1 Abrams Main Battle Tank, the Multiple Launch Rocket System, the Bradley Fighting Vehicle, and the new Crusader Mobile Gun System, were just too heavy. The Air Force C-5 strategic transport (the Air Force's largest) could carry two M1 tanks.[4] The newer long range C-17 can carry only one. The C-130 aircraft that provides tactical airlift cannot carry it at all. Neither could it carry the Bradley, current self-propelled artillery, the planned Crusader gun, or the Multiple Launch Rocket System nor engineer heavy support equipment. It was all too big, too heavy, or both. Indeed, even the C-17 could carry either one Crusader mobile artillery piece or its ammunition support vehicle, but not both at once. On the other hand, light forces (such as an airborne or Light Infantry Division) were highly deployable but once on the ground lacked staying power, lethality, and tactical mobility.

The logistical requirements of deployed forces of all kinds were unacceptably large, in part due to the Army's inventory of multiple types of equipment, the sheer number of which drive up the requirements for repair parts. The "iron mountain" of supplies that supported the first Gulf War had been an amazing achievement, but it was incredibly difficult and expensive. The same is true of the second war, and, again, it took months of buildup before the hostilities. It probably could not be done against serious opposition.

General Shinseki's solution was to transform the entire Army by emphasizing key characteristics (responsiveness, lethality, survivability, sustainability, deployability, agility, and versatility) to create a new "medium" division that was rapidly deployable and could dominate the full spectrum of operations, replacing both light and heavy divisions.

It was a bold vision. The technologies required were incredibly complicated and could cost as much as $100 billion. It would take at least 31 million lines of computer code to run the Future Combat Systems (FCS) and its suite of new manned and unmanned machines, all loaded with the latest sensors, roaming the air and ground. Software had to be developed that would process sensor data, identify friend and foe, set targets, issue alerts, coordinate actions, and guide decisions. New kinds of wireless communications devices were required—controlled by still more software and relaying communications via satellites—to allow seamless links between units.[5] With minor exceptions such as special operations units, the entire Army would be organized this way. The plan offered by his predecessor to recategorize the Army as Special Operations forces, Strike forces, Contingency forces, and Campaign forces/ homeland defense died a quiet death having been pretty much ignored by everybody.

Certain analysts pointed out that the Army had an unhappy history of designing divisions for deployability. This had happened in World War II but most notably with the "Light Division" concept and the high-tech 9th Division (Experimental); both produced highly deployable units that lacked firepower, mobility, and sufficient support. These concerns were dismissed as the complaints of chronic naysayers. All Army divisions would be transformed to this new type of organization called the Objective Force, and the critics be damned.

If achieved and fully operational, hopefully sometime between 2012 and 2015, the Objective Force would meet the goal of a combat capable brigade on the ground, ready to fight, anywhere in the world in 96 hours followed by a division in 120 hours and five divisions in 30 days. The more ambitious part was the call for the lead division in 120 hours, versus the previous goal of 288 hours (12 days). But the truly remarkable figure was that of five divisions within 30 days when the most optimistic 1999 estimate was 75 days. It was a remarkable ambition since in 1999 it was flatly impossible. Four years later, during the preparation for the second Gulf War, it would take months to move three heavy divisions into place. Being able to deploy as rapidly as the general asked meant the Army needed to acquire some critical abilities. This in turn required some scientific and technical advances that were by no means guaranteed, notably:

- Combat vehicles of radically reduced weight but with increased lethality.

- Increased deployability of the entire force without sacrificing survivability.
- Greatly reduced requirements for logistic support located with the force.

What the Chief wanted was no mean feat. Take the example of the Future Combat Vehicle, the new lighter fighting vehicle that was the centerpiece of the FCS. It had to be about 70 percent lighter and 50 percent smaller than the current main battle tank, the M1A2 Abrams. The M1A2 weighs 60 to 70 tons depending on the configuration and load. The new fighting vehicle had to be about 20 tons at the most, ideally less than that. The internal volume of the M1A2 is about 650 cubic feet; the new vehicle could not have an internal volume of much over 300–400 cubic feet. Of course, the new vehicle also needed to be able to survive on the battlefield, lethal in its own right, fully netted with C4ISR (command, control, communications, computers, intelligence, surveillance, and reconnaissance) systems of all the services and be logistically supportable. The Army hoped to have answers to these technological challenges, at least in the form of research and development plans, by 2003. The pace of progress toward technological solutions and availability of resources, especially funding, would be key factors.

Down at the Infantry Center in Fort Benning, Georgia, a large group of soldiers were not at all surprised by the General's remarks. More than a month's frantic work

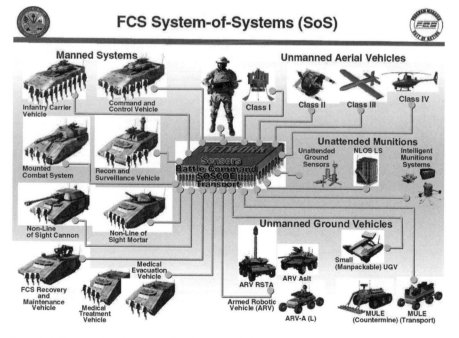

Army briefing graphic depicting the elements of the Future Combat System with the network as the central feature.

had gone into the initial brigade concept before Shinseki's October announcement. Intensive modeling and simulations of various infantry force structures had been conducted by the Infantry Center and its Dismounted Battlespace Battle Lab. An extensive after-action review followed each simulation, and Major General John Le Moyne, Fort Benning's commanding general, was briefed on the results. Le Moyne then briefed the senior U.S. Army Training and Doctrine Command (TRADOC) leadership on an almost nightly basis. All this went on behind closed doors up until the Chief's October announcement.[6]

One requirement that emerged from the Fort Benning discussions was for the replacement of current armored vehicles with wheeled vehicles in order to reduce weight and simplify maintenance and support for the new units. The first priority was to find existing wheeled armored vehicles that would replace the traditional tracked tanks and armored personnel carriers and reduce tonnage by 50–70 percent. Since 90 percent of the Army's deployability problem was due to its logistic requirements, the obvious solution was to reduce those requirements. Allegedly, wheeled vehicles required fewer parts and less service than tracked.

Because the Air Force did not expect to see any new types of transport aircraft for at least 20 years, new systems would not only have to be strategically deployable by the current C-17, but also be able to fit inside a C-130 aircraft for tactical intra-theater lift.[7] The C-17 would be able to carry four to six of the projected new FCS vehicles vs. a single M1A2. Overall logistic needs would be further reduced through common platform/common chassis/standard caliber designs to reduce the stockpile of repair parts. As a measure of his urgency, General Shinseki ordered the Army to immediately begin to seek ground and air platforms (vehicles) that were smaller, lighter, more lethal, yet more reliable, fuel efficient, and more survivable. It was to actively promote technologies that will provide survivability through low observables, ballistic protection, long-range target acquisition, deep targeting, early attack, and first round kill with smaller caliber weapons.

In order to meet the general's requirements, the Objective Force needed the same lethality and survivability as the heavy force it would displace, but the agility and transportability of a medium weight force. In order to meet his timeline, technology exploration needed to conclude sometime in 2003. This would allow the Interim Phase to begin in 2003–2004 with the transformation of five to eight more brigades including at least one National Guard brigade.

This transformation did not, however, mean the immediate abandonment of the Army's heavy armored elements. Until the Objective Force was achieved, plans were to retain portions of the current Army, known as the Legacy Force. Priority for the limited modernization went to the III (U.S.) Corps. This is the force that would go to war if the need arose during the next 15 years or so.

The bridge between the Legacy Force and the Objective Force was the Interim Force. In 2000, initial Brigade Combat Teams were formed at Fort Lewis, Washington, to validate an organizational and operational model for the Interim Force. Based on this validated structure, the Army would field the Interim Force in 2001, using current, off-the-shelf technology. An Interim Armored Vehicle, for example, would be used to equip Interim Force units until the advanced Future Combat Vehicle (FCV) of the Objective Force could materialize. The goal was to have one "interim brigade" at Initial Operating Capability by 2001 and fully operational by 2003, built around a common unit design and common family of combat systems.[8] This new, medium weight unit would hopefully achieve Shinseki's goal of around the world deployability within 96 hours and be capable of sustained combat upon arrival. With its usual love of terminology, the Army fretted over what to call the new formations, beginning with medium brigades, and then calling them "initial brigades" before finally settling on "Initial Brigade Combat Team" (IBCT).

General Shinseki promised that the Army would stand up the two new model brigades, at Fort Lewis, Washington, "as quickly as we can." In fact, the 3rd Brigade, 2nd Infantry Division, and 1st Brigade, 25th Infantry Division, had already been earmarked as the Army's Initial Brigades and their commanders discreetly advised of the fact.

If all went as planned, the IBCT organization would enable the brigades to conduct operations across the full spectrum—from small-scale contingencies such as Bosnia and Kosovo, to major theaters of war. Although the IBCTs were supposedly deployable units, their main purpose was to act as test-beds for organization, methods, current technology, and off the shelf equipment. As FCS surrogates for the Interim Force, they could stimulate doctrine development, organization design, and leadership training. Ultimately, heavy and light forces would converge on similar capability in a family of systems (the Future Combat System) loaded on a common platform (the Future Combat Vehicle), whatever that turned out to be. When technology permitted, transformation to the common FCV platform would erase the line between light and heavy units, leaving an Army whose combat forces consist almost entirely of multipurpose medium brigades. The fact that those future brigades were designed chiefly to fight conventional military forces bothered almost no one.

By military procurement standards, the Army responded with lightning speed. Backed by the personal pressure of the Army's senior leader, in December the procurement system brought the first of the "off-the-shelf" equipment to the Armor Center at Fort Knox, Kentucky, for testing, 35 medium armored vehicles in the 20–25 ton weight class from France, Turkey, Canada, Switzerland, Singapore, Germany, and the United States. Scout, tanker, mortar, and engineer crews representing Fort Knox, Fort Lewis, Washington, Fort Benning, Georgia, and Fort Leonard Wood, Missouri, tested the sample vehicles as candidates to outfit the Interim Brigades. The machines were tested in off-road and on-road driving, live firing, swim capabilities, loading and unloading the vehicles onto C-130 transport planes, railheads, and railcars, as well as in other tactical training.[9]

No decision on an interim vehicle was expected until midsummer 2000, a date that soon slipped to "sometime" in the fall. Meanwhile, something needed to be done right away. So, the Canadian Armed Forces were approached to loan 32 of their Light Armored Vehicle (LAV) IIIs, an eight-wheeled vehicle manufactured by General Dynamics Land Systems– Canada (formerly General Motors Defense) and

General Dynamics Land Systems Division of USA. The GDLS-Canada LAV III 8x8 light armored vehicle had been in Canadian service since 1999. The LAV III is itself a version of the Piranha III built by Mowag of Switzerland.[10]

The LAV III was already designed to fit in the C-130 and featured a lightweight hull design with ballistic protection and higher performance in terms of payload versus gross vehicle weight. Electrically welded high hardness steel plates were presented as armor against light and heavy machine gunfire, antitank mines, and artillery shell splinters. According to Mowag, "the vehicles are equipped for peace keeping and peace enforcing roles," not full-spectrum operations, but it still seemed like a good start on the characteristics desired of the FCV.[11]

By February 2000 the LAVs were arriving at Fort Lewis, Washington, as the 3rd Brigade began to turn in its Abrams tanks, Bradley fighting vehicles, and heavy artillery. The Army assured competing vehicle manufacturers that the LAV IIIs were not necessarily the equipment that would be seen in future brigade motor pools across the Army. But, given Shinseki's fast track approach to transformation, they were necessary as short-term stand-ins for whatever interim armored vehicle would eventually be selected for the new brigades. In the meantime, these vehicles would be used to develop the tactics, techniques, and procedures for the initial brigades.[12]

Given the intention to simultaneously field the modernized legacy force (Force XXI) and the Interim Force, Shinseki seemed to be asking for two armies at once. Funding would be a problem. Accordingly, the fiscal year (FY) 2001 Army budget request included decisions to restructure or "divest" a number of programs in order to provide resources to support transformation and achieve the ambitious deployment goals outlined in Shinseki's October 1999 speech. The restructure slowed two programs that fed into Force XXI and the Objective Force (Crusader and the Future Scout and Cavalry System). The "divestitures" included Heliborne Prophet (Air), Multiple Launch Rocket System (MLRS) Smart Tactical Rocket, Stinger Block II, the Command and Control Vehicle, and the Army Tactical Missile System Block IIA all intended for Force XXI units.

The Initial Brigades

Very early it was decided to give the new organization an old name, Brigade Combat Team. As explained by Colonel Joe Rodriguez, TRADOC's director for the transformation at the time:

> The normal brigade in the US Army today is not organized as a brigade combat team. They get mission-tailored and task organized when they go to combat, or when they go to train. But when they're in garrison, they're in garrison as a pure brigade. This [new] brigade lives, eats, and sleeps as a Brigade Combat Team. All the different combat arms, combat support, combat service support in the brigade, all these people are rated by the colonel commanding the brigade.[13]

But, caveats aside, the BCT was essentially a conventional infantry brigade designed to have two core qualities—mobility and the ability to mount and provide fire support for dismounted infantry assault. The planners started with the standard, long-standing Airborne and Air Assault Infantry organizations as the basic structure and added personnel, weapons, and equipment to enhance mobility, lethality, and force protection.

The first two IBCT's did have some real differences from the Army's ordinary brigades. Each consisted primarily of three infantry battalions, an artillery battalion and a reconnaissance battalion. The reconnaissance battalion, now to be called the RSTA squadron (Reconnaissance, Surveillance, and Target Acquisition), significantly increased the intelligence gathering capability of the brigade. The new brigades also would have organic engineer, military intelligence, and signal companies. Another significant change was that, like the brigade, the battalions and companies of the brigade were to be combined arms teams, consisting primarily of medium armored gun systems (replacing tanks), infantry, and mortars. Previously, Army companies and battalions were organized as pure tank or infantry units, then task organized based on mission requirements.

As designed, the RSTA Squadron was unique in its organization as well. Unlike previous reconnaissance squadrons, it featured larger scout platoons, unmanned aerial vehicles, and counterintelligence soldiers in each scout section to gather human intelligence. The squadron's job was to provide information to the brigade commander so he would have situational understanding as well as situational awareness, all building toward the holy grail of "dominant awareness."[14]

Initial Brigade Organization

- Three Infantry battalions of three companies each. These were new combined arms companies with both indirect- (mounted 120 mm mortars) and direct-fire weapons systems (mobile gun systems or MGS).
- A Reconnaissance, Surveillance, and Target Acquisition squadron consisting of three RSTA troops and a Sensor troop with an Unmanned Aerial Vehicle, Nuclear Biological Chemical Recon Platoon, and a Ground Surveillance Radar Platoon.
- One antitank company.
- One field artillery battalion.
- One engineer company.
- One brigade support battalion.
- One military intelligence company.
- One signal company.

As noted, the new brigades were equipped with Interim Armored Vehicles (IAVs), the Canadian supplied Land Attack Vehicle III, each carrying a nine-man infantry squad and a two man crew. The actual interim vehicle (LAV III had not been officially adopted yet) would come in several configurations—mortars, antitank, fire-support, reconnaissance, etc. As described by Major David Pound, chief of the

Concepts Analysis Division at the Infantry Center, "It's similar to going to a car dealer. You can get several different models of Ford. They are all Fords, and they all look about the same. But each is tailored to meet individual requirements."

Artillery support for the brigade was initially provided by the High Mobility Artillery Rocket Systems (HIMARS), a smaller wheeled version of the standard MLRS. Among other things, the HIMARS was air transportable and able to fire the long-range Army Tactical Missile System guided missile, delivering 950 baseball-sized M74 antipersonnel antimateriel submunitions to ranges exceeding 165 km.[15] This would eventually be replaced by a new weapon, a self-propelled howitzer based on the Lightweight 155mm (M777) cannon system and mounted on the common chassis for all IBCT vehicles. HIMARS, however, was not slated for production until 2003 with fielding in 2005, well beyond the 2003 deadline for an operational IBCT.

Each infantry battalion kept the same reconnaissance platoon as a conventional battalion, capable of conducting limited simultaneous mounted and dismounted reconnaissance. There was a four-gun 120 mm mortar platoon also equipped with four 81 mm mortars to support dismounted operations. One new and unique organization was a 10-man sniper squad assigned to each battalion. The squad was to provide the infantry version of precision fires using heavy, medium, and light caliber sniper systems—medium (M24—7.62mm), light (match grade M16—5.56mm), and heavy (XM107—cal .50). Each rifle company had three rifle platoons, a MGS platoon and a section of two 120 mm mortars mounted on IAVs. The mortar section was also equipped with two 60 mm mortars to support dismounted operations. Each company also had a three-man sniper team. Each rifle platoon consisted of three nine-man rifle squads and a weapons squad, the former with rifles and grenade launchers, a light machine gun, and a Javelin antitank missile launcher (called a "CLU" for command launch unit). Every weapons squad had two three-man M-240B medium machine gun teams and two Javelin gunners with CLUs.[16] It was a more complicated scheme than conventional companies, battalions, and brigades (more special skills, more kinds of equipment, more maintenance and training requirements), and there was some question as to how well a small battalion headquarters could handle that many resources. But on paper at least it was a very capable organization with far more reconnaissance ability than ever before, more mobility, and significantly more ability to place fires on target.

Wheels Instead of Tracks?

The most attention-getting feature of Shinseki's plan was his almost offhand proposal to get rid of the Army's tanks (and other tracked vehicles) in favor of a "wheeled gun platform." Proposals for wheeled fighting vehicles had surfaced from time to time over the years but had never received much enthusiasm from either the Army's leadership or its rank and file. For many the idea of wheeled combat vehicles was something close to blasphemy, for road patrol and peacekeeping perhaps, but to replace main battle tanks? And that was just the interim proposal. As if that were not enough, the Objective Force "tank" was not expected to be a tank at all, but a system of systems called the Future Combat System—several devices (including robot vehicles) separately running around the battlefield, but all acting together to produce the same result as a tank.

The main battle tank was the image of the Army and close to being its raison d'etre. The ability to conduct sustained ground operations under the most intense combat conditions was the defining characteristic of the Army. It was the role that distinguished it from the other services, and the tank was central to making it possible. As one officer put it, "Without tanks, we're just a big version of the Marine Corps."

Lacking an interim armored vehicle of any kind, much less one that met the Chief's requirements, a substitute had to be found in order to meet the goal of an initial operational capability by 2001. That meant an entire brigade set of vehicles, more than 380 of them, by March 2001. To meet this interim requirement, the Army provided funding in the FY 2001 budget to identify and field an existing Medium/Interim Armored Vehicle as a common baseline capability for the BCT. Confusingly, this was termed the Medium Armored Vehicle (MAV), which seemed to be the same thing as the IAV.

The ideal vehicle was one that combined mobility, lethality, and survivability with lower weight and smaller size than standard U.S. armored vehicles. In concept, this was to be achieved by using a lightly armored vehicle whose real protection came from the enemy's inability to locate and target it. It would be designed not to be hit, with weaponry that can defeat armor, and used "low-observable" technology to avoid being targeted. Several families of medium platforms existed or were under development throughout the world that, with slight modification, could meet the initial MAV/IAV requirement for a base system. Finding a surrogate for the MAV was the reason for the trials held at Fort Knox in the spring of 2000. Until new vehicles could be designed and built, an existing one would have to serve the purpose.

As described by the Army, the MAV Infantry Carrier Vehicle (ICV) needed to provide direct, supporting fires to assault infantry in order to destroy hardened enemy bunkers, machine gun, and sniper positions. It would be supported by a separate MGS whose primary armament must defeat a standard infantry bunker and create an opening in a double reinforced concrete wall, through which infantry can pass. The same armament needed to be capable of firing 7–12 rounds per minute for at least 2 minutes. A laser range-finder, shoot-on-the move capability was also required, able to defeat main battle tanks (up to T-72M, the standard Soviet tank) out to at least 2000M and preferably 4000M. Given the poor record of lighter wheeled vehicles carrying cannon (they tended to tip over when the gun was fired), it was another amazing set of specifications.

The brigade's SP Howitzer would be based on the Lightweight 155mm (M777) cannon system (then in development) mounted on the common chassis for all IBCT vehicles and be capable of firing all currently fielded and developmental U.S. and North Atlantic Treaty Organization (NATO) Standard 155mm munitions and propellants. In addition, the system had to be able to reach a range of 30 kilometers with a maximum rate of fire of no fewer than five rounds per minute.[17] At least the howitzer vehicle would presumably be able to stop and deploy some sort of anchor system before firing, an advantage denied the MGS.

But all this depended on having the MAV/IAV, and that remained no more than a concept. The trials for an interim armored vehicle dragged on past summer 2000 and into the fall, much to the displeasure of General Shinseki. The delays, he believed, would threaten the momentum necessary to achieve his transformation goals. Finally, in November, the Army announced to the surprise of no one that the LAV III would be the Interim Armored Vehicle. This conferred some advantages, chiefly that the vehicle was already in use by the interim brigades giving it a big boost toward meeting Shinseki's schedule. But it also raised some problems. First of all, the General Motors/General Dynamics partnership that had been created specifically to produce LAV IIIs could not meet the production goals for 14 to 17 months, pushing the initial operational capability date back as far as May 2003 rather than the original date of December 2001.[18]

The Army initial requirement for interim vehicles was projected as 1740 systems to equip five brigade-size units of 348 systems each. However, it could go as high as 2131 vehicles if all variants were purchased. Additional ones would be required for training purposes, maintenance floats, and spares. Eventually, there could be an additional 10 brigades or as many as 5,000 more vehicles.[19] The IAV contract had a value of about $4 billion over six years, plus $2 billion more for systems and weapons to be installed on the machines. This made it a very lucrative contract with a possible lifetime of more than 30 years and well worth fighting over. As soon as the LAV III award was announced, United Defense LP, a competitor for the contract, lodged a formal protest with the General Accounting Office claiming the Army had failed to consider its own criteria in choosing the LAV III. This added further delay. According to one Army general, "The Chief is not happy with the schedule we are bringing in."[20]

Then there was the problem of the MGS. The LAV III variants for the new brigades were supposed to include an autoloading 105mm gun system based on the M68A1 cannon being developed at Watervliet Arsenal, New York. This would add some badly needed punch to the smaller caliber weapons of the brigade. However, neither the gun nor LAV III versions to carry it were anything like ready for fielding. Worse, once the vehicle-gun marriage was achieved, it would be at least two years before production could begin. The same was true of the fire support vehicle and the nuclear-biological-radiological (NBC) reconnaissance vehicle. That, of course, would mean that the initial brigade combat teams would be "operational" without their principal direct-fire weapon and less than optimum indirect fire support. The interim solution was to equip the Anti-Tank Guided Missile version with "bunker busting" rounds. A HMMWV (Humvee) equipped with a laser designator would be used as a substitute fire direction vehicle, and handheld sensors would have to substitute for the NBC vehicle. Later the brigades received the Army standard M93 Fox chemical reconnaissance vehicle, itself a modified armored car based on an older European model.

What About the Network?

A great deal of attention was paid to the hardware that would go into the Interim and Objective Forces. But none of this would work without the "network" to tie it all together. Somehow, this elusive network was going to achieve unheard of "situational awareness" by commanders at all levels and a "shooter to sensor link." This was briefed incessantly, but somehow most of the attention went to the Interim Armored Vehicle and the various accoutrements of the Interim Brigades. Most people did not understand the electronic connectivity issues and were willing to just trust in the assurances of the briefers that the network piece was under control. But it was not all as simple as that, and those involved in creating the promised system of systems faced a huge challenge. For example, the global information grid of the Department of Defense (DoD) was based on the Defense Information Infrastructure (DII), created in the early 1990s and already inadequate and outdated.

In order to work as required, the network had to provide a voice, data, and video communication, command, and intelligence system that could link unit commanders at all levels within the unit of action including the individual vehicles and dismounted soldiers. That was hard but doable with a slight stretch of current technology. But the net also needed to link all participants with all sources of intelligence, including unattended ground sensors, dismounted soldiers, ground vehicles, aircraft, and space satellites. Furthermore, net members were to link with all sources of combat firepower, including systems both inside and outside the unit regardless of the services that own them. Also, it had to link with joint, interagency, and/or multinational coalition elements that might be relevant. At the moment, many of the components required for such a system either did not exist at all (e.g., mobile relays and unmanned ground vehicles) or were in the design stage. On top of that, many of the existing systems that might be incorporated, especially radios, were incompatible.

That was the first layer of needed capabilities. In order to perform those functions, the IBCT/FCS network had to be able to obtain and fuse imagery and other data from national and commercial assets (e.g., satellites), Army assets both within the unit of action and above the unit of action, and other services' assets. Finally, the net needed to access and manage enough scare bandwidth to transfer vast amounts of information. Two complementary programs—Joint Tactical Radio System and Warfighter Information Network–Tactical—were supposed to enable the interoperability and the increases in bandwidth, but they did not exist either.

The Critics Gather

When the Army first ran simulations pitting hypothetical medium-weight brigades against the Yugoslav Army, on Kosovo terrain, the results were less than stellar. "In the first few runs, the loss ratios were pathetic," observed an Army officer involved with the tests. "They were like 1-to-1. We prefer 10-to-1 and even much greater." At a 1-1 loss ratio, the projected force was likely to run out of assets long before the enemy did.[21]

The thin-skinned medium-weight vehicles had a basic problem in that they were vulnerable to first hits from Yugoslav tanks. As soon as the opposing force realized this, they began to stage armor ambushes. The U.S. medium weight force took heavy losses moving through ravines and other choke points in the rugged Balkan terrain. The U.S. vehicles were also subjected to a fierce pounding from enemy artillery.

The simulated bashing revealed a number of new concerns with the medium-weight brigades. The vulnerability of the 20-ton fighting vehicle to a first shot meant that the new unit would have to find and kill enemy tanks, artillery, and other armor defeating weapons before they can target U.S. vehicles. Information would substitute for armor.

That made intelligence, reconnaissance, and target acquisition ("situational aware-ness" in techno jargon) an even higher priority than before. The medium weight force could not afford to simply advance until it bumped into the enemy. Its effec-tiveness lay in its ability to find and target an enemy without being located itself, and this came through loud and clear in the war games. Said an Army officer who helped shape the games, "We dramatically increased the number of UAVs [Unmanned Aerial Vehicles], to make sure there was nothing going on we didn't know about." These were, of course, hypothetical UAVs since the Army had no standard UAV in production and no firm design for one.

Critics inside and outside the services identified three central objections to Shin-seki's vision. Allegedly, some of the changes were too marginal, others were too dependent on unproven technology and, finally, others might ultimately leave the Army with less combat power than it had before. Andrew F. Krepinevich, a retired Army officer serving as executive director of the Center for Strategic and Budgetary Assessments, a Washington, D.C., think tank said, "It sounds like this thing isn't sup-posed to fight. It's just supposed to get to Albania in four days. They ought to be given a pat on the back, but there are a lot of holes there."[22]

Furthermore, the Army still had not clearly stated what the new units are supposed to accomplish. Full-spectrum dominance was a nice phrase but so far that is all it was. Like many analysts, Krepinevich believed that the Army should be experi-menting with different force designs, each tailored to the various kinds of conflict likely to be encountered in the future—one for urban warfare, another for deep strike missions using precision artillery and attack helicopters, and perhaps a third operat-ing in an environment where the enemy has cut the logistics tail. Asking for one standard design, medium weight unit to be all things in all possible conflicts was just asking too much.

But perhaps the most telling criticism was that the technology was not there and would not be anytime soon. It was possible that General Shinseki's vision of a capable full-spectrum all-wheeled ground force simply could not be provided in the time frame imagined, i.e., 15 years. According to some analysts, near-term technological development offered little hope for the emergence of a medium-weight or wheeled vehicle able to confidently take on the most demanding and dangerous of combat missions. The best one could hope for was that the advance of science and technology could solve these problems in time—say, 30 or 40 years.[23]

Who Picks Up the Bill?

Then there was the cost of transforming the Army—already something like $70–$100 billion over 10 to 20 years and likely to rise. This would certainly collide with other high-profile military programs in all of the services. Within defense circles, Army Chief Shinseki received good reviews for his transform initiative, but only so long as the Army could pay for it. The idea of parallel development within transformation meant maintaining older "legacy" systems until the new ones were ready. The Army intention was to sustain and modernize its existing heavy forces until the new "objective force" was ready for deployment throughout the Army. As explained by Army Secretary Louis Caldera: "Until the objective force is fielded throughout the Army, it is likely that we will need to maintain heavy, digitized divisions (i.e. Force XXI) with the capacity to win against Soviet-era armor that may be employed against us in places like Korea or Southwest Asia."[24]

Congress was not enthusiastic about paying for two armies, and neither were the other services that might be tapped for funds. In March 2000, Senate Armed Services Committee Chairman John Warner (R-VA) warned the Army leadership that its modernization plans were in "jeopardy," because there was not enough money to build lighter, strategically deployable forces and continue procuring all the other updated weapons the service wanted for its current forces. Defense Secretary William Cohen told senators that no additional funds would be provided and that the Army should focus on transformation within its current resource allocation. Since about 1990, each service's share of the total defense budget had been relatively fixed: 25 percent for the Army; 29 percent for the Air Force; 31 percent for the Navy/Marine Corps; and 15 percent for the defense agencies. The other services were obviously unwilling to change the ratio to benefit the Army since they had their own transformations to fund. The Marine Corps was gearing up for urban warfare and the Navy shifting to "network-centric warfare." None of this was expected to be cheap.

One obvious place to save money was on manpower. Soldiers were expensive; annual personnel costs for a single Army division in peacetime were over $2 billion. Furthermore, soldiers had no corporate advocates. The big defense contractors are all high-tech providers and long range; big-ticket projects are their bread and butter. They all promised wonderful new capabilities, and their presentations emphasized that technology could substitute for soldiers.

But even normally friendly commentators questioned how the Army could expect to fund two forces at once, transformation and the status quo. The pro-defense *Armed Forces Journal International* editorialized, "If the Army isn't willing to cut the old to pay for the new, just how dedicated is the Army to transformation? If the

Army is unwilling to pay a high price for change, it's doubtful the Army is committed to change in the first place."[25] More cruelly, they were also ready to argue that the Army already had enough money, if the Army actually transformed itself.

Transformation the Air Force Way

The Air Force predictably had the greatest heartburn with the prospect of increasing the Army's share of the defense pie. As the airmen saw it, the USAF had transformed itself into an all-weather, night-fighting, highly precise weapon with no help from anyone. Because of good management, most of its fighter-bombers were already equipped with laser guidance. In the Yugoslav/Kosovo operation, satellite-guided bombs, refined by last-second radar updates, hit points precisely in all weather conditions. Future air attacks would increasingly be from standoff distances, far from surface-to-air defenses. Using an array of precision guided weapons, aircraft would be able to strike targets currently restricted to expensive cruise missiles at far lower cost. Most Air Force fighter-bombers would have these capabilities within the decade—if nothing interfered with planned funding.[26]

And, as for "legacy systems," the USAF had its own. In fact, most of the year 2000 Air Force consisted of older aircraft like the F-16 and the venerable B-52, kept effective through constant upgrades. More cogently, this had been accomplished quietly with available funding over the past ten years. Why could the Army not do the same?

In truth, the Air Force had been ruthless in its management of change. The emphasis on nuclear weapons was gone. The Strategic Air Command had been disbanded and the number of ballistic missiles cut in half, with more reductions planned. Learning from the private sector, the Air Force slashed management layers. Air divisions were disbanded and staffs reduced to a maximum of 100 people. Education and training bureaucracies were integrated into an Air Education and Training Command. Aerial refuelers were combined with airlifters as the new Air Mobility Command. System development, maintenance, and modernization were all gathered into the Air Force Materiel Command. Even the basic wing and squadron structures were reorganized across the Air Force.[27] Furthermore, the USAF had to replace every satellite it owned by 2010. Here the service planned to not merely replace them, but also increase its space capabilities, revamp its space power doctrine, and integrate its air and space communities into a single team.

The airmen claimed to take the money for these and other changes out of hide—and believed the other services should do the same. If the Army had been less forward-looking, well, that was its own fault. It did not mean that the ground pounders deserved special treatment. Everyone understood that if the Army tried to tax the other services to solve Army problems, a savage interservice fight would be inevitable. In the next Quadrennial Defense Review (QDR), the Air Force was prepared to argue that any such move would shortchange America's chief asymmetrical advantage—dominant aerospace power. The airmen also continued to voice dissatisfaction over the secondary place their service occupied in military doctrine. The editor of *Air Force* (an organ for USAF views published by the Air Force Association) commented that "The Air Force often seems to fare better in battle than it does in peacetime in the corridors of power in the Pentagon. War plans and joint doctrine emphasize ground operations. Not even the Gulf War, in which it was generally agreed that air power was the decisive element, managed to change that. The joint planning models in use today discount the effectiveness of air power. Air Force operations not in support of surface forces are considered "un-joint." [28] In other words, the whole U.S. doctrine for the use of military forces needed some serious rethinking.

As far as the Air Force was concerned, there was some doubt that the Army actually understood the concept of "transformation." For the airmen, transformations were not spectacular, all-inclusive, one-time changes. For them, continual change was a fact of life, part of everyday business and integral to the way modern organizations operate. Successful organizations routinely allocate money for transformation. Modern business learned to emphasize the ability to change. It is the way everyday business gets done. Taking modern business as a model, military leaders needed to exploit new fields and new ways of doing business.

By the end of 2000 the competition between advocates of air power and those of ground warfare continued to sharpen. The October 2000 issue of *Armed Forces Journal International* featured an article coauthored by retired Brigadier General Huba Wass De Czege, one of the Army's leading theoreticians and an architect of AirLand Battle doctrine. In it, Wass De Czege characterized Operation Allied Force (OAF) as a proven failure and called for the continuing primacy of land power and a shift in funding to support the Army transition, including the strategic lift assets the Army would need for rapid deployment (i.e., cargo aircraft). Directly attacking the Air Force's emphasis on precision bombing, he argued that ground forces could be more precise than bombing from three miles up, cause less collateral damage, and result in fewer casualties than a strategically coercive air-centric campaign.[29] The U.S. Air Force quickly shot back in the December issue of the same journal with a letter from Colonel Ron Dietz, the USAF chief of doctrine. Colonel Dietz replied that OAF was in reality a "joint/combined campaign" (presumably alluding to the presence of naval aviation and aircraft from NATO allies) and, unlike the idealized ground campaign envisioned by General Wass De Czege, operated under real world political constraints.

Matters were not helped any when *Newsweek* magazine surfaced what it claimed was a "suppressed" U.S. Air Force report showing that the 1999 air campaign in Kosovo was militarily ineffective. As reported by the magazine, Allied bombing blew up hundreds of cars, trucks, and decoys, but barely dented Serb artillery and armor. By *Newsweek's* account, the report credited only a tiny fraction of the targets claimed at the time: 14 tanks, not 120; 18 armored personnel carriers, not 220; 20 artillery pieces, not 450. "Out of the 744 'confirmed' strikes by NATO pilots during the war, the Air Force investigators, who spent weeks combing Kosovo by helicopter and by foot, found evidence of just 58." [30]

George W. Bush Adopts Transformation

Transformation advocates had cause to celebrate when Republican presidential candidate George W. Bush took up the flag of military revolution and planted it in the center of his military policy. It was not exactly a surprise. After all, Donald H. Rumsfeld, Bush's campaign advisor on defense, was a well-known advocate of transformation and a revolution in military affairs (RMA)–based military. But it was still the most emphatic pro-transformation statement yet from a national leader.

Speaking before the Corps of Cadets at the South Carolina's Citadel Military College on September 23, 1999, Bush delivered his transformation manifesto. As reviewed by Nicholas Lemann of the *New Yorker,* it sounded like "an unremarkable Republican fusillade." However, "If you owned a secret decoder ring, the speech was highly significant: Bush had endorsed the Revolution in Military Affairs."[31]

The first part of the address was pretty unremarkable. Threats were identified: weapons proliferation ("the contagious spread of missile technology and weapons of mass destruction"), terrorism, information warfare, and "the unconventional and invisible threats of new technologies and old hatreds"; promises were made: "better pay, better treatment and better training for the volunteer military—a billion dollars in salary increases" as well as the end of "vague, aimless and endless" deployments. Peacekeeping missions, in particular, received the back of the candidate's hand.

For military futurists, however, the thrilling moment came when Bush invoked the magic word "transformation" and promised, "to take advantage of a tremendous opportunity. . . to extend the current peace into the far realm of the future. A chance to project America's peaceful influence, not just across the world, but across the years."

> This opportunity is created by a revolution in the technology of war. Power is increasingly defined, not by mass or size, but by mobility and swiftness. Influence is measured in information, safety is gained in stealth, and force is projected on the long arc of precision-guided weapons. This revolution perfectly matches the strengths of our country—the skill of our people and the superiority of our technology. The best way to keep the peace is to redefine war on our terms.

Candidate Bush went on to condemn the Cold War "industrial age" military and promised armed forces organized "for information age battles." The real goal, he said, was

> to move beyond marginal improvements—to replace existing programs with new technologies and strategies. To use this window of opportunity to skip a generation of technology. This will require spending more—and spending more wisely.

There would, he said, be a sweeping review of Defense Department programs. Furthermore, he promised, "I will commit an additional $20 billion to defense R&D between the time I take office and 2006."

It was a rousing endorsement of military transformation, or at least those were all the right words. But when it came to specifics, the speech provided only a few vague ideas of what transformation ought to look like. The Air Force was indirectly praised with a brief endorsement of its current doctrine—the ability "to strike from across the world with pinpoint accuracy—with long-range aircraft and perhaps with unmanned systems." Bush also mentioned the need to "protect our network of satellites," presumably an Air Force prerogative.

The Navy received a bare mention advising the service to "pursue promising ideas like the arsenal ship." But the Army was viewed critically—Army units needed to be lighter and more easily deployable, and light forces must be more lethal. And all these forces needed to be organized in "smaller, more agile formations, rather than cumbersome divisions."

On the other hand, most Army officers were pleased at the candidate's condemnation of "peacekeeping" and "nation-building" operations like Bosnia and Kosovo and his promise to put a stop to "vague" missions of this sort. Peacekeeping and nation building had emerged as important Army roles since the 1970s with soldiers sent to support uneasy peace agreements or assist in restoring devastated countries from Somalia to Haiti, Bosnia, and the Sinai Desert. These not-quite-peace and not-quite-war operations were generally detested within the Army, and candidate Bush was clearly promising to put an end to them.

The services were less pleased when the candidate sounded a disturbing note,

> I will expect the military's budget priorities to match our strategic vision—not the particular visions of the services, but a joint vision for change. I will earmark at least 20 percent of the procurement budget for acquisition programs that propel America generations ahead in military technology. And I will direct the Secretary of Defense to allocate these funds to the services that prove most effective in developing new programs that do so.

The emphasis on "jointness" was not necessarily welcome to uniformed observers, given the deep divisions between the services and their competing interests, especially the struggle for a share in the defense budget. But, nevertheless, "jointness" (staple of DoD's nominal policy for years) would be a major theme of Bush's defense policy.

Finally, the speech was also a triumph for Andrew W. Marshall, a sort of vindication after all his years of little-noticed labor deep in the Pentagon. Marshall was probably the most important promoter of the RMA in the U.S. defense establishment. "Bush's speech showed the fingerprints of Marshall's allies and endorsed Marshall's main ideas."[32]

Writing in *Foreign Affairs,* Condoleezza Rice, the candidate's national security advisor-designate and later Secretary of State, promoted the same theme. She argued that nation building and operations of this sort rob the military of its conventional combat skills. "The military", she wrote, "cannot, by definition, do anything decisive in these 'humanitarian' cases," and runs the inherent risk of mission creep (military operations that escalate beyond a sustainable level and lack discernible strategic ends).[33]

Candidate Bush became President Bush in a hotly contested election and, after taking office, wasted no time making transformation a presidential policy.

Alas, this was of limited help to the Army. A January 2001 General Accounting Office (GAO) report pointed up a basic problem with transformation—the risk involved in planning an Objective Force based on hoped-for developments in technology and doctrine. Since it was clearly possible, perhaps even likely, that the required developments would not meet the transformation timeline, the report recommended a more gradual approach in stages, incorporating worthwhile new capabilities but planning to keep the Legacy and Interim Forces "longer than anticipated." In effect, it was endorsing something closer to the gradualist approach of Force XXI, rather than the leap ahead that Shinseki and others thought necessary. The Army replied that GAO was ignoring the Army's "holistic" approach and concentrating solely on technology. This answer, of course, ignored the fact that, if the technology failed to materialize, the rest of the "holistic approach" was probably irrelevant if not actively dangerous.[34]

General Shinseki was unbowed by the report. On March 1, the Chief of Staff plowed ahead by announcing that the Objective Force needed to be fielded by 2010 vice 2012. "Our intent is to accelerate the transition to research and development by collapsing traditional lines." There would be no waiting for the development of better systems if it meant slowing down the transformation process. "This is about speed," he said. Actually, it was about bureaucracy. If the FCS program was funded and in progress, it would acquire a constituency among the bureaucrats and defense contractors involved. With vested interests to support they would fight for transformation during the rough times to come. Shinseki proposed to add funds to the Future Combat System program for fiscal years 2003 to 2008. In April 2003, FCS progress would be reviewed to identify the technologies and concepts with the best prospects for rapid success. "We will make the tough calls," the General said, "we will shift resources to the most promising technical solutions." The second milestone would be the development and demonstration of a prototype FCS model beginning in FY 2006.[35]

The QDR of 2001

By late spring 2001, the worst forebodings of the Army's senior leadership were coming true. The dreaded Quadrennial Defense Review was coming fast, and the service was in trouble. General Shinseki's transformation imitative was meant to keep the Army on the leading edge. He was committed to the concept and four programs that he viewed as essential to that process: the IAV, the Crusader Mobile Artillery System, the Comanche reconnaissance/attack helicopter, and the FCS. Now all four were under pressure from the Secretary of Defense (SecDef) for either reduction or outright elimination. The 75-ton Crusader self-propelled gun had even been singled out by the president as an example of an outdated system. It seemed that, among the civilian defense leadership, these programs were viewed chiefly as a source of funds for other "leap-ahead" technology programs.

A strategy review conducted by Andrew Marshall's Office of Net Assessment had already called for a shift in geographical focus from Europe to Asia. Rumsfeld was believed to be concerned with the expected rise of China as a near-peer competitor and allegedly wanted a China-framed QDR. Both he and Marshall emphasized the military leverage afforded by long-range bombers and space systems. Early drafts of the review did not even mention ground forces.

Another review by the Defense Secretary's conventional-forces panel endorsed similar priorities, suggesting that cuts in ground forces could free up money for investment in futuristic weapons. A transformation panel reviewing technology programs proposed $100 billion in increases through 2007, but allocated less than 10 percent of the money to Army programs. Like the other services, the Army had been largely excluded from these administration reviews of military strategy and priorities. But, unlike the other services, the news for the Army was uniformly bad.

Among the senior defense leadership, only General Shinseki and Army Secretary Thomas White were staunch supporters of ground-based military power. Under their leadership, the Army began to prepare for a battle in the QDR.

Some of this was the service's own fault. As an institution, the Army remained convinced that land power was self-evidently the most important component of national military power. The Army had rejected trendy theorizing about future warfare and focused its "military revolution" thinking on improvements in the way it did business. Army Transformation was really about how to fight conventional wars in a more efficient and effective manner. Despite a decade that began with the successful air campaign in the Persian Gulf and ended with a similar air power success in the Balkans, the Army clung to its belief in the obvious, enduring value of land power. This value was less obvious to outside observers. Even the eminent military historian John Keegan concluded that Operation Allied Force heralded a new age of aerospace power.

Finally convinced that its back was to the wall, the Army prepared to enter a Quadrennial Defense Review that by summer's end would determine the fate of America's oldest military service. As perceived by the Department of the Army, the underlying agenda of the 2001 Defense Review was to justify cuts in the Army force structure in order to buy leap-ahead systems more rapidly for the other services. In a series of June meetings, the Army headquarters staff formulated its responses to the draft terms of reference for the QDR.

The Army offered four basic counterarguments.

First of all, it argued that policy makers were overestimating the value of precision-strike weapons. "There are no single-dimensional military solutions to strategic challenges," the Army warned. Overreliance on technological "silver bullets" would not work with adaptive enemies who could avoid or withstand being targeted from the air.

Second, it argued that the assumption that no major wars would occur in the near-term (through 2006) was unfounded. "History demonstrates that serious threats develop with very little warning." Because "investment strategies that ignore current or near-term challenges expose the United States to unacceptable risk," the Army contended, "we must maintain readiness while we transform."

Third, the Army leadership rejected the assumption that future wars would be brief, not requiring sustained operations. It argued "the advent and duration of future conflicts and war cannot be predicted," and that conflicts caused by failing nations could not be resolved by "air or sea power alone."

Finally, it argued that there was insufficient appreciation of land power among policy makers. Pointing out that ground forces were far better suited than other forces for prolonged operations in "complex terrain" such as mountains, cities, or jungles, the Army asserted its unique capabilities were "an essential complement to the rest of the Joint Force."[36]

A Battle Joined

The other participants in the QDR immediately rejected these points, dismissing the Army thinking as backward looking and out of date. The long-term future might be unknowable, but it was also of little consequence. The services had their own short-term agendas to pursue.

The Air Force's fleet of aircraft was rapidly ageing, and the airmen sought accelerated investment in new aerospace and information technologies they believed would yield a versatile force capable of quickly achieving victory in most conflicts while risking few American lives. There was the F-22, of course, still the crown jewel of Air Force's future, but there was also the Joint Strike Fighter program. These two planes, the USAF argued, were the real transformation.

The Navy had similar ideas based on a concept of network-centric warfare featuring standoff munitions launched from warships operating in littoral regions. The Marines argued that they were better postured than the Army for rapid response to overseas contingencies, given the Marines' lesser dependence on land bases and more modest logistical requirements.

Even when key players such as Deputy Secretary Paul Wolfowitz and Deputy Under Secretary Stephen Cambone accepted the abstract logic of the Army's position, they remained intent on finding money for "transformational" capabilities. Although the Army might be correct in the long run, the present seemed to be a time of diminished danger. If risks had to be taken for the sake of transformation, this seemed the time to take them.

Discouraged by the response in the Pentagon, the Army began to look for allies outside the government. Formerly disdainful senior officers suddenly became interested in meeting with defense intellectuals and even with reporters. The Association of the U.S. Army issued a series of uncharacteristically harsh attacks on emerging Pentagon priorities. In early August, 82 lawmakers—including a majority of members on the House Armed Service Committee—sent a letter to Rumsfeld, warning him not to cut Army force structure below the existing level of 480,000 active-duty personnel. This demarche was not well received in the SecDef's office, and rumors began to circulate that Army Secretary White was in trouble with his boss.

Meanwhile, senior Army leaders inside the building went on an offensive to educate the senior civilian appointees on how overextended the service was in supporting

numerous peacekeeping and peace-enforcement obligations. In a visit to the Army
Operations Center, Wolfowitz was briefed that a relatively small peacekeeping force
of 5,000 soldiers in Bosnia required a commitment of almost 20,000 personnel—
5,000 on the ground, 5,000 training to go, 5,000 retraining and reintegrating upon
their return, plus thousands more in support functions or displaced by the deployment of primary units. Given that 293,000 of the Army's active-duty force of
480,000 personnel were available for deployment at any given time, Bosnia was tying
up one out of 15 deployable troops. It would not take many such obligations before
the Army's already dubious capacity to wage two major theater wars was reduced to
one and a half, or less.[37] Few of the Defense Department's senior policy makers were
persuaded to action by the Army's arguments, but a combination of bureaucratic
resistance, political pressure, and uncertainty about the future helped reinforce its
position.

Back at the 4th ID

Despite struggles, shortcomings, and setbacks, the 4th Infantry Division (Mechanized) was officially pronounced the world's first fully "digitized" division. The
4th ID had now been conducting force-on-force training, map exercises, and endless
drills with the Force XXI Battle Command Brigade and Below (FBCB2) system since
1995, including several rotations at the National Training Center.

The main object of attention was the FBCB2, which would enable the Tactical
Internet system that would create the networked system at the heart of transformation. Its purpose was to network soldiers and airmen across the battlefield and provide complete situational awareness, the long sought "common operational
picture" that will precisely locate and identify friendly and enemy troops. Communications would take place within seconds rather than minutes, and everyone would
have the same information. Despite all the work that had gone into it, FBCB2, the
electronic heart and soul of digitization, still suffered from teething problems.

First of all, it was proving exceedingly difficult to keep the complex computer systems operating under simulated combat conditions. Jouncing in the back of tanks
and armored personnel carriers, subject to constant heat, dust, and vibration as well
as unpredictable variations in electrical current, just was not an environment well
suited to complex networked computing. When enemy electronic countermeasures
were added to the picture, it became nearly impossible. Anyone who had attempted
to keep such a system running in the relatively benign environment of an air-
conditioned office complex could sympathize.

Another important shortcoming was the type of commercial encryption used. It
did not meet National Security Agency type-1 standard encryption standards, limiting the transmission of some command and control and classified data. Furthermore,
in the real world, the satellite communications "pipe" turned out to be significantly
narrower than the line-of-sight radio communications for which FBCB2 was originally designed. It was the bandwidth problem again. The satellite link lacked sufficient bandwidth and became overloaded, further hindering data transmission.

Voice-recognition software also ran into difficulty when the commercial products tested could not cope with the noisy confines of armored vehicles.[38]

There were also training and maintenance problems as constant patches, upgrades, fixes, and other changes were factored into the system. Fortunately, there were at least a few young soldiers who had grown up with computers. They were well accustomed to the vagaries of computer systems and often amazingly resourceful in finding solutions to unexpected problems. They were extremely helpful, but there were not that many of them and they could not be counted on as a long-term solution.

Undaunted, the 4th ID continued its grinding schedule of exercises and evaluations. Division Capstone Exercise I at the National Training Center at Fort Irwin, California, during April 2001 saw the tanks, helicopters, and armored personnel carriers testing the effectiveness of the new command and control systems across miles of open desert. Division Capstone Exercise II, a division-level command post map exercise was held in October. Despite difficulties, the Army pronounced the exercises a success and plans went forward to convert the 1st Cavalry Division to the Force XXI structure by 2003, followed by the 3rd Armored Cavalry Regiment at Fort Carson, Colorado.[39]

An initial operational test and evaluation was postponed from late 2002 as work was still needed to interface other communications systems with FBCB2. Problems persisted, and a year later FBCB2 was still considered a developmental system, not approved for acquisition.[40]

CHAPTER 6

THE DIGITAL ARMY AT WAR

Transformation and George W. Bush

I will begin creating the military of the next century.
—Presidential Candidate George W. Bush[1]

If he thinks he's going to change the culture of the military overnight, he ain't seen nothing and he ain't been nowhere.
—Admiral (ret.) William Crowe[2]

The Era of Bush and Rumsfeld

Once in office, the new President, George W. Bush, told Secretary Donald Rumsfeld to carry out the promised "review of the United States military, the state of our strategy, the structure of our forces, [and] the priorities of our budget."[3] Rumsfeld's principal assistant and leader of the review would be none other than Andrew Marshall himself, the prophet of transformation. Pentagon insiders had no doubt Marshall would deliver on time—as one civilian staffer observed, "he's been working on that report since 1973."

The newly elected President used the occasion of Rumsfeld's appointment to lay out his expectations in blunt terms:

> Our nation is positioned well to use technologies to redefine the military. And so one of Secretary Rumsfeld's first tasks will be to challenge the status quo inside the Pentagon, to develop a strategy necessary to have a force equipped for warfare of the 21st century.[4]

So Donald Rumsfeld arrived at the Pentagon with a mandate to "challenge the status quo and envision a new architecture of American defense," as one of President Bush's campaign speeches put it. Change, the Secretary of Defense (SecDef) said, will not come easy for America's military. "You can count on me to lead these changes in a spirit of respect and gratitude for the military and its traditions."[5]

Two weeks later, in a speech at Norfolk Naval Air Station, the President further hammered home his message of change.

Our goal is to move beyond marginal improvements to harness new technologies that will support a new strategy....Our defense vision will drive our defense budget, not the other way around.[6]

The new SecDef was a vocal advocate of ideas like transformation and rapid dominance, as well as a believer in air power; he was suspected to be ready to finance his agenda through force cuts, especially cuts in ground forces. It was transformation, but not "Army transformation." Indeed, it looked more like anti-Army transformation. What the President and Rumsfeld espoused was more of an ideology than a plan. It gathered sundry elements of the revolution in military affairs (RMA) under the umbrella of "transformation," emphasizing speed, precision, and flexibility with precision munitions as its primary symbol. Precision weapons and space-based missile defense were transformative. Army tanks and artillery were not. The very tenets of transformation were threatening to ground forces, especially the emphasis on speed.

As described by General Tommy Franks, the Commander, U.S. Central Command, the defense secretary emphasized early that there were two immediate strategic problems. First of all, the sanctions against Iraq were collapsing, and the 1991 coalition had dwindled to the United States and Great Britain. Containment was no longer working. Rumsfeld wanted a plan to deal with Iraq. The other big issue was terrorism and Usama bin Laden. The frustration with "pinprick, standoff retaliations," what the President had described as "swatting at flies," was building within both the Pentagon and the intelligence community.[7]

Rumsfeld's appointment was received without enthusiasm in the Army corridors of the Pentagon. This was reinforced when rumors emerged from the secretary's office that Rumsfeld would like to reduce Army strength by two more divisions. He was also known to believe that each of the services emphasized certain big-ticket weapons systems because they enhanced the role of that particular service, not because they made strategic sense. This was worrying because the new SecDef had clout. He was close to the President and a principal architect of Bush's military policies. As if that were not enough, Rumsfeld and the President were both former military aviators (Bush in the Air National Guard), and Vice President Richard Cheney was considered an air power enthusiast. All this, plus the new SecDef's experience in the government bureaucracy would make it hard to defeat or deflect his initiatives when they threatened the Army.

In March Rumsfeld and Marshall briefed top military leaders on the results of the review. The reaction was reportedly not good, and by May rumors were rife that Rumsfeld and the Joint Chiefs of Staff were openly at odds. General Shinseki, in particular, was reportedly unhappy with the approach taken by the Defense Secretary and his Office of the Secretary of Defense (OSD) staff. Army Transformation,

Shinseki's initiative, had been underway for almost two years, but somehow it was not what the secretary meant by "transformation." Exactly what Rumsfeld did mean was not entirely clear, but it certainly did not seem to be anything that would help the Army. In the end Rumsfeld's strategic review came and went with few programmatic changes and not much lasting impact.[8]

Armed Against Whom and With What?

If changed threats included terrorism, nonstate actors, insurgencies, and more effective weapons in the hands of all these, it was hard to see how the proposed transformation would help. Despite the invocation of Full Spectrum Dominance and ritual bows to asymmetric threats and terrorism, the transformed military was not designed to counter those threats. Just exactly whom it was intended to fight was not clear, but transformation really meant a better way to defeat old fashioned enemies—the armies of nation states.

Military information networking did take a big step forward in 2001 when the Department of Defense (DoD) announced its first "enterprise architecture," the Global Information Grid (GIG). As the concept of network-centric operations continued to take hold, the Pentagon established the GIG to replace the outdated Defense Information Infrastructure. GIG was described as communications "scaffolding" to carry the defense information network around the world. Once the various subsystems were in place, U.S. forces would be able to reach into the network via satellite and pull down information services anywhere in the world.[9]

Despite such tangible advances, Rumsfeld's plans ran into steady opposition from doubters and those with vested interests. Within certain senior circles at the Pentagon the transformation initiatives sparked an unspoken rebellion accompanied by bureaucratic resistance and general foot dragging. The major visible effect was the sudden inclusion of the magic word "transformation" in hundreds of Pentagon planning and procurement documents. Weapons and other systems that had been planned and programmed for years were suddenly portrayed as "transformational." Even the heavyweight Crusader Mobile Gun System—the poster child for an overpriced, overweight, undeployable "old-think" system—was now branded "transformational," much to Rumsfeld's disgust.

By the summer of 2001, the secretary appeared headed for an early departure. The question was not whether President Bush would let Rumsfeld go, but when. As early as April, the on-line magazine *Slate* offered a Rumsfeld "death watch" and reported that "it's rumored there's a pool at the Pentagon to guess when Rumsfeld will go."[10] On September 7, a *Washington Post* columnist opined, "the sweepstakes have already begun" on who might succeed Rumsfeld. He was criticized for his managerial style, he was slow in filling top positions, and his approach to transformation alarmed entrenched interests in the defense industry and on Capitol Hill. Analysts argued that Rumsfeld's transformation really meant concentrating on a "few high-tech weapons controlled from the White House."[11] According to the Washington grapevine, he was autocratic, ineffective, and losing Bush's confidence.[12]

The Whole World Changes

Bush's presidency was generally judged to be struggling as well. Political commentators had began to speculate that he might be a one term president when, on September 11, 2001, the whole world changed. Al-Qaeda terrorists flew two hijacked airliners into the twin towers of the World Trade Center in New York City, a third crashed into the Pentagon, and a fourth dove into an open field in Pennsylvania. As he rallied America's forces and promised retribution, the President seemed full of energy and conviction.[13]

Among the things that changed on 9-11 were Bush's political prospects. According to *ABC News* and *Washington Post* public opinion polls, the President's job approval ratings soared within 24 hours of the attacks from 55 percent to an astounding 86 percent.[14] September 11 certified George W. Bush as President, not necessarily for anything he had done, but because of the awful burden that fell on him and because American lives suddenly depended on his leadership.[15]

Rumsfeld's reputation also benefited from the events of 9-11. When the hijacked airliner struck the Pentagon, the secretary ignored his security detail's attempt to rush him from the building and instead began directing rescue efforts. He immediately started the services on planning a military response. What had looked like autocratic single-mindedness now looked like decisive leadership.

Another thing that changed was the attitude in Congress and the DoD toward defense spending. As Loren Thompson, a defense analyst with the Lexington Institute remarked: "The whole mind set of military spending changed on Sept. 11. The most fundamental thing about defense spending is that threats drive defense spending. It's now going to be easier to fund almost anything."[16] Congress moved with exceptional speed to provide $40 billion in emergency spending to rebuild from the attacks and prepare for a long-term, sustained campaign against terrorism.

On September 20, President Bush addressed a joint session of Congress to declare a "global war on terrorism." "Whether we bring our enemies to justice, or justice to our enemies, justice will be done," he said.

It did not go unnoticed that his global war was a complex and dangerous campaign of undefined scope and duration, but the fact did nothing to dampen the general enthusiasm. What did go unremarked was the damage to the rationale for transformation. Prior to September 11, Shinseki, Rumsfeld, and their associated staffs and planners all believed that the United States was in a period of strategic pause with no serious enemies on the horizon. It was an opportunity to take risk by accepting less present capability and investing the savings in future capability. The strategic pause was clearly over. Troops were alerted for deployment, and, according to the *Washington Post,* CIA covert operations began in several countries.[17]

Nevertheless, in the midst of the reaction to September 11, Bush's administration took another step forward toward the President's transformation ambitions. Army General Hugh Shelton, the Chairman of the Joint Chiefs of Staff reached the end of his term on September 30. The President elected to replace him with Air Force General Richard B. Meyers, the vice chairman. The replacement of an

Army general with an air power advocate was duly noted in the Army corridors of the Pentagon.

The QDR (Finally)[18]

The attacks effectively derailed the 2001 Quadrennial Defense Review (QDR), and there was some opinion that it should be delayed, but in the end defense leaders decided it would be too painful to reopen the entire process. The 2001 QDR went to Congress on September 30 and was released publicly on October 1.[19] Instead of the expected lightening bolt of transformation, it was a hasty post-September 11 rewrite of the final draft. "The report is pabulum at best," said one of those involved in preparing it. The "guidance was 'just do no harm,' and we adopted that as our role." There was talk of the transformation of the U.S. military to address "asymmetric" threats, but little direction on how the services might prevent or respond to these threats.[20] As Congressional Research Service defense analyst Ronald O'Rourke put it, "Nothing was cut from the QDR, with no plans on how to pay for anything."[21]

Much of the previously fashionable thinking about global security and future warfare now looked naive, even foolish. In retrospect, the 1990s had been a lucky decade, a fool's paradise. And much of what the Army had been saying suddenly looked profoundly perceptive. Major threats really could emerge without warning. The character of future threats really was unknowable.

To meet these threats, the United States had a much smaller force than a decade earlier. Between the end of the Persian Gulf War and September 11, 2001, the active military lost 40 percent of its strength: eight Army divisions, more than 200 Navy ships, 15 Air Force fighter wings, and about 700,000 personnel.

This may have been what led the QDR to its most important change. Since the end of the Cold War official policy held that U.S. forces were capable of fighting two major regional conflicts while simultaneously continuing a range of other missions. Without explicitly rejecting the classic "two war" strategy, the QDR began a shift in favor of a more realistic assessment called the 1-4-2-1 strategy. Like the two war approach, it was actually a force sizing method rather than a strategy. It called for defense of the homeland (the "1") while deterring forward in four regions (the "4"). At the same time, the armed forces would be able to swiftly defeat adversaries in two overlapping campaigns (the "2"), winning decisively in one of them for an enduring result (the second "1"). There would also be enough capability left over to engage in a limited number of lesser contingencies. The force structure to support two simultaneous major conflicts just was not there. But even allowing for some of the four deterrence operations to be conducted solely by air forces, it was an open question whether there was enough structure to accomplish the 1-4-2-1.

The QDR held that forward-deployed forces must be capable of deterring or defeating enemy forces with minimal reinforcements from home. The report also addressed the related problem of limited access to Asia, saying the current concentration of U.S. assets in Western Europe and Northeast Asia "is inadequate for the new strategic environment." In one of the few decisions presented in the document, the

QDR directed Air Force Secretary James Roche to "increase contingency basing in the Pacific and Indian Oceans, as well as in the Arabian Gulf."[22] But, reformulating military strategy did not change the existing force structure. After an extensive, painful series of more than 50 studies, panels, and reviews, Rumsfeld apparently concluded the force structure and acquisition program bequeathed to him was OK.[23]

Reality continued to vindicate the Army's long-held positions. It really was dangerous to be unprepared to fight on short notice. Excessive emphasis on a handful of warfighting technologies really was risky. In a war against terrorism, the capacity to fight in jungles, mountains, and cities began to look more useful. Terrorists were too elusive to be remotely targeted using precision munitions, and weapons of mass destruction could not be reliably eliminated without combat forces on the ground to find and destroy them.

But thoughtful observers drew another insight from the aftermath of September 11. It was just possible that the U.S. reliance on high technology had sent some adversaries the message that America was weak. Usama bin Laden certainly thought so and had been saying so in interviews for some time. In a widely circulated e-mail after the September attacks, former United Nations relief worker Richard Kidd offered this observation based on his experiences in Afghanistan: "After the absolutely inane missile strikes in 1998, the overwhelming consensus [in the region] was that we were cowards, who would not risk one life in face-to-face combat. Rather than demonstrating our might and acting as a deterrent, that action and others of the recent past have reinforced the perception that the US does not have any 'will' and that we are morally and spiritually corrupt."[24] The only way to signal resolve to terrorists and other anti-American elements in the region was through infantry operations—not to hold ground, as the Soviets tried to do two decades ago, but to demonstrate that America will risk lives when necessary to defend its interests.[25]

This was a basic argument the Army had often made over the years, without notable success. But with Army Special Forces targeted against Afghanistan and the National Guard patrolling key domestic assets, observers stressed, "it's a safe bet any ideas about shrinking the Army are off the table. In fact, if policymakers decide to launch a definitive campaign to eliminate weapons of mass destruction in places like Iraq, the Army's recent assertion that it needs 40,000 more troops to meet overseas commitments may end up looking too modest."[26]

Newly confident Army officials assured outsiders that the enhanced, near-term quick-reaction capability of the Interim Armored Vehicle (IAV) made it a sure thing for increased funding. The IAV was the Army's most important initiative for rapid deployability, but other key modernization priorities such as the next-generation Crusader self-propelled howitzer, the Future Combat System (FCS), and the stealthy Comanche armed reconnaissance helicopter seemed safe. All three programs, plus the upgrades of legacy systems, fed into the "Objective Force." Given the new and focused sense of danger, it was even possible that the Army could add new programs such as the Marines' V-22 tilt rotor. In any case, it seemed clear that the Army had survived America's post-Cold War demobilization with its most critical capabilities intact.

Army Secretary Thomas E. White was nearly ebullient, "...land power is back with a vengeance, because reality has intervened to remind Americans why countries that can't prevail on the ground also can't secure their most vital interests."[27] White went on, "these Interim Brigades will do 35–40 miles an hour cross country. They'll have their own organization....They'll be supported by Comanche helicopters and Crusader indirect-fire systems—it'll be a wonderful time to be a part of the Army. It really will. I'm looking forward to it."[28] As events developed, Secretary White, his vision of the future, and the systems he championed would not long survive.

Afghanistan: Operation Enduring Freedom

When we find out who did this, they're not going to like me as president. Somebody is going to pay.[29]

—George W. Bush

Rapid Dominance and Rapid Decisive Operations were both accepted as the way to apply the RMA to warfighting, but their application to Afghanistan was not obvious. The country was ruled by a radical Islamic faction called the Taliban, an Arabic word meaning "students" or "seekers." The group had been organized by religious students in Kandahar in southern Afghanistan during 1994, mostly in reaction to the bloody anarchy created by factions struggling for control of the country. Under their leader, Mullah Mohammed Omar, the Taliban imposed a form of Islam based on the traditional practices of some Afghan tribes. In application it was so strict that it was recognized by few other Islamic leaders. Human rights violations abounded. Women were not allowed out of the home without a male escort and could not work, pursue education, or access public health care facilities.[30]

By this time the CIA had been tracking the Al-Qaeda leader for about five years, and a CIA-trained paramilitary team was attempting surveillance of bin Laden and his top lieutenants.[31] The Agency had also been supporting the anti-Taliban resistance in Afghanistan, a ramshackle coalition of warlords and local militia leaders called the Northern Alliance. Also known as the United Front, it was based on the remnants of the government ousted by the Taliban in 1996 and various warring factions that struggled for control after the Soviets left in 1989. Many of the alliance followers were former mujahideen guerillas that fought the Soviets in 1979–1989. The Alliance's military effectiveness was no better than marginal. It had been stalemated for years and was struggling to hold the roughly ten percent of the country it still controlled. This loose coalition, with its confusion of conflicting internal agendas, would provide the ground forces for the U.S. war.

Early in the planning after September 11, President Bush had announced a worldwide campaign against terrorism, not one confined to the perpetrators of the 9-11 attacks. This raised the issue of Iraq. There was a body of opinion in the Pentagon, led by Deputy Defense Secretary Paul D. Wolfowitz, which held Hussein was determined to buy, steal, or develop weapons of mass destruction. In their eyes, Hussein was the real threat.[32] Saddam Hussein was a sponsor of terrorists; should not any campaign against terrorism make Iraq a target?

President Bush appreciated the problem of Iraq but took a first-things-first approach. He demanded that the Taliban turn over bin Laden and the top members of Al-Qaeda, presumably knowing full well that the Afghan government would refuse. Indeed, such was bin Laden's power and influence in the country, the government probably could not have surrendered him even if the Taliban leaders wanted to do so. Bush swore to bring Al-Qaeda to justice and if the Taliban stood in the way, so much the worse for them. The stage was set for Operation Enduring Freedom (OEF), the war in Afghanistan.

Preparing for War

Prior to September 11, the Bush administration favored a smaller Army, relying more on special operations forces, high-tech weaponry, and air power. Afghanistan, they believed, provided an opportunity to test that vision. Since the Taliban appeared willing to engage in something close to conventional positional warfare, Operation Enduring Freedom was an ideal, relatively low-risk proving ground for the elements of transformation—weapons systems under development, experimental sensor platforms, new operational concepts, and communications links between the military services.

Actually getting those systems to the war was a different matter. This was the job of Central Command (CENTCOM) in Tampa, Florida, commanded by Army General Tommy Franks and responsible for military operations in West Asia. But CENTCOM had no standing operations plan for Afghanistan—one would have to be built from zero and quickly. It was difficult for several reasons, but the first one was lack of usable information, not just intelligence but even detailed terrain data. Surprisingly, for an area that had been of U.S. interest since the Soviet invasion of 1979, there was not much useful intelligence on Afghanistan. Nearly all the CIA contacts were in the north, and the agency had never been tasked to develop the sort of information needed to support a war. Even less was known about the southern part of the country. Few targets had been identified. There was little militarily useful infrastructure in the region, or for that matter, much infrastructure at all. On top of that, winter was coming.

Franks thought they would need perhaps 50,000 troops, but it would take months to assemble the forces and get them halfway around the world. This was exactly the kind of slow-motion conventional planning that transformation was supposed to replace. Rumsfeld was unsatisfied, telling Franks that he wanted action in weeks, not months. Both Rumsfeld and the President believed that the Pentagon needed to be pushed into new ways of thinking.[33]

The SecDef wanted a transformational war, one that would exploit U.S. technology with reconnaissance drones, armed unmanned aerial vehicles (UAVs), air-delivered precision weapons, and a large deployment of Special Forces. On September 25, he called in his chief commando, Air Force General Charles Holland,

Commander of the U.S. Special Operations Command (USSOCOM), for a meeting together with the Joint Chiefs. The same day he was quoted as telling reporters, "A lot of it will be special operations. There's no question but that the people who, God bless them, who have volunteered for that work and trained themselves for it, are important to our country. They're unconventional, and we're dealing in an unconventional time. And we may very well need more."[34]

Unfortunately, SOCOM had no better idea of where bin Laden was than anyone else. Despite the usual collection of very expensive collection systems, there was the issue of actionable intelligence—there was not much and by the time it got to SOCOM it was usually too old to be worthwhile. It was not good enough to know where bin Laden was yesterday or even today. To take action they needed to know where he would be a week from now. Rumsfeld was disappointed; he wanted a more aggressive attitude and more action, the sooner the better.[35]

In the meantime, a small number of CIA paramilitary teams contacted the Alliance to coordinate supplies and gather information on the available indigenous forces. Agents began to bribe Taliban commanders into switching sides, dispensing large amounts of cash while funneling intelligence back to the United States.

Having announced a covert war on terrorism, the next problem was to find the resources to fight it. The official U.S. covert action arm was the CIA's paramilitary office. But that organization, never large, had atrophied over the years. According to open press reporting, the entire paramilitary section numbered no more than about 75 persons. Rumsfeld agreed to beef up the capability by loaning enough Army Special Forces and Navy SEALs to double the section. There was considerable debate about this since Title 50 U.S. Code required a presidential "finding" before any CIA covert action. In other words, every such action had to be personally approved by the President, but military special operators did not fall under the same requirement. What was the legal standing of a mixed team of military special forces and CIA paramilitary officers? Nobody knew with certainty, but that was not allowed to stand in the way.[36]

An increased role for special operations forces (SOF) as unconventional forces may have been desirable, but the Rumsfeld version sometimes seemed to miss the point. The secretary wanted to emphasize the "global role" of these units, not see them dedicated to specific geographic areas. This matched the commando image of such units, but it ignored an important truth. The effectiveness of SOF depended to a large degree on knowledge of the culture, language, and geography of a specific area. Lacking that, they were just elite light infantry.

During a televised speech on September 19, the President told the nation to expect a lengthy campaign: "unlike any you have ever seen" with both overt and covert elements. He also called for patience. On September 24 he announced an Executive Order to freeze the finances of terrorist organizations and groups that supported them, including several nonprofit and charitable organizations. The war on terrorism might be progressing, but militarily nothing much was happening.

In Afghanistan the limits of strategic air power quickly became obvious, especially the need for forward bases. The president of Pakistan, General Pervez Musarraf, publicly sided with America and agreed to provide support, including limited over-flight and, very quietly, basing for small numbers of special operators and certain "low-profile" support elements. However, the Taliban had strong support within Pakistan's own clandestine intelligence service. Moreover, a significant portion of the country's population outright opposed any U.S. attack on Afghanistan. Pakistan could provide important forms of support, but not large-scale basing and especially not basing for offensive operations. If Musarraf did so, he would risk the fall of his government and the rise of a fundamentalist Islamic state in its place.

Until CENTCOM could capture and rebuild the former Soviet air base at Bagrham, AF, there was no way to get even modest numbers of Army boots on the ground. But for the Army there was at least the special operations option, which did not require anything like the basing or support needed by large conventional forces. The USS Kitty Hawk was ordered from port in Yokosuka, Japan, without its fighter squadron. America's only permanently forward deployed aircraft carrier took on Special Forces and SEALs plus their long-range helicopters to become a floating base for special operations in Afghanistan.

Lacking even the carrier and special operations options, the Air Force was in an embarrassing position. If the idea was to use American aircraft in support of indig-enous ground forces, then most of those planes would be fighter aircraft. In order to use fighter aircraft, the Air Force needed bases near the operational area, echoing the call in the 2001 Quadrennial Defense Review for more air bases in South Asia. The closest readily available bases were in England, Turkey, Saudi Arabia, and Diego Garcia—none particularly near Afghanistan.[37]

Not only did the USAF lack the right bases, but political considerations made neighboring states unlikely candidates as hosts for attack aircraft. Furthermore, air-fields could not just be plunked down in any available spot. The existing sites used for forward-deploying bombers (Diego Garcia, Guam, and Fairford Air Base, Eng-land) were workable for long-range bomber missions, but the distance was prohibi-tive for fighters. The best fighter location was probably aircraft carriers off the coast of Pakistan, but that meant leaving much of the air war to the Navy. It was a prospect too dreadful for the airmen to contemplate.[38]

A great deal of effort had gone into creating and selling the ideas of Rapid Decisive Operations (RDO) and Effects Based Operations (EBO) featuring air power. Since the Army could not bring effective force to bear quickly, this should have been a priceless opportunity for the Air Force. EBO's idea of considering and coordinating effects across various elements of power might have merit at the strategic level where the various elements came together. But, despite a plethora of proposals and papers, there was no real doctrine, especially concerning the "how" part of EBO. It seemed to be concerned with what and why but gave few clues to operational and tactical commanders. In other words, it did not answer the two vital tactical questions: "how are we going to do it?" and "who is going to do what tasks by when?"[39]

Unfortunately the EBO idea of analyzing the enemy as a system of systems did not seem to have much application below the strategic level. Despite reconnaissance by satellites, aircraft and UAV targets proved elusive. Unless the plan was to just bomb and hope for the best, worthwhile targets had to be found, and there did not seem to be very many. According to Rapid Dominance and RDO doctrine, striking critical nodes should be the highest priority. As usual, the Taliban and Al-Qaeda failed to cooperate by providing "command-and-control nodes" or "logistics hubs" to bomb. Their military consisted principally of loosely organized militia infantry using civilian trucks and buses. The relatively small numbers of tanks and artillery were scattered and beneath the notice of an air intensive Rapid Dominance Operation. Their air defense was thin, and they had no ports or industrial centers. The transportation network consisted mostly of dirt roads and trails. Even General Meyers was skeptical. Scanning the available choices, he concluded, "You're not going to topple a regime with this target list."[40]

There was another, related, problem. The idea was to topple the Taliban, bin Laden, and his cronies, not pound Afghanistan into rubble. Collateral damage had to be very limited. Much of the population already hovered on the edge of desperation, fed mostly by international aid. A number of those agencies warned that military action would disrupt vital food shipments and create a massive humanitarian disaster. This gave rise to the idea of dropping food to the population while bombing the leadership. Ideally, the population would be untouched and the leadership forced out. It was a targeting nightmare that demanded complete and precise intelligence, bringing the problem full circle. Without soldiers on the ground it was impossible to develop that kind of precision intelligence.

There was yet another serious issue. If the United States was to perform regime change in Afghanistan, and it obviously was, what would the follow-on regime look like? The country could not simply be turned over to the feuding warlords of the Northern Alliance; their ceaseless warring had wrecked Afghanistan and led to the rise of the Taliban. The obvious answer was to use American troops to stabilize the country, provide security, assist in reconstruction, and generally midwife the transition to some kind of Afghani run government. The problem was that candidate Bush had made it abundantly clear that combat troops were not to be used in "nation-building." But lack of that kind of commitment after the anti-Soviet War in Afghanistan had helped create the Taliban and made the country vulnerable to Al-Qaeda.[41]

Reduced need for troops was a central ingredient of the Bush-Rumsfeld military transformation. Because of high technology, everything could be done with much smaller military forces, but it was difficult to see how that would work in postwar Afghanistan. There was a daunting list of things to be done, and lots of manpower was required; food production had to be restored, a health system created, schools reopened, and new ones built. There were no services or education for women, the monetary system was broken, and the country was scattered with landmines.

The doctrinal solution was to enlist non-DoD agencies, other nations, nongovernmental aid groups, and international organizations, such as the World Bank, to help. After all, was not the idea to approach warfare as a policy issue, not merely a matter of defeating an enemy? But everyone agreed that security was the one indispensable requirement before any other initiative could succeed. Until the enemy was defeated, nothing else was going to happen. Al-Qaeda and the Taliban understood that non-military support for reconstruction was the weak link of any U.S.-led operation. They began to strike at vulnerable aid workers whose organizations consequently became more and more reluctant to assist. Countering the threat would mean soldiers were needed, lots of them. Well, perhaps the United States could quickly create an Afghan National Army. That would answer the security problem while avoiding a massive commitment of American forces. At least it sounded like a plan. Meanwhile, Rumsfeld prepared to ask the President for authority to call up as many as 300,000 reserves, rather than the currently approved 50,000.

At the same time, General Franks and the CENTCOM staff huddled with CIA officers and USSOCOM to figure out the special operations piece. The anti-Taliban Northern Alliance and a few small elements in southern Afghanistan had been identified and contacted by CIA paramilitary teams. The Agency would coordinate air drops of food, medical supplies, and so forth. Once the CIA operators had made arrangements for their reception, military special operators (mostly Army Special Forces) would arrive to identify targets and provide the kind of highly specific "eyes-on" target that would allow the precision guided munitions (PGMs) to do their work.[42]

As it emerged, the war planning held some major disappointments for the Army. First, the LAV-equipped Interim Brigades, the centerpiece of Army Transformation, were not ready, and in any case there was no obvious role for them. Likewise, the Army's other major transformation effort, the heavy "digitized" 4th Infantry Division (Mechanized) was never even seriously considered. The most conspicuous piece of the Army involved was the relative handful of Special Forces, a few hundred people at the most. No matter how effective the SF might be, it was not going to justify budget and force structure for "big Army" (the conventional forces). Besides that, there was a tendency in Congress and the civilian leadership of the Pentagon to see special operations forces as part of the Tampa-based USSOCOM, not properly part of the Army at all. Finally, to make matters worse, the first major ground forces in Afghanistan would be U.S. Marines, the Army's direct competitor as an expeditionary force.

A Golden Opportunity for Air Power

In the south, the basing problem was initially solved with a "lily pad" technique—airfields that could be used as flexible, temporary locations rather than full-fledged permanent bases.[43] Uzbekistan finally agreed to let combat search and rescue operate out of their country. By now about 80 countries had offered to help, but only a few were willing to provide combat elements and only in very limited numbers. The early effort was developing into a kind of special operations Olympics as Canada, Germany, Australia, Great Britain, New Zealand, Norway, Denmark, Turkey, and France (among others) all promised to assist with their elite special units, but no more than a few dozen personnel each and then for limited periods.[44]

The war began in earnest on October 7, when U.S. and British aircraft launched a wave of attacks against the country's few "strategic" targets: air fields, air defense sites, radar installations, and a handful of previously identified terrorist training camps.[45] Shortly after the first wave of strikes a humanitarian food drop was made, emphasizing that the war was against the Taliban and Al-Qaeda, not the Afghan people. Leaflets were also dropped warning in Pashto, Dari, and English: "The Taliban are using civilian areas to hide their equipment, endangering everyone in the area. Flee any area where military equipment or personnel are located."[46]

Bin Laden replied with a smuggled videotape, aired by the Arabic TV news station Al-Jazeera. "God has blessed a group of vanguard Muslims," he said, referring to Al-Qaeda as "the forefront of Islam, to destroy America." The good news was that Tajikistan agreed to allow the United States to operate from three old Soviet-era air bases in their country, greatly increasing the potential for U.S. special operations and tactical aircraft to strike into Afghanistan.[47]

There was not merely a lack of suitable targets for rapid dominance; there was a serious shortage of military targets period. A CIA Predator was flying in the north and getting some results, but there was only one of them. Plus the single Agency team on the ground lacked laser equipment and had no direct communication with the bombers. According to General Meyers, "Our [tactical aircraft] are loitering, waiting for emerging targets identified by Predator." As described by Bob Woodward:

> It was an incredible moment, barely imaginable in the annals of modern warfare. After a day of strikes, the airborne might of the United States was just...lumbering around the sky...waiting for targets of opportunity.[48]

According to diplomatic and intelligence sources, the bombing so far had not only failed to paralyze the Taliban with shock and awe, they were not impressed at all. It looked like more of the same old policy: bomb a few targets from high altitude and announce a success. After about two weeks, Air Force and carrier-based Navy planes exhausted their list of "strategic targets." The Air Force added Special Operations AC-130U gunships to their force mix. Based on the C-130 cargo plane, the U models are armed with a 25mm Gatling gun (capable of firing 1800 rounds per minute), a single-barrel, rapid-fire 40mm Bofors cannon, and a 105mm Howitzer. A lot of firepower seemed to be expended on targets of minimum value.

By mid-October the Special Forces (SF) teams still were not on the ground in Afghanistan because of a combination of bad weather and deployment delays. Without the SF teams to "lase" ground targets with their laser designators there was little application for the air delivered PGMs, and no tactical progress was being made. In fact, it was unclear what was happening, but the Northern Alliance forces remained in place, reluctant to attempt even local advances against the Taliban. In the south, there was no organized resistance, and the CIA was having a very hard time recruiting any. The only bright spot came on the night of October 16–17 when the 160th Special Operations Aviation Regiment flew hundreds of miles through mountains and a dust storm to deliver an eight-man Special Forces contact team to Northern Alliance headquarters near Mazar-e-Sharif. Then, on October 19 the first SF A Teams, Teams 555 and 595 of the Army's 5th Special Forces Group, finally touched down in northern Afghanistan.[49]

The same night, AC-130 gunships led a predawn assault on "Objective Rhino," a Taliban-held air base southwest of Kandahar, deep inside southern Afghanistan. Elements of the Army's Third Ranger Battalion staged a spectacular nighttime parachute drop to seize the airfield. Simultaneously, CH-47 "Chinook" helicopters from the 160th Special Operations Aviation Regiment disgorged a reinforced Delta Force Special Mission Unit mounted in 6x6 assault vehicles at a nearby complex used by Mullah Omar, the Taliban leader.[50]

The Pentagon immediately provided videotape of the Rhino operation to the news media. Later that day, General Myers termed the operation "flawless." He told reporters that the Special Operations Forces did meet resistance but "were able to deploy, maneuver, and operate inside Afghanistan without significant interference from Taliban forces."

A few weeks afterwards, Pulitzer Prize winning journalist Seymour Hersh told a different story. In Hersh's version the assault on Mullah Omar's complex was such a "near-disaster" that future Special Forces operations inside Afghanistan might not take place. According to his article in the *New Yorker,* 12 commandos were wounded, three seriously. "The unexpectedness and the ferocity of the Taliban response 'scared the crap out of everyone,' and caused the United States Central Command to back away from the use of special operations forces. This is no war for Special Operations . . . at least, not as orchestrated by CENTCOM and its commander, General Tommy R. Franks, of the Army, on October 20th."[51]

General Franks immediately countered, saying "we had no one wounded by enemy fire" and the only "wounds" sustained were "scratches and bumps" from the parachute landing on rocky ground.[52] Based on conversation with members of the special operations community, the truth apparently lay somewhere in the middle. In fact, the Ranger raid on the airfield went off well despite resistance. However, the Delta/Ranger attack on Omar's compound allegedly ran into problems when an Al-Qaeda and Taliban reaction force began showering them with automatic weapons' fire and rocket propelled grenades. It turned into exactly the kind of stand up fight the lightly armed commandos seek to avoid. While there was reportedly no thought of canceling special operations missions, there was also little taste for another high-profile raid. As a demonstration of capability, it was impressive but otherwise not notably helpful. The Northern Alliance formations were still not moving while they waited for U.S. bombers to hit the Taliban lines. Meanwhile, the number of enemy fighters crowding to the front had almost doubled since the start of the war.[53] It would be up to the SF teams in the north to take the war to the Taliban.

The basic operational concept of the ground war depended on the Northern Alliance. The Alliance could muster perhaps 20,000 fighters serving various warlords and armed almost entirely with rifles, machine guns, and RPG-7 antitank rocket launchers. Otherwise, their equipment was limited to a few jealously hoarded tanks and artillery pieces, a small number of aircraft, and a very few helicopters—barely operable relics leftover from the anti-Soviet war of the 1980s. Many of the leaders, moreover, were nothing more than petty local tyrants, thugs, smugglers, and drug dealers. The Alliance forces were also outnumbered at least two to one by the Taliban and Al-Qaeda.[54]

So far a handful of CIA operatives had been infiltrated into the country during October followed by the two Army SF teams, each accompanied by a USAF combat air controller. Their mission was to supply and support the principal warlords of the Alliance and assist them in their fight against the Taliban and Al-Qaeda. The special operations soldiers and airmen on the ground would direct air strikes in lieu of the tanks and artillery that the Alliance lacked. As soon as the SF teams were in contact with the enemy, they began to identify targets on the Taliban front lines. The first bombing was a disappointment since six separate attempts by a circling B-52 bomber failed to put a single smart bomb near the target.[55] On the other hand, the Afghans were astonished that the team could actually produce a bomber, especially on short notice.

Enemy convoys could be seen moving back and forth within easy range of the teams' laser designators. However, it soon became obvious that the teams on the ground were not getting priority for air strikes. In obedience to Rapid Dominance doctrine the Air Force was still working off CENTCOM's list of fixed targets, pounding "vital" targets like the Tora Bora cave complex near Jalalabad.

Finally, on October 27, Rumsfeld ordered that 70 percent of the air effort be dedicated to the tactical ground war, striking Taliban units opposite the Northern Alliance. Despite the shift in emphasis, late October was discouraging with the capture and execution of a key anti-Taliban organizer in the south and reports that Northern Alliance units were beginning to retreat. The inevitable finally occurred when U.S. bombs twice struck a Red Cross warehouse in Kabul. No one was injured but the news media seized on the incident.[56] As recounted by Woodward:

> Rumsfeld felt he had issued unprecedented, even draconian orders not to shoot or drop bombs unless there was specific intelligence about the targets, preferably US eyes also having verified the target.[57]

Special operations forces on the ground were the answer to the targeting question and getting more SF teams in a major concern. Weather delays were part of the problem, but also the Tajik air bases were not ready and the Uzbeks were proving troublesome as were some elements of the Northern Alliance. Pakistani support continued to be firm, but General Musarraf made it plain he would prefer a quick end to the fighting. It was an unfortunate fact that the strategy of ad hoc basing and fighting through surrogates tended to make the U.S. hostage to other agendas.

The few Special Forces that had been infiltrated were scoring some dramatic successes. With satellite radios, global positioning, and laser-targeting systems, the SF could illuminate targets for a range of aircraft including fighters and heavy bombers. Navy and Air Force fighters could fly out and answer calls for air support, but their time over target was limited. The real performers were the Air Force bombers that could loiter for hours and deliver ordnance against a number of different targets.

The Taliban were unprepared for this kind of onslaught. After years of static, stalemated war with the Alliance, their tactical positions were poorly chosen, typically located on exposed ridgelines without cover. Near Bisbqab, in the north, SOF elements identified Taliban targets from more than eight kilometers away. Because of the new PGMs, they were obliterated by SOF directed air strikes. Their trench lines, bunkers, and fixed positions became death traps. However, neither Taliban nor Al-Qaeda were about to sit and be tamely slaughtered in obedience to Transformation doctrine. Instead, they quickly began to adjust. Camouflage appeared and enemy forces began making careful use of cover and concealment while moving. When Predator came over, they hid under dusty blankets. Nighttime movement became common.[58]

Rumsfeld kept pressing for more SOF involvement and made a special visit to Fort Bragg, home of the U.S. Army Special Operations Command, owner of most of the U.S. SOF. While there he also visited the Joint Special Operations Command (JSOC). JSOC was a relatively small (1,500 person) state-of-the-art command capable of dispatching small groups of highly trained operators anywhere in the world on short notice, including the famed Delta Force and the Navy's counterterrorist SEAL team. JSOC's Task Force 11 was already in Afghanistan and preparing to hunt for so-called high-value targets, including Usama bin Laden. This was Rumsfeld's ideal for the future—small, fast-reacting, rapid-deploying, effective, and enabled by advanced intelligence and communications networking. Also, it should be added, expensive and hard to duplicate.

The first of about 2,000 Marines from the 26th Marine Expeditionary Force began landing at Kandahar airport on November 26, the first conventional ground troops to arrive. It was not a happy moment for the Army generals.[59]

Precision strikes depended on precise location and that become more and more difficult. Al-Qaeda, in particular, learned very rapidly to conceal fighting positions, preventing the SOF from directing PGMs against them. A late November counterattack by Al-Qaeda at Kunduz penetrated allied positions and forced American SOF teams to withdraw three separate times to avoid being overrun. During combat along Highway 4 in December, Al-Qaeda forces concealed their defenses in culverts and burned out vehicles littering the roadside. They remained undetected until their concentrated fire drove back advancing Alliance units. They also began to take advantage of terrain, advancing counterattacks to within small arms range before revealing themselves.[60]

The Battle for Tora Bora[61]

Seeing that fighting the Northern Alliance plus U.S. air power was a very different proposition than fighting the Northern Alliance alone, the Taliban and Al-Qaeda began to change their approach. Sometime around November 12 bin Laden and the senior Al-Qaeda leadership made its way into the foothills and rugged slopes of Tora Bora, about 30 miles southeast of Jalalabad. Situated between two high ridges in the White Mountains, Tora Bora consisted of a large network of tunnels and fortifications used by Afghan rebels during the anti-Soviet war of the 1980s. The complex was described as being virtually invisible from above.[62] Targets were hard to identify, and most of the technical collection systems (e.g., satellites, remote radar, and photography) were not very helpful. It was quickly clear that bombing alone would not do the job.[63]

Digging the veteran fighters out of their bunkers and caves would be a classic infantry task but not a welcome one. For one thing, it was the sort of ugly combat that transformation methods were supposed to avoid. For another, it would inevitably mean casualties, perhaps heavy ones. The preferred method so far had been to use local warlords and their troops as surrogates for U.S. infantry, backed up by Special Forces to provide supplies, support, and direct precision bombardment. But this was to be the first important battle to include allies from Afghanistan's Pashtun majority. Afghan warlords were not enthused about attacking Tora Bora with or without U.S. support and talked about "asking the Arabs to leave," not about attacking them outright.[64]

While CENTCOM tried to persuade the warlords to fight, bin Laden apparently walked away from the complex and headed into Pakistan. This may have began a slow exodus of bin Laden's foot soldiers as many followed the example of their leader and, often aided by local villagers, worked their way across the border into Pakistan. Meanwhile, the United States pressured General Musarraf to move Pakastani troops into blocking positions along the Afghan-Pakistan border near the Al-Qaeda complex. This was complicated by the reality that the border area was largely ungoverned by either country and most of its inhabitants did not regard it as a border at all.[65]

It was not until December 5 that U.S. and Coalition special operators were able to persuade the Pashtuns to attack the shrinking group of Al-Qaeda in Tora Bora. On the ground command and control was performed by Delta Force, the most capable special operations unit and the one whose training and equipment were judged best suited to a fight in the high, cold mountains. About three dozen additional special operations troopers from U.S. Army and Coalition special forces waded into the battle with the Afghans. Leaving tactical command to the Afghan warlords, the special operators tried to manage the fighting and "paint" targets for the warplanes with their laser designators. American B-52s rained bombs down on the mouths of caves and bunkers where the remaining fighters were hidden.[66]

The Afghan fighters on the Coalition side were unable or unwilling to maintain anything like a siege of the area and Al-Qaeda's Arab and Chechen foot soldiers continued to leak away. Most of them disappeared along smuggling routes through mountain passes and into Khost Province, some of them moving farther south into Afghanistan and others across the border into Pakistan.[67]

Tora Bora got most of the attention, but it was not the only battle in the war. Elsewhere, Alliance forces advanced, supported by U.S. SOF and tac air every step of the way, squeezing the Taliban and Al-Qaeda back toward their original stronghold at Kandahar. On the night of December 6, Mullah Mohammed Omar and the Taliban leadership abandoned their last stronghold and fled. Taliban armed resistance crumbled and the remaining Al-Qaeda faced an unappetizing choice—surrender, die in the trenches, or retreat. Choosing the least odious option, they gave up the defense of their camps near Kandahar and scattered.

Despite precision bombing and close support from AC-130 gunships, the gun battles at Tora Bora went on while Arab fighters continued to bribe, threaten, and negotiate their way out of the area, at one point having an Afghan translator radio, "Our guest brothers want to find safe passage out of your province." On December 11 Defense Secretary Donald Rumsfeld expressed public doubt about the effectiveness of the Pakistani units supposedly blocking escape routes across the border. "It's a long border," he said. "It's a very complicated area to try to seal, and there's just simply no way you can put a perfect cork in the bottle."[68]

Afghan fighters on the Coalition side finally took the last of the Tora Bora caves on December 17, but fighting continued to sputter in the nearby valleys. Haji Zahir, an Afghan warlord and leader, found only 21 bedraggled Al-Qaeda fighters who were taken prisoners. "No one told us to surround Tora Bora," Zahir complained. "The only ones left inside for us were the stupid ones, the foolish and the weak."[69]

Charles Heyman, a British military analyst, delivered an epilogue to the battle,

> There appears to be a real disconnect between what the US military was engaged in trying to do during the battle for Tora Bora—which was to destroy Al Qaeda and the Taliban—and the earlier rhetoric of President Bush, which had focused on getting bin Laden. There are citizens all over the Middle East now saying that the US military couldn't do it—couldn't catch Osama—while ignoring the fact that the US military campaign, apart from not capturing Mr. bin Laden was, up to that point, staggeringly effective.[70]

After Tora Bora, Tommy Franks made a fundamental change in his approach to the war. The much ballyhooed new way of fighting using local surrogates, precision air power, and a few special operators had turned out to be real but limited. Calling for reinforcements from the United States, he began to quietly raise the number of American troops in the country. It would be months before he would rely solely (or even principally) on local forces to carry the fight. From then on, U.S. and Coalition soldiers would be on the ground as first-line combat units.[71]

Operation Anaconda

I had no reason to doubt the intel until about six to eight hours before we launched.
—Major General Franklin Hagenbeck, Commander, 10th Mountain Divison and Task Force Moutain[72]

Although the Taliban were officially defeated and their government collapsed, the Al-Qaeda and Taliban fighters had scattered into the mountains along the Pakistan border, so the hunt for them went on. During early 2002, information gathered by special operators indicated a large group of Al-Qaeda holdouts were operating in the Turgal Gar Mountains. All available targeting assets including UAVs, satellite imaging, precision radar, and electronic intercept equipment were focused on about

100 square miles of mountains and the adjoining Shah-i-Kot Valley, searching for enemy strongholds.

Part of the intelligence and targeting problem was at least mitigated when the Army's Intelligence and Security Command (INSCOM) was brought to bear. Building on the lessons of Desert Strom, INSCOM was able to link operational commanders with important intelligence assets including communications intercepts from the National Security Agency and overhead imagery from the National Imagery and Mapping Agency. The Army was able to deploy six Trojan satellite downlink terminals (the basic link for "reach-back" intelligence from U.S.-based national systems). The terminals were in support of a relatively small force equivalent to about a reinforced division of U.S. and Coalition troops. A force of about one-tenth the size of the one in Desert Storm was receiving almost ten times the support from national collection and analysis systems. Most importantly, it was a big increase in the ground commander's ability to task those systems for specific tactical needs.[73]

Finally, after weeks of intensive reconnaissance by ground and air, allied forces located a large concentration of Al-Qaeda in the mountains and the Shah-i-Kot Valley near Gardez. The valley floor ranged from 7,000 to 8,000 feet in altitude. Rugged mountains that reared to an altitude of 11,000 feet ringed it. The temperatures ranged from a high of 60 degrees Fahrenheit to a low of zero with an average wind chill of minus 20. In effect, the temperature could drop 80 degrees in 24 hours. This was where Al-Qaeda chose to make a stand. The Al-Qaeda fighters apparently believed that the rugged terrain and their intimate familiarity with the ground would negate the American technology, forcing the morally and physically inferior American soldiers to fight and die.[74]

In March, the Americans launched Operation Anaconda to dig them out. Special operations teams went in first, late in February, climbing the frozen ridges unseen despite hundreds of enemy fighters in the area. One of their first discoveries was an enemy DShK heavy antiaircraft machine gun set up to cover the 700 meter gap American helicopters would have to fly through to enter the valley. Despite having "every national asset" including spy planes and satellites looking at the valley, the gun had gone undiscovered until two SEALs crawled up on it.[75]

The remainder of the force, called "Task Force Mountain," was a mixed bag of local forces, U.S., Canadian, and other special operators and about 1,200 infantrymen from the Canadian Battle Group, 10th Mountain and 101st Airborne Divisions. The operation opened with repeated precision air strikes against the identified objectives. Task Force Mountain helicoptered into the valley, supported by Army utility and attack helicopters, Air Force, Marine, and Navy warplanes, and the infantry's own mortars.[76] A special point was made to include 300–400 Afghan militia but not as the centerpiece of the battle. They were referred to as the "main effort" only for purposes of information operations (i.e., propaganda).

When U.S. and Afghan forces landed in the area, they immediately came under fire and were pinned down by unsuspected enemy positions. Helicopters mistakenly deposited one group of soldiers from the U.S. 101st Airborne Division almost directly on a hidden enemy strongpoint. Nearly every helicopter was hit by enemy ground fire but still managed to land the troops. It quickly developed that the enemy was not where it was expected, but had moved up into the nearby mountains. Despite more than a week of bombardment, Al-Qaeda holdouts survived to engage approaching allied infantry. As enemy positions were found, the Americans on the ground directed punishing air attacks against them. One dug in enemy command post was hit with at least five 2,000 pound bombs, but U.S. infantry finally had to assault by fire and maneuver to quell resistance from the position.[77]

It took the participation of U.S. and Canadian infantry plus their Afghan allies to finally turn the tide in "an essential load of old-fashioned close combat against surviving, actively resisting opponents...without this essential close-combat capability the outcome in Afghanistan could have been very different."[78] The battle even produced an example of air-mech operations courtesy of the 3rd Battalion of Princess Patricia's Canadian Light Infantry. On March 15, 2002, the Canadian Battle Group used U.S. Army CH-47D helicopters to air assault their armored and tracked BV-206S vehicles into the fight as part of the 2nd Brigade, 10th Mountain Division.

Despite the enemy's refusal to tamely submit, American casualties and aircraft losses were light—far lighter than feared. Air power proved tremendously effective in the unglamorous role it had long shunned: attacking enemy ground forces.[79]

Anaconda also provoked another skirmish in the Army–Air Force battle within DoD. Under Pentagon insistence that he deploy as lightly as possible, the commander of the 10th Mountain Division left behind his air support operations squadron deployed to Afghanistan. When 10th Mountain ran into a tougher-than-anticipated Al-Qaeda enemy in Operation Anaconda, Air Force officials—left out of the planning—had to piece together tactical air support teams and, with the Navy and Marine Corps, find enough aircraft at the last minute to support ground troops in trouble.[80]

Later, when the 10th Mountain commander complained about lagging Air Force support in the *Field Artillery* journal, air officials were outraged. But Air Force Chief of Staff General John Jumper sought to bridge the growing fissures and initiated an effort with Army Chief of Staff General Eric Shinseki to review the Anaconda campaign.[81] The two leaders created some operational fixes that were applied during the war in Iraq, including the placement of an Air Force general at the coalition ground force headquarters as a high-ranking air component representative.[82]

During the hostilities, Pentagon sources repeatedly reminded the press that Enduring Freedom would help Rumsfeld fulfill President Bush's directive to comprehensively transform the U.S. military into more agile, flexible, and efficient fighting forces equipped with increasingly sophisticated weaponry. As described by the Pentagon, it was proof positive of Transformation. Officially, U.S. forces drew on all available resources to identify targets and attack them as rapidly and precisely as possible, allowing for relatively small numbers of troops to rapidly subdue their foes. That was true, but the implication was that those resources were primarily high-tech miracles, not old fashioned soldiers.[83]

U.S. CENTCOM deployed the Predator and the new $31 million Global Hawk UAV in a reconnaissance role. Those two systems alone required much greater bandwidth than was used for Operation Allied Force in Kosovo. Lieutenant General Harry Raduege Jr., director of the Defense Information Systems Agency, observed, "In Operation Enduring Freedom, we're supporting one-tenth the number of forces deployed during Desert Storm with eight times the commercial SATCOM bandwidth." Additionally, "Global Hawk consumed five times the total bandwidth used by the entire US military in the Gulf; and operations in Kosovo used 2.5 times what was used in the Gulf War."[84]

Operations in Afghanistan were also portrayed as exemplifying "jointness," defined as the willingness and the ability for the armed services and various government agencies to work together. "One of the most important features of this operation is how well the services are working together. Everyone has something to bring to the table and cooperation has never been better."[85]

Allegedly, special operations forces from each of the military services and CIA operatives worked side-by-side in harmony and close cooperation from the earliest days of the operation. In fact, cooperation was sometimes uncertain. As reported by members of the elite forces, there was a great deal of tension bordering on hostility between the CIA and the military special operations forces. Nor was the relationship between the various service elites notably smooth. Army Special Forces did not always embrace the idea of including Air Force combat controllers in their missions. Air Force leaders tended to feel that, since in their view the war was about guiding PGMs against targets, they should be in charge, not the Army. Reportedly, it took the intervention of USSOCOM to ensure cooperation between the storied Delta Force commandos and their opposite numbers in the Navy.[86]

It is important to note that both Taliban and Al-Qaeda conducted something much closer to conventional positional warfare than to guerrilla operations. They sought to take and hold ground and to defend key geographic points. When attacked by less well trained Alliance troops, they commonly held on and repulsed the attackers despite U.S. air support. At Bai Beche, for example, Al-Qaeda held on during two days of intense air attacks, refusing to withdraw. Many of their positions survived and drove back an attack by Northern Alliance troops. A second round of air strikes was planned, but as related by Stephen Biddle, miscommunication led Alliance cavalry to attack too soon, while SOF directed PGMs were still in the air. As a result, the cavalry charged in seconds after the ordnance hit, attacking through billows of dust and smoke. Seeing themselves overrun and about to be encircled, the Al-Qaeda fighters finally abandoned their positions. The victory resulted from extraordinarily tight coordination of air and ground attacks, far closer than would ever have been permitted on purpose.[87]

Initially, the Afghanistan campaign appeared a great success. Using local allies, a relatively small number of special operators, and a plentiful supply of precision guided munitions, the Taliban had been defeated in two months. Army Secretary Thomas E. White pronounced himself satisfied with the Army performance as validating the existing force structure and its plans for the future. Under the headline "Afghanistan Validates Army Way," the secretary enumerated the lessons of the Afghan conflict. "Lesson number one is that it validates the balanced force structure we have in the Army. The effect we want is the destruction of that terrorist network and we're aiming all of our resources at achieving it. We've got the flexibility to do it very differently if more heavy forces are required, or more conventional forces." The obvious conclusion, of course, was that the Army structure of ten divisions centered on heavy forces was the right answer. But this made his next comment something of a non sequitur. "Our whole new concept of fighting with our Interim Brigades and ultimately with the objective force is absolutely the right course to take."[88]

White took pains to underline the role played by ground forces as part of the precision strike team. The Army, he said, wished to achieve long-range precision strike in accordance with the QDR. Afghanistan was an application of the current technology but "it still depends on tough, resourceful people on the ground that can make sure we pick out the right targets to achieve the results that we seek. And consequently there will always be a significant role for ground elements in long-range precision strike."

The MAV/IAV Becomes the Stryker Vehicle

The Army sets great store by naming things, and in February 2002 the Interim Armored Vehicle was officially dubbed the "Stryker" in honor of two Medal of Honor recipients: Pfc. Stuart S. Stryker (World War II) and Specialist Robert F. Stryker (Vietnam). The Interim Brigade Combat Teams (IBCT) accordingly would be known as the Stryker Brigades. The Army also renewed its commitment to field six IBCTs with more than 300 Strykers in each. In October 1999, the Army had promised the first two IBCTs, located at Fort Lewis, Washington, would be equipped and ready for deployment during fiscal years 2003 and 2004, respectively.[89] It still sounded possible, but the timing would be tight since fiscal year 2003 actually began in September 2002.

In the wake of Afghanistan, Army transformation took a serious blow when Rumsfeld announced that he was terminating the Crusader, one of Shinseki's prized programs. After the fight to preserve the Stryker armored vehicle, both the chief of staff and the Army secretary, Thomas White, were convinced the cancellation was a serious mistake. Crusader, the Comanche helicopter, and Stryker were all essential to the Army vision of its future self. It looked like another step in a general attack on the Army, part of a larger diminishment of ground operations.

The response was a classic example of bureaucratic warfare, fought in the halls of Congress and the Pentagon and on the opinion pages of major newspapers and obscure journals. White and Shinseki had planned to buy 480 Crusaders and their accompanying armored ammunition vehicles at a total cost of about $9 billion. That was not an amount to be taken lightly. The vehicle's manufacturer, United Defense Inc. of Arlington, Virginia, and two Republican stalwarts, Senator James Inhofe and Representative J.C. Watts (both of Oklahoma) took up the fight. It resulted in an extended public furor that included Congress, the Defense Department, and the Army. Secretary Rumsfeld was reportedly infuriated and, more determined than ever, ensured that the Crusader stayed canceled.[90]

The Crusader battle still was not over. On July 26, 2002, the Under Secretary of Defense for Acquisition, Technology, and Logistics signed a memorandum directing the U.S. Army to take "prudent and deliberate" actions to bring about an orderly termination of the Crusader program. Thirty-two million dollars was to be transferred from Crusader to the FCS. The same day, Shinseki submitted "The Army Indirect Fires Report" to Congress stating that the cancellation of Crusader would cost the Department of Defense $18 to $24 billion over 14 years to replace the artillery capability lost.[91]

It did not save the Crusader, but the Indirect Fires Report did result in a permanent rupture in relations between the Secretary of Defense on one side and Shinseki and White on the other. Rumors quickly spread that Rumsfeld had already chosen Shinseki's replacement, a move that was taken as a slap in the face for the general who still had 15 months on his term as Army chief.

Operation Mountain Sweep[92]

The Afghanistan war ground on in the late summer of 2002. Taliban remnants, local tribesmen opposed to the foreigners, and even a few Al-Qaeda were still operating inside Afghanistan, ambushing patrols and setting off the occasional bomb in the cities. Most of the activity centered around the Pakistan border near the cities of Khost and Gardez, but technical intelligence was of no help and the United States had few human intelligence resources to offer. Special Forces teams had been working in the area since March turning up a few caches, but their major goal was the slow process of winning trust from the local villagers. Then, in mid-August an Australian patrol came under heavy fire outside Khost. The fight continued for about five hours until American C-130 gunships arrived and the insurgents fled, leaving ten dead. It was the heaviest contact with anti-Coalition forces in months and seemed like a heaven-sent opportunity. Accordingly, Coalition commanders quickly organized a large scale operation called Mountain Sweep in the hopes of flushing out the enemy fighters and capturing badly needed intelligence. The operation provided an object lesson in the difference between conventional warfare and the unconventional kind.

Mountain Sweep was a major operation involving more than 2,000 Coalition soldiers including elements of the Army's 75th Rangers and 82nd Airborne Division. Because of the Army ability at rapid airlift, helicopters were able to mount five air assault missions as targets of opportunity arose during the week-long operation. But the crux of the problem was not mobility—it was information. Coalition, primarily U.S., soldiers had the risky chore of rooting through Afghan homes for clues to the whereabouts of Al-Qaeda. And that was the problem. Special Forces soldiers were initially assigned the job of dealing with the locals. Having learned through hard experience that the Afghans were inclined to distrust foreigners and had a difficult sense of honor, they operated carefully. They dealt only with the senior male members of each village and allowed the women to stay out of the gaze of strange men. After searching a village, they would usually have tea with the leaders and express thanks for their cooperation. In their view a friendly and cooperative village was worth more than a few hidden AK-47s. Rifles were cheap in rural Afghanistan, but cooperation was precious. It was a painstaking business but at least in the minds of the special operators it was slowly gaining friendship. Bits and pieces of intelligence began to accumulate, and villagers would sometimes point out landmines or mention the location of insurgent caches. But in the judgment of the Coalition command it took too much time for too few results. Besides, after the experience of Tora Bora, there was little faith in the cooperation of local peasants.

In Mountain Sweep the task was soon taken over by regular soldiers, trained in entirely different methods. Where the SF were schooled in patience, the paratroopers were used to direct methods. In one illustrative incident a Special Forces captain was finishing his introduction with the village headman when he saw six paratroopers force their way into a nearby house. When the panicked farmer tried to run, he was slammed to the ground. The captain ran to intervene, and inside the hut he found the paratroopers trying to frisk the women. By the time he ordered the soldiers to leave, the family was in "a state of shock." "The women were screaming bloody murder," the captain recalled. "The guy was in tears. He'd been completely dishonored."[93]

From the Coalition point of view, Mountain Sweep was at least a qualified success. Several arms caches were destroyed and a dozen suspects detained for questioning. But, when the SF leaders submitted an after-action report complaining that the main result was to terrify innocent villagers and ruin months of carefully built rapport, it feel on deaf ears. The hard won flow of human intelligence, they reported, had dried up completely.

Events in Afghanistan were not cheering in the late fall of 2002. First of all, the transition authority was beset by the usual Afghan devils of tribalism and warlordism. Moreover, Taliban remnants, including Mullah Mohammed Omar, still operated from sanctuaries in Pakistan. Taliban guerrillas continued to make sporadic incursions, killing soldiers and aid workers. The battle at Tora Bora and Operation Anaconda had broken Al-Qaeda and driven it largely from the country while forcing the Taliban into a very low-level guerrilla war. But nearly a year after the fall of Kabul and Kandahar the United States and the Northern Alliance had still failed to pacify the country, and the U.S.-installed central government seemed to have little influence outside the capital. Commentators were starting to ask if the country was slipping out of control. The high-tech methods that had been so devastating in force-on-force battles were of little help. Even General Myers felt obliged to acknowledge, "We've lost a little momentum there, to be frank."[94]

Defense Secretary Donald Rumsfeld arrived in Kabul to welcome UN participation and signal a shift in priorities from "major combat" to "stability." But within days of his announcement, multiple guerrilla attacks forced the United Nations to suspend mine-clearing operations. Eighteen months after the fall of the Taliban regime, the guerrilla resistance continued to hang on stubbornly.

The Karzai government had not managed to disarm the warlords or unite Afghanistan's varied regions, but then no one ever had. As had been true for centuries, local warlords paid as little attention as possible to the central government. Enriched by the resurgent drug trade, collecting "taxes" and "customs duties," and with perhaps 200,000 armed followers, they had little incentive to cooperate.[95] The scarcity of reconstruction aid contributed to the problem. Although the national army struggled to keep its recruits, militias thrived. Herat Governor Ismail Khan supported 40,000 soldiers and a solid infrastructure. Until real security arrived, Afghans were likely to keep their AK-47 rifles. And without funding for crop substitution, farmers would see that the country retained its status as the world's leading opium producer.[96]

The struggle against Al-Qaeda and the Taliban went on. Neither could hope to eradicate the U.S.-led Coalition, or even eject it by force. But they could make the country ungovernable and destroy the legitimacy of the Coalition-installed government. The best way to accomplish that was to interfere with the country's first-ever national election scheduled for June 2004. If enough Afghanis could be threatened, persuaded, or forced to stay away from the polls, the shaky national government would lack legitimacy not only in the eyes of Afghans, but in the world community as well.

The burden of supporting governmental legitimacy fell on U.S. Army Civil Affairs teams and multiservice, multinational Provincial Reconstruction Teams (PRT), but both faced an uphill struggle. In Afghanistan, the central government had never had much influence on the daily lives of most people. A PRT provided generator or farming equipment had a huge impact on their daily lives and at least in theory showed the benefits and good intentions of the government in Kabul. But as usual, the need had not been anticipated. There were too few Civil Affairs units, and the PRTs were operating in only 3 of 32 provinces.[97]

PRTs were predominantly military organizations of 50 to 100 persons, including a few civilian representatives to provide political and developmental expertise. The original intention was that the PRTs would coordinate the reconstruction process in PRT areas. The planners, however, reckoned without the prickly nature of various international "civil" assistance agencies and organizations. UN agencies and nongovernmental assistance groups denounced the plan and especially the use of the word "reconstruction." They demanded that the military confine itself to the issue of security, narrowly defined as the use of force, and especially objected to the teams taking assessments of village needs. Nevertheless, with or without the cooperation of the international civic community, the armed PRTs were the only assistance organizations capable of operating in high risk areas. Numbering in total less than 1000 persons, they had their work cut out for them.[98] Meanwhile, the war degenerated into an affair of ambushes, rocket and mortar attacks, and patrol actions. After the futile and costly attempt at positional defense in late 2001 and early 2002 the Taliban and Al-Qaeda had adapted.

None of this diminished the Pentagon's satisfaction with the cleverness and agility shown by U.S. armed forces (especially Special Operations Forces). OEF was labeled a success and the result of military transformation. If the Army no longer needed to haul around heavy weapons with long logistics tails (a conventional armored division has as many as 10,000 vehicles), forces could be deployed around the world more quickly and easily. For the moment, the Air Force looked like a big winner in the endless battle for dollars and glory. But there was grumbling that pilots were being turned into truck drivers, simply flying over and dumping out precision guided weapons.[99]

The Stryker Brigade Combat Teams

The Interim Brigade Combat Teams, now renamed Stryker Brigade Combat Teams (SBCT), were still experiencing a rough ride as the vehicle, the interim brigade concept, and FCS all remained under scrutiny.

On April 12, 2002, Army Chief of Staff General Eric Shinseki went to the Anniston Army Depot in Alabama to unveil the first Strykers manufactured in America. They were the first installment on GM GDLS Defense Group's $4 billion order for 2,131 of the vehicles. Two unfortunate facts hung over the ceremony. First of all, testing had revealed that the vehicle's armor did not provide the advertised protection against 7.62mm and 14.5mm machine gun fire. What antitank weapons (or enemy tanks) would do to it did not bear thinking. Still worse, the vehicle stubbornly remained overweight. Despite strenuous efforts by an "aggressive weight management team," Stryker was 4,000 pounds over the 38,000 pound weight requirement, still too heavy for airlift. A month later the machines were delivered to the initial operational units—3rd Brigade, 2nd Infantry Division, and 1st Brigade, 25th Infantry Division, both at Fort Lewis, Washington.[100]

In July General Dynamics followed up the infantry-carrying Strykers with the first of eight preproduction Mobile Gun Systems (MGS). This was the second of the two major variants of the new vehicle. Each SBCT was to include 31 MGS but these first eight were handmade prototypes, testing and development models only. Conscious of the transportability issue, program representatives were careful to state that MGS "is in the research and development phase; its weight cannot be specified," but they assured DoD that MGS "will be in compliance" with Army and Air Force "weight profiles."[101] The fact that the gun system was also too tall to fit aboard C-130 aircraft was largely ignored.

As described by prime contractor General Dynamics the "MGS design carries a General Dynamics 105 mm tank cannon in a low-profile, fully stabilized, shoot on the move turret. Its armor protects the three-soldier crew from machine-gun bullets and mortar and artillery fragments on the battlefield. It operates with the latest command, control, communications and computers intelligence, surveillance and reconnaissance (C4ISR) equipment as well as detectors for nuclear, biological and chemical weapons. The Stryker mobile gun system carries 18 rounds of 105 mm main gun ammunition; 400 rounds of .50 caliber ammunition; and 3,400 rounds of 7.62 mm ammunition." The use of the present tense was perhaps a bit optimistic since the first operational gun had yet to be fielded. Furthermore, the planned 105 mm close support round for the MGS had not even entered development.[102]

Until an MGS design was finalized, the first two Stryker brigades would have to be satisfied with the Army standard TOW antitank missile. It was not revolutionary, or even transformational, but at least it provided a measure of protection against enemy armored vehicles.[103]

Developmental difficulties were not the only problems; there were also political pressures to contend with. Convinced that the Army was predisposed to select a wheeled vehicle, United Defense L.P., the M113A3's manufacturer, and its supporters waged a furious campaign in the press, Congress, and the Pentagon to halt or reduce the Stryker program. In the 2001 Defense Authorization Act, lawmakers had ordered the Army to conduct a side-by-side evaluation pitting the Stryker against "a tracked vehicle already in the service's inventory"—before allowing the Army to purchase vehicles for the fourth, fifth, and sixth Stryker brigades. The only such vehicle was Stryker's principal competitor, the 1960s vintage, tracked M113A3 armored personnel carrier. The General Accounting Office rejected a formal protest by United Defense. But Congress insisted on the side-by-side test.[104]

The Army responded with its own furious public relations campaign to oppose a new round of evaluations but finally settled for a stipulation that Secretary Rumsfeld should have the right to cancel the test. At about the same time, rumors began to surface that some members of the Office of the Secretary of Defense would like to cut Stryker procurement significantly. The Stryker Brigade Combat Teams were at the heart of the Army transformation initiative. But some defense officials were quoted as publicly wondering if the Brigades were "truly transformational." According to the rumors, the OSD wanted to use the brigades' funding to finance the Future Combat System.[105]

This led in turn to an effort to convince Rumsfeld of the vehicle's value, including a Stryker ride at Fort Lewis. The effort was ineffective and in September 2002 the Interim Combat Vehicle was tested against the M113 yet again. An e-mail campaign sprang up among industry analysts, Pentagon budget specialists, and retired Army officers to challenge the Army's statements about the Stryker's capabilities.

Stryker's problems continued during the field portion of the Millennium Challenge 2002 joint exercise held at the National Training Center in the Mohave Desert and at Fort Polk, Louisiana. The Army found that the Stryker needed an Air Force waiver to deploy aboard C-130 aircraft. The waiver allowed no more than four men to accompany the Stryker, so the rest of the infantry squad would have to travel on another aircraft.[106]

According to an Army memo quoted in the press, the vehicle was both too wide and, with antennas, too tall. It could not be loaded without stowing the vehicle's Remote Weapons System (RWS) and removing all antennas. The crew also needed to remove smoke grenade launchers and "compensate for an immature height management system." The Army noted in the memo that the vehicles experienced several "challenges" from desert heat and terrain during the exercise, including 120 degree temperatures inside the vehicle and numerous tire failures as well as electrical and optical failures.[107] As developmental problems went, these were fairly minor (except for removing the RWS and the problems with tires) and to be expected, but they lent fresh ammunition to those opposed to the whole idea of wheeled armored vehicles.

Perhaps more seriously, soldiers reported the vehicle was too cramped to don protective clothing and equipment, or to wear the fighting load. Also, the tight space made it difficult to access ammunition and load their individual weapons. These problems were inherent in the design of the vehicle and not something that could be cured with a few tweaks during development.

Nevertheless, the Army took an optimistic view and preferred to dwell on Stryker's successes rather than its failures. "We've been able to fly [the Strykers] on combat missions across a full spectrum of potential threats and operational scenarios [during testing] at Fort Irwin and Fort Polk, Louisiana," according to Major Amy Hannah, an Army spokesperson. The testing at the National Training Center, she said, focused on "a desert environment under mid- to high-intensity combat conditions," while at Polk, "testing focused on mid- to low-intensity...including urban operations."[108]

The Army was not quick to publicize another lesson from Millennium Challenge. Establishing the network and keeping it running is a highly specialized talent. According to observers, the digital units operated in a digital box that included extensive provisions to compensate for the static and brittle nature of the network. Even when working with plenty of support from civilian experts, the digital tools were spotty, enough to question their battle-worthiness.[109]

A number of major weapons programs were under review by the OSD for cancellation or major cuts, including the Comanche, the V-22 tiltrotor, and the F-22. Speculation grew that Stryker could be part of the list. Rumors began to swirl around the Defense Department that the entire Stryker program might be canceled. According to unnamed officials interviewed by the *Army Times,* there was considerable skepticism about the utility of the Stryker Brigade Combat Teams, especially in light of their price tag, $1.5 billion per brigade. Army officials professed themselves totally unaware of any such rumors, but there was a scent of blood in the budget waters.[110]

At issue, once again, was the ability to transport the vehicle by C-130. The whole rationale for a lightweight armored vehicle began with the need for rapid deployment by air. According to the unnamed official, "It barely fits into a C-130 [Air Force transport plane] with inches to spare. Plus, it's so heavy that most of the time we may need two 130s to carry each Stryker—one for the vehicle and the other for fuel, ammunition and crew. One [Stryker] with all that stuff can go on a 130, but then the plane can't fly very far."[111]

Former House Speaker Newt Gingrich (R-GA) added to the high-profile controversy when he counseled that Stryker "should either be canceled or limited to one test brigade that will never be air-transported but that could be used" to evaluate new electronics.[112]

Within the 1st Battalion, 23rd Infantry Regiment, at Fort Lewis, training exercises for the Stryker brigade began to take on the flavor of a possible war with Iraq. At Yuma Proving Grounds (YPG), the team configuring the Stryker for desert conditions received instructions to hurry work. YPG officials told reporters that two shifts were working, each ten hours a day, six days a week. "It's very unusual," said Wayne Lucas, a YPG engineer for 15 years and a team leader for the Stryker program. "I don't know that it's happened ever."[113]

The Army's fears were confirmed in October when a Pentagon working paper advocated trimming the Stryker force to three brigades, saving $4.5 billion. Three brigades, it was argued, would be enough to handle small-scale contingencies and offer an experimental base for the future Objective Force. Army officials countered that all six SBCTs were needed to fill the gap between the current force and the FCS, still at least a decade away.[114]

Army Secretary Thomas E. White reacted quickly and ordered four Strykers flown to Andrews Air Force Base near Washington, D.C., for an audience of defense establishment figures and former Congressman Gingrich. The vehicles demonstrated their ability to load and unload from both a C-130 and the larger C-17 and quickly configure themselves for either transport or combat. The dignitaries were then invited to a series of presentations on the Stryker's capabilities, hosted by the Army Secretary who touted the system as "a new capability, a new way of fighting."[115] White also expressed his belief that six Stryker brigades would be fielded by 2007 and the first Objective Force unit in 2008.[116]

General Shinseki lent his weight to the debate, saying "the Stryker must be fielded to provide soldiers the capabilities they've needed for the last 12 years. It's time and the right number [of brigades] is six." The Chief also pledged that Army forces would field a PGM capability with the Non Line-of-Sight cannon as part of the FCS program. Shinseki went on to accuse Stryker opponents of spreading disinformation and pronounced himself "confident" the transformation process had achieved "irreversible momentum."[117] Meanwhile, the 4th Infantry Division ended its role as an experimental unit and returned to the pool of operational units in September 2002 as the first fully digitized division.

In late November, the Army and the Office of the Secretary of Defense finally achieved a hard-fought compromise to field the original six Stryker Brigade Combat Teams, but with strings attached. The last two Stryker Brigades were scheduled for 2007–2008. To satisfy the OSD, they needed to look more like the Objective Force and less like a souped-up remnant of the Legacy Force. Exactly what that meant was not specified, but for most observers it certainly implied improved C4I systems as well as better surveillance and reconnaissance capabilities, an air and missile defense element, as well as more precision munitions and unattended sensors. Where all this would come from was uncertain, but the Stryker Brigades were safe, at least for the moment.[118]

Planners also considered adding an aviation detachment to the Stryker brigades. The Apache Longbow was the obvious choice but adding helicopters equally obviously added to the time and resources required to deploy the brigade. For Transformation, the preferred possibility was the RAH-66 Comanche, but that system was under scrutiny from budget cutters and in any case would not be available until 2008–2009.[119]

Meanwhile, replacement of weapons expended in Afghanistan and preparation for the expected war with Iraq provided a new bonanza for the defense industry. Boeing stepped up production of its Joint Direct Attack Munitions—the most widely used smart bomb in the Afghan war. Raytheon added a third shift and announced that production for its laser-guided bomb had been accelerated by five months "to support the warfighter in the war on terrorism." Alliant Techsystems, the largest supplier of ammunition to the U.S. military, received a $92 million contract to make 265 million rounds of small-caliber ammunition for the Army.[120]

The Stryker Test

The test comparing Stryker to the 1960s era M113 armored personnel carrier finally ended in January 2003. On the balance Stryker was judged superior, but not the startling advance one might expect over a vehicle designed in the 1950s. The Army Test and Evaluation Command report gave comfort to Stryker advocates when the new vehicle was found superior in speed, armor, gas mileage, noise, comfort, and target acquisition. Nevertheless, the M113 performed better in turning, operating in water, and range. Although the M113 covered a greater range of terrain, Stryker performed better on roads, secondary roads, and trails. The two vehicles were also judged on projected price and cost of operation and maintenance. One M113A3 would cost $3.1 million to operate and maintain through 2023 while Stryker was cheaper at $2.9 million. But when the M113's $300,000 purchase price was factored in (vs. $14 million for a Stryker vehicle) the M113 came out way ahead.[121]

The test started another round of sniping between armor partisans and transformation advocates. Relations between the OSD and the Army leadership went from strained to little short of hostile.

CHAPTER 7

THE WAR WITH IRAQ

Any time you make a plan that requires the enemy's cooperation, you're in trouble.
—Ancient maxim of the infantry

By mid-2002 the war in Afghanistan had largely settled down to sniping, skirmishes, and intermittent rocket and mortar attacks. The number of American soldiers slowly inched up as the United States shouldered the task of assisting recovery and patrolling the rugged, ill-defined Pakistan border. Nevertheless, the situation seemed to be contained; after all, Afghanistan had been the graveyard of foreign armies. No modern force had done as well as the Americans; overall it counted as a success.

Despite continued fighting in Afghanistan, Iraq remained on the minds of Washington policy makers. U.S. Central Command (CENTCOM) had been updating and revising its Iraq war plans since late 2001. It had also steadily improved its forward facilities in Kuwait and Qatar, but all at low key. In the spring of 2002, Vice President Richard Cheney and Defense Secretary Donald Rumsfeld had begun in earnest to build the case against Iraqi dictator Saddam Hussein. International economic sanctions had been in place for 12 years with little evident effect on Hussein. However, the impact on Iraq's civilian population was harsh. A UN "Oil-for-Food Program," started in 1997, provided little relief to Iraqis, and the humanitarian crisis continued. It also appeared that cash from the Oil-for-Food Program was used by Saddam for everything but food. The Iraqi dictator used the UN provided funds to buy weapons, finance terror, build palaces, and encourage pro-Iraqi figures in France, Libya, Syria, Indonesia, and Russia. By now the restrictions were being regularly violated and their only effect was the continuous punishment of the Iraqi people for the intransigence of their dictator. There was great international sentiment for relaxing the sanctions or lifting them entirely.[1]

The point of the measures was to force Saddam to comply with the disarmament agreements made at the end of the Gulf War. UN inspection teams had been at work to see that Hussein was stripped of offensive arms, especially missiles and weapons of mass destruction (WMD). But the inspections were dubious since they were never truly no-notice and there was plenty of time to move or conceal offending items (if any). Also, the dictator often exercised the privilege of declaring various military and secret police facilities off limits, including many of his "palaces." In any event Hussein had forced the UN inspectors out of the country back in 1998. Now it looked as if he was poised to break out of the sanctions box entirely. Obviously there was something to hide and, at least in the minds of some observers, that something was WMD. In simplest terms, the administration argued that Saddam had not eliminated his weapons of mass destruction as agreed at the end of the 1991 Gulf War. His continuing refusal to honor these promises to the United Nations constituted grounds for war.

Later, after the end of major operations in Iraq, when no evidence of significant WMD was found, there was great controversy over the use of a WMD threat as a *causus belli*. In fact, prior to the war, intelligence officials worldwide generally believed that "Iraq had, in varying degrees, ongoing programs for the development and deployment of weapons of mass destruction."[2] The presence of such weapons, at least chemical ones, seemed to be, in the words of the American CIA, "a slam dunk."[3]

After the UN Security Council demanded renewed inspections of Iraqi weapons production in November 2002, Hussein "did everything possible to make it appear he had something to hide."[4]

The U.S. Senate had elucidated over 20 reasons for hostilities with Hussein, but it was far easier to feature WMD as a cause for war than to explain the political complexities. President George Bush's advisors believed that Saddam was a threat to the region, a threat to the United States, and a bloody, repressive dictator to boot. Bush also suggested a link between Saddam and Al-Qaeda. Public opinion polls that summer and fall showed more than two-thirds of Americans polled consistently favored military action.[5]

Several observers, notably including retired General Brent Scowcroft, national security adviser to Bush's father, were less sanguine. They predicted that a U.S. invasion would lead to an explosion on the Arab "street" galvanizing anti-American sentiment and endangering any allies that supported the United States. Others feared a conflict would result in terrorist attacks against the West, heavy Iraqi civilian casualties, and a humanitarian crisis.

Russia, France, and even normally staunch allies like Germany vehemently opposed any U.S. attack while public opinion throughout Europe was overwhelmingly against military action. When the United States failed to win UN approval for a new war on Iraq, most remaining international support likewise vanished. With only Britain providing a major troop contribution, Bush was committed to what amounted to a unilateral war.

On September 16, 2002, Defense Secretary Rumsfeld confirmed that coalition aircraft had been responding to antiaircraft fire with a systematic degradation of Iraq's air defense, a necessity prior to any action against the Hussein regime.[6]

At about the same time, the Army began a crash program to deliver thousands of computers to units earmarked in the Iraq operations plans. High-bandwidth links were set up for intelligence units in the field. One of the high priority items was a new tracking system called Blue Force Tracker (BFT) that marked the location of U.S. fighting vehicles and even allowed text e-mails to reach certain frontline vehicles. Importantly, it operated via satellite rather than ground-based radio. BFT had earned rave reviews in testing and would prove to be one of the digital stars of the war.[7]

Unfortunately, it was not a simple matter of passing out new computers, and the idea of fully digitizing the units was discarded almost at once. Only the 4th Infantry Division had the latest equipment and software; the remainder of the Army was a digital hodgepodge. The new devices and applications were worthless unless they could exchange data ("talk to each other") but interoperability was not an easy goal. Existing systems not only could not communicate, they often did not speak similar languages. Even within Army units digital systems were at different levels of maturity ranging from the fully digitized and largely tested 4th ID to units with no digitization beyond ordinary office automation. The partially digitized ones suffered from incompatibility among systems, communications media, radios, operating systems, and even simple physical incompatibility between wiring types and connections. Even the Advanced Field Artillery Tactical Data System, used since the 1980s, proved troublesome when updated software turned out to be incompatible with earlier versions.[8]

Furthermore, voice communications also suffered from incompatible systems. Multiple voice networks with names like Defense Switched Network, Tri-Tac Tactical Voice, MSE Voice, and Gray Voice were built according to differing policies, using different techniques and different operating protocols. Sometimes, the telephones themselves were not interoperable.[9]

The buildup to war brought another clash between the office of the Secretary of Defense (OSD) and General Shinseki. Appearing before the Senate Armed Services Committee, the Army chief was pressed to estimate the number of troops needed to stabilize postwar Iraq. Based on his experience as NATO commander in Bosnia, Shinseki placed the number at over 200,000. Shinseki's words would later prove prophetic, but it was the wrong answer as far as Department of Defense (DoD) policy was concerned. Deputy Defense Secretary Paul Wolfowitz dismissed Shinseki's estimate as "wildly off the mark." In the official version, far fewer would be required.[10]

In August President George Bush approved the overall war strategy for Iraq—"goals, objectives and strategy." The plan was to win quickly and decisively. Victory would answer all doubts. A speedy American victory would negate most of the opposition, and the spectacle of Iraqis cheering their liberators would answer critics of the war. Since it was expected to be a "liberation" greeted by enthusiastic Iraqis, there would be no need for a large occupation force. Phase IV of the planning, the postwar occupation, was treated as an afterthought.[11]

At about the same time, long range surveillance teams began cycling though the theater to acclimate them to the terrain, weather, and culture. In Afghanistan, U.S. interrogators continued to press for any information about Iraqi military units and dispositions.[12]

In November, CENTCOM's forward operations center went up at Camp As Sayliyah, a 262-acre U.S. military "forward positioning" site in the Arab ministate of Qatar. The move was billed as a routine exercise called "Internal Look," a test of CENTCOM's "standing deployable headquarters." No combat forces were involved, but about 600 CENTCOM staffers and 400 personnel from subordinate commands were sent to Qatar. CENTCOM noted in a press release that, even though the exercise was scheduled for one week, some personnel would stay longer. "You have to allow for the advance party, set-up time, and take-down time," explained one CENTCOM spokesman.[13]

Located in the open desert outside Qatar's capital, Doha, the center consisted of 24 portable "elasti-shelters" hardened against biological, chemical, and conventional attack. A year earlier this had been considered a long-term, advanced project for the Raytheon Company. But DoD's emphasis on transformation had turned it into a short-term reality, a transportable expeditionary headquarters with the full panoply of high-tech command and control—laptops, satellite uplinks, special encrypted communications lines, cameras for video conferencing, and connections with video cameras on remote-controlled platforms including the Predator unmanned aerial vehicle (UAV).[14] As Sayliya already contained enough equipment for an armored brigade including M-1 Abrams tanks, Bradley fighting vehicles, and other armored personnel carriers,

According to DoD spokespersons, "War is not imminent, and the exercise is not a prelude."[15] Outside Kuwait International Airport another construction project was underway—Camp Wolf, a large staging area for troops and cargo. Observing the preparations, retired Marine General Anthony Zinni, CENTCOM Commander from 1997 to 2000, guessed that there was "a 70 percent chance that we're going to go" [to war].[16]

The same month, on November 3, an Al-Qaeda leader and five alleged terrorists were killed by a Hellfire missile fired from a CIA-operated Predator in Yemen. The Predator was controlled by CIA operators using the TV camera on the UAV. They watched Al-Harethi and the suspected Al-Qaeda members from 160 miles away at a French military base in Djibouti.[17] It was an impressive display of technology and intelligence and gave a boost to proponents of the UAV as a star of the transformation process.

By the eve of the second Iraq War, Rapid Deceive Operations doctrine was still unknown to the general public, but the phrase "shock and awe" had become part of the public lexicon.[18] The idea was that Iraq's command and control would collapse under shock and awe's hurricane of shock, wonder, and disbelief. A firestorm of cruise missiles and aircraft-delivered precision guided munitions would crash down to paralyze the Iraqi leadership with a display of explosive firepower whose psychological impact would be as important as its destructive effect.

It made a powerful image, and statements from military pundits and the Defense Department bristled with such references. As phrased by Secretary Rumsfeld, "There is always a risk in gradualism. It pacifies the hesitant and the tentative. What it doesn't do is shock, and awe, and alter the calculations of the people you're dealing with."[19] Shock and awe was the first step toward "rapid dominance." High-tech Coalition forces would dominate the enemy through superior information and air-delivered, precision guided munitions. The war would demonstrate the ability of relatively small, powerful, highly mobile ground tactical units, supported by air power, to employ precision fires and fight almost independently over incredibly large distances.

Richard Perle, a senior adviser to Rumsfeld, predicted the United States would easily "detect and destroy with precision strikes the critical elements of Saddam's military power." U.S. forces, he said, working "alongside Iraqis eager to liberate their country [will cause] Saddam to crumble far more quickly than the critics of preemption expect."[20]

Thomas McInerney, a retired Air Force general, said that the war would be won with "an intensive, 24/7 precision air-centric campaign" using "time critical targeting ...to achieve rapid dominance in the first 72 hours of combat, focused on regime-change targets. Most of the army does not want to fight for Saddam, and the people want a regime change," McInerney asserted.[21] The judgment that Hussein's army would not fight for him and the Iraqi people would welcome a liberating force was shared by Pentagon officials and became an important element in planning for the war.

The planners at CENTCOM were not so convinced that the war would be a walkover. Even though "Rapid Decisive Operations" was something of a mantra, no one there thought the regime would suddenly collapse regardless.[22] First of all, it was not easy to plan a countrywide campaign using a greatly reduced number of "transformed forces." Traditional military planning required a strength advantage of at least 3 to 1, three attackers for every defender, for an attack to have an even chance of success. This created a real problem since the paper strength of the Ba'athist regime's military was more than 450,000 troops. Even if the regular armed forces shattered as in Desert Storm, the core of the Iraqi forces (paramilitary units, the Republican Guard, and the Special Republican Guard) were expected to fight. This still left the Coalition at a probable 3 or 4 to 1 disadvantage. In towns and cities the added advantage to defenders would raise the ratio to about 6 to 1.

The CENTCOM staff and the commander, General Tommy Franks, had been hard at work on Operations Plan 1003, the standing operations plan for Iraq, commonly referred to as "ten-zero-three." The so-called "back to Iraq" plan was developed in the years immediately following the end of Gulf War I. CENTCOM planners believed then that, sooner or later, they would need to finish what was started in 1990–1991 by going all the way to Baghdad and ejecting Saddam and his minions. Following the terrorist attacks of 2001, planning was stepped up in the expectation of war with Iraq.

In the beginning, General Franks's planners prepared a conventional campaign a lot like Gulf War I. The plan seemed to suggest that the experience Franks and CENTCOM had gained in the Afghanistan War had little bearing on the problem of Iraq. As an organization, the Army was still skeptical that the success in Afghanistan could be applied elsewhere, especially a very different sort of war on the Arabian Peninsula.

In the months before the second Gulf War, 1003 was a low-risk, high force level plan calling for, in Franks's words, "a whole bunch of divisions, a whole bunch of jets, a whole bunch of bombs and a whole bunch of aircraft carriers." "A whole bunch" meant something like 250,000 troops including three heavy divisions with thousands of vehicles. Lighter divisions included the 101st Airborne Division plus a Marine Corps division and various smaller fighting organizations. On top of this, of course, went all the support elements needed to sustain the units in combat. In CENTCOM's view, this was still a relatively light force, less than half the size of the one that chased the Iraqis out of Kuwait in 1991. The problem was that the force structure for a significantly larger force did not exist. An invasion force of 300,000 or more would be almost impossible to generate and clearly impossible to sustain. The force structure just was not there. Besides that, a huge force would inevitably offer many more points for friction and opportunities for serious errors.

In practical terms it meant a slow deployment followed with a deliberate advance by mass armor formations supported by heavy air bombardment. There was very little transformational about it.

This was exactly what Rumsfeld and his OSD team did not want. As seen by the OSD, the entire plan was cumbersome and too conventional. The Secretary of Defense pushed hard for Franks to adopt a scheme that incorporated Rumsfeld's notions of shock, awe, and rapid dominance. The idea was to place the enemy's top-to-bottom structure, military and governmental, under a variety of constant, nonlinear, unpredictable pressures until the system collapsed. Speed and precision were the answer—they brought a quick, nearly bloodless victory in Afghanistan and would do so again in Iraq. The preferred recipe called for an air-heavy plan to deliver precise devastation guided by a relatively small number of special operations soldiers on the ground. The entire ground force would be about 80,000, divided between heavy Army forces and a lighter contingent of Marines. This force would conduct a decapitating strike, rapidly occupy Baghdad, kill or capture Hussein and his chief henchmen, and still leave the rest of the country largely untouched.[23]

Reportedly Franks met shortly after that with retired Army General Peter J. Schoomaker, formerly head of the U.S. Special Operations Command, a meeting that presumably was brokered by the OSD.[24] According to news reports, the two met at Franks's headquarters in Tampa where the former commando general discussed the role special operations units could play. Allegedly, the meeting strongly influenced Franks's subsequent thinking. Schoomaker did not make the discussion public but he did tell reporters that Franks was "a quick study" who "understands joint warfare." After that, special operations took a lead role in the new war plan.[25]

The Bush administration's concept of the war went well beyond simply defeating the Iraqi military and ejecting the dictator. Although that remained the overriding concern, there were several subordinate objectives. First was a desire to prevent as much "collateral damage" as possible, meaning a minimum of civilian casualties. This was, after all, a war against Hussein and his supporters, not the Iraqi people. Low collateral damage also meant avoiding attacks on civil infrastructure (roads, bridges, power plants) needed to restore Iraq after the war. Equally important, it meant protecting the oil fields that were the country's principal resource. If oil money kept flowing in, then Iraq could supposedly finance much of its own reconstruction. Furthermore, CENTCOM was to fight the war without inflicting massive casualties on the enemy army since it would be needed to maintain order after the war.

As viewed by CENTCOM, the OSD concept had several problems, principally that it required the Iraqis to cooperate by not fighting too hard, and it presumed that air power could do the job almost unassisted. Franks reportedly responded by recalling the first Gulf War when the bombing did nothing to prevent Saddam's forces from torching the oil fields in Kuwait. "How long," he asked, "did it take to get Iraqis out of Kuwait?" They did not leave until U.S. Army tanks drove them out.[26]

Norman Schwarzkopf, the general who commanded U.S. forces in the 1991 Gulf War, became a public spokesman for the Army's strong reservations. In January he gave Thomas Ricks of the *Washington Post* an interview criticizing the Defense Secretary's war plan and called Rumsfeld's micromanagement "scary." "When he makes his comments, it appears that he disregards the Army," Schwarzkopf said. "He gives the perception...on TV that he is the guy driving the train and everybody else better fall in line behind him—or else." With unacknowledged foresight, Schwarzkopf was also skeptical about the Bush administration's readiness to deal with the aftermath of the war. "I would hope that we have in place the adequate resources to become an army of occupation," he warned, "because you're going to walk into chaos."[27]

The final plan was a compromise between the Rumsfeld version of transformed warfare and CENTCOM's conviction that the secretary's notions of lightweight war were very risky. The initial ground force would consist of roughly 100,000 troops, including heavy armor, supported by overwhelming air power. But this force would be backed up by a contingent of perhaps three more divisions. If Rapid Decisive Operations (RDO) and Effects Based Operations (EBO) did not work as planned, the follow-on force would be ready to enter the theater with old-fashioned devastating force. President Bush blessed the plan, but politics delayed the start of hostilities. When the war actually began, the initial force had about doubled in size due to the arrival of an additional 100,000 "contingency" forces, closer to Frank's original plan even though much of that number was out of the actual fighting.

In January, President Bush announced the creation of the Office of Reconstruction and Humanitarian Assistance within the Department of Defense, an "expeditionary" office to prepare for "the coordinated, balanced progress of economic and security reconstruction in a post-conflict Iraq." "Expeditionary" was another buzzword greatly favored by transformation advocates, meaning able to function with minimal outside support. The announcement was another triumph for Rumsfeld and the OSD, pushing aside the State Department and its "Future of Iraq" postwar planning project. Postwar operations would be led by Jay Garner, a retired Lieutenant General who helped lead the 1991 humanitarian relief operation in northern Iraq.

It was a move that seemed contrary to the tenets of Effects Based Operations that called for interagency cooperation and coordination. Although there were doubts that EBO could be effective at operational and tactical levels, this move was at the strategic level where it was supposed to be most important. Garner would, in effect, be the American viceroy for Iraq.[28] A big part of his plan was to provide postwar security by retaining a large part of the Iraqi Army. Furthermore, in accordance with RDO doctrine, postwar security and reconstruction would be handled by the UN and nongovernmental organizations assisted by the tens of thousands of international troops promised by his civilian superiors. In the real world it was unrealistic to expect large troop contributions from allies given the general public opposition to the war in most of those countries.

All that was part of the despised "nation-building" that the U.S. military simply was not going to do. Most American forces would rapidly return to the United States or elsewhere within a few months of the inevitable victory.

Also in January, a few select National Guard units were called up without fanfare, such as Orlando-based Charlie Company, 2nd Battalion, 53rd Infantry Brigade (Florida National Guard). In February, the 2/53 began predeployment training at Fort Stewart, Georgia. By then the total number of U.S. reservists from all services on active duty was reported as 150,000.[29] It was the largest reserve call-up in more than 50 years. Since Korea the DoD had opposed large-scale activation of the reserves, but now it was impossible to fight without them. The active-duty strength just was not there.

February 14, St. Valentine's Day, was an eventful day. At the United Nations, weapons inspectors delivered yet another inconclusive report on their findings in Iraq. The U.S. and British delegations again failed to convince the Security Council to enforce its own resolutions. Al-Jazeera, the Qatar-based Arabic-language TV news network, rebroadcast an audio tape purportedly from Usama bin Laden. In it the Al-Qaeda leader called for Muslims to fight alongside Saddam Hussein and to inflict the largest possible number of casualties on the Americans. The same day, DoD officials reported that there were 200,000 U.S. troops, Army and Marines, in the Gulf region. Almost half of Kuwait had been declared a military training area to accommodate the "warp speed" buildup of American and British forces.[30]

Units arriving in Kuwait were still being hurriedly supplied with computers and Blue Force Tracker, the system that enabled each vehicle to broadcast its Global Positioning System (GPS) coordinates and an ID code. This critical stream of data was displayed at CENTCOM headquarters in Qatar on a large plasma screen, allowing Franks to monitor locations in real time. Some other commanders in the field also had access to it, thanks to last-minute installations.[31]

The war was now scheduled to begin following the nighttime insertion of about 350 Army Special Forces troopers on March 19. The SF teams would have 48 hours inside the country to prepare for conventional operations to begin on March 21. There would be no extended Gulf War I style air campaign. It was too likely to cause an unacceptable number of civilian deaths and spur opposition to the war. Instead, Navy and Air Force aircraft and missiles would begin the much-anticipated shock and awe air bombardment, concentrating on government and military command and control targets.

As conceived by Harlan Ullman, shock and awe were not obliteration but an attack on the enemy's will: stunning one's opponent into realizing that your might was so enormous, so unbeatable, that the fight was as good as over. The Iraqi command paralysis would allow the U.S. forces inside the enemy decision cycle where they would remain until victory. It was a heady vision, and it briefed really well.[32]

Shortly before dawn the next day, ground forces would enter Iraq from Kuwait and Turkey, rolling toward Baghdad as fast as treads could carry them.

Paratroopers of the 173rd Airborne Brigade would attack in the north, flying from their base near Aviano, Italy. This would have been a wonderful opportunity for an air-transportable, medium-weight brigade—i.e., a Stryker brigade—to land on a paratrooper secured airfield and lend punch to the lightly armed airborne unit. But Stryker was not ready.

Instead, the heavy mechanized 4th ID would attack from Turkey and link up with the 173rd. Together they would seize the oil fields at Kirkuk and then proceed toward Baghdad, destroying the two Iraqi divisions guarding the northern approaches to the city. At the same time, the Army's 3rd ID and the First Marine Expeditionary Force would enter Iraq from the south. The 3rd ID would attack toward Baghdad while the Marines secured the Rumaila oil fields and made a supporting attack up the Euphrates Valley toward the capital. Tactically it was all fairly routine for a contemporary military operation.

The exception lay in the role of the 3rd Infantry and the Special Forces. The 3rd ID was to dash directly up the road to Baghdad, stopping for nothing. The speed required, the distance to be covered, and the difficulty of the terrain would make it the longest and most audacious combat movement of a U.S. Army division since General George Patton slashed across North Africa in pursuit of the Afrika Korps. But unlike conventional campaigns, the heavy tanks and armored personnel carriers were to avoid taking ground or securing key locations. There were no follow-on forces to secure the division's rear and guard its supply lines. If rear units were attacked or supply lines were threatened—so the theory went—the technology would allow commanders to see the problem as it developed and dispatch a response. Information would replace a massive troop presence on the ground.

Besides, if enemy forces collapsed quickly as anticipated and the Iraqi population proved welcoming, there was no need for large numbers of U.S. soldiers. On the eve of the war Vice Admiral Lowell E. Jacoby, director of the Defense Intelligence Agency said, "We're prepared for a situation where the Iraqi military offers stiff resistance. There is a very real likelihood, though, that resistance could collapse very quickly."[33]

An information campaign was planned to ensure such a collapse. Radio broadcasts urged soldiers to abandon Hussein's "corrupt" regime, and more than 40 million leaflets were dropped across southern Iraq. The leaflets and broadcasts also warned them not to use weapons of mass destruction and not to destroy Iraq's oil infrastructure. Other aspects of the "perception management" campaign included a series of public-diplomacy activities that failed to generate much return. As Osama Sibliani, the publisher of *Arab American News,* noted: "The United States could have the Prophet Muhammad doing public relations and it wouldn't help."[34] Considerable lip service was given to "psyop," also called information operations, during the planning phase but it never seemed to be terribly important except to the practioners. Although General Franks considered the "information campaign" one of the four fronts in the war, he barely mentions it in his memoir of the war, *American Soldier.*

During the buildup to war Coalition psyops did make innovative use of mobile phone text messaging and e-mails sent directly to key decision makers in the Iraqi regime. Although most Iraqis could not access the Internet, most of the leadership did. Coalition psychological operators used this means to make sure each understood the cost of supporting Saddam, both for Iraq collectively and for themselves personally.[35]

The concentration of power in a few hands seemed to make Iraq a perfect target for a decapitating strike. Saddam Hussein was the strategic center of gravity, all power began with him, and influence stemmed only from his personal authority. Obviously, the planners thought, if Hussein were removed, the rest of the Iraqi leadership would falter without him. With a bit of luck the entire government might even fall. With this in mind, President Bush directed the CIA to take covert action against Hussein before the war started. Ideally, Iraqi officers or citizens would kill Saddam themselves.[36]

Amatzia Baram, a leading Israeli expert on Saddam at the University of Haifa, supported the "fragile leadership" theory. "A nice price on his head once the war begins will have a better chance than the one offered for Osama bin Laden. Saddam is surrounded by men who seek pleasures in this: power, women, prestige and money. They are more likely to sell him down the river."[37]

The CIA and Defense Intelligence Agency argued Saddam's hold was "brittle"—infected with disloyalty and with worries about personal survival. Privately, the analysts were not all so sure. Saddam had a cohort of absolute loyalists close to him who had not only benefited enormously from the regime, but also been intimately involved in its most horrific acts. They had every reason to fight fiercely for the government that protected them. Furthermore, regardless of the British and U.S. forces' announced intention to liberate Iraq, they were still an invading army that would inevitably kill many Iraqis. Given time for nationalist sentiments to take hold, they might not receive the enthusiastic welcome planners hoped for.[38]

Skepticism and the FCS

Despite the immanency of war, the policy process ground on, as did research and development. The General Accounting Office (GAO) was finishing up a year-long evaluation of the Future Combat System (FCS), the cornerstone of the Objective Force. The report was expected in April, and rumors held that the results would not be favorable. FCS proponents had even more reason to be apprehensive in March when Secretary Rumsfeld appointed a panel of experts from the Institute for Defense Analysis to review the program. The panel chairman was former Air Force chief of staff, retired General Larry Welch, a staunch air power advocate and hardly one to view FCS sympathetically. The timing seemed suspicious, too, shortly after the expected critical GAO report was due and only 60 days before the FCS program was scheduled for its next phase of development. Included on the panel was General Schoomaker, the retired special operations commander. Speculation in the press centered on Rumsfeld's decision to reexamine the Future Combat Systems only three months before General Shinseki's retirement.[39]

It was also believed in some Army circles that the probe was a retaliatory move against Shinseki. Any recommendation for canceling FCS would be a huge embarrassment not just to the chief of staff but to the entire Army. The same circles were not comforted by having a retired Air Force general lead the review, nor were those lawmakers that had supported transformation with hundreds of millions of dollars. *National Defense* magazine reported one senior staff member of the defense appropriations subcommittee as describing the situation as "scary."[40]

The GAO report, "FCS Program Issues," came out on schedule and, as predicted, the results were not encouraging. In polite language the report complimented the Army on its innovative approach, but concluded that the timeline for FCS development and deployment was unrealistic. The report assessed 31 critical FCS technology areas that, if not available, would result in "significant degradation." However, the technologies required were at "levels considered immature by best practice standards." Furthermore, if the network capability fell below some (undetermined) critical mass, it could be fatal to the units. Some of the most fundamental systems, including fuel efficient propulsion, water purification, and hybrid electric power systems were some of the least likely to be developed in the short term. "Even with a longer schedule, [design and development] is still a significant challenge for such a vast scope-completion of technology development." In other words, FCS as initially conceived was not going to happen.

On May 10, 2003, the Institute for Defense Analysis issued the report of the Independent Assessment Panel for Future Combat Systems, immediately christened the "Welch Report." By comparison to the GAO report, it was a burst of sunny optimism. The panel did not comment on the feasibility of specific equipment needed for FCS. Instead, the report restrained its skepticism and settled for calling attention to the dependence of FCS units on external means to operate as a high-performance system of systems. It also noted that the software required to produce the "system of systems" was still speculative. Nevertheless, the panel concluded, the Army was on a "logical track" to transform its "contribution" to the joint fight.[41]

A week later, the Under Secretary of Defense (Acquisition, Technology, and Logistics) approved $14.92 billion for the development and demonstration phase of the FCS. Rather than take the opportunity for a serious re-look at the program, the Army chose the less painful option, requested, and was granted, two more years for development. However, the undersecretary also directed the Army to provide an update on progress in November 2004 before he would grant authority to continue development and authorize prototype production. The Future Combat System was behind schedule and over budget, but still alive.

Prepping the Special Operations War

1,400 US special operations troops, almost certainly including Army Special Forces, were exercising in the country as part of Exercise Early Victor '02, which began on Oct. 6. Jordanian, Omani, Kuwaiti and British troops also took part in the exercise. It is likely that significant Special Forces elements remain in the country.[42]

With the help of the Iraqi opposition both inside and outside the country, CIA operatives had three other covert initiatives running in 2002. The maximum effort was to eliminate Hussein. Large rewards were offered to anyone who could provide advance information on the dictator's whereabouts, but without useful results. The Agency had conducted a similar effort in Afghanistan with warlords, who provided vital information that helped topple the ruling Taliban regime in 2001. But even a $25 million reward offer failed to produce timely and accurate information on the location of Al-Qaeda leader Usama bin Laden. CIA operatives also monitored Saddam's presidential palaces in Baghdad and his hometown of Tikrit.[43] CIA Crisis Operations Liaison Teams were organized for deployment to CENTCOM, specifically tailored to work side-by-side with special operations and conventional forces. Eventually a total of 12 such CIA teams would be supporting military operations in Afghanistan and Iraq.[44]

Another initiative was to induce Iraqi military officers to surrender outright or at least keep their forces out of combat. The third was to find and recruit anyone— soldiers, scientists, or administrators—with knowledge of Saddam's chemical, biological, and nuclear weapons. Inducements included large cash payments and offers to relocate the families of those who assisted the Coalition. The first and second initiatives seemed to hold promise; at least some military officers seemed to seriously consider the possibilities. The third effort had less success.[45]

At Fort Bragg, Joint Special Operations Command (JSOC) was busily reviewing operations in Afghanistan. Rumsfeld was unhappy with the hunt for top Al-Qaeda and Taliban figures. A number of smaller fry had been captured or killed as well as a few important leaders, but the really big fish, bin Laden and Taliban leader Mullah Mohammed Omar, were still not located. "How do we organize the Department of Defense for manhunts?" he asked querulously. "We are obviously not well organized at the present time." The JSOC response was to create Task Force 20, built on experience in Afghanistan and aimed at capturing leading figures in Saddam Hussein's regime. At the Delta Force compound on the other side of Fort Bragg, small teams of commandos poured over maps and models of likely Saddam hideouts and memorized pictures of the dictator as he might appear in various disguises. The Army's elite force was preparing to hunt and, if necessary, kill Saddam, his sons Qusai and Uday, and more than a dozen other top Iraqi military and political leaders.[46]

Later, Delta Force commandos and CIA operatives moved to covert locations in Kuwait, Jordan, Saudi Arabia, and northern Iraq as they prepared to storm Saddam's presidential palaces. "The expectation is to kill him within days" of the start of the war, a senior Pentagon official told reporters. "It's what Delta has been training 24/7 to do." An executive order signed in 1976 by then-President Gerald Ford and still in effect prohibited assassinations of foreign leaders in peacetime. But once the war began, neither U.S. policy nor international law restricted military operations against enemy leaders, particularly if forces are acting in self-defense.[47] If the Delta Force got a clear shot at the Iraqi leader, they were ready to take it. But their activities had been widely reported in the American media, so planners had to assume the Iraqis were fully aware of the preparation, too.

For an allegedly secret undertaking, the hunt received more than its share of publicity. New reports revealed that six U.S. spy satellites passed over Iraq each day to photograph Saddam's suspected hideouts. Two other satellites, along with an RC-135 Rivet Joint surveillance aircraft, were dedicated to intercepting telephone conversations of Iraqi leaders. Supposedly the information was relayed to Delta Force operatives in Iraq who were prepared to call air strikes on the suspected hideouts. Since high-ranking Iraqis had access to western news media, they presumably knew of the surveillance and stopped talking when the satellites were overhead.[48]

It is believed that Delta Force commandos took advantage of darkness to drop by UH-60 helicopters at preselected sites in Iraq before the war began. The plan was that the soldiers would hack into and shut down Iraq's communications and power facilities using laptop computers. "Special forces have now been trained so that they can break into land lines and monitor what's going on inside those systems or feed in false information," said military analyst Anthony Cordesman of the Center for Strategic and International Studies, a think tank in Washington, D.C. The idea was to keep Saddam from communicating with his subordinates, especially anyone who might help him escape or might be ready to trigger biological, chemical, or nuclear weapons.[49]

As revealed by the *Christian Science Monitor,* CIA operators cooperated with the commandos and "reached out to members of Hussein's regime that might become informers."[50]

Using the CIA developed information, the military special operators would call air strikes on specific targets, including Saddam's hideouts. The goal was to minimize civilian casualties, preserve the city's infrastructure, and maintain goodwill with ordinary Iraqis. After the bombing, the commandos were to begin a systematic search of the targets, taking DNA samples to determine whether Saddam—or his three reported doubles died in the attack.

Shock and Awe in Action

Will it rely heavily on shock and awe? Yes.
       —Anthony Cordesman, Center for Strategic and International Studies[51]

Rumsfeld and adherents of revolution in military affairs (RMA) were quick to argue that precision weaponry—especially precision munitions delivered by aircraft—combined with America's array of advanced satellite communications, sensors, and spy drones would increase military capability exponentially. Furthermore, the cumulative power of having all the services fight as an integrated team meant far less manpower was required. "We can do far, far more with far less," said Harlan Ullman. In short, the generals who wanted more troops simply failed (or refused) to recognize the strides made in high-tech warfare since the first Gulf War.[52]

Although not expecting a quick regime collapse, CENTCOM was apparently convinced that relentless pressure on multiple fronts could overwhelm the Iraqi ability to react. A rapid, combined-arms campaign would seize the initiative with "shock and awe." Pressure combined with continual maneuver should not only keep the Iraqis off-balance, but make it much harder for them to use their chemical and biological weapons. Most importantly, an ineffective Iraqi response would compensate for the risks and vulnerabilities in the U.S. plan.[53]

In the days leading up to the invasion, Donald Rumsfeld promised a war that "will not be a repeat of any other conflict. It will be of a force and scope and scale that has been beyond what has been seen before...Iraqi soldiers and officers must ask themselves whether they want to die fighting for a doomed regime or do they want to survive, help the Iraqi people in the liberation of their country and play a role in a new free Iraq."[54] Not everyone was impressed with the concept. They were particularly alarmed when Ullman unwisely used the 1945 atomic bombing of Hiroshima as an example of shock and awe. A growing chorus of antiwar critics called the new strategy a blueprint for killing thousands of civilians in Baghdad and predicted a humanitarian disaster.[55] Ullman replied that speedy surrender would reduce overall casualties and collateral damage.[56]

It is axiomatic that no war goes as planned, but Operation Iraqi Freedom underwent a major change before the war even began. The Turkish parliament was dominated by the Islamist A.K. (Justice and Development) Party, and the upcoming war was deeply unpopular among most Turks. After extended diplomatic maneuvering, Turkey's parliament made it final: no U.S. forces would attack Iraq from Turkish soil. This meant that the "transformed" 4th ID could not attack from the north but instead needed to reposition to Kuwait, a process that would take weeks.

Now the responsibility for the entire northern front fell on the Combined Forces Special Operations Component Commander. His forces already included the special operators assisted by the anti-Saddam units of the Kurdish peshmerga militia, but now, for probably the first time ever, a special operations commander was in tactical control of a conventional U.S. Army brigade—the paratroopers of the 173rd. The hope was that they would be enough to delay the repositioning of Iraqi heavy forces.

Even the revised Operations Plan did not survive the first day of the war. On March 16, President Bush made the final decision to launch the invasion and the following day delivered an ultimatum to Saddam Hussein. He and his sons were given 48 hours to leave Iraq, but, of course, few expected that would actually happen. The special operators were ready to enter Iraq by ground and air. Conventional forces prepared to cross the border from Kuwait. By 3 PM Washington time on the March 19, U.S., Australian, and Polish special operations forces (SOF) were inside Iraq.

But at the same time agents in Iraq were reporting that Saddam Hussein was at the Dora farm complex near Baghdad, a known Hussein facility.[57] This was the decapitation opportunity they had been wishing for. Bush, Rumsfeld, Central Intelligence Agency Director George Tenet, and their advisers weighed the possibilities of civilian casualties against the chance to take out Hussein. Would it compromise the special operators now in Iraq? The President gave the order and two F-117 stealth fighters were launched from Qatar, each carrying a pair of EGBU-27 bombs designed to penetrate underground bunkers. A salvo of Navy cruise missiles was also fired at the farm. Saddam survived the attack, apparently wounded but alive. "We almost got the bastard," said an intelligence source at V Corps headquarters.[58]

Shortly afterward, General Franks learned that Iraqi armor had entered the Rumaila oil fields. "We decided to go...early when we saw three oil fires burning in the Rumaila fields," Franks said. Since the "decapitation strike" had already started the visible part of the war, the ground offensive was pushed up. There would be no preliminary air campaign and the "shock and awe" would be delivered by ground as well as air forces.

The Invasion Begins

The change threw off the timing of everything from ammunition resupply to the air-tasking order that determined what aircraft were to support forward troops. Commanders and soldiers scrambled to make the change, but at 6 AM Iraqi time on Friday, March 21, the 1st Marine Division and the Army's 3rd Infantry Division (Mechanized) rolled across the Kuwait border into Iraq. It was a tribute to the professionalism of the soldiers and Marines and a small sample of their future performance.

The Iraqis performance began with a trickle of surface to surface missiles from Al-Basara, aimed at the Coalition advance and the assembly areas holding the 101st Airborne Division. Several went astray into the ocean or the desert, and the others were destroyed by Coalition antimissile batteries. It was a microcosm of the way the war would go.

The 3rd ID (really a task force) began its advance with five days supply of food, fuel, and ammo and was to cover more than 228 miles in less than 48 hours. The goal was to put tanks and mechanized infantry within a day's march of Baghdad quickly, seize the international airport, and force Saddam to capitulate, all without messy house-to-house fighting in the city. The first serious problem occurred almost immediately when the fast-moving 3rd outran its communications.

All of the advanced digital "transformative" systems (including the supply system but also the All Source Analysis System, Maneuver Control System, Joint Early Warning System, Advanced Field Artillery Tactical Data System, and the Automated Deep Operations Coordination System) relied on the Army's standard Mobile Subscriber Equipment (MSE) in order to communicate. These were all intended as on-the-move systems to support units maneuvering over extended distances in combat. MSE had been improved by packing it on smaller vehicles and by increasing bandwidth. But in order to employ the system, the division's signal battalion had to stop and set up their equipment. As soon as they did, the rapidly advancing units promptly outran the system's 15-mile radius. According to the division's after-action report, the digital systems "struggled" with communications, seriously handicapping the advanced network systems.[59]

One brigade of the 3rd ID reported that whenever the unit moved, everything would fail except the Blue Force tracking system. Every few hours the unit would stop, hoist up its antennas, log back onto the network, and attempt to download whatever it could. But software and bandwidth problems would lock up its computer system for 10 to 12 hours at a time, rendering it useless. Perversely, in three cases, U.S. vehicles were attacked while they stopped to receive intelligence data on enemy positions.[60]

> March 23, 1233—No comms with 3rd ID, would be interesting to see if they have this info [possible large scale counterattack]. The 3rd ID liaison officer in our TOC [tactical operations center] does not have comms.
> —Internal e-mail from 101st Airborne Division intelligence analysis element[61]

Division leaders were also hard pressed to maintain communication with their brigade combat teams advancing toward Baghdad. When possible, information was passed verbally, over FM radio. But at other times vehicles outran even their radio connections. This left just one means of communication: e-mail. By a fortunate circumstance Blue Force Tracker, in addition to position data, also enabled text-only e-mail. The system was intended as a supplement, but it wound up as the primary method of control. At times, it was used for issuing basic orders to units that were otherwise out of contact.[62]

Not least of all, the service and support elements lacked the information they needed to supply the combat forces. Many units spent all 21 days of continuous combat operations without receiving a single repair part. Troops made do by cannibalizing broken-down equipment, towing what they could not repair, and abandoning what they could not tow. Reports concluded that the communications strain was a significant contributor to the logistical difficulties in getting food, fuel, and ammunition resupply to the troops—a task "accomplished with much difficulty."[63] According to the division after-action report, route congestion and extended distances "contributed to confusion, frustration and worry." But "the inability to transmit data while on the move...fed the downward [logistics] spiral and made it nearly impossible to recover."[64]

Troop ingenuity came to the rescue, creating limited on-the-move communications by cobbling together Tactical Satellite, International Maritime Satellite, Force XXI Battle Command Brigade and Below (FBCB2) systems, and the tactical artillery networks. It was not until the division finally halted outside Baghdad that the system was able to catch up. Reporter Joshua Davis traveled with the Army 11th Signal Brigade, the unit responsible for maintaining the network in Iraq. He found an

> unsung corps of geeks improvising as they went, cobbling together a remarkable system from a hodgepodge of military-built networking technology, off-the-shelf gear, miles of Ethernet cable, and commercial software. And during two weeks in the war zone, I never heard anyone mention the revolution in military affairs.[65]

Lieutenant Colonel Norman Mims, the 11th Brigade's intelligence officer, was responsible for placing forward signal units in secure locations. "If it's a question of the network going down, we get helicopters, air support, tanks—whatever we need [to restore it]. Signal has become a lot more complicated in the Internet age. We used to only have to worry about radios. Now it's about providing enough bandwidth to power streaming video and monitor real-time troop and vehicle movement."[66]

Troop ingenuity, however, could not solve the problem of extended and lightly secured supply routes. Supply lines remained a nagging problem, and parts resupply for Bradley fighting vehicles, M1A1 Abrams tanks, and HMMWVs (Humvees) was "a total failure," soldiers said.[67] Logisticians in Kuwait used the military's Secure Internet Protocol Router Internet to relay orders directly to the United States. In addition, the Defense Logistics Agency had learned a trick from private shipping companies, which can track a parcel en route. Each war shipment carried a radio frequency identification tag that told commanders the product's exact location.[68] This was an excellent step, but the other half of the problem was to marry the supplies with the appropriate unit at the appropriate time. When all the pieces are moving at once, this becomes very difficult.

American ground troops drove so fast to Baghdad they sometimes outran even the most basic supplies including bottled water and packaged rations of Meals Ready to Eat.[69] Roads were clogged as convoys fought to bring supplies and support elements up behind the fast-moving combat forces. Fuel was a constant struggle: a single pipeline snaked forward out of Kuwait, and refuelers brought their big tank trucks forward to rendezvous with the convoys and keep the supply trucks rolling. The ground forces needed about 2 million gallons of fuel a day. Supplying it would not have been possible without GPS positioning and Blue Force Tracker to guide them, but some vehicles still ran out of gas and stalled in the desert. The pace was brutal on humans and machines alike. After 30 hours of relentless advance, drivers and commanders were all fighting sleep. Accidents happened and coordination became spotty. After 48 hours the supply routes were marked with overturned cargo haulers, stalled fuel trucks, and broken Humvees. There were not enough soldiers to maintain the rate of advance, and on the third day commanders finally had to allow the exhausted troopers to sleep.[70]

At the same time, soldiers from the 101st and 82nd Airborne Divisions had to be diverted from their intended missions and used to secure the long supply routes against paramilitaries. The rear area attacks from Iraqi irregulars were little more than minor skirmishes, but they were dangerous and hindered operations. Opposing them was a mission that would have been accomplished by military police and armored cavalry units, but these had been left behind. The diversion of the airborne units meant, in turn, that these light forces were not available to secure key infrastructure, including water treatment plants, hospitals, and power plants.[71]

Retired marine Major General Bernard Trainor followed the progress of the war and saw a developing problem.

> ...what is not going well, although the administration won't admit it, is that the Americans aren't being greeted with open arms as they had anticipated. ...The Americans wanted to gain propaganda value out of being greeted going into Basra, with everyone running into the streets and hugging and kissing Americans. They are not even in Basra. Why? Because there's hostile fire coming out of Basra. The same situation exists with Nasiriya. They haven't taken that either. So we have a long supply line through Shi'a territory which was supposed to be so compatible with us. [The Shiites] are not being very cooperative. As a matter of fact, it is just the opposite.[72]

Securing the supply lines would have been a natural mission for the Stryker Brigades, but there was still some hesitation to deploy the first of those, the 3rd Brigade of the 2nd Infantry Division at Fort Lewis. As the centerpiece of Army transformation, a lot hung on the performance of the 3rd Brigade. But after an initial push to have the brigade included in the war plan, there seemed to be a lot less hurry.

Meanwhile, in Qatar and Kuwait, CENTCOM had information problems of their own. If connectivity was bad at the tactical level, it was too good at the command level. They received so much data from some of their airborne sensors that they could not process it all; at some points, they had to stop accepting feeds.[73]

The night of March 26 was cloudy and moonlit, not perfect for a parachute assault but good enough. Within 25 minutes 1,000 troopers of the 173rd were in action on the ground at Bashur in northern Iraq. Ninety-six hours later all of the brigade task force's 400 vehicles and another 1,200 soldiers had been safely delivered. Five M1 Abrams tanks, and two platoons of M113s arrived with them to add a punch to the lightly equipped paratroopers.[74]

The brigade quickly employed its two USMC Dragon Eye UAVs, delivered shortly before the jump. The hand-launched Dragon Eye is a very small UAV, little more than a radio-controlled model airplane with a miniature video camera and transmitter on board. It lacked the sophisticated capabilities of the larger UAVs, but it was easy to use and required little maintenance (one reportedly crashed on landing and was repaired with duct tape). More importantly, it was available and gave the brigade a look-around-the-corner capacity it otherwise lacked.

The next day a communications team from the Army 509th Signal Battalion landed and began to install secure and nonsecure Internet, secure and nonsecure teleconferencing, and telephone service. They were also able to set up a temporary Internet café so soldiers could exchange e-mail with family and friends at home.[75] The Army's Intelligence and Security Command delivered a Trojan satellite downlink terminal (the basic link for "reach-back" intelligence).

Fifty-two of the now familiar Trojan antennas were dotted throughout the theater (only 13 had been deployed for Desert Storm). They reached down to division level and provided 60 percent more bandwidth than in Gulf War I. It was an important improvement that, for the first time, gave field commanders at the division level their own capability to tap national level intelligence resources.[76]

Camp Udairi, 15 miles from the Iraqi border was the centerpiece of the digital networks. It was very different from CENTCOM's forward headquarters at As Sayliyah. It had been built primarily as a staging area for troops going forward, but the camp also held dozens of antennas and satellite dishes belonging to the 11th Signal. The center of the site was a standard Army tent festooned with cables leading to and from the antenna array. When the air conditioning faltered in the baking heat, Private First Class Michael Boone swept the bank of electronics with an ordinary home vacuum cleaner. "This equipment was never meant to be run in this kind of environment." Boone said. "When a dust storm comes through here, the tent is totally useless. We'll have a person vacuuming the switches and servers around the clock, which helps. But none of it's going to matter if it gets hot."[77]

Boone's servers were built to function in climate-controlled rooms. But in the desert, the military pushed them to their limit, demanding every possible bit of bandwidth. When a network runs that fast, it becomes unstable at temperatures past 100 degrees. In computer terms the war was a race against the coming of summer. When daytime highs hit 125, the whole system could crash.

Computer servers were one linchpin in the operation; another was providing tactical information for those computers. UAVs were kept busy in Iraq, although perhaps not in the numbers generally supposed. The Army's A Company, 224th Aviation, was able to launch Hunter UAVs within two hours of a request and operate up to four Hunters simultaneously. For the first time imagery feeds from the UAVs fed directly to a joint analytical control element (JACE) in real time where they could be analyzed for targeting information. Also for the first time, the UAVs and the JACE were able to provide "oven-fresh" imagery, but the problem lay in getting the data to the combat units moving forward.[78]

Not to be outdone in its own medium, the Air Force's Predator flew its first networked operations with four simultaneous orbits over Iraq and one over Afghanistan. Three of those orbits were controlled by remote stations back in the United States. Armed Predators fired Hellfire missiles against Iraqi targets and even flew escort missions with Army helicopters.[79] The improved Tier II+ version of Global Hawk made its operational debut, with 24 hour loiter times at altitudes above 60,000 feet. Global Hawk was virtually undetectable from the ground and provided day/night all weather reconnaissance using electro-optical sensors and synthetic aperture radar.

Hunter, Predator, and Global Hawk were impressive improvements over the UAV's combat debut in Desert Storm, but were still a long way from the goal of total intelligence support down to the foxhole level.[80]

Nevertheless, when the system worked, the results could be spectacular. During a blinding sandstorm that lasted from March 25 to 27, a JSTARS aircraft detected an Iraqi Republican Guard unit maneuvering near U.S. troops. Bombers attacked using satellite-guided bombs unaffected by poor visibility. And the vehicle-tracking system (Blue Force Tracker) ensured that commanders knew the locations of friendly units.[81]

Omar Khalidi, a captain in an Iraqi missile unit, described a Coalition air strike that hit his unit in the midst of the sandstorm. "We were hiding and thought nobody could find us. When the big bombs hit, the vehicles just melted." Most of the Iraqi officers were sure it was done through spies, because, they believed, it was impossible to find the unit through satellite or aircraft. "Even if you drove by it, you couldn't find it," Khalidi said.[82] But clearly, it had been found.

There was a harbinger of things to come at about 10:40 AM on Sunday, March 30, when a civilian taxi stopped close to a U.S. checkpoint north of Najaf and the driver waved for help. When soldiers from the 1st Brigade, 3rd Infantry Division approached, the car exploded, killing the driver and four soldiers. It was the first such attack of the war, and Iraqi government television called it "the blessed beginning." Minutes after the bombing, three other taxis tried to bolt through another, nearby, 3rd Division checkpoint and were riddled by 25mm fire from a Bradley fighting vehicle.[83] It was the debut of the suicide car bomb, VBIED (vehicle borne improvised explosive device) in military jargon, probably the most effective weapon to be used against the Coalition in future months.

By April 1, the war was in its twelfth day and the Division's lightning drive to Baghdad had paused near Najaf to rest, refit, and allow supplies to catch up. Army logistics units hurried forward while Air Force C-130s used stretches of highway to land critical items for soldiers and marines. This caused great alarm in the press, but to an objective observer the war was going amazingly well. The British were encircling Basra, and the U.S. Marines, having won the battle of Nasiriyah, were moving towards Kut on the right flank of the advance. Further back, a brigade of the 82nd Airborne Division secured the rear and seized an air base near Nasiriyah, allowing Coalition aircraft to operate forward. Half the total U.S. inventory of Tomahawk cruise missiles had been fired. There was no refugee crisis and no WMD had been used. On April 2, the 3rd Division resumed its advance and crossed the Euphrates River to attack the Republican Guard.

One Republican Guard division, the elite Medina al Munawara, or Medina the Luminous, was specified as a target for the 3rd ID. Tactically, it was the Iraqi ground force center of gravity, guarding the southern approaches to the Iraqi capital. If the Medina chose to stand and fight, CENTCOM meant to annihilate it. This would speed the conclusion of the war by illustrating the hopelessness of armed resistance. But heavy air strikes and attacks with rocket artillery eviscerated the Medina before the U.S. division could even launch their main assault. An attack across the

Euphrates by a single brigade of the 3rd Infantry was sufficient to defeat the remnants of the much larger Iraqi unit. By twilight on April 2, lead elements of the 3rd ID were ten miles from Baghdad.

"We never really found any cohesive unit of any brigade of any Republican Guard division," said Colonel William F. Grimsley, the commander of the attacking 1st Brigade. What his soldiers encountered, he said, was a mixture of Baath Party fanatics, paramilitary fighters, and bits and pieces of different Republican Guard units.

Coalition air forces took advantage of their air superiority and ranged across the country challenged only by antiaircraft fire. They (chiefly the RAF and USAF) launched between 700 and 1000 sorties on an average day, most against Iraqi ground forces. The Iraqis were unable to move troops and equipment because of devastating air power, combined with the disruption of communications among commanders. Under cover of the air umbrella, the 173rd Airborne Brigade was poised to threaten Baghdad from the north while elements of the 101st Airborne assaulted forward by helicopter on the left of the advance to flank the Medina Division.

By mid-April Coalition Special Forces and U.S. Army Rangers operated freely in the former Scud zone of western Iraq, seizing a third western air base for forward operations. Other special operations units including British and Polish special operators, Delta Force, the Army's 160th SOAR, SEALs and Special Boat Teams from the Navy, USAF Combat Controllers, and Pararescue men carried out operations throughout the combat zone. Every Air Force special operations aircraft in the inventory took part, including AC-130 gunships, big MJ-53J Pave Low helicopters, and the EC-130E Commando Solo, used for psychological operations broadcasting. Lead elements of the 4th Infantry Division were ashore in Kuwaiti ports awaiting the arrival of their heavy equipment. In the United States the 1st Infantry and 1st Cavalry Divisions prepared for deployment.

Once they arrived in Baghdad, the 3rd Mech provided another form of shock and awe. A tank column from the division's 2nd Brigade was sent barreling through Baghdad on what commanders called a "thunder run." The big tanks were fired on by all manner of weapons including a hailstorm of rocket propelled grenades and returned the fire as they rolled into the center of the city. Not a single tank was destroyed and only one was stopped, the crew escaping unharmed. It was a demonstration of U.S. might on the eve of the thrust into the heart of the capital, and it achieved the intended result: shocking Iraqi defenders and weakening their resolve.

> It's somewhat ironic that when we went into southern Iraq, which we thought we would be welcomed much more—much better than we were—the fedayeen and others put up some resistance, and the conventional wisdom that once we got north to Baghdad, and God forbid Tikrit, the elite Republican Guard would dig in and fight to the last man. It just hasn't happened.[84]

After such a resounding defeat, many Iraqis believed that there must have been some kind of deal between the U.S. military and Republican Guard commanders. In fact, the CIA had worked hard to strike just such a deal but with limited success. General Ghanem Abdullah Azawi, Iraqi army air defense command, had a simpler explanation: "The army didn't believe in it," he said, "because it wasn't a war, it was suicide." As senior army commanders saw it, "this war has no result, only death," he said. "Why should we fight to save Saddam? That's why most of the commanders told their soldiers not to fight, just withdraw."[85] That sounded remarkably like shock and awe—not the all encompassing nation-crushing type planned for—but still an important psychological effect on the enemy.

"It was just as if that last battle had no effect," Khalidi said. "Everyone was surprised that a military force could pass through all the Republican Guard and Special Republican Guard forces surrounding the [presidential palaces], and everyone became afraid." With the forays into Baghdad came "unimaginably heavy bombing," including the use of low-flying A-10 Thunderbolt tank killers, Khalidi said.[86]

Even senior Iraqi military leaders failed to grasp the technological gap they were facing. U.S. air power, opposed only by the weak Iraqi air defense, was equally devastating to military equipment and the will to fight. When combined with the heavy armored attacks from the 3rd Mech, they really did create a version of shock and awe, at least on the tactical level. On April 9 the U.S. Army and Marines swept into central Baghdad. The major cities of Mosul, Kirkuk, and Tikrit were still held by the enemy and combat continued for the remainder of the month, but the Hussein government was in collapse. "In the end, when [U.S. troops] entered Baghdad, everything was messed up," Captain Khalidi said. "There were no orders. We didn't know where the commanders went. We didn't know what to do. So everyone just went home."[87]

John Keegan, perhaps the most famous and respected modern military historian, described the battle this way:

> The capture of Baghdad had been in many respects a model of a modern military operation, cunningly planned with every electronic aid, skillfully executed by highly trained troops.[88]

As always, the cost of the victory had been paid by the dead, American, British, and Iraqi. Still the butcher's bill was astonishingly small. Iraqi civilian casualties were far lower than many expected because of the Coalition policy of avoiding urban fights and the careful precision of their bombing. Civilians certainly suffered, but in far lower numbers than might have been expected. The number of Iraqi military casualties was also small since even the Republican Guard managed to avoid most heavy combat. The highest toll was among the fedayeen including Hussein's political militia, die-hard Ba'athists, and foreign fighters come to oppose the "Great Satan." The number of their dead is uncounted, but it must have been in the thousands.[89]

Making sure that the Pentagon would control every aspect of postwar reconstruction and the formation of Iraq's new government, Rumsfeld rejected a team of postwar administrators proposed by the State Department. Decisions on the postconflict government appeared to be entirely in DoD hands, especially those of Paul D. Wolfowitz, the Deputy Secretary of Defense. This was no small annoyance to General Garner, who was nominally in charge in postwar reconstruction.

By then the Army had the equivalent of about five and one-third divisions in Iraq where they would stay for a year. Had all the Iraqis given up and welcomed the Coalition as liberators and saviors, things would have gone well. But they did not, and the country descended into looting and chaos that the available forces were too few to stop.[90]

The 4th ID Goes to War

If the Iraq war was to be the showpiece of transition, the 4th Infantry Division (Mechanized) was slated for the starring role. Accordingly, the 4th ID received a "warning order" early in the planning process to prepare for action. Designated "Task Force Iron Horse," the division and its supporting elements would lead the ground war, punching across the Turkish border with Iraq to open a northern front. At Fort Hood, division commander Major General Raymond T. Odierno and his staff were ready. For eight years, from the commanding general down to the lowliest rifleman, their division had trained and prepared for high-tech warfare.

"The timing's perfect for our division, because we have just come off three National Training Center rotations," said Odierno. "The digital capability that we've been working on and invested in for the last five to eight years has come to fruition and now we're going to deploy this division. We are changing what I call the 'personality of the division' to a war-fighting division."[91]

Back at the Pentagon, the Department of the Army was equally enthused. "That's where the armed forces are going—we're going digitized," said Major Amy Hannah, an Army spokeswoman. "And the 4th Infantry Division is the most prolific of all of them with the high-tech gear it has."[92]

The Army's most advanced systems were to make their battlefield debut with the 4th ID. The division was the best-equipped unit in the Army, complete with advanced M1-A2 battle tanks and Bradley fighting vehicles and the Shadow 200 RQ-7A, the Army's first standardized tactical UAV (the Hunter was considered experimental). The division also boasted the AH-64D Longbow Apache equipped with "fire-and-forget" Hellfire antitank missiles and digital communications. It would be the Army's combat laboratory, ready to prove digitization and transformation on the battlefield and demonstrate the relevance of heavy conventional forces. The division would go into action with the full digital capability of the FBCB2 system and its painfully developed Tactical Internet mated with the Ground and Airborne Radio System and Enhanced Position Location Reporting System line-of-sight radios.

Their deployment orders came down on January 20. Task Force Iron Horse, comprising 16,000 soldiers from the 4th Infantry and 24,000 supporting troops from ten bases, was to deploy to the Persian Gulf.[93] Eight years of testing and training were about to bear fruit.

The 4th ID's task had been to invade Iraq from the north, launching from Turkey. But Turkey, a Muslim state, was not eager to be seen as taking part in an attack against a fellow Muslim government. Meanwhile 30 ships laden with the division's

14,000 pieces of equipment slowly steamed in circles off the Turkish coast while the troops languished in the United States. After weeks of discussion, the Turks finally refused permission, and the ships carrying the 4th ID's high-tech equipment headed for Shuaiba Port in Kuwait.

The first vessel arrived April 12, two months later than planned, more than three weeks into the war. The port at Shuaiba could handle only five ships at a time, and each ship took two or three days to unload. Then the high-tech gear had to be unpacked, reassembled, and tested before being certified combat-ready. That took another week, with backlogs, shortages, and electrical failures to overcome.[94] Part of the problem was that many of the 4th ID's digital systems had not been officially fielded, meaning they had not undergone operational trials, yet the division was going to war with them.

"If this division had been available from day one of the war, it would have been a good test case," said Patrick Garrett, a senior fellow with GlobalSecurity.org, a military research organization. "Now there's still sort of a question mark as to what the 4th ID is going to be able to do."[95]

The 4th ID finally saw combat on April 16, fighting Iraqi paramilitaries and armed men in civilian clothes near an airfield north of the capital. "Mostly we're just destroying their equipment as we secure the airfield," said Colonel Don Campbell, commander of the 4th Infantry's 1st Brigade.[96] Later in the war the 4th ID would see its share of combat, but for now the division Rumsfeld had described as "America's hammer" found itself relegated to cleanup operations.

The Special Operations War

Special operations forces were tightly incorporated into the U.S. Central Command's planning from day one. More special operations commandos and air crews were assigned to more missions and integrated more thoroughly into conventional military operations than in any other war in American history. All told, more than 9,000 special operations personnel were involved in the conflict. "This was the largest and most comprehensive integration of Special Operations and conventional forces that I've ever seen," said Colonel Randy O'Boyle, commander of the Joint Special Operations Aviation Detachment for southern Iraq.[97]

Navy Seals and Army Special Forces spent days living in ditches and holes deep in enemy territory, watching critical routes near the Karbala Gap. The missions were dangerous, became tedious, and lacked any trace of glamour, but they provided valuable intelligence to the Marines and the Army 3rd Infantry Division, as they rumbled north toward Baghdad.

Placing the 173rd Airborne Brigade under the command of JSOTF-North (Joint Special Operations Task Force) was a first, but not without its problems. From the CENTCOM point of view it enabled the SOF to seize and hold contested ground, something SOF teams were inherently unable to do. Using these assets, JSOTF-North was able to seize and hold Kirkuk and the nearby oil fields, a major goal of the northern campaign.

Integrating the SOF and conventional operations was troublesome because the two types of force did not view the battlefield from the same perspective. Further, SOF normally supported a conventional effort. Reversing this relationship put a strain on command and control relationships. Army doctrine did not address the problem in any useful way, and the units had not trained together. As a result, the infantry and SOF elements "did not readily accept each other's intelligence and operational assessments" and did not always understand each other's operational activities. As usual, it was up to the soldiers on the ground to work through these "friction points."[98]

For special operations commanders who wanted to prove that their small units could play a significant role in a large-scale conventional campaign, the war was an experiment that largely succeeded. They ignored the fact that Debecka Pass was a thoroughly conventional mission and not a special operation at all. They also ignored the more important fact that this reduced the special operators to the role of elite conventional infantry, a role already filled by the regular Army and the USMC. The special operators did receive a backhanded sort of compliment in 2005 when the Army began to field five-ton armored "gun trucks" very similar to those jury-rigged by the Special Forces for operations in Western Iraq. Credit for the idea was given to "operations in Vietnam."[99]

The 2003 conflict with Iraq serves as a graphic example of both the strength and the shortsightedness of transformation as an organizing principle. To a large degree, U.S. and British operations against Iraq showed what could be done with a relatively small military force enabled with new technology. But the aftermath also showed the serious shortcomings of that force.

CHAPTER 8

AFTERMATH

The Tyrant has fallen...the United States and our allies have prevailed.
—U.S. President George W. Bush, May 1, 2003[1]

The U.S. military had fallen in love with an idea—transformation. Now it seemed that that love was requited. On May 1, 43 days after the start of the war, U.S. President and former fighter pilot George W. Bush landed on the deck of the aircraft carrier *USS Abraham Lincoln.* Speaking in front of a banner that read "mission accomplished," the President said, "Major combat operations in Iraq have ended." The war, he went on, had been carried out "with a combination of precision and speed and boldness the enemy did not expect, and the world had not seen before."[2]

Secretary Donald Rumsfeld could hardly wait to castigate the pundits and armchair generals who had been so critical of his approach to the war. "Never have so many been so wrong about so much."[3]

Shock and awe were not exactly implemented and the air campaign was severely truncated, but it was without doubt a rapid and decisive operation. In exactly three weeks, the enemy capital had been taken and the regime overthrown—less than half the time of the 1991 Gulf War, with fewer than one-third of the strikes and with one-tenth the number of bombs. It seemed to realize the Office of the Secretary of Defense (OSD) vision of smaller, agile forces empowered by new technology and supported by precision firepower, from the air. Coalition military aircraft flew 15,825 strike sorties and dropped 27,250 weapons. Coalition ground forces fired tens of thousands of artillery and mortar projectiles, rockets, and tank-gun rounds. Firepower, it was argued, had replaced manpower. This, of course, ignored the fact that the forces finally used were at least as close to Frank's original plan as they were to Rumsfeld's.

A few old soldiers and one or two analysts brought up Vietnam, the last time America had tried to substitute firepower for boots on the ground. The results had been less than desirable and turned many local civilians against the Americans. These critics were told that Iraq is not Vietnam and attempts to equate the two in any way were not only irrelevant and outdated but smacked of defeatism.

Losses among the Coalition forces and Iraqi civilians had been remarkably low by any standard. Only 402 Coalition deaths were reported, including 351 U.S. troops and 51 British soldiers, Marines, and airmen. The Associated Press reported that at least 3,240 Iraqi civilians were killed, based on records from Iraqi hospitals.[4]

Nevertheless, amidst the general exultation, officers at U.S. Central Command (CENTCOM) noted some puzzling things about the victory. First of all was the failure to find weapons of mass destruction (WMD). Perhaps the WMD had been hidden, perhaps smuggled out of the country, or perhaps did not exist at all. No matter which it was an intelligence failure of the first order.

Then there was the anticipated popular uprising that failed to materialize, even among Hussein's long-time victims in the heavily Shiite south. Richard Perle's promised "Iraqis eager to liberate their country" also failed to turn out and join the Americans. The regime had not quickly collapsed under punishing air strikes, and there were no mass surrenders on the model of 1991. However, mass demonstrations and marches did occur among the Shiite civilian population. Along with celebrating their liberation, the Shiites immediately began calling for a Muslim state and demanding U.S. troops go home. Among the minority Sunni things were going bad very quickly. By May 1, there had been three days of deadly violence in the city of Fallujah, evidence of an orchestrated effort against American forces led by radical clerics and former regime officials. But perhaps that was an aberration. This was not how the war was supposed to go. Although the WMD failure got most of the attention, the absolute misreading of the Iraqi civilian response to the invasion was a far worse failure of intelligence.

There had been no large-scale, organized military resistance, and few prisoners were taken. Prewar planners had expected anywhere from 16,000 to over 50,000 enemy prisoners, but the actual result was far lower. According to the 1st Marine Division after-action report, many Iraqi units tried to surrender when approached by British and U.S. main force units. However, since the speed of the advance precluded handling large numbers of enemy prisoners, they were often simply ignored. Equally often, the Iraqi Army seemed to just melt away. By the time 3rd Division tanks crossed the Euphrates River on April 2, much of the Iraqi regular army had ceased to exist. Instead of surrendering, Iraqi soldiers simply took off their uniforms and went home. The vast majority left without any personal experience of combat; they were dispersed, but not defeated.[5]

The tenacity and ferocity of the Iraqi paramilitaries were important and unwelcome surprises as was the continuing inability to locate and track enemy forces, especially the paramilitaries. In part, because of this lack of information, the Iraqis had forced the Army and Marines to fight in cities they had planned to bypass or take in stride. Would the Iraqi irregulars learn from this and continue to seek combat in the cities?[6]

And what about the assorted munitions Hussein had purchased and scattered in hundreds of large and small depots across central Iraq? Large amounts were known to exist but not the thousands of tons that were found. Moving it all to safe locations and destroying it would be a monumental task. Who would do that, or, for that matter, who would guard these huge ammo dumps? In the end most of them went unguarded and tons of munitions disappeared into hands violently opposed to the American presence.

Another surprise was the refusal of many Iraqi civilians to act as if there was a war going on. Repeatedly, civilian cars and vans, including whole families, would drive into firefights and speed through roadblocks, oblivious of the danger. U.S. and British soldiers had to make split-second decisions with no way to tell the difference between a car full of innocent civilians and one full of armed fedayeen or a suicide bomber.[7]

Then there was the civilian looting. A certain amount of disorder was expected, but what actually happened was unprecedented. Baghdad fell on April 9, symbolized by the destruction of a huge statue of Saddam Hussein in Fridos (Paradise) Square. Much of the city's population celebrated their liberation with a rampage of looting duplicated across Iraq's major cities.

The destruction caught the relatively small number of U.S. and British troops completely unprepared. Except for guarding a few vital sites (e.g., the Oil Ministry), they could only stand by and watch the spectacle of a country destroying its own infrastructure. Kanan Makiya, an Iraqi exile and Bush administration adviser termed the situation "very messy and complicated." The most pressing need, he believed, was a U.S.-trained Iraqi security force that could carry the administration's message of a new democratic state. This force, Makiya said, should have been ready as soon as Baghdad fell. Instead, local clerics took leadership, organizing people to direct traffic, pick up garbage, and arm themselves to deter looters. The mosques often filled the security and services needs of ordinary Iraqis, accruing political clout as they did so.[8]

When questioned at a press conference on April 11, Donald Rumsfeld dismissed the pillage, saying, "stuff happens." He blamed the wreckage on "pent up feelings" and criticized the media for exaggerating the extent of the damage. "The images you are seeing on television, you are seeing over and over and over," he complained. "It's the same picture of some person walking out of some building with a vase and you see it twenty times. And you think, my goodness, were there that many vases?"[9]

Unfortunately the theft was not limited to a vase or two, or even several. Iraqis began with government ministries, stealing everything while scattering and destroying the files and records needed to restore a functioning government. Unsatisfied, the looters turned to hospitals and schools, carrying off everything that was portable while hospital staff armed themselves to protect their dwindling medical supplies. Even the rickety electrical, water, and communications infrastructure fell apart when the thieves began to systematically strip telephone networks and electrical systems. As described by Jay Garner, "not only did they take everything out of the buildings, but then they pulled all the wiring out of the buildings, they pulled all of the plumbing out of the buildings, and they set it on fire."[10]

When it was believed (wrongly) that thieves had emptied the Iraqi National Museum of its treasure trove of antiquities, the story led to what John Keegan characterized as "wild denunciation of the invasion in the Western press."[11] These claims further hurt the legitimacy of the occupation, but there was no effective information plan to counter them.

The chaos went on for weeks and then gradually subsided as opportunities for booty vanished. But the damage had been done. Seventeen of Iraq's 23 government ministries were burned and looted out of existence. The Coalition's intention had been to quickly restore a minimally damaged government and a largely intact infrastructure. That possibility disappeared with the pillage. The lack of clean water and electrical supplies became constant irritants making reconstruction more difficult and bringing the ire of ordinary Iraqis down on the Coalition.

If Gulf War II was an illustration of Rapid Decisive Operations, it showed the critical weakness of such methods. As conceived, Rapid Decisive Operation doctrine should require less stabilization and reconstruction since it at least hopes to avoid the destruction of most basic infrastructure. But the near-simultaneous collapse of the regime and its security forces also means an abrupt halt to internal security functions, emergency services, public services of all kinds, transportation, and much infrastructure (e.g., electricity). The result is a power vacuum.[12]

Both Rapid Decisive Operations (RDO) and Effects Based Operations (EBO) looked to international military and civil support to shoulder most of the burden of postwar reconstruction and stabilization. The authors of the doctrine had never considered what might happen if the United States undertook a war without significant international approval. U.S. war planners expected 150,000 additional troops from supporting nations to aid the U.S.-led operation, General Tommy Franks said in a postwar interview. Lacking UN, NATO, or any other international sanction, most of the supposed donors felt no moral or legal compulsion to assist. There was little help, and it was slow to arrive.[13]

Finally, RDO and EBO had produced military dominance without actually defeating the enemy. Much of the Iraqi military and paramilitary establishment was untouched. If it could be turned to reconstruction and internal security functions, that would be fine. But the danger was that it could also become a source of armed resistance. Outside elements and anti-Coalition forces were quick to take advantage of the general collapse of government and order. In the absence of border controls, the Al-Qaeda network became active, bringing foreign jihadists into the country. Iran moved quickly to take advantage of the power vacuum in southern Iraq. The Tehran-backed Supreme Council for the Islamic Revolution in Iraq flooded the Basara area with religious agitators, fanning the flames of anti-Americanism. Covert assistance flowed from Syria and Iran while Hezbollah, the Lebanon-based, terrorist group, declared U.S. "occupation forces in Iraq" to be fair game. For many, perhaps most, Iraqis, the United States was a foreign invader. No matter how much they hated Hussein's government, growing numbers of Iraqis were willing to fight what was increasingly perceived as a foreign occupation.

Prompt control of the postwar public information flow might have made an important difference, but the strategic planners apparently gave little thought to postconflict information operations. In the absence of local Iraqi media, people needed information and, especially, reassurance after the turmoil of war and the trauma of occupation. This was an opportunity for psyops to make a great difference, but it was largely missed and the little that did occur was often ad hoc. As a result, the information vacuum was filled by anti-Coalition or at least strongly pro-Arab media including the influential satellite news station *Al-Jazeera*.

The United States responded by hurriedly contracting with companies to broadcast almost anything to fill the void and offer an alternative to the virulent anti-American and anti-British messages in the Arab media.[14] It would not be until February 2004 that the U.S.-sponsored Alhurra satellite television station began broadcasting Arabic language news and information programming. By then it was too little and too late.

In his Senate confirmation hearing, the candidate for Army chief of staff, General Peter Schoomaker, remarked that he might need more soldiers on active duty. "Intuitively, I think we need more people," he said, cautiously allowing that he was going to "take a little risk" in stating the obvious. "I mean, it's just that simple." Rumsfeld reacted immediately, replying that "...the analysis that's been done [on troop strength] indicates that we're fine." The persistent, stubborn refusal to raise troop levels became a major feature of reconstruction policy in Iraq.

Continued widespread violence and devastation were accompanied by protracted delays in restoring electricity, water, and medical care. In southern Iraq, an area dominated by the Shiites, the country's largest ethnic group, mass demonstrations and marches continued to call for a Muslim state and the immediate removal of American troops.

"Victory is at risk," said Senator Richard Lugar (R-IN). Senator Christopher Dodd (D-CT) was more direct: "To be quite honest, it is very hard to fathom what the administration's strategy is with respect to the immediate stabilization of the situation, let alone the longer term reconstruction in Iraq."[15]

But according to Major General Buford Blount, commander of the 3rd Infantry Division in Baghdad, "about 90 percent" of the security problem "is common criminals—the looters, the car thefts, attempted bank robberies, et cetera—and only about 10 percent...is a holdover from the previous regime."[16] The general seemed unaware of the growing insurgency and his estimate would prove overly optimistic, but that was not clear yet.

The CIA briefed in June 2003 that a "classic insurgency" was underway in Iraq, a conclusion that was denied by Rumsfeld—"I don't use the phrase 'guerrilla war' because there isn't one"—until he was corrected by his field commanders that, yes, they were in the midst of a guerrilla insurgency. Nevertheless, the Iraq War was still treated as an unqualified triumph for Rumsfeld and his idea of transformation.[17]

The war had shown that the United States and Britain could sweep aside even a very large but third-rate enemy. Now was the opportunity to show that military might could transform Iraq into a friendly, democratic regime, a proving grounds for change in the Middle East. But very little in U.S. military training, organization, or doctrine even addressed the issue. This was the dreaded nation building, the very thing Bush and Rumsfeld swore to avoid.

Before long, the Bush administration looked seriously worried. The orgy of looting was replaced by increasingly serious armed attacks against Coalition forces. The particular targets were the American units located in the so-called "Sunni triangle" of cities around Baghdad in central Iraq. Now there seemed a real danger that civil order might collapse, making reconstruction impossible. General Garner's plan, coordinated with the British in Southern Iraq, had been to use parts of the Iraqi regular army as an internal security and reconstruction force. Around 15 battalions of Iraqi troops, 100,000 soldiers, were to go to work on behalf of the Coalition rebuilding and providing security, especially in the Sunni areas. In Garner's words, "we were going to hire them and make them, for lack of a better word, reconstruction battalions and use them to help rebuild the country."[18] But before any of this could be implemented, Garner was hastily replaced with former ambassador L. Paul Bremer III. General Garner later contended "the plan was for me to put a team together, take it over there, and hand it off to a presidential appointee, which was exactly what happened."[19]

Perhaps, but under the circumstances it looked as if Garner had been shown the door as a damage control move by a badly worried administration. In any case, Ambassador Bremer came in on May 10, and Garner's careful prewar planning was immediately scrapped in favor of a "new plan from the interagency."[20]

Bremer proceeded at once to order that the Iraqi Army be disbanded in order to remove a center of opposition influence. The first result was to remove any possibility that it could be used for reconstruction and internal security. The second was the creation of a huge pool of discontented young men, former soldiers, resentful, undefeated, and now without employment. It also meant that thousands of Iraqi families lacked any means of support. As a recruiting device for resistance fighters, it was first rate.

This would have been less serious if enough Coalition manpower had been on hand to take over security functions, at least in the major cities. But the relatively small force that had been so successful at war was proving far short of that needed to cope with the uneasy peace. Furthermore, the robust international assistance force that had been hoped for stubbornly failed to materialize. Well, then, perhaps an all-Iraqi security force was the answer. New soldiers and police could be trained for the interim government and used to stabilize the country. How hard could it be?

The War in Washington

After a series of well-publicized disagreements with Army Secretary Thomas White and outgoing Army Chief of Staff General Eric Shinseki, Rumsfeld seemed to have lost patience with the Army. He made his displeasure plain on May 1 by finally firing White and attempting to replace him with the Secretary of the Air Force, James G. Roche. Another disciple of Andrew Marshal, Roche was an air power advocate, an articulate supporter of transformation, and a trusted Rumsfeld man who could "fix" the problems in the Army.[21] The selection was received with amazement and alarm in the Army, but the choice of Roche underscored Rumsfeld's determination to steamroller Army resistance and the secretary was in no mood for subtlety.[22] Neither was Congress where White had been well regarded by the armed services committees in both houses. The Senate was in no mood for an early confirmation of Roche so an interim appointee, Les Brownlee, formerly a deputy to White, was named acting secretary.

The decision to replace White as Army secretary reportedly stemmed from disagreements with the White House and OSD over its vision of a faster, lighter military. White did not necessarily agree that the old must be sacrificed to bring in the new. When Rumsfeld wanted to cancel the Crusader artillery system, preferring precision to firepower, rumors flew that White was working behind-the-scenes to support those trying to save the program. Also, White conspicuously failed to correct General Shinseki when the general told Congress that a large number of soldiers would be needed to stabilize Iraq. This did not endear him to Rumsfeld, who called the figure an exaggeration.

Shortly after taking office, the new acting secretary of the Army asked a Defense Department–funded think tank, the Institute of Defense Analyses (IDA) for a new study on transformation. The budget vise—and the attempt to produce arms to face a world of uncertain threats—originally sparked the drive for transformation. But an $11 billion increase for defense in 2002 and another $48 billion increase in 2003 allowed hard decisions to be put off. Now the Future Combat System (FCS) was on the block again. The new study, the second in two years, was taken as evidence of unhappiness with the FCS approach to transformation.[23]

The effort to confirm Roche and other moves seemed calculated to emphasize the Rumsfeld vision of lighter forces that fight "jointly," reinforcing each others' combat efforts. The Secretary was said to be impressed by Roche's push to move the Air Force in more of a joint direction and make it support air-to-ground tactical operations (long anathema to air-minded strategists).[24] Roche and Rumsfeld had known each other for years and reportedly shared a close relationship. Within the OSD it was believed that White and Shinseki failed to make a coherent case for their programs and policies. But as far as Army leaders were concerned White and Shinseki were champions of land power who stood up to Rumsfeld, who did not understand transformation and declared war on the Army in order to finance his vision.

"Rumsfeld doesn't hate the Army," a Pentagon official said. "He is frustrated [and] sees in the Army as impervious to change."[25] Many in the Army objected that the service had invested as much effort, money, and brainpower as any other in transforming itself. But, as a ground-based force, it faced different problems from the other services.

The Army leadership saw themselves as the fathers of transformation—but defense officials under Rumsfeld regarded them as reluctant practitioners. White and Shinseki balked at Rumsfeld's vision of air-centric transformation and, worse, actively opposed parts of it (e.g., cancellation of the Crusader) that they saw as wrongheaded or even hostile towards the Army. Rumsfeld's unwavering demand for innovative, small-footprint wars in Afghanistan and Iraq was seen as dangerous.[26]

On the other hand, Roche and Air Force Chief of Staff General John Jumper were stalwart advocates of the Rumsfeld vision, especially an increased role for air support. He and Jumper pushed Air Force generals to be innovative with UAVs, to retire B-1 bombers to improve mission-ready rates, to keep A-10 attack planes, and to lease tanker aircraft. They revamped educational and command curricula, sacked senior officers who failed to perform, and cut billions of dollars in future spending.[27]

Rumsfeld's staff wanted the Air Force to buy more B-2 stealth bombers and reduce its F-22 purchase to 180 jets. Roche countered that the Air Force did not need more slow, pricey B-2s, but did need the F-22. In order to prove his point, he dramatically accelerated changes, repackaged the plane as the F/A-22 (A for attack). No longer billed chiefly as an air superiority fighter, it was presented as a "transitional" ground attack platform for delivery of smart ordnance.

Rumsfeld continued to leverage his newly enhanced stature to press for change. "He's flying high, and he's going to put his own stamp on" Army leadership, Bernard Trainor, a retired Marine Corps three-star general, said. "Rumsfeld will have his way, and the people who are selected [for top Army posts] will be people who will comport with his thinking."[28]

Despite events in Iraq the belief that the Army was over strength and ought to be "transformed" into a smaller, lighter, more agile force was still alive and well in the OSD. The possibility of reducing the Army from ten divisions to eight was also raised again but received little support outside the secretary's office. Reductions were hard to justify in view of current events. First of all, significant forces, perhaps a division's worth, were still tied down in the mountains of Afghanistan. Second, of course, was Iraq, the big problem. Garner's original notion that the Iraqi Army should be preserved as an internal security force had been overturned; the new Iraqi police were incapable and often ran from a fight when they did not actively assist the insurgents. The other short-term solution was to solicit troop contributions from partners and allies. This course provided an added benefit by "internationalizing" the conflict and showing that Britain and America did not stand alone. These appeals had been going on for some time with little worthwhile result. The Coalition contained 32 "contributing" nations, but except for Britain and the United States most contributed no more than a handful of soldiers, and the Pentagon had to resort to extended tours of duty for regular soldiers and reservists. "There are challenges greater than we anticipated," said a White House official, insisting "In time; the benefits of our actions will be quite obvious."[29]

And despite five months of searching, a 1,200-strong military and CIA team led by CIA weapons expert David Kay still had not found the predicted stockpiles of chemical, biological, or nuclear weapons.[30] This should have been a warning sign on the road to transformation—if the best national resources, including an on-the-ground team of searchers and experts, could not find the elusive WMD, what did that say about the ability to produce actionable intelligence? If everyone believed the WMD were there when they really were not, was that any better?

Intelligence, reliable analysis of near-real-time information, was a foundation stone of the entire transformation concept. But the intelligence problem was not anywhere as near to solution as transformation advocates claimed.

By late summer 2003, approximately 130,000 U.S. ground forces were tied down in what appeared to be a protracted occupation. In the Sunni Arab regions of the country a full-fledged insurgency was underway. In the midst of all the turmoil, on August 1, 2003, General Peter J. Schoomaker became the 35th Chief of Staff, United States Army. The same month Secretary Rumsfeld announced that he foresaw no need to increase troop strength in Iraq.[31]

In mid-August the President began to revise his public views on events in Iraq. In an interview with Armed Forces Radio on August 18, President Bush explained that "combat" operations were still going on, attempting to make a distinction between "major" combat operations and the continuing conflict in Iraq, which he described as a "different kind of combat." In the same interview he made the same distinction with regard to the war in Afghanistan. "We've got about 10,000 troops there." This number, he said, was "down from, obviously, major combat operations." In fact, as pointed out by the *Washington Post* (among others), the 10,000 American soldiers in Afghanistan was the highest total number of U.S. troops in the country since the war began. When the remnants of the Taliban government fled in December 2001, there were no more than 3,000 U.S. soldiers and Marines in Afghanistan. That number rose to 5,000 during the last major battles against Al-Qaeda and the Taliban in March 2002. When the President spoke, a multinational International Security Assistance Force, led by Germany, had about 4,600 soldiers securing the capital, Kabul. But the United States alone was carrying out significant military operations in the remainder of the country.[32]

A similar situation was developing in Iraq where Poland had agreed to provide about 2,400 soldiers, the Ukraine 1,640, and Spain about 1,300. After a terrorist attack on the eve of the Spanish national election, Spain hurriedly withdrew its forces. Eleven other countries including Japan, Hungry, Romania, Latvia, Estonia, El Salvador, Honduras, Mongolia, and the Philippines agreed to send token contingents. It was enough to cobble up an understrength multinational "division." However, if the object was to have as many flags represented as possible, it did succeed in that, even though the burden of combat remained heavily on the United States and Great Britain.[33]

Political Maneuvers

In turn the U.S. Congress and others began to question Department of Defense (DoD) assurances that the current U.S. troop level was sufficient. Rumsfeld acknowledged, "There are some recommending that more US forces go in," and added that the troop level needs to be reviewed "fairly continuously." But he stressed that CEN-TCOM commander, General John Abizaid, had not asked for more soldiers.[34] "If we got the recommendation from the combatant commander that he thinks he needs more forces, he'll have them," Rumsfeld said. "If more troops are needed in Iraq," the secretary said, "then the effort should be on developing additional Iraqi capabilities rather than additional (US and coalition) capabilities beyond those that have been committed."[35]

On September 4, the White House informed Congress that President Bush would seek a $60 to 70 billion budget increase to cover the cost of occupation and reconstruction in Iraq. This followed a $79 billion budget supplement passed in April to support the fighting in Afghanistan and Iraq. The new request was almost double earlier estimates and was taken as proof that the administration had badly underestimated the difficulties in postwar Iraq.[36]

From May 1 through September Saddam loyalists, foreign fighters, and anti-Coalition militia had killed more than 60 Coalition soldiers, mostly with roadside bombs and rocket-propelled grenades. That month the *Washington Times* printed excerpts from a secret report prepared for the Joint Chiefs of Staff that laid the blame for setbacks in Iraq on "a flawed and rushed war-planning process that 'limited the focus' for preparing for post-Saddam Hussein operations." Senior U.S. officials, including Deputy Defense Secretary Paul Wolfowitz finally conceded that an unanticipated guerrilla war was underway in Iraq. The Pentagon was forced to scrap its original plan for rebuilding as violence increased and basic services were slow to resume.[37]

In a masterpiece of understatement the report concluded that (contrary to EBO doctrine) the interagency process, such as between the Pentagon and State Department, "was not fully integrated prior to hostilities." Before the war, "Phase IV objectives were identified but the scope of the effort required to continually refine operational plans for defeat of Iraqi military limited the focus on Phase IV." In other words, the demands of planning for the transformational war overwhelmed planning for the postwar period. This was hardly surprising since the emphasis of transformation is entirely conventional warfighting; nothing in the concept really addresses issues such as postwar occupation.[38]

At the same time, Congress began to receive an increasing series of complaints blaming the climbing casualty rate on the low force levels, the shortage of body armor, and the lack of armored vehicles, especially up-armored HMMWVs. In the military procurement system armor for soldiers and HMMWVs were "non-priority" items, like tents. In response to questions about the lack, acting Secretary of the Army Les Brownlee simply stated that the attacks in Iraq "differed from our expectations."[39] They certainly did, and that was the point.

In November it was announced that U.S. troop strength in Iraq would drop to about 100,000 by May 2004 as new units rotated in. The reduction would be accommodated by an increase in the size of Iraqi security forces from about 115,000 to some 171,000. By the end of 2003, 19 of the Army's 33 combat brigades were committed around the world. For months it had been obvious that the U.S.

armed forces were stretched to the breaking point by the stress of fighting two wars simultaneously. When May rolled around without the promised decrease in Americans or increase in Iraqis, Congress began to call for a big increase in the size of the active-duty military for the first time in 16 years.[40]

This might be welcome among the overstretched soldiers, but from the OSD perspective it was disastrous. Larger forces would cost money, and at least part of that money would inevitably come from transformation programs. Rumsfeld insisted that Pentagon analysis did not justify any expansion in the force. And, he argued, it would be the most expensive solution and prevent the Pentagon from spending much-needed money to transform the rest of the military. The United States was spending roughly 3.5 percent of the gross national product (GNP) on defense, or about $400 billion. It seemed like a lot of money and it was, but it was still less than half the percentage of GNP spent on defense 40 years before.

The OSD continued to heavily promote the idea that battlefield successes in Afghanistan and Iraq had validated the secretary's ideas on transformation for twenty-first century warfare. These conflicts allegedly demonstrated the overwhelming value and necessity of transformation. But during the early summer of 2004, the U.S. Army quietly began to move more Abrams tanks to Iraq. Transformation looked good on briefing slides, but armor was still welcome on the ground. Few things demonstrated capability and resolve like 70 tons of tank rumbling down a city street.

By June 15, 2004—two weeks before the United States was scheduled to hand off authority to a provisional Iraqi government—the internal situation continued to worsen within the disputed areas. Six government ministers were attacked in the first half of June. Then insurgents shot and killed the deputy foreign minister on June 12 and the deputy education minister on June 13. Also on June 12, five U.S. soldiers, two Coalition soldiers, and two Iraqi policemen were injured in separate bomb attacks. Three hostages taken the previous week were found dead. The White House warned that even this level of violence might increase as the transition of sovereignty approached.[41]

In Turkey, President Bush met with NATO leaders hoping for pledges of assistance. The only cause for optimism was a Dutch promise to keep their 1,400 soldiers in Iraq and South Korean's confirmation of their pledge to provide an additional 3,000 troops.[42]

Remarkably enough, the military leadership and the defense industry apparently drew one primary lesson from the Iraq experience—they needed more of the new technology. From this judgment they produced a grand new wish list of military hardware based on the war's supposed "lessons." Despite the escalating insurgency, they remained resolutely fixed on the conventional warfighting phase of the operation. Iraq was an inept opponent, they argued. Future wars will demand lighter vehicles, smarter weapons, stealthier fighters, longer-range missiles, better satellites, and more communications bandwidth. The idea that it might require more soldiers was not mentioned.[43]

A Special Operations Renewal

Because of its success in northern Iraq and in clandestine missions, the U.S. Special Operations Command emerged as a major beneficiary of the second Iraq war. After being relegated to a thoroughly secondary role in the first Gulf War, special operations forces ended the second one as an important player. Earlier that year, in January, Secretary Rumsfeld had announced a new plan for U.S. Special Operations Command (USSOCOM). From now on the Special Operations Command elements formerly under each regional commander would have their own authority under USSOCOM to conduct clandestine (and perhaps covert) counterterrorist actions. Special operations forces could now act immediately to locate and capture or kill terrorists.[44]

According to Arthur K. Cebrowski, the Pentagon's director of the Office of Force Transformation, "The broad strategic thrust of the nation is to move from being reactive to being preventative. You have to be engaged around the world. The general rule is that small forces with a depth of local knowledge have more power than very large formations that come from [elsewhere]. Certain characteristics of our Special Operations forces are enormously valuable, and we would like to see them spread more into some of the other forces," he said, adding that the characteristics include ease of insertion, depth of local knowledge, and small-unit agility. "That's been a strength of special operations forces. The summary answer to what the US needs is more Special Operations Forces (SOF)-like forces, a higher ISR [intelligence, surveillance and reconnaissance] fraction and more focus on the weapons of mass destruction problem."[45]

The problem, of course, is that SOF qualities are not entirely the product of agility, tactics, or equipment; they are accompanied by maturity, experience, and training that are probably impossible to duplicate in a force much larger than the current strength of U.S. SOF. The U.S. Army's Special Operations Command found it impossible to meet even relatively modest prewar strength goals without lowering its traditional requirement for experience and recruiting directly from the civilian population.

In the wake of Special Operations' well-publicized successes, Defense Secretary Rumsfeld strongly endorsed SOF as the global force of the future. Encouraged by the secretary's enthusiasm, USSOCOM sought and received $6.7 billion for 2004, a 47 percent increase over its 2003 budget, by far the largest increase in its history. Of that, $2.2 billion would be spent to increase the number of commandos and elite troops to 49,000 active and reserve members by the end of 2004, an increase of about 10,000. The House Armed Services Committee responded by declaring that SOCOM "is clearly a treasured national asset in the war on terrorism and our best asset in disrupting the enemy in foreign lands." Together with the Senate, they doubled SOCOM's authorized 2004 spending on new equipment for the growing force.[46]

Nor should it be supposed that the special operators were immune to the siren call of new-tech. Among the costliest items on SOCOM's 2004 shopping list were

$675 million to upgrade long-range helicopters, $390 million to modify four AC-130U gunships, $214 million for other C-130 modifications, and $109 million to buy Special Operations systems such as terrain-following/terrain-avoidance radar for use in two test CV-22 Osprey aircraft. Nevertheless, SOCOM spending was heavily weighted toward improving existing, proven systems.

The funding increase was remarkable not only for its magnitude but also because it was largely unquestioned. The new spending could significantly expand the reach of the Army's Special Forces, Delta Force, Navy SEALs, and other Special Operations forces, enabling the U.S. Special Operations Command in Tampa "to locate and track individual terrorists across the globe and conduct small surgical operations [in foreign countries] with minimal risk to forces" assigned to missions, according to congressional testimony by Lieutenant General Bryan D. Brown, deputy commander of USSOCOM.[47]

"By operating 'in the seam' between peace and war," Brown told the Senate Armed Services Committee, "Special Operations Forces can address transnational and asymmetric threats," which would include actions by small terrorist groups. The Joint Chiefs of Staff were equally ready to support a SOF expansion. "A robust cadre of humint [human intelligence] forces organic to SOF would give us perhaps the most important aspect of operations-intelligence fusion that one could get in the field, in direct support of counterterror," said Lieutenant General Norton Schwartz, director of operations for the Joint Chiefs of Staff. Others advocated that SOF include a new, secretive, and ethnically diverse intelligence cadre capable of tracking down sophisticated terrorist networks.[48]

The CIA was quick to respond to possible competition complaining that SOCOM was receiving an unlimited "license to hunt worldwide." It did sound like an overlap with the clandestine paramilitary operations carried out since the 1950s by the Agency's special activities division within the Directorate of Operations (now called the National Clandestine Service). Special operations officers responded by pointing out that the Agency often recruited former special operators for these tasks and borrowed active-duty ones. The new mandate, they said, would just cut out the middleman. Meanwhile, according to press reports, the CIA also received large amounts of new money for its paramilitary activities in the 2004 budget. Although the number, as with the entire CIA budget, is classified, SOCOM's new budget was probably roughly that attributed to the CIA, which is thought to be near $4.5 billion.[49]

Back at the Stryker Brigades

Despite modifications, the Stryker armored vehicle continued to struggle with the basic contradictions of weight and deployability versus armor and lethality but did demonstrate its political survivability. The House Armed Services Committee tried and failed to withhold $300 million from the Stryker program until the Army and the Defense Department solved the problem of a vehicle that weighed too much for rapid deployment, but was apparently too light to survive in combat.[50]

In addition, the Stryker's light armor and rubber tires made it vulnerable to weapons like rocket-propelled grenades. It was again proposed to add attack helicopters and perhaps tanks to Stryker brigades. That would improve their punch, but would not solve their deployability problems. In fact, it would recreate the problem Stryker was intended to solve. And the Army still had difficulty developing an adequately lethal gun for the vehicle.

It was disheartening for the people on the Stryker project. A lot of progress had been made in meeting the deployability requirements for the Stryker Brigades. By using the lighter vehicle and reducing overall support and sustainment requirements, the brigades were almost 50 percent lighter than a conventional heavy brigade equipped with Abrams tanks and Bradley fighting vehicles. Nevertheless, a Stryker unit's airlift requirements were still considerable—300 Strykers, 1200 other vehicles and pieces of equipment plus 3,900 soldiers made a sizable load.

In June 2003 the General Accounting Office (GAO) issued a pessimistic report on Stryker Brigade deployability. Shinseki's original Transformation Plan required that the Interim Brigades (now called Stryker Brigades) deploy to any spot in the world within four days. As time went by, that seemed less likely, and the Army changed it from a requirement to a "goal or objective." The GAO report allowed that the Army had made significant progress and that the Stryker Brigades could be deployed more rapidly than heavy armored forces. However, even if Stryker's weight and size problems were solved, the four-day deployment goal was probably still impossible.

> Meeting the 4-day worldwide deployment goal of a brigade-size force would require more airlift than may be possible to allocate to these brigades; at present, it would take from 5 to 14 days, depending on brigade location and destination, and require over one-third of the Air Force's C-17 and C-5 transport aircraft fleet to deploy one Stryker brigade by air. Because airlift alone may not be sufficient, the Army is planning to use a combination of airlift and sealift to deploy the brigades. However, if sealift were used ...deployment times to many global regions would be significantly longer....[51]

If four days were impossible for a Stryker Brigade, how could an FCS unit expect to cut that by two-thirds?

The report also mentioned that a Stryker Brigades airlift requirement was about twice that of a light infantry brigade.

Then there was the issue of the brigade's high-powered 105mm Mobile Gun Systems (MGS). The MGS was to be the principal striking power of the Stryker Brigade Combat Teams (SBCTs), but it continued to have problems. The vehicle chassis had been lowered to fit inside a C-130. That helped with the fit problem but created a new difficulty. The lower chassis brought the cannon muzzle closer to the front of the vehicle, resulting in blast damage when the gun was fired. The blast also created a burn hazard to the crew and nearby personnel, especially if the vehicle's hatch was open.[52] Reportedly, the vehicle also tended to topple over when the gun was fired.

The weight issue returned as well. In order to reduce MGS's weight for airlift, it was decided to produce a lighter-weight barrel for the 105mm gun, saving about 108.8 kg (approximately 217 pounds) toward the 18,733 kg (approximately

41,213 pounds) weight limit for C-130 flight. The manufacturer, General Dynamics Land Systems, also tackled a host of minor but annoying issues such as obstructions that battered crew members whenever the vehicle moved. It also developed that spent casings ejected from the vehicle's machine gun wedged the commander's hatch closed. Troops solved the problem effectively but inelegantly by taping torn pieces of cardboard MRE (meals, ready to eat) packs to the gun mount, deflecting empty brass over the side of the vehicle.

The first U.S. Army Stryker Brigade had been certified for initial operating capability in May, two years behind schedule. But even that late date was chiefly for public relations purposes since the Army admitted that "additional testing" would be required before the brigade's equipment and 3,900 troops could be ready for deployment.[53] In June the Army was still reporting development problems with the Stryker. The Single Channel Ground and Airborne Radio System radios, Enhanced Position Location Reporting System, commander's video display terminal, and Force XXI Battle Command Brigade and Below system (FBCB2) were all installed more-or-less successfully but only on some command vehicles. This meant that the much-advertised "situational awareness" had to be transmitted the old-fashioned way, by voice radio.

Congressman Jim Saxton (R-NJ), a member of the House Armed Services Committee, continued to question the MGS. Saxton criticized the "danger to the crew when the gun is fired because of the muzzle velocity, and the recoil and the relatively lightweight of the vehicle for purposes of handling the recoil from the gun." A 108 page report on Stryker and the MGS written for Saxton's office was merciless. The Congressman went on to cosponsor an amendment to the House version of the 2004 defense-spending bill that directed the Army to provide extra information on Stryker brigade lethality and sustainability.[54]

On July 23rd, the 3rd Brigade of the 2nd Infantry Division—SBCT—learned that the unit was scheduled to make its combat debut in Iraq. A lot hung on the success of the Stryker Brigade in Iraq. The Stryker units were the Army's most important symbol of transformation, the first new vehicle for a lighter, rapid-deployment Army. Defense Secretary Rumsfeld had agreed to buy 2,131 of the new vehicles by 2006. It was a big commitment and a heavy bet on the Stryker Brigades to show what new technology could do.

Officially the Army insisted that the Stryker and its array of high-tech communication and vision-enhancing equipment were ideal for Iraq. Privately, some were not so certain.

Everyone agreed that the Stryker's armor was too weak to withstand some of the weapons used by Iraqi insurgents, especially the ubiquitous rocket-propelled grenades (RPGs). All 309 Strykers bound for Iraq had to be fitted with new, heavier armor designed to withstand the homemade bombs and mines, as well as rocket-propelled grenades the Iraqis were using. The new armor added protection but also created the old bugaboo—extra weight that made the vehicle heavier and slower. Upgrades also could not solve another problem—the vehicle had not been designed for urban warfare and was unable to turn in tight areas or climb over rubble.[55]

"Strykers were marketed to Congress and elsewhere as being capable of 'Full Spectrum Warfare' which palpably was not true," said Victor O'Reilly, a defense consultant, in a report on the Stryker for the House Armed Services Committee. "They cannot stand up to heavy machine-gun fire, are still entirely vulnerable to rocket-propelled grenades, and the weight of their increased armor impacts negatively on speed, reliability and off road performance."[56]

Regardless, on October 9, 2003, the vehicles of the 3rd Brigade (SBCT) began to roll aboard transport ships at the port of Tacoma, Washington. The first operational Stryker unit, the new showcase of Army transformation, was bound for Iraq, on its way to combat. Despite having been developed at great trouble and expense for air transportability, it would arrive via ship through the port of Kuwait City.

Shinseki Departs

Shinseki's retirement ceremony was held on June 12, 2003, at Fort Meyer, near the Pentagon. Former Army Secretary White was present but neither Rumsfeld nor any of the DoD's top civilians attended. The general took the opportunity for a final critique of Rumsfeld's plan to reduce the size of the Army, saying, "Our soldiers and families bear the risk and the hardship of carrying a mission load that exceeds what force capabilities we can sustain."[57] At the moment he spoke, about 130,000 Army soldiers were still in Iraq, and it had just been announced that the 3rd Infantry Division would not leave as originally scheduled.

More than a dozen senior Army generals supposedly guilty of old-think were shuffled off to retirement along with Shinseki. The acting chief of staff, General John Keane, who was also retiring, thanked them for their services and told them it was time to go. Allegedly, most of the retired officers were asked to leave in order to open up positions that were key to Army Transformation.[58]

By late summer, Rumsfeld's lean-warfare approach to postwar reconstruction seemed badly offtrack. The war in Iraq was placing enormous strains on Army forces; five months after the fall of Baghdad about half the service's combat power was still deployed in Iraq. About 150,000 U.S. soldiers and Marines were engaged in the Iraqi occupation, helped by no more than 21,000 from other countries, most of those British. Except for the British armored division near Basra, international forces had been slow to arrive. Additional troops were still in short supply, with India, Pakistan, and Turkey indicating that they wanted UN authorization for peacekeepers.

Secretary Rumsfeld was growing publicly exasperated with the situation. According to reporters, when pressed by Congress on his plan to deal with the growing insurgency, he finally burst out, "I keep hearing, 'What is the plan, there is no plan.' That is plain not true," he told a Democratic congressman during a hearing on the Bush administration's request for funds to finance reconstruction in Iraq. "Success is the plan."[59] It was a vintage Rumsfeld answer, pungent, quotable, and nonresponsive.

The secretary was not the only one frustrated. U.S. and British troops had been kept well past their expected rotation date and were vocal in their displeasure.

Electricity was still not working in the Iraqi capital, and clean water remained in short supply. The country's major airport remained out of operation. The oil fields expected to pay for reconstruction were still not working, and even gasoline was hard to find.

There was relative calm in the north and south of the country but deadly attacks continued in the so-called "Sunni Triangle" between Baghdad and Tikrit. The toll of American or British wounded and dead continued to creep upwards until, on August 26, the number of postwar deaths reached 140, more than the 138 service members killed during "major combat operations." Ten days later a car bomb detonated outside Najaf's Imam Ali Mosque, killing Ayatollah Mohammed Bakr Hakim, the main Shiite cleric in Iraq, and more than 100 of his followers. Hakim had been one of the few prominent Shiite leaders to advocate compromise with the occupying forces.[60]

Congress urged the President to bring in more international troops, and the Congressional Budget Office reported that America's army was just too small to garrison Iraq for very long. Without soldiers from elsewhere, the Pentagon faced some unattractive choices: reduce numbers in Iraq and Afghanistan, activate more National Guard units or stretch out tours of duty for those already in Iraq. The British also reportedly had long insisted that the project required more troops. In turn the U.S. Congress and others began to question DoD assurances that the current number of U.S. soldiers and Marines were enough. Rumsfeld acknowledged, "There are some recommending that more US forces go in." But he continued to stress that the CENTCOM commander had not asked for more soldiers and was training the Iraqi security force.

Developing additional Iraqi capabilities was a sensible idea if a bit late. However, the original notion had been to use the Iraqi Army for postwar internal security so there was no need to plan a massive train-up for local security forces. Then the Iraqi military was disbanded, leaving a security vacuum to be filled by the understrength Americans.

Even President Bush's ardent supporters were calling for more troops in Iraq, believing the vision of a democratic Iraq (and a transformed Middle East) would perish without them. Rumsfeld remained adamant about holding the line on U.S. troop strength, but the "boots on the ground" need not necessarily be high-tech American boots. What was needed was basic soldiering to provide the long-sought stability and security that would enable reconstruction. International forces could do the job, but that meant cooperation with the United Nations, which was more than somewhat dubious about the entire enterprise.

In the first week of September, President Bush finally announced that he was ready to give the United Nations "a larger responsibility." The offer to give the United Nations some meaningful control marked a big shift in foreign policy—and a victory for Colin Powell and the State Department. In a nationally televised prime-time address, President Bush described a grinding, extended conflict far different from the celebrated lightning campaign that unseated Hussein. Acknowledging the continued pressure of guerrilla attacks from Hussein loyalists and "foreign fighters," he promised to ask Congress for $87 billion in emergency spending for military operations and reconstruction in Iraq and Afghanistan, and added that Iraq had now become "the central front" in the campaign against terrorism.[61]

He said he would ask the United Nations for additional international troops for Iraq and Afghanistan. He also called on "Europe, Japan and states in the Middle East" that "will benefit from the success of freedom in these two countries" to "contribute to that success." It was a tacit admission that the United States could not go it alone and maintain its current level of American troops in both Iraq and Afghanistan.

It was a commendable effort, but it failed to produce any significant number of soldiers. In a much less publicized move, the Army extended overseas tours for thousands of National Guard and Army Reserve forces in Iraq and Kuwait. The new order, issued without any formal announcement, required 12-month tours on the ground in Iraq or surrounding countries. The practical effect for Guard and Army Reserve troops was to extend their original yearlong mobilizations for anywhere from one to six months.[62]

After a year of inconsistent efforts to create Iraqi police and military, a Shiite uprising broke out in April 2004. Rebel fighters appeared in Baghdad's sprawling Shiite slum known as Sadr City and the city of Fallujah. Led by the radical Shiite Mehdi Army and other opposition groups (including Al-Qaeda), they launched a series of hit and run attacks on U.S. garrisons and supply lines, but the real object was the administrative and police authority of the Iraqi interim government.[63]

It was the first serious test of the new Iraqi security forces, and they failed miserably. Large parts of the security forces broke and ran while others surrendered and handed their U.S.-supplied weapons to the insurgent militias. A wave of desertions swept through the 150,000-strong Iraqi army, border guard, and police. Fighting spread to the northern oil city of Mosul and Ar Ramadi at the western tip of the Sunni Triangle. After six days U.S. troops were ordered to pull back from the rebel held areas to prevent an unacceptable level of civilian and troop casualties. The rebels were left in charge of Sadr City, Falllujah, and several smaller areas.[64]

According to Anthony Cordesman of the Center for Strategic and International Studies:

> The United States wasted a year (at least from May 2003 to April 2004) in trying to create effective Iraqi military and security forces. Training effective Iraqi military, police, and security forces is not a luxury or sideshow. It is the only way to ensure Iraqis feel secure and see the effort to create a new government as their own. Regardless of how many Iraqis did or did not welcome the fall of Saddam Hussein, one public opinion poll after another shows that Coalition forces quickly came to be seen by many Iraqis as occupiers, and as occupiers that could not bring security.[65]

After the debacle of the April uprising, Lieutenant General David Petraeus was returned to Iraq in May 2004. Petraeus had commanded the 101st Airborne in Mosul and was considered the most able tactical commander of the war. His job now was to take charge of a new Multinational Security Transition Command with responsibility for the training of all Iraqi security personnel. In a vital change of policy, it had been agreed that properly screened officers of the old Iraqi Army could be part of the new forces. The Iraqi Defense Ministry began open recruiting of former members of Hussein's army, appealing for whole units to reenlist. It was late, but it was a start.[66]

Stryker in Iraq

In January 2004, Stryker vehicles in Iraq were outfitted with additional protection, a "cage" of slat armor, which encircles the vehicle as protection against RPGs. The grillwork was a high-tech version of the "chicken wire" used in Vietnam for the same purpose, to trigger rocket-propelled grenades before they could strike the vehicle. The armor added about 7,000 pounds to the vehicle. The tires were overinflated to compensate for the extra weight, which meant the Central Tire Inflation System could not be used. The overinflated tires tended to sink into soft ground and get stuck. Furthermore, the recovery winch on the vehicle was not designed to pull a Stryker with add-on armor; this meant a tow truck or tank recovery vehicle sometimes had to be used.

It also developed that the slat armor made the vehicle noticeably wider on each side. Now they could not pass side by side on typically narrow two-lane roads. One driver had to pull off the road to make room for the other vehicle to pass. When he did, the vehicle would sink into the dirt and require another vehicle to recover it.[67] As usual the solution came from the soldiers involved who developed a simple barrier of heavy steel mesh fence material on a frame of whatever material was available. It was lighter, cheaper, less cumbersome, easier to replace, and reportedly as effective as the slat armor.[68] But this would not take as many hits as the slat armor and was declared a "non-solution." The official answer was to continue adding 7,000 pounds of slat armor.

At least there was good news from the Stryker Brigade in northern Iraq. The 3rd Brigade (SBCT), 2nd Infantry Division was first placed in the city of Samarra, about 50 miles north of Baghdad and well within the infamous "Sunni Triangle." Combat patrols began there in December where one vehicle was destroyed by an improvised explosive device. The crew escaped with minor injuries, but the unit was soon withdrawn and reassigned to Mosul in the friendlier, Kurd-controlled area well north of Baghdad. Stryker proved vulnerable, but, contrary to predictions, it did not fail miserably in combat. Casualties had not been high, and enemy RPG gunners failed to wreck the predicted carnage.

According to the Army, Strykers equipped with FBCB2 and Blue Force Tracker really did make for a better, more coordinated response. The FBCB2 "battlefield Internet" had been improved since the forced march up to Baghdad in 2003, and, at least in theory, each vehicle's computer was now linked to all the others via satellite. The Stryker units would, in theory, be able to respond quickly and bring coordinated flexible firepower to bear. It is interesting, however, how few of the soldier accounts of Strykers in combat mention the use of these systems. The impression gained, at least from these accounts, is that the vehicles were valued for their speed and armor, and the actual fighting was accomplished by eyesight and coordinated over voice radio. Of course, the brigade's static deployment to one relatively quiet area for months contributed to the unit's performance.[69]

On March 28, an RPG gunner managed to slip one past Stryker's slat armor, severely damaging the vehicle but leaving the crew uninjured. By April about a dozen Strykers had suffered serious damage from roadside bombs and several were totaled. But thanks to the up-armoring and added RPG screen, only one was destroyed by the ubiquitous rocket-propelled grenades. The most serious incident had been the death of three crewmen when a dirt embankment collapsed underneath one vehicle, rolling it over.[70]

Stryker's size proved to be somewhat of a problem; it was as big as a small bus with a turning radius too wide for many of the city streets it operated in. It was also top-heavy with a tendency to roll over. But in action, Stryker proved to be faster than the armored M-2 Bradley tracked infantry vehicle, was quieter, and provided a smoother ride. This last was a real plus for infantrymen used to being jounced and bruised for hours inside tracked vehicles. Tactically more important, the relatively quiet Stryker provided an advantage on raids, or just patrolling. The road wheels and metal pads of a tracked vehicle made a lot more noise. "The Iraqis are unnerved by silent Strykers sneaking up on them," claimed military analyst James Dunnigan.[71]

Silent Strykers or no, the Iraqi insurgency gained steam in the summer and fall of 2004, and Mosul lost its status as a relatively quiet zone. Instead, the city became a focus of insurgent activity including what appeared to be specific attempts to destroy or capture one of the Stryker vehicles.

In one instance a very large car bomb exploded next to a moving Stryker, flipping it over and sending it skidding about 30 feet. The exterior of the vehicle was seriously shredded, but none of the four soldiers inside were badly injured. Everyone involved agreed that it was certainly a lot better to be in a Stryker than a HMMWV, even an up-armored one, when a roadside bomb went off.[72] In another instance a suicide bomber drove an explosives laden truck directly into a Stryker, disabling it. One soldier was killed but the other occupants survived with injuries.[73] General Schoomaker later referred to the incident, endorsing the Stryker as "the most survivable vehicle in Iraq today."[74] Not everyone was impressed, and the Israeli Defense Force, a prospective customer for Strykers, criticized it as having too many blind spots and not being maneuverable enough as well as top heavy and prone to rollovers. In the words of one IDF officer, "it's a piece of junk."[75] The Canadian Defense Forces, on the other hand, agreed to purchase at least a few of the vehicles to complement its existing fleet of LAV IIIs, the original form of the Stryker.[76]

Was That the Transformation?

We got nothing until they slammed into us.
            —Lieutenant Colonel Ernest Marcone, whose battalion was struck without
                                warning by the largest counterattack of the war[77]

Even as the Army's 3rd Division and the Marine Corps Expeditionary Force fought through the streets of Baghdad, Vice President Dick Cheney was presenting the conflict as "proof positive" of the success of "transformation." Across the Potomac, in the corridors of the Pentagon, Rumsfeld partisans hailed the victory as another validation of his vision. In the new conventional wisdom, Tommy Franks had been determined to refight the last war until led to the light by Secretary Rumsfeld. Perhaps, it was admitted, there had been a few hiccoughs, accidents, and surprises such as the resistance by fedayeen irregulars, but overall it had been a triumph of the new thinking championed by the Defense Secretary.

The war against Iraq focused on speed, flexibility, and use of real-time intelligence data. In this case, as in Afghanistan, transformation meant the use of precision guided weaponry, special operations forces, and long-range air power. The Rumsfeld doctrine of speed, real-time intelligence, and flexibility was the new orthodoxy. Unfortunately for proponents of transformation in the OSD version, things were not so neat.

The connectivity between CENTCOM in Qatar and the Pentagon may have been excellent, but connectivity in Qatar did not lead to data for the troops in the Iraqi desert. It was a problem all the ground forces suffered, Army and Marines. Some units outran the range of high-bandwidth communications relays. Downloads took hours. Software locked up. Reconnaissance systems were not always available, and the enemy often took pains not to be found in the first place.[78]

> During Operation Iraqi Freedom, despite unparalleled intelligence assets, most of the fighting on the ground was characterized by the participants as resulting from meeting engagements-battles in which American forces unexpectedly bumped into the enemy.[79]

Shortly before dawn on April 3, the largest counterattack of the war struck a battalion of the 3rd Divison's 69th Armored near a key bridge on the Euphrates River southwest of Baghdad. As described by the battalion commander, Lieutenant Colonel Ernest Marcone, "Next to the fall of Baghdad that bridge was the most important piece of terrain in the theater, and no one can tell me what's defending it. Not how many troops, what units, what tanks, anything. There is zero information getting to me. Someone may have known above me, but the information didn't get to me on the ground."[80]

Marcone was told that a single Iraqi Brigade might be moving in his direction, but no sensors or no network warned him of the reality. At about 3:00 AM his unit was struck from three directions by not one brigade but three: 25 or 30 tanks, more than twice that many armored personnel carriers, artillery, and between 5,000 and 10,000 Iraqi soldiers. It was just the kind of conventional, massed force the situational awareness system was designed to detect. Yet, "We got nothing until they slammed into us," Marcone recalls. "It is my belief that the Iraqi Republican Guard did nothing special to conceal their intentions or their movements. They attacked en masse using tactics that are more recognizable with the Soviet army of World War II."[81]

The Iraqi brigades descended on a single U.S. battalion, about 1,000 soldiers supported by 30 M1 tanks and 14 Bradley fighting vehicles. When the sun rose, the
Iraqi units had been decimated at a cost of eight Americans wounded. Better training, better equipment, air support, and just plain better soldiering made the difference. Information was not armor; armor was armor.[82]

A report prepared by the RAND Corporation confirms that "there appeared to be
a 'digital divide.'" At the division level or above, the view of the battle space was
adequate to their needs. But among frontline commanders in the Army and Marines,
"Everybody said the same thing. It was a universal comment: 'We had terrible
situational awareness.'"[83] This was empathically not the transformation version of
warfare.

The lack of situational awareness was not entirely a problem of communication.
The Iraqis took several steps to deceive Coalition intelligence efforts as to their disposition and intent. They positioned inoperable equipment as decoys and went out of
their way to attract attacks on unmanned derelicts, some left over from the first Gulf
War. Some units were hidden and others placed near targets the United States and its
allies would prefer to avoid—mosques, schools, and hospitals. To the extent possible
they concealed their communications by using cell phones, low power radios, and
couriers. Not all units took these measures, but those that did were able to conceal
air defense weapons, tactical headquarters, maneuver systems, and tactical missiles
with some success.[84]

The ability to discern what the Iraqis intended "remained illusory." Despite a
plethora of assets, the Coalition found it nearly impossible to track militia and fedayeen movements.

The pace of Coalition maneuver took the enemy by surprise and at least to some
degree managed to get inside his decision cycle. But the fabled "shock and awe"
was small scale at best—the regime did not collapse until driven out, and elements
managed to hang on long after "major combat operations" were declared ended in
May 2003. Shock and awe is part military technique and part psychological games-
manship. Instead of publicizing early surrenders and repeatedly stressing the Iraqi
military failures, the U.S. administration stressed the possible difficulties of the
war. Seen in this light, it was really more a part of the generally lackluster information campaign conducted by the United States. Concentrating on "information
dominance" in the military sphere, insufficient attention was paid to gaining psychological dominance. Instead of dominating public information in Iraq, the Coalition
allowed the Iraqi government to continue propaganda broadcasts right up until the
fall of Baghdad.

The U.S.-led force certainly accomplished more with less, but with equal certainly
it failed to prove that the day of heavy industrial age ground forces was over. Furthermore, the postwar stabilization turned out to be a much more serious military problem than anticipated by transformation enthusiasts. Heavy armor in the form of M1
tanks and Bradleys played an indispensable role in both the war and the irregular
fight that followed it, not only for firepower but also for its psychological effect.
There are other problems with the notion of the Iraq conflict as an entirely or even

mostly new form of warfare. For one thing the scale of forces involved, although much smaller than the first Gulf War, still did not qualify as light. After subtracting the members of the 1991 Coalition included for cosmetic purposes, the difference narrows even further.

Also, the abysmal state of the Iraqi armed forces limited the value of any lessons from the war. Even by comparison with their sorry state in 1991, both the regular army and the elite Republican Guard were ragtag formations with faulty equipment, low morale, and poor leadership. Underlying all this was a culture of self-deception in which military and civilian leaders consistently lied to one another about everything from the condition of their equipment to the presence of U.S. forces inside Baghdad.[85]

CENTCOM had the great advantage of strategic initiative in its war planning. This meant that the United States could undertake an 18 month buildup of logistic support facilities and a gradual inflow of troops in the months before the war lasting from the fall of 2001 until major combat operations began on March 19, 2003. Hostilities would begin where and when the United States and its Coalition partner Great Britain decided. Iraq had months of unequivocal warning as U.S. and British forces entered the region, but there was essentially nothing they could do about it. If the Coalition needed more time, it was available.[86] Impressive as the combat performance was, it hardly qualified as a rapid-deployment war.

Furthermore, the idea of destroying a regime by a rapid stroke to seize the capital was hardly an innovation. It could be argued that the technique of a rapid armored thrust supported by air power looked more like the 1940 German *Blitzkrieg* in France than anything truly "transformational."

Finally, the scale and persistence of the Iraq insurgency challenged the validity of the military victory. The U.S. military had insisted on preparing for the war they preferred, not the one they were likely to face. This meant that very little in training or doctrine dealt with counterinsurgency and even less with the political environment it occurred in. Those who tried to introduce that kind of consideration were ignored or dismissed. But future wars may well be fought in urban zones by low-tech fanatics who do not follow the old rules. They are unlikely to array themselves as convenient targets for the United States to detect and destroy. Indeed, a leading cause of death among U.S. soldiers in Iraq became improvised bombs targeting passing vehicles such as Humvees. Furthermore, the enemy adapted as friendly forces did. Up-armoring of vehicles in Iraq was met by larger and larger improvised explosive devices.

Some networking technology is useful against insurgents. Using methods that are closer to police techniques than military ones, suspicious vehicles can be tracked, and their connections to other people and locations determined. UAVs can monitor suspicious areas and deliver video feeds from urban settings as well as battlefields. Acoustic sensors help find snipers, and jamming devices can sometimes block radio-controlled detonation of roadside bombs. But most of the progress against the insurgents has been made by human intelligence, old-fashioned tips from humans. "Our networks don't really have the sensitivity to keep up with unconventional enemies. All the network does is move information around, but the information itself is the key to victory," said Loren Thompson, chief operating officer of the Lexington Institute, a think tank in Arlington, Virginia. "It's a little hard to derive meaningful lessons from networked war fighting when you are dealing with such modest threats."[87]

The principal instruments of U.S. power in the continuing fight were the heavy armored units and conventional infantry disdained by transformationists. Michael O'Hanlon, of the Brookings Institution, observed, "the urban battles revalidated not just tanks but the guys operating them and the guys covering them with rifles in their hands."[88]

Arthur Cebrowski, retired vice admiral and director of the Pentagon's Office of Force Transformation, argued that it would be a mistake to use the network problems in Iraq as an argument for retaining heavy armored forces. The real problem was that the network was hurriedly grafted onto old-fashioned command and control systems. The result was time delays and the magnification of individual communications failures.[89]

Owen Cote, associate director of the Security Studies Program at MIT, followed the progress of transformation in the Iraq conflict with considerable interest. "If there is this 'revolution in military affairs,' and if this revolution is based on technologies that allow you to network sensors and process information more quickly and spread it out quickly in digestible form, we are still just scratching the surface of it," says Cote. "If you look at the performance of a lot of the components of the first efforts in that direction, it's a pretty patchy performance."[90]

It is often said that generals have a tendency to fight the previous war. In Iraq, there may have been too much eagerness to fight the next one.

CHAPTER 9

THE NEXT ARMY

Don't confuse enthusiasm with capability.

—General Peter J. Schoomaker

The Modular Army: Taking Transformation "In Stride"[1]

Attempts to streamline and lighten the divisional structure usually involve the shifting of assets to other echelons and in the creation of a division that needs to be reinforced again before it can fight effectively.

—U.S. Army Combat Studies Institute, 2000

The Secretary of Defense had not managed to get the Army he wanted out of his previous leadership team. Now, Donald Rumsfeld's handpicked Army chief of staff had the task of turning 480,000 overstretched conventional soldiers into an agile, flexible, networked force. The secretary wanted fundamental change in the way the Army did things. In his view the service urgently needed to become an expeditionary force like the Marine Corps, but with more firepower and the staying power to fight large land wars. A key question was how the service intended to match force structure to the administration's emerging "4-2-1" strategy of being able to deter forward in four theaters, halt aggression in two, and decisively defeat in one—all at the same time.[2]

General Peter J. Schoomaker, however, had more immediate problems. When he took over as chief of staff, 70 percent of the Army's combat strength (including activated reservists) was at war, was preparing to deploy, or was returning. Four of the Army's ten divisions and a Stryker Brigade were in Iraq or Afghanistan, and elements of three other divisions were en route to the Gulf region. Another, the 10th Mountain Division, was refitting at Fort Drum, New York, after duty in Afghanistan.

The only untouched division was the 2nd Infantry, permanently stationed in South Korea, and one of its brigades was slated for Iraq in 2004. Of course, the Army was not alone in this situation; 60 percent of Marine Corps power was deployed overseas, mostly in Iraq. Half of the Navy's aircraft-carrier battle groups and the bulk of the Air Force's B-1 and B-2 heavy bombers were engaged there as well.[3]

Iraq was the urgent problem. The insurgency was, if anything, gaining momentum, and occupation was going to be a primary duty of the Army for years. Units that expected to be deployed for perhaps six months were there 12 months or more, testing their endurance. But with only ten divisions and a handful of independent brigades, the numbers just did not work. At the time of the first Iraq War in 1991 the U.S. Army had 18 divisions and 706,000 personnel. At the end of "major combat operations" in Iraq in 2003 it had ten divisions and 476,000 people. The Navy had 580 ships in 1991; it had 306 in 2003. The Air Force, which had 165 air wings in 1991, had 91 by the end of Gulf War II. President George H. W. Bush, President Bill Clinton, and Congress saw the end of the Cold War as the end of the era of large standing armed forces. President George W. Bush, a staunch advocate of military transformation, had seen no reason to change this policy. As a result, the armed forces, especially the Army, were stretched dangerously thin.

Reportedly, things were so tight that when Lieutenant General John Vines, the senior U.S. commander in Afghanistan, called for one more Army battalion service leaders could not find one in the active force.[4]

Furthermore, the 2004 National Military Strategy called for meeting threats close to their sources. "Our primary line of defense remains well forward. Forces operating in key regions are essential to the defense of the United States and to the protection of allies and US interests."[5] That meant continuing overseas deployments, and there just was not enough Army to go around. Somehow more capability had to be generated from the existing force structure. The service was already planning to convert about 10,000 military jobs to civilian positions in 2004 and 2005. It also had plans to conduct public-private competitions of 226,000 positions by September 30, 2009. That would eventually free up additional soldiers for strictly military duties, but not all of those would go directly to additional combat strength. The answer was to field more units by making them smaller but, hopefully, without any loss in capability. It was a tall order and led to the most sweeping change in Army organization since the Korean War.[6]

General Schoomaker was more than willing to take on the task. "As far as I'm concerned, there is not a damn thing sacred about what we are doing in the Army except our values.... I'm often asked, how far can I move the Army? I tell them as far as I can. The Army is tremendously resilient." Reorganization was required and according to the new chief, "you can't fool around on the margins if we're going to change. We're going to move very quickly."[7]

Schoomaker moved aggressively without waiting to develop a constituency for his plans. Instead, he acted at once to make the reforms he believed were needed. One of his first moves was to free up additional personnel by "dis-establishing" a number of field artillery, air defense, engineer, and armor units (eliminating 24, 10, 11, and

19 battalions, respectively, both active and reserve). Most of the positions (but not necessarily the personnel) would be reassigned to increase the types of units needed in the immediate future, chiefly military police and special operations forces but also transportation, civil affairs, and psychological operations units. Exact numbers were not presented, but the total was believed to exceed 100,000, more than 10 percent of the total Army.[8]

The loss of the artillery units was especially hard to take since field artillery was usually regarded as the fighting army's most important force multiplier. Additionally, the advent of precision artillery rounds was expected to give the Army a toehold in the precision munitions business, now wholly dominated by the Air Force. But, nevertheless, given the changing missions the Army was called upon to perform, Schoomaker apparently believed his service could cut as many as 40 artillery battalions across the active and reserve components. Traditional tube artillery, ammunition, and the trucks to transport them amount to about 50 or 60 percent of the gross weight of a heavy division. Reducing the artillery and replacing it with air support is an obvious way to reduce the weight and bulk of the division.[9] If the Army was going to become more "joint" (meaning in this case more dependent on air power for close combat support), they needed less tube artillery. But if Iraq and Afghanistan were examples of future conflict, there would be a definite need for more military police.

It also fit nicely into the Department of Defense (DoD) push for transformation and "jointness." Unfortunately, neither the Army nor the Air Force was completely pleased with the idea. Traditionally, only airmen guide Air Force assets to ground targets, and the airmen were not eager for that to change.

On June 30, the Army Training and Doctrine Command issued its newest version of the basic manual for the operation and organization of the Objective Force. It was obsolete even before it hit the streets as Schoomaker plowed ahead with his agenda. The very term "Objective Force" was discarded. The Shinseki terminology of Legacy Force (combat forces as they existed prior to transformation), Interim Force (the brigades equipped with the Stryker vehicle), and Objective Force, which included the Future Combat System (FCS), was all changed. The new Army chief mandated a new set of terms: "Current Force" replaced "Legacy and Interim Forces," while "Objective Force" was replaced by "Future Force."[10] To go with all this, a U.S. Army Futures Center was established to supply the training and doctrine piece.

The Modular Army

In late September, Schoomaker explained his plan to generate more deployable units by drastically redesigning Army combat forces, starting in early 2004 with the 3rd Infantry Division (Mechanized) and 101st Airborne Division (Air Assault). His plan was to recast the Army along the general lines suggested by Colonel Doug MacGregor and others—the division would no longer be the basic tactical building block of the combat forces. The Army would become brigade-based by making the brigade a much more capable formation. This would be accomplished by turning the maneuver brigades (the ones that actually fight) into scaled-down versions of the conventional division. Since this would create very similar building blocks, it was referred to as a "modular" approach.

The new brigade design would actually give up some of the strength of a conventional brigade by losing one of its combat battalions. But they would have their full quota of specialist units (e.g., military intelligence) that normally would not be a permanent element of the brigade. The 2004 Army contained 33 combat brigades. By subtracting a battalion from each to make up additional brigades, the service could in theory field as many as 43 reorganized brigade combat teams by 2006 and 48 by 2009. Applying the same logic to the reserve components could eventually almost double that number. In an Army strapped for deployable units, the arithmetic was very appealing.

As usual, the new plan would cost money, billions of dollars annually at least. That immediately sparked speculation that the Army would back away from its commitments to the Future Force in general or the FCS program in particular. In what might have been an excess of optimism, senior Army leaders predicted that substantial supplemental budgets would enable the Army to improve its current force without shorting the future force. Publicly, they blasted speculation that FCS might have to be delayed by several years. "That is not true. Hell no, we're not doing that." [11] Privately, it was rumored that one of the new chief's goals was to "put FCS out of its misery."

But the first priority was the reorganized brigades, now called "Units of Action (UA)." As part of this new taxonomy, divisions and corps would both become Units of Employment–X (UEx), and higher echelons would become Units of Employment–Y. A Unit of Action was officially defined as "brigade-like maneuver unit of action with assigned support and service support elements to provide...combatant commanders more deployable/flexible forces for employment." Subordinate formations were to be force "modules." [12]

Shortly afterwards, the term "Unit of Action" was judged too generic and a pointless departure from tradition, so the new units were tagged with the unwieldy appellation Brigade Combat Team Units of Action (BCTUA). This bit of semantic adjustment was largely ignored in the working Army and, except for briefing slides, the new units were referred to simply as new brigades or the even more reductionist "brigades." Likewise the UEx (formerly division) was called a Division UA and the UEx (formerly corps) was generally referred to as a Corps UA, commonly shortened to just division and corps, respectively. This practice was officially discouraged, and to distinguish among UEx's, the division-sized ones were called two-star UEx's and the corps-sized ones were called three-star UEx's (reflecting the ranks of their commanders). The taxonomy of reorganization finally became so complex that the entire business was informally encapsulated in the term "modularity," which became shorthand for the whole reorganization process.

Even though the new brigades would lose one-third of their combat power, so the theory went, they would make that up by adding a reconnaissance unit, some formerly division-level assets and digital networking. The last would not only raise combat efficiency but tie-in support from other Army, joint and allied units.[13] The brigade UA's reconnaissance, intelligence, military police, and other new assets would be taken from the division, making the division headquarters more purely a command and control element. The division commander's ability to influence the battle directly (e.g., by means of division artillery) would be markedly reduced. This was an important change since it would decrease the central warfighting role held by the division.

This change was, of course, made possible by the network. Once the magic of information enabling was invoked, the new brigades would be gifted with situational awareness so acute that each one could deliver the combat effectiveness of a conventional division. But the changes could not wait for the network because the brigades were needed now, not a decade from now. They would still be based on M-1A Abrams tanks, Bradley fighting vehicles, and Apache attack helicopters. If the digital "system of systems" failed to materialize, they could still rely on old-fashioned armor and firepower, not the high-tech bag of tricks required for FCS.

In addition to the infantry, medium (Stryker) and heavy BCTUAs, five other types of UA would be organized as multifunction Support Brigades—aviation, fires (artillery), sustainment (logistics), maneuver enhancement (engineer), and RSTA (reconnaissance, surveillance, and target acquisition). Overall it looked like a combination of the Interim Force concept of independent brigades married to a somewhat modified version of the Force XXI initiative. Change would be incremental and not predicated on the great technological leap of "transformation" Shinseki style.

Schoomaker's new Brigade Units of Action were very similar in concept to the planned structure for the Interim Brigade Combat Teams planned four years earlier as part of Shinseki's transformation plan. The term "Unit of Action" was not new either; it had been used in Army doctrine, simulations, and concept papers for several years as the generic name for units created under the Objective Force (now called the Future Force). Yet, it was a bolder move than it might first appear. The changes might not seem startlingly original (similar proposals had been floating around for at least a decade) but boldness does not require originality. What Schoomaker proposed was to change the fundamental way the Army organized for combat.

Since the Civil War, the basic fighting unit of the U.S. Army had been the division. By World War II, these divisions were commonly organized as three combat brigades (the maneuver elements) and various supporting elements. The organizational concept called for support assets (such as artillery and engineers) to be pooled at division level and parceled out to the brigades as required to make up task forces. It was also argued that this arrangement allowed for more flexibility since division commanders could tailor their brigade task forces. But the brigades always needed their combined arms support. Furthermore, it was also accepted that these units functioned best when they habitually worked with each other, when the same support units were continuously associated with the same brigades. It had long been agreed that the ideal relationships between the brigades and their combat support elements would be permanent, making them all part of a single standing task force. Still, to accomplish this degree of decentralization would mean more assets were needed overall. It was an expensive proposition, and Army budget needs were better served by pooling a more limited number of assets at division level.[14]

Creating the new brigade combat teams broke with this tradition by making brigades the basic fighting unit, but it did so expensively. It meant more support was needed since common assets were no longer shared among the brigades of a division. But not only would the new brigade teams have more subordinate units, there would be more brigades.

All the combat brigades in the Army were to become Brigade Units of Action and each of the ten active duty divisions would add at least one more BCTUA, giving each division four or five brigades instead of the traditional three. Of the initially planned 43, 20 would be heavy, 9 light, 5 medium-weight (Stryker brigades), 4 airborne (in the 82nd Airborne Division), and 4 air assault (in the 101st Airborne Division). The Army National Guard's structure would change from 15 enhanced separate brigades, 19 brigades within divisions, and 1 separate brigade, to 32 brigade combat teams plus one Stryker brigade combat team.[15] By the time the entire Army including support elements and reserves was converted, the total could reach as many as 82 brigade teams, all without adding significantly to the Army's end strength. Some of the planners even believed that a cut in overall Army personnel numbers might be possible.[16]

The new modular Units of Action (brigades) were to be assigned their own support elements. This was not much of a change since any U.S. combat brigade designed to operate outside a division would normally have its own cavalry (reconnaissance) troop, engineer company, military intelligence unit, military police platoon, artillery battalion, and support battalion. But now there were more of each, except for artillery. In theory this made the brigade UA much more independent of higher commands and much more flexible. Since there would be no need to assign and integrate support units before deploying the brigade, they would also be more responsive. The basic differences were a reduction in artillery, the loss of a combat battalion, and the switching of one combat battalion for a different type (e.g., infantry brigades traded an infantry battalion for an armored one and vice versa). However, the increase in numbers and types of subordinate elements also made the brigade UAs more difficult to control and support.[17] It also did little to speed deployment.

There was more reshuffling and renaming, of course. The RSTA squadron, for example, was redesignated as a cavalry squadron but with no change in mission. The Aviation Brigade Units of Action became Multi Functional Aviation Brigades for no obvious reason.

To the unbiased observer it looked like a serious reduction in combat power. A reorganized brigade would lose a battalion, one-third of its combat power, and replace it with a cavalry squadron—a light reconnaissance battalion mounted mostly in up-armored HMMWVs.[18]

The major function of the two-star "Unit of Employment–X" (formerly the division) would be to provide command and control for two or more of the remodeled brigades. As originally designed by Schoomaker, each two-star UEx would gain one or two brigades but lose most of the division level support assets to the brigades, while acquiring some assets formerly assigned to the three-star UEx (formerly corps). For example, under the so-called "Marne Plan" for the 3rd Infantry Division, the division would be reorganized as a headquarters with five similar maneuver brigades, one aviation brigade, division artillery, and a division support brigade, each of the maneuver brigades being rebaptized as a BCTUA. Taking this as a prototype, each two-star Unit of Employment (division) would have five maneuver elements:

4 BCTUAs (combined infantry/armor/artillery/support) and one Aviation Brigade Unit of Action.

A typical Division UE would be organized as follows.

Four or Five Brigade Units of Action each with—

Brigade Headquarters
1 Inf Bn 1 Armor Bn
1 Cavalry Squadron (two motorized companies in Humvees, a dismounted recon unit plus a section of three M2 Bradley's and another in the Squadron headquarters)
1 Artillery Bn
1 Fwd Spt Bn (Supply, Maintenance and Medical)
1 "Troop" Bn: includes an engineer, military intelligence and signal company and a surveillance scout unit.

One Aviation Brigade Unit of Action/Multi-Function Aviation Brigade with—

Avn Brigade HQ
1 Bn of AH-64D Apache Longbow Attack helicopters
3 Bn of UH-60 Blackhawk utility choppers
An Aviation Support Bn to maintain and service the helicopters.

One Fires Unit of Action with—

Division Artillery Headquarters
1 Field Artillery Bn.

And—

A Space Support Element (SSE) (receives satellite provided information).
A Sustainment Unit of Action with Engineer, Quartermaster and Chemical units.
A Special Troop Battalion with everything else (e.g., military police and the band).

Another organization called the Battlefield Surveillance Brigade was mentioned in the Army literature but without a detailed explanation. Briefing materials suggested that the Surveillance Brigade was intended as a larger and more capable version of the reconnaissance, intelligence, surveillance, and target acquisition battalion.[19]

Although the reorganized Brigade Unit of Action was actually larger than a conventional brigade, it still looked much like one. Most of the differences came from tinkering with the force mix, not from fundamental changes. One change came from the increase in "overhead" support units formerly attached to the brigade but not part of the permanent organization. On the other hand, the fighting parts of the brigade were notably smaller than before. For example, each brigade normally can expect to receive an attached artillery battalion of 24 guns. Under the new configuration, each BCTUA would field just 16 guns. The loss of eight guns and all their associated crews, vehicles, and equipment noticeably lighten the brigade, hence making it more deployable. Presumably the subtracted guns were required to fill out the new BCTUAs. In principle, fewer guns, but firing more accurately, meant less ammunition needed and a reduced burden on ammunition resupply all the way back to the depots in the United States (which would, of course, be smaller than before).[20]

Initially, the new structure eliminated much of the air defense capability from the brigades and division.[21] This was based on the optimistic assessment that no serious air threat could be expected in the foreseeable future. After reevaluation some air defense assets were added back in.

All of this does indeed reduce the need for outside support, making the unit more expeditionary. Unfortunately, there were some issues—for example, the planned precision rounds were not available and BCTUA guns would fire the same unguided rounds as before. Probably for this reason, Major General William Webster, commander of the 3rd Division, opted to retain all his artillery battalions.

On January 28, 2004, General Schoomaker briefed the House Armed Services Committee on his restructure plans, beginning with the 3rd Infantry Division (ID), back at Fort Stewart, Georgia, after more than a year of combat in Iraq. By 2005, the three brigades of the division and supporting units were to be reorganized into five maneuver UAs, "combat ready, trained and prepared to execute the OIF 3 [Operation Iraqi Freedom] rotation, or any other mission assigned."[22]

Schoomaker's approach may have lacked the ground-breaking innovation of Shinseki's but was probably much more acceptable. For the most part, it was a straightforward reallocation of assets normally found within a conventional division. Schoomaker's initiative was much more closely aligned with the Force XXI process of incremental change than the radical innovations promised by his predecessor.

Furthermore, it was based on bits and pieces of ideas that had been floating around for some time and were at least familiar to most Army leaders. In fact, the entire concept harked back to the World War II Regimental Combat Team (RCT). Like the Unit of Action, the RCT had been designed to function as an independent organization. Similarly, it had three maneuver battalions (but all infantry), a field artillery battalion (105mm howitzer), an engineer company, and various smaller specialist attachments.[23]

Speaking pure Pentagon-ese, General Schoomaker told the House Armed Services Committee, "We are in a very serious mood right now, looking at modulizing the Army, standardizing it, developing an Army that's more lethal, more agile, more capable of meeting the current and future operating environment tasks." The service, he added, is implementing Secretary Rumsfeld's January order to add 30,000 new people, "growing the Army as fast as we can grow the Army."[24]

In July 2004, Schoomaker's vision came a step closer to reality. Congress had funded the 30,000 new soldiers, giving the Army a total authorized strength of about 512,000. Despite concern in Congress, the Office of the Secretary of Defense (OSD) and some analysts remained certain the increase was not only unneeded but possibly counterproductive. Analyst James Carafano of the Heritage Institute called the troop increase "wrongheaded." Permanent increases, he argued, would be extraordinarily expensive and make it harder to modernize and transform the force. The result would resemble the "hollow Army" of the 1970s. Besides, by the time new forces were available (probably about two years), the need for additional troops in Iraq would likely subside.[25] General Webster of the 3rd ID estimated that he needed about 4,000 additional soldiers to fill out the new five brigade structure. The other commanders would presumably require about the same number. There was a shortage of trained infantry, and reshuffling support units would not produce them. Eventually reorganization in the rest of the Army might free up enough additional positions, but positions are not the same as trained soldiers needed to flesh out the new UEx design. At least in the short run the 30,000 troop increase was badly needed.

Rumsfeld was not happy at the prospect, and Schoomaker was brought back on-message stressing that the increase was only temporary. But it made it much easier to man the 13 to 15 new units of action the general's plan called for. After the 3rd Infantry Division, and the 101st, the 4th Infantry Division (digitized), now back at its home station in Fort Hood, Texas, added a BCTUA. Some divisions including the 82nd Airborne would go from the traditional three brigades each to four while the two brigade 10th Mountain Division would add a third and a fourth. The 25th Infantry would go to five brigades with other divisions expected to follow suit later.

The interesting part of all this was not just the much hyped new brigade but also the much maligned "old-think" division. Some proposals had called for eliminating the division altogether in favor of a flatter structure with the brigade combat teams controlled directly by the next level up, the corps headquarters (or three-star UEx). Another plan had been to flatten the command structure by eliminating the corps. Some of its functions would migrate to the divisions and some to the theater army. However, the Army was not ready for such a radical step, and there was considerable doubt as to whether a corps could manage and support eight or more combat brigades. There was still need for an intermediate echelon to actually manage the battle and that brought planners back to the division.[26] The idea was to create more deployable, expeditionary units that still had the endurance and combat power of conventional units. This created a serious problem. Reducing the size of the unit made it more deployable but worked against endurance and combat power. Current technology just did not make up the difference—possibly someday but not right now. Even if the two-star Units of Employment–X (i.e., division headquarters) lose most of their combat support assets to the new brigades and shift virtually all logistics responsibility up to the corps, a robust headquarters is still needed.

The two-star UEx (division) fills the role of a command-and-control entity able to deploy without subordinate units. Previously a deploying division headquarters would, for example, remove elements from its military intelligence (e.g., an analysis control element), the signal battalion and division artillery units, and others. Nevertheless, the reduced division headquarters still had a lot of baggage with three, fully manned, mobile command posts (CPs) built in as well as mobile-command-communications assets for each of those CPs. Unfortunately, a division headquarters that deploys without a division faces the unappealing possibility of being tapped to run a task force composed entirely of modular brigades that are total strangers, both to the headquarters and each other.

To make life even more complicated, the two-star UEx (division) gained some brand new assets to manage, prominent among them Space Support Elements (SSE). SSEs were a great new capability—the division could tap directly into space-based services like imagery and weather information. But it was one more information flow that had to be managed to support the BCTUAs. And one more set of mouths to feed, gas tanks to fill, and communications links to provide. Furthermore, someone needed to manage the battle and control assets "borrowed" from the corps for specific needs, e.g., a heavy engineer battalion for bridging a river. Finally, other considerations aside, it is by no means certain that a stripped down division headquarters can command and control four or perhaps five brigades in "nonlinear" combat. As a result, the "stripped" two-star UEx (i.e., division head-quarters) grew to an estimated 2,000 persons.

To add to the confusion, the two-star UEx was to receive some assets formerly assigned to the corps (or three-star UEx). Exactly what assets and how they would be employed were vague. Just as the BCTUA looked like a scaled-down division, the two-star UEx began to look like a scaled-down version of the old corps structure.

Then there were the dull but necessary rear area support functions. The U.S. Army is the only force in the world that can generate, deploy, and sustain significant land combat power for an indefinite period. But it can do so only because of "below-the-line" units that deploy to support the combat force. These include area support units, terminal service units, mortuary units, port detachments, fuel and water supply systems, and many others, all the apparatus that supports and sustains the "above-the-line" forces, the combat and direct support units actually in the fight. Further, these are not requirements that can somehow be reorganized away. Federal law (USC Title 10, Chapters 6, 303, and 305) includes a long list of support responsibilities the Army must accomplish not only for its own units but those of other services as well.[27] The emphasis on jointness made these functions all the more important, and someone had to perform them: by law that someone was the Army.

Logisticians would dearly love to eliminate the Desert Storm–style iron mountain of supplies needed to sustain forces in combat. But the iron mountain existed for a reason. The requirements of combat units could not be predicted except in a very general way. When a fighting brigade needs critical resupply, it needs it now, and just-in-time can easily become just-too-late. Two critical areas caused supply problems during the Iraq invasion in 2003. "The first was our inability to see the requirements across this vast battlespace in real time—to know what kind of ammunition was being consumed, to know how much fuel was being used, to know exactly what spare parts were required where," according to Lieutenant General Chris Christianson, the Army's deputy chief of staff for logistics. "In the case of repair parts, when something goes bad on an airplane or you need a transmission on a tank—those requirements aren't easy to predict. Those are the ones that caused the largest problems for us."[28]

"[The second problem was] the ability to respond to that [need]," he said. "Even if you knew what the problem was, reaching out and delivering support to the precise place on the battlefield where it is needed is very difficult. We don't have a structure today that is distribution based. The need is for 'FedEx on the battlefield.'"[29]

Colonel David Fastabend is a combat engineer and military doctrine writer. Working with an earlier but similar version of the brigade-based system, he estimates that, even using optimistic assumptions, it is hard to imagine a tooth-to-tail ratio of less than 1.3:1 or about 1,300 support troops for every 1,000 soldiers in combat units. This is a vast improvement on earlier supporters-to-fighters ratios that went as high as 20:1 in some cases, but it is still a large support element that, of course, generates its own support needs. Rear echelon soldiers still need food, housing, medical care, and so forth.[30]

In 2001, the Army had addressed this shortfall in the Stryker Brigades by creating 205-person combat service support companies to be attached to the 392-person brigade support battalions in each Stryker Brigade Combat Team (SBCT). These companies were primarily transportation, maintenance, and supply augmentation. It was a valiant attempt to come to grips with the problems of light force versus adequate logistics. However, it did nothing to relive the need for a theater supporting structure that would service the Stryker Brigade support battalions.

The reorganized brigades were essentially taken "out of hide," created by reorganizing the pieces of a standard division into smaller elements. The result is more brigades and larger ones, but with fewer maneuver elements—in other words, fewer teeth and more tail. Whether the remaining teeth will be sharp enough to make up the difference remains to be seen. The 3rd Division, which had been so successful in Operation Iraqi Freedom fought with its brigade combat teams reinforced to 5,000 or more troops. Compare this to the 3,700 end strength estimated for a Brigade Unit of Action. As troop strength declines, each soldier becomes correspondingly more necessary and valuable, and the impact of a loss is harder on the unit's ability to perform.

The Future Combat System Reexamined

All these changes would cost money, lots of it, and none had been budgeted for them. The Army's budget issues could be summed up in three letters—FCS, the Future Combat System. In February 2004 General Schoomaker had decided that the Army could not afford its long gestating Comanche attack/reconnaissance helicopter. Instead, the $14 billion scheduled for Comanches would go to upgrade more than 1,400 aircraft and buy almost 800 new helicopters for the Guard and Reserve. The decision fed rumors that FCS might be next.

There had already been considerable skepticism in the OSD about Army transformation and especially the FCS. The schedule now called for 15 FCS brigade-sized Units of Action by 2020—about one-third of the active force. Total cost to develop and produce that many was estimated at $92 billion. It was risky and very expensive.

Skepticism came to a head in April 2004 when Paul L. Francis of the General Accountability Office (GAO) testified before Congress.

> FCS is at significant risk for not delivering required capability within budgeted re-
> sources. Three-fourths of FCS' needed technologies were still immature when the pro-
> gram started. The first prototypes of FCS will not be delivered until just before the
> production decision. Full demonstration of FCS' ability to work as an overarching sys-
> tem will not occur until after production has begun. This demonstration assumes com-
> plete success—including delivery and integration of numerous complementary systems
> that are not inherently a part of FCS but are essential for FCS to work as a whole.[31]

FCS already had all the money it could reasonably expect, and that was not enough. It dominated the Army's entire budget for decades to come, crowding out other programs, including needed maintenance and upgrades for existing equipment. Furthermore, simply throwing more money at the problem would not work anyway. The program was just too ambitious. It was compounded by the fact that FCS really was a "system of systems" just as advertised. Either it all worked or none of it did.[32]

Outside analysts agreed. "It's one thing to strive for transformation, but another thing to expect a near-miracle. That's what we're talking about here, nothing short of a miracle," said defense analyst Eric Miller, of the watchdog group Project on Government Oversight.[33]

After the Paul Francis testimony and the GAO and Welch reports of 2003, the new chief of staff took a careful look at the program.[34] In August 2004, he began to carefully back away from the FCS, at least as previously conceived. Loren Thompson, chief operating officer at the Lexington Institute in Arlington, Virginia, pointed out that the Army's adjustment of the FCS program and schedule marked a major restructuring, a multiyear delay in deploying the system and a 25 percent increase in acquisition costs. "The Army is correctly billing that it is accelerating some of the fielding of FCS technologies," Thompson was quoted as saying. "But it is just as accurate to say that the service is delaying some of the elements."[35]

The announcement was headlined with a statement that the service expected to fully fund the FCS network and its 18 core systems, light manned vehicles, and robotic air and ground vehicles. But the fine print stated that whatever FCS capabilities were ready by 2008 would be tested by an experimental unit (possibly the final Stryker brigade).

Of the 18 core systems required for FCS, only four were expected by 2008 and some of those would be achieved by scaling back capabilities. One critical system was the Non-Line-of-Sight Launch System (NOLS), commonly referred to as "rockets-in-a-box." NOLS was needed to provide the fire support that would protect the thin-skinned FCS vehicles with loitering attack munitions and precision attack munitions. Now, only the precision rockets were expected. No prediction was made as to when the needed antitank loitering munition might be expected.

Three more of the core systems were planned for 2010 and three more in 2012. But the most important element, the network, and eight other core systems would not be ready until 2014. As FCS capabilities developed, they would be filtered into the BCTUAs as further upgrades until 2014 when the first fully equipped Future Force Unit of Action was to be operational, much less capable than originally planned and well behind schedule. It was also noted that a significant increase to the current development funding of $14.78 billion would be required.[36] If that increase was not forthcoming it could easily push FCS back indefinitely.

Given the uncertainty surrounding the debut of FCS as an operational system, any near-term conflicts would be fought by the Brigade Combat Team UAs. This meant that the Army would probably fight much the way conventional formations have fought since the "maneuver" revolution of World War II, a manner derived from Air-Land Battle concepts.

Air Force Transformation

In February 2004, the U.S. Air Force issued its "Transformation Flight Plan," an update of the 2002 version. The 2002 plan had sought to convey "that the Air Force has always been transformational just by its cultural nature." Unfortunately, the plan was so unclear that the service issued a 20-page pamphlet to "explain the concept of transformation to the service's uniformed airmen and civilian employees."[37]

The Air Force also published its Posture Statement for 2004 containing the predictable pitch for the F/A-22, now repackaged as both an "air dominance" fighter and a "precision strike" aircraft. The Posture Statement also helpfully pointed out that "fifth-generation advanced aircraft with capabilities superior to our present fleet of frontline fighter/attack aircraft are now in production."[38]

At about the same time there was an interesting development in the field of air-to-air combat. The USAF's 3rd Fighter Wing lost decisively in ten days of mock-combat against the Air Force of India. Called "Cope India" it was the first joint U.S.-India exercise and pitted U.S. F-15s against India's aging fighter force, composed chiefly of Vietnam-era MiG-21s and a few modern Sukhoi-30s. The American defeat received a great deal of international publicity with headlines like "Aging IAF Shoots Down USAF Top Guns" (*Times of India*) and "War Games in India Show Up US" (BBC). But it came at a suspiciously convenient time.[39]

This sudden vivid demonstration of the desperate "need" for the embattled F/A-22 was skeptically received in defense circles at home and abroad since it came at a time when the Air Force was desperately trying to protect its next-generation fighter from the budget knives. Even the *Times of India* remarked that it all seemed rather too convenient.[40]

Meanwhile the Air Force was having other modernization problems.[41] One way to help assure a controversial program lasts is to implement it incrementally as proto-types, test units, and so forth. On July 1, 2004, the airmen and the Defense Department sought to shore up the future prospects of the F/A-22 Raptor by ordering 22 new copies of the fighter from Lockheed Martin with delivery in October 2006. Given a contract value of $2 billion that brought the flyaway cost of the F-22 to about $100 million per copy. The Air Force already owned 51 F/A-22s. With the additional aircraft it would have about three squadrons of the new planes, nearly enough to constitute a "wing," the usual organization for operational deployment. Altogether that amounted to a substantial number of aircraft and made additional procurement that much harder to stop.[42]

Although protecting the cherished F-22 with a tenacity that bordered on mania, the USAF was not blind to its problems. If it was billing itself as the military arm of decision, able to deliver precision ordnance anywhere in the world and conduct halt phase operations that would bring ground forces to their knees, the Raptor was not the solution. In cold fact, the Air Force was not structured to do that. In written testimony for the House Armed Services Committee, the service's vice chief of staff pointed out that in Operation Iraqi Freedom aircraft were able to operate from bases close to the battlefront. There was no reason to believe that luxury would exist in the future.[43]

Simply put, as the land-based air arm, the USAF needed bases. Most of its inventory consisted of 2,400 "short-legged" tactical fighters, the F-15, the F-16, and the A-10. Its long range inventory was limited to about sixty 1970s vintage B-1s, 21 B-2 stealth bombers, and 85 B-52s that were older than the pilots that flew them. Both the B-1 and the B-52 could carry large bomb loads over intercontinental ranges but were vulnerable to enemy air defense systems. Two B-1s can carry as much ordnance as a squadron of F-16s (24), while needing only eight aircrew instead of 24 and using less than half the fuel. Even without refueling, the B-1 can operate from much farther away from the battle area, reducing or eliminating the demand for operating, maintaining, and defending forward airfields.

The stealthy B-2 existed in only 21 copies (all based in the middle of the United States) and carried less ordnance than either of the other two bombers.[44] To operate as advertised, the airmen needed either forward bases or lots of very long range aircraft. In recognition of these facts, on April 29, 2004, the USAF asked industry for ideas to "substantially" improve its long range strike capability in the near term, either by upgrading existing bombers or fielding a new weapons system. The new capability needed to be operational by 2020, the request stated. This was amazingly quick by normal procurement standards.[45]

John P. Jumper and James G. Roche said they were becoming increasingly convinced of the need for "an interim long-range strike system...not necessarily a bomber" (i.e., a bomber) to cover the gap between the current small and aging bomber force and a next-generation platform, which might not enter service for more than two decades. Given the expected lag time, the flyers suggested they would need yet another version of the F-22.

The requirement called for substantially greater payload capacity and unrefueled range than existing fighter/attack jets yet not as large, costly, or complex to operate and maintain as the B-2. Proving themselves nothing if not single-minded, air power advocates immediately proposed a bomber version of the F/A-22 as the ideal interim replacement.[46] There were several alternatives (conventional warheads on ICBMs, an arsenal plane, a UCAV) but as the Congressional Research Service noted dryly, the

FB-22 "appears to be the only bomber concept that Air Force leaders are discussing with any enthusiasm."[47]

Unfortunately for USAF budgeteers, the ground support issue could not be resolved by repackaging the F-22. The Army had been pressing for more close support aircraft, and accordingly U.S. Air Force Chief of Staff Jumper announced that the service would like to buy the F-35 Joint Strike Fighter (JSF) STOVL (Short Takeoff Vertical Landing) variant, ostensibly to provide close air support, particularly for Army ground troops. In September, they pegged the number of STOVL F-35s at "hundreds." This was a sharp reversal in USAF budgeting since the plan had been to buy 1,763 close support JSFs, all in the conventional takeoff and landing configuration. If it freed up funds for the F-22, who was the loser?

Meanwhile, the "industry team" making the F-22 began a series of newspaper ads, emphasizing that over 1,000 companies in 43 states were involved in building the fighter plane. Obviously, this covered a lot of Congressional districts, and the impact was not likely to be ignored by lawmakers.

Stryker Under the Magnifying Glass

Regardless of questions about Stryker, on March 4, 2004, General Dynamics Land Systems received an Army order for 212 of 300 vehicles need to form a fourth Stryker brigade in 2006. The price tag was $282.4 million not including the cost of the additional 88 vehicles needed for the brigade.[48]

Stryker's troubles continued unabated as the GAO and the Senate both continued to critique the program. The GAO reported that the vehicle was still too heavy to transport any reasonable distance on the C-130. Further, GAO confirmed reports that Stryker did not roll out of the aircraft ready to fight, but instead required time-consuming preparation before it entered combat. In addition, the costs of the program had soared 22.5 percent in just three years.[49]

Senator John Warner (R-VA) and Senator John McCain (R-AZ), the two highest-ranking Republicans on the Senate Armed Services Committee (SASC), reacted with an announcement that the committee was "gathering information on inadequacies of the Stryker program" and would hold hearings on the program. Stryker was a huge, and hugely critical, procurement program for the Army. And the vehicle's woes could no longer be explained away as typical development pangs in a new program. The Stryker program was well along, and even strong criticism from Congress had not prompted the Army and the contractor to produce solutions.[50] Adding insult to injury, it also turned out that when a Stryker was loaded on a C-130, a second aircraft was needed for most of its fuel, ammo, appliqué armor, and operational equipment. According to the *Washington Post,* some in Congress felt they had been lied to about the system.

Warner, the SASC Chairman, spoke of Stryker in the past tense, as he recalled how Pentagon planners envisioned its signal role in the new Army. The Stryker "was a system that was going to be the centerpiece for the reorganization of the Army." It was supposed to be the herald of a new era of lighter, more capable, highly deployable

Army vehicles. Instead, it was turning out to be a somewhat better-than-average armored truck and less deployable than some of the tracked vehicles it was to replace.[51]

The Stryker had been sold as part of a transformational move away from the ponderous weapons of the past, in favor of light, swift, and agile systems. Allegedly, Rumsfeld was not a big fan of the program, and he certainly did not enjoy being raked over the coals about it by Congress. Stryker seemed poised to become another of the Army's failed programs along with the Crusader artillery system and the Comanche helicopter. One OSD staffer observed privately, "the problem isn't that Rumsfeld is canceling Army programs, but that the Army keeps coming forward with programs that either meet no-longer-relevant requirements from the '80s or '90s [e.g., Crusader and Comanche] or that meet relevant requirements in unrealistic or just plain bad ways."

The concept of Stryker brigades as the Army's first response to serious conflict had apparently been abandoned. Still, there was a feeling that the Army had gone too far down the road with Stryker to turn back, and in October 2004 General Dynamics received the go-ahead for at least limited production of all the Stryker variants. The troubled Mobile Gun System received only a "limited low-rate production" green light for 14 vehicles. This number would allow further development of "selective redesign" while additional reliability testing was performed on two of the original eight engineering prototype Mobile Gun System (MGS).[52]

Of all the new BCTUA, the number of Stryker Brigades was now pegged at five plus a sixth to function as an experimental unit for FCS. Evidently, they were no longer the wave of the future. The other Units of Action Brigades would have Force XXI equipment like the rest of the Army, improving it incrementally until the Future Combat System became reality, if it ever did.[53] The remainder of the nearly 2,100 planned Strykers would be assigned to these BCTUAs as conventional vehicles, that is, without the elaborate networking systems of the SBCTs.

Stryker's fate as a fairly conventional armored vehicle was underlined in an odd move in early 2005. The Army ordered that 16 Strykers, minus the elaborate network, be diverted to a Ranger unit. The vehicles scheduled for delivery to the 2nd Cavalry Regiment (BCTUA) would go instead to the 2nd Ranger Battalion, scheduled for Afghanistan. In a typically convoluted move, it was stressed that the Rangers were "borrowing," not buying, the Strykers but that "it is unclear when the Rangers will return the vehicles." The mystery was further deepened when plans were revealed to somehow create a seventh Stryker BCTUA in U.S. Army Europe. Despite removing 16 vehicles from the system for the Rangers and still more for the new seventh unit, it was promised that all units would receive their Strykers on schedule, although it was unclear how that might be accomplished.[54]

In northern Iraq, the 1st Brigade (SBCT) of the 25th Infantry Division was urgently calling for early fielding of the Stryker Mobile Gun System. The intended stopgap, tube-launched optically tracked, wire-guided, antitank missiles mounted on infantry Strykers, was not working. The antitank missiles just did not have the firepower needed against fast-moving insurgents in Mosul. But their hopes were disappointed in June when the Army announced that the first 14 of the new MGS prototypes, with a redesigned ammo handling system, would not even be ready to begin testing until October.[55]

Personnel Problems

October 2004 marked three years of Operation Enduring Freedom in Afghanistan with 18,000 Coalition forces still on duty there, about 8,000 more than at the fall of the Taliban. There had been real improvement. After delays, the country's first national election was scheduled for October 9 and over 10 million Afghans, 40 percent of them women, were registered to vote. But after three years of effort former Taliban and other insurgents still contested some areas outside the major cities, especially in the south and west and along the rugged Afghan-Pakistani border. An International Security Assistance Force (ISAF), a NATO force operating under a United Nations mandate (UNSCR 1386, 1413, and 1444), had been established in 2003 to take over security duties in Kabul and vicinity, relieving U.S. troops of security duties to hunt insurgents. By 2004 ISAF included more than 8,000 soldiers, sailors, and airmen from 36 nations and expanded operations outside Kabul to help stabilize selected areas in advance of Afghan national elections.[56] This did nothing to reduce the American military presence; it just shifted it to less stable areas.

In Iraq the insurgency still ground on. During September, 29 Iraqi and multinational troops were killed by car bombs. U.S. and Iraqi forces undertook a drive to restore enough control so national elections could be held in January. The main focus of the operation was the rebel held cities including Najaf, Fallujah, and the Sadr City section of northeastern Baghdad.

As of October 5, 2004, there had been 1,205 Coalition deaths, 1,066 Americans, 68 Britons, 6 Bulgarians, 1 Dane, 2 Dutch, 1 Estonian, 1 Hungarian, 19 Italians, 1 Latvian, 13 Poles, 1 Salvadoran, 3 Slovaks, 11 Spaniards, 2 Thai, and 9 Ukrainians.[57]

In late 2004 it was finally inarguable. Even the diehards in the OSD admitted that the armed forces were running out of personnel. The 30th Heavy Separate Brigade (North Carolina), the first National Guard Brigade to deploy since World War II, was fighting in Iraq. Combat units from the Florida National Guard were in the Middle East, and squadrons from the Air National Guard supported Coalition troops in Afghanistan and Iraq. More than 188,000 reserve component service members were on active duty.[58]

The United States Army had 340,000 soldiers deployed around the world. About 145,000 were in Iraq including two entire divisions (the 1st Cavalry and the 1st Infantry Divisions) and six brigade combat teams—the equivalent of two more divisions—plus an infantry regiment, an armored brigade, and a separate combat engineer company. More than 40 percent of the U.S. troops in Iraq were National Guard and reserve members with the total expected to reach 50 percent by the end of the year.[59]

Another 13,500 were in Afghanistan, including the equivalent of a division and elements drawn from five different aviation regiments (all the aviation units came from the National Guard). The remainder was deployed around the world from Korea to Kosovo. A battalion of the New Jersey National Guard was on peacekeeping duty in the Sinai.[60]

Meanwhile, three Guard Brigade Combat Teams and a division headquarters had been called up and were training to replace units in Iraq. The head of the U.S. Army Forces Command recommended that another four National Guard Brigades be mobilized for unspecified duties in "the fight against terrorists." Last but not least, General Schoomaker's brigade reorganization plan needed more infantrymen than the current Army force structure could offer, about 1,000–1,2000 more per new brigade.[61] The Air Force and Navy were being tapped for personnel to fill holes in the Army roster in Afghanistan and Iraq. More than 4,000 Air Force personnel were assigned new roles (including drivers, interrogators, prison sentries, and gunners on supply trucks) and dispatched to combat zones for longer tours of duty—as much as 12 months rather than the Air Force's usual 4 months. Like the airmen, several thousand sailors were assigned to "nontraditional" roles to free up Army personnel in Iraq, in Afghanistan, and at the military prison at Guantanamo Bay, Cuba. To say that the Army was overstretched would have been a considerable understatement.

One of the reasons for the enthusiasm over future force concepts is that they promised to reduce personnel requirements. People are the most expensive part of the U.S. military because they require the greatest amount of support. This made it very tempting for the budget cutters of the 1990s to reduce personnel as a first priority. Given the breakup of the USSR and the assumption of a strategic pause in which the United States could expect no major military engagements, it made sense. Money that would be spent on housing, medical care, training, and so forth could be used to fund the expected future technologies that would in turn enable an even smaller force.

It was an enviable feedback loop but it did not work out in reality. The strategic pause turned out to be ephemeral, beginning with the first Gulf War. But, even that war brought only a brief, temporary halt to the strength cuts. Units were still returning from the desert when the cutting began again. It did, however, teach planners a false lesson. Since reserve units (especially the National Guard) played only a small role, there seemed no reason to worry about them. Here again economy was the order of the day as units were disestablished and the survivors consolidated.

When the reduced Army was called on to fight simultaneously in two locations, it could barely manage to do so even with the reserve units. As a result, by October 2004, nearly 234,000 reservists had been called to active duty, about 168,340 were currently mobilized, and more were expected. Since the other services were also using their reservists at an unprecedented rate, a GAO report concluded that "it is possible that DoD will run out of forces."[62]

The problem was not just short-term. For reservists repeated mobilizations were not an attractive prospect. Accordingly, retention and recruiting rates were dropping in both the active and the reserve forces. In high demand specialties, the attrition was even more serious. In the Army Reserve the retention rate for military police went from about 67 percent in 2000 to 49 percent in 2003. The rate for National

Guardsmen with aviation skills dropped from 80 percent in 2000 to about 30 percent in 2003 according to the GAO.[63]

When the war began, there was little debate about the length of combat tours because the Pentagon did not expect to deploy large numbers of troops for more than a few months. But as the unexpected insurgency grew, the 12-month rule was adopted for both active-duty and reserve units, and a few units were ordered to stay even longer. Over the following year, the toll taken by the constant level of danger and tension and the continual trickle of casualties resulted in a call for shorter combat tours, 9 or even 6 months instead of 12. General Schoomaker replied that he would prefer shorter combat tours in Iraq but that could not happen as long as the roughly 135,000 troops were required there to fight the insurgency. The well was quickly running dry. Perhaps things would be better in another year when more Iraqi police and soldiers had been trained.[64]

Training Problems

In the BCTUA-based Army the problem would be exacerbated by the training requirement created by the proliferation of digital networked systems. Common sense, ordinary experience, and reports from the field all confirmed what should have been obvious: digital skills are hard to acquire, tend to be very perishable, and require a steep learning curve for both soldiers and leaders. According to one training officer, "It takes a long time for human crews to learn how to intuitively operate" these complex systems-of-systems. What is more, the emerging generation of complex digital tools is not only more complex but there are more of them. This adds to an already heavy individual and collective training burden. Both the Army as an institution and individual commanders need to make some hard choices about the kind and amount of training soldiers receive.[65]

The lack of an institutionally based, Army-wide digitization training strategy makes the situation worse. The result is a trade-off between training time for soldier skills and technical skills. In the real world civilian contractors field the systems and their numerous modifications and do most of the training. This is not a viable long-term solution.[66]

Special Operations Forces in the New Army

In January 2003, Secretary Rumsfeld had proclaimed a new order of things in special operations. Not only would U.S. Special Operations Command (USSOCOM) headquarters be expanded, but special operations forces (SOF) would run their own counterterrorist operations. The in-theater Special Operations Command (T-SOC) units (formerly subordinate to the regional commanders) would have authority to plan their own missions under the supervision of USSOCOM, requisition the materials required, and execute the missions. It was another huge change in the way SOF did business. No longer did SOCOM need to go through a torturous and usually unfruitful approval process before conducting antiterrorist operations outside a war zone.[67]

> By organizing at SOCOM headquarters in Tampa, as well as at smaller Theater Special Operations Commands in regional theaters, the Special Operations Command will have the tools it will need to plan and execute missions in support of the global war on terror.[68]

Needless to say, this announcement was received with a marked lack of enthusiasm among those who supported the old command arrangement (especially Combatant Commanders) and those who opposed special operations on general principles. There was also reluctance among the other services to support what was perceived as essentially a ground combat (i.e., Army) organization. In fact, very little of substance had happened since General Charles R. Holland received his original marching orders shortly after the 9/11 attacks. Much of the blame for the slow pace of change was placed on Holland, who was reluctant to enter the kind of knife fight that would be needed to wrest power from the theater commanders and accept the authority given to him by Rumsfeld. Now the advisers of the Secretary of Defense were telling him that "Charlie's got a case of the slows."[69]

As a result, SOCOM received a new commander to go with its new responsibilities—when Holland's term at SOCOM expired in September 2003, he was replaced with Army Lieutenant General Bryan "Doug" Brown, a long-time special operator and Holland's former deputy. Rumsfeld ordered General Brown, to speed up SOCOM's transition into a fully operational command. The command was to "plan strategically" and execute operations around the world. SOCOM and the T-SOCs would also receive upgraded command, control, and communications facilities to plan and execute operations worldwide.

The changes meant that Special Operations Command would perform fewer special airlift missions, counterdrug operations, and routine foreign military training and civil support. That was another change welcomed in the special operations community where such "ash and trash" missions were often viewed with disdain. Other U.S. forces or agencies could pick up those missions.[70]

Any reference to special operations forces was curiously downplayed in public descriptions of Schoomaker's reorganization, curious because of the widespread publicity given the participation of SOF in Afghanistan and Iraq. However, no one needed fear that the special operators would be left out. In past wars SOF and SOF-like units had been formed and then either diminished or abolished altogether. But now, because of the biggest budget increase in its history, SOCOM was poised to become the major player in ill-defined "global war on terrorism." Funding was projected to increase by as much as 20 percent per year for the next five years, 4,000 people would be added as well as dozens of new helicopters and fixed-wing aircraft. The personnel increase will include not only the well-known commandos (e.g., Navy SEALs, Army Special Forces) but also the Army's psychological operations and civil affairs troops, and a new 85-man USMC Special Operations unit, Det 1, which deployed to Iraq in April 2005.[71]

Earlier enthusiasm for giving SOCOM a new intelligence role had not waned either. The command began adding 700 intelligence analysts and related skills to its U.S. and overseas regional headquarters. According to statements made to the press, the new resource would analyze intelligence—gathered by its own forces as well as by CIA agents, spy satellites, and other means—and plan Special Operations–led missions with an emphasis on agile responses to short-term intelligence.[72] SOCOM also began building a new "warfighting hub," for "planning, supporting, and executing Special Operations in the war on terrorism," according to General Brown.[73]

The new emphasis was part of Secretary Rumsfeld's endless search for "actionable intelligence." An official quoted in the press stated, "For too long, the shooters have left intel for the spooks to do. Our philosophy is: Everybody's an intelligence agent." Armed with the secretary's instructions to carry out capture or kill missions against terrorists both SOCOM and USASOC wasted no time in spending the money. The U.S. Army Special Operations Command quietly opened an intelligence-training center at Fort Lewis, Washington. The command had operated its own specialized intelligence training at Fort Bragg, North Carolina, since 1986, but the new school was allegedly a more advanced program. Published reports state the school focuses on how to create collection networks and how to handle informants. "You're not supposed to know what they do," according to a publicly quoted source. "They say it's an advanced intelligence course, kind of like the 'Farm' [CIA training center]."[74]

The issue of an increased paramilitary role for special operations units took on particular importance when the 9/11 Commission delivered its final report in June 2004. In it, the commission made several recommendations to improve intelligence and related matters, including the role of USSOCOM. Citing the model of CIA-SOCOM cooperation on covert and clandestine operations in Afghanistan, the commission called for standing, closer cooperation between military special operations and the CIA. More pointedly it made the specific recommendation that "lead responsibility for directing and executing paramilitary operations, whether clandestine or covert, be shifted to the Defense Department" under "the Special Operations Command."[75] Defense Secretary Rumsfeld was not enthusiastic about taking over the CIA's paramilitary tasks and then-acting CIA Director John McLaughlin was vociferously against it.

Much of the issue hung on the definition of "paramilitary." The OSD was apparently willing, perhaps even enthusiastic, about undertaking clandestine *military* operations, meaning those conducted secretly by U.S. military forces with or without the cooperation of local national troops. But "paramilitary operations" as conducted by the CIA involve persons that are not part of the armed forces of the United States. Often the missions do not have any direct military effect and are aimed at strengthening and encouraging foreign elements considered desirable by the United States. (In practice, military personnel may be temporarily assigned to the CIA, and CIA personnel may temporarily serve directly under a military commander.)[76]

As explained by the Congressional Research Service:

DOD special operations are frequently clandestine—designed in such a way as to ensure concealment; they are not necessarily covert, that is, concealing the identity of the sponsor is not a priority. The CIA, however, conducts covert and clandestine operations to avoid directly implicating the US Government.[77]

In fact, there was great similarity between the CIA functions and the SOF ones, and the differences were as much a matter of degree as kind. Especially since, according to the Congressional Research Service, the CIA often needed military support. There was no clear right or wrong answer, but it was one of those ideas that would not go away.

Another QDR

In the midst of turmoil in Iraq and continuing combat in Afghanistan loomed the specter of yet another Quadrennial Defense Review (QDR) in 2005. As always, the QDR was a high stakes game for all involved. But this time the "Terms of Reference," a classified document spelling out the basic assumptions underlying the process was written by none other than Secretary Rumsfeld himself, reportedly without input from the service chiefs. Nevertheless, the Army had cause for optimism. Regarded earlier as the service of the past, the Army was now heavily engaged. It was obvious that high-tech sensors and weaponry would not locate Al-Qaeda fighters along the Pakistan border or insurgents in the Sunni Triangle. That was a job for foot soldiers and even old-fashioned heavy armor. In the past the Army had been willing if not eager to accept force cuts to finance transformation technology. Now, stretched thin by operations in Afghanistan and Iraq, a compelling case could be made for more troops. Since the Army had already been authorized a temporary strength increase of 30,000, any redivision of the budget might well sacrifice Air Force fighters and Navy ships to pay for the Army's strength boost. Furthermore, since the Army's burdens were not likely to lessen soon, it might be necessary to make the increase permanent at an annual cost of about $3 billion.

But President Bush had announced that he expected to reduce the national budget deficit in part by cutting back defense spending. Since the operations and maintenance and personnel budgets were off-limits, that left procurement. Defense Department budget documents leaked to the press confirmed the fears of the other services that they were about to be sacrificed on the altar of Army shortfalls. Cuts of $55 billion over six years were proposed, mostly from the Navy and Air Force including F/A-22 procurement, to be reduced by 96 planes, well below what the airmen claimed to need. Navy submarine purchases would also be reduced, and even President Bush's prized missile defense system would be cut. The Army, on the other hand, wanted additional $25 billion through 2011 to finance Schoomaker's BCTUAs.[78]

Through the last half of 2004, OSD representatives began meeting with service counterparts in order to "get ready for the Quadrennial Defense Review and exchange information so that we're working with each other, not against each other," said one official who participated in the discussions. Not that anyone actually expected that to happen. The Army and the Air Force had both maintained full-time QDR offices since 2001, preparing for the inevitable bloodletting of the 2005 report.[79]

This was brought into stark focus in February 2005, when Schoomaker told the House Armed Services Committee that, in addition to the annual $5 billion or so for the "modularity" reorganization, $3 billion more was needed for personnel to man the new Modular brigades and another $4 billion to reset forces returning from Iraq and other locations overseas.[80]

Afghanistan and Iraq

Real progress was being made in Afghanistan, if not at the pace critics would have preferred. The transitional administration had adopted a national development framework and budget, a constitution had been drafted, and a new national currency, the afghani, was already stable. The International Monetary Fund estimated that the economy had grown by 28 percent in the past year; over 2 million refugees returned to Afghanistan and millions of children were in school, some for the first time. After 23 years of war these were significant achievements, but the security situation was still not good. Antigovernment elements continued to demonstrate their ability to strike even the capital Kabul.[81]

For months the U.S. forces, the Taliban, and Al-Qaeda had waged war over the legitimacy of Afghanistan's first national election, scheduled for October 9. The Taliban and Al-Qaeda warned everyone to boycott the election, boasting that they would reduce the polls to chaos and bloodshed. The primary counter was the ad hoc U.S. and NATO-led Provincial Reconstruction Teams that sought to bring at least a degree of progress and security. New Zealand and South Korea had been persuaded to contribute, and the teams were operating in 20 of Afghanistan's most populated areas by September 2004.[82] In some of the most dangerous areas similar actions were carried out by the Army's CAT-A teams (Civil Affairs Team–Alpha) doing their best to help give legitimacy to the new central government one road and one school at a time.[83]

U.S.-led operations continued with soldiers and marines pursuing guerrillas as part of a winter offensive in frozen Patika Province along old-time smuggling routes that crossed Afghanistan's eastern border.[84]

Elsewhere there was little respite for the American armed forces, and Iraq was the reason. In October, Secretary Rumsfeld declared that no large American redeployment could be expected before Iraqi security forces were strong enough to maintain order throughout Iraq. When he spoke, there were about 100,000 trained and minimally equipped Iraqi security forces. An additional 50,000 were expected by the January elections.[85] Rumsfeld said the goal was to have 200,000 to 250,000 trained Iraqi security troops. It was an incredible demand to put on General David Petraeus —the well-established and equipped training base in the United States would have been hard-pressed to produce that many soldiers. To do it in Iraq would call for another miracle, and none was forthcoming.[86]

U.S. troops there celebrated Halloween 2004 with the news that about 6,500 of them would be extended for at least two more months for the next round of Iraqi elections scheduled for late January. Troops from the 1st Cavalry Division and the 1st Infantry Division (who would have gladly foregone the honor) were selected to "maintain continuity of forces in the theater during the election period." It was the second extension for the 1st Cavalry troopers. On the other hand, soldiers of the 3rd Infantry Division, scheduled to replace 1st Cavalry troopers, would deploy on schedule, sooner if needed. Meanwhile the 42nd Infantry Division (New York Army National Guard) was scheduled to become the first division-level National Guard deployment into combat since World War II. By that time, more than 40 percent of the U.S. force in Iraq was Guard or Reserve, and the insurgency continued unabated.

Finally, on October 8, 2004, Secretary Rumsfeld issued Defense Directive 3000.cc "Defense Capabilities to Transition to and from Hostilities." In it he directed the services to provide a more robust stabilization and reconstruction capability.[87] Importantly for the Army it ordered that the Land Component Commander (i.e., the Army) in any campaign would have the primary responsibility for stabilization and reconstruction.[88]

Until now the idea had been to push off postconflict responsibilities to civil agencies and international relief groups. But those had proven reluctant.

Rumsfeld's directive was a necessary public relations move and probably as close as the secretary could come to admitting a mistake. Less impressively, he also placed the responsibility for the robust capability in the already overstretched reserve components. Presumably that would at least mollify the most vocal critics and still maintain the momentum for transition in the active services. Quick to read the handwriting on the wall, the services immediately made "post conflict stabilization" the phrase of the day.

At the beginning of November the count of U.S. military deaths in Iraq stood at 1,119, and it rose rapidly as fighting escalated in the insurgent-held city of Fallujah and insurgents struck back in other cities and towns. Since the start of the war, 8,287 U.S. service members had been wounded, 5,000 seriously enough to prevent them from returning to duty. The majority of the deaths in Fallujah were U.S. Marines killed in action as the 1st Marine Expeditionary Force led the house-to-house fighting along with elements of the Army 1st Cavalry Division and 1st Infantry Division and several battalions of U.S.-trained Iraqi troops.

The insurgents had proven more deadly and resilient than expected and the newly trained Iraqi security forces less capable than hoped. After the Fallujah offensive, insurgents continued to attack in other parts of Iraq, like Mosul and Babil Province. At the same time, a sizable U.S. force was needed in Fallujah to stabilize the city and attempt to restart reconstruction. Experienced combat-hardened forces were needed against the insurgents and to put steel behind the faltering Iraqi security forces. Squads of U.S. soldiers or Marines were stationed inside police stations in hopes they would stiffen the resolve of local forces and prevent routs like that in Mosul, where newly minted Iraqi police officers fled when attacked by small numbers of rebels. All of this meant that still more soldiers and Marines were needed on the ground.[89]

By December 2004 about 650,000 American soldiers were on active duty worldwide (including 185,000 reservists), a total that was well above the Army's legally authorized strength of 480,000. About 200,000 were engaged in combat or peacekeeping, almost entirely in Iraq and Afghanistan. The Pentagon announced in December that an additional 12,000 troops were required to quell insurgent attacks and provide security for the Iraqi elections on January 30. The 6,500 troops had already been extended in October. This brought the total number of military in Iraq to 150,000, the highest level since the invasion. If the war had gone as originally planned at this point there would be no more than a single division left in Iraq.[90] Instead, DoD found itself extending the tours of about 10,400 soldiers and marines, even as their replacements began to arrive. On top of these numbers, two battalions of the Army's 82nd Airborne were altered for movement to Iraq in early January 2005.

Despite insurgent attacks more serious than those in Afghanistan and threats more credible, the January 30, 2005, elections came on schedule. Insurgents attacked polling stations with bombings and mortar volleys that killed more than 40 people, including nine suicide bombers. In one spectacular video a long line of Iraqis wound around a polling place and snaked down the street. When insurgent gunfire broke out, the crowd scattered, but when the shooting stopped they reformed their line and resumed patient waiting for their turn to vote. By most estimates about 8 million people voted, roughly 60 percent of those eligible. Under the circumstances it was a remarkable demonstration.

> This was not a perfect election, but that it was held is the thing.
> —Shehab, Iraqi teacher and journalist, Basra[91]

Successful as they may have been, the elections did not eliminate the insurgency. The next day, a suicide bomber killed 21 people in Baghdad. For the United States, the manpower crunch was more serious than ever as the third rotation of troops to Iraq began, including the last of the National Guard's combat brigades. The troops held past their rotation date could now leave for home, but that did nothing to relive the situation. The Pentagon response was to consider rewriting the rules for reserve call-ups, permitting National Guard and Reserve members to be mobilized beyond the existing two-year limit. Lieutenant General James Helmy, head of the Army Reserve, lashed out in response, warning that the Reserve was rapidly turning into "a broken force." No one was invoking the image of elite commandos, deep air-mech strikes, or small, agile information-enhanced units now. The need was for ordinary, mundane soldiers with unglamorous trucks and HMMWVs.[92]

In Afghanistan the situation was somewhat better as the long-sought international relief force finally began to materialize as thousands of NATO (principally British and Canadian) soldiers arrived to expand local security. Nevertheless, 2005 was the deadliest in Afghanistan since the Taliban was ousted in 2001. About 1,600 people were killed, including 91 U.S. troops, double the total in 2004. By mid-2003, NATO troops (principally) were expanding cautiously into the volatile southern areas where the Taliban welcomed them with a fresh series of attacks. This did not mean that the United States was leaving. About 2,500 American soldiers were redeployed, but further scheduled draw-downs were halted when the Taliban resumed their sporadic offensive in 2006.[93]

CHAPTER 10

THE DIGITAL ARMY

[The Army] cannot simply be what it was, and think that it is going to be relevant for this new, complex world that is emerging.
—John Hamre, Deputy Secretary of Defense[1]

The Bridge to the Future Force[2]

Electronic connectivity between and among all echelons in the Army will result in such speed and precision in communication that the entire organization's situational awareness and agility will far exceed that of today's forces. This greatly enhanced connectivity, speed, precision, and agility will result in significantly improved lethality, survivability, tempo, versatility, sustainability, and deployability in the force.
—4th Infantry Division (Mechanized) Force XXI Briefing, April 2000

The improvements promised in the Force XXI briefing proved to be real, even if considerably short of the all-encompassing changes that had been promised. But digitization and transformation were no longer at the top of the agenda. Because of the continuing, unexpected demands of the fighting in Iraq and Afghanistan, the problem was finding enough troops. The new "modular" Brigade Combat Team Units of Action (UAs) were the Army's solution and were accepted with far less resistance than Future Combat System (FCS) and transformation. Perhaps this was because they were the most straightforward, combat brigades being generally more similar than different. The sort of reshuffling General Peter J. Schoomaker called for was fairly simple to conceptualize. However, despite the avowed "expeditionary" and modular nature of these new units, the fact was that they could still not go to war without a great deal of support. The changes made to accommodate that above

the brigade and division level were less straightforward because at the corps level
and above units were sufficiently different to preclude a simple rearrangement of
assets.

Prior to the Schoomaker shuffle and the introduction of the confusing and unnecessary Units of Employment–X (UEx), Units of Employment–Y (UEy), and so forth,
the active duty Army contained four corps, the First, Third, Fifth, and Eighteenth
Airborne Corps. Above these were eight "armies" or Army Service Component
Commands. Whatever the names, these organizations are responsible for logistics
and administrative functions but are not in the direct chain of command between
the regional commander and the Army corps in the field.

In general, a three-star UEx (corps) was made up of two or more divisions, commonly three. It is the highest echelon concerned with warfighting per se. In Army
manuals it is common to say that the corps functions at the operational level, meaning that it sets the conditions for combat success by its divisions, the formations that
actually fight. Corps have more resources than divisions, and, if skillfully used, these
resources (missile and artillery fire, intelligence, logistic support, etc.) can be of enormous aid to divisions in combat.

Under the planned reorganization some of the corps' capabilities migrate to the
two-star UEx (division). Those remaining merge with the Service Component Commands, creating the UEy. The idea was that this would eliminate the corps, removing
an entire level of hierarchy and streamlining command and support arrangements.
This change raises important questions of how corps and theater support functions
will be accomplished since the change was inaugurated without accompanying doctrine, and so far it has proven untenable. However, the present discussion is more
concerned with the combat employment of these units. For that reason, the issue
of theater support will not be addressed except in passing.[3]

General Kevin Byrnes, the Army's chief of training, described division support this
way:

> The [conventional] division headquarters—in order to deploy—must pull support from
> its signal battalion up to division headquarters, pull a lot of intelligence out of its intelli-
> gence battalion, pull fires out of the division artillery, pull engineers, and form a larger
> entity. Our division headquarters [the future UEx] will...not rely on subordinate or
> higher headquarters for manning...[the headquarters] will be formed and trained as a
> deployable entity.[4]

This is interesting since it implies that the division UEx may not lose most of its
capabilities to the Brigade Combat Team Units of Action (BCTUAs) after all. It
leaves open the question of where the Army will find enough additional resources
to fill out the support requirements for the expanded brigades.

The U.S. Army's III Corps at Fort Hood, Texas, was considered the prototype for
the reorganized corps. All of III Corps deployed to Iraq in 2003 where it fought as a
Force XXI unit, an industrial age formation with digital enhancements.

As a new three-star UEx, III Corps (and its component UEx's) were designed to be
"Joint from the start." It is "joint connected" with an organic, standing capability to

operate with other services—i.e., have multiservice connectability via the Global Information Grid. This sounds good but, like all the new network intensive approaches, it brings problems of its own.

Success in combat requires commanders to visualize the battlefield and to see the enemy, the terrain, and themselves in time and space. That, in a nutshell is the point of all the rhetoric of information dominance. However, this has been difficult for higher echelons like a corps because of time required to receive and process operations reports (information about what friendly forces are doing) and intelligence (information on what the enemy is doing). New information technology (IT) has improved situational awareness at all levels. But advanced technology alone is insufficient and perhaps even counterproductive without doctrine to integrate the employment of new systems. Unless doctrine and organizations evolve together, the Army will simply be preparing to replay the second Gulf War.

Because the principal strength of these units still lies in their M1 main battle tanks and Bradley fighting vehicles (with digital upgrades), the temptation is to create doctrine that is not very new, an updated version of AirLand Battle. This temptation to tinker around the edges of old doctrine (with cosmetic changes) is enhanced by the fact that updated doctrine and updated equipment require each other. However, the Army is and will for the foreseeable future be very unevenly modernized. For example, the Army has about 7,600 Abrams in its total inventory (active and reserve). However, there are limits on the amount of upgrading the Army can afford. The fiscal year 2005 budget request limited both the M2 Bradley upgrade and M1A2 Abrams tank upgrade to save money for the Future Force program.

By preference, the service would field two digitized versions of the Abrams, each matched with Bradley variants carrying comparable technology. But spending on Future Force and the cost of fighting in Afghanistan and Iraq has slowed those programs down from their already slow pace.

The 2005 National Defense Authorization Act allotted only $292 million for enhancements to the M-1, barely enough to upgrade about 67 M1A2s. Only $51.5 million was provided to enhance the Bradley fighting vehicle. The result of all these machinations is a ground force in a variety of states of upgrade with all the consequent problems of training, maintenance, and support. Gone is the neat vision of a fairly uniform "legacy" force with digital upgrades, a very uniform "interim" force based around Stryker, and a "future" force with all the high-tech accoutrements featured in defense industry pamphlets. Instead, the prospect is for a hodgepodge of equipment that is unlikely to be nearly as networked as hoped.

The new "digitized" vehicles are intended to fight as networked systems rather than individual platforms in order to increase combat power by an order of magnitude. The expected increase in tempo, precision, lethality, and survivability will allow Army combat units to dominate battlefields well into the future. In theory, combat power will continue to increase as multiple combat systems are linked to a network of information sharing and synchronization. This idea of having a complete view of the battlefield, or at least that portion the soldier is concerned with, is called situational awareness. Commanders will build on this synergy to focus combat power, maneuver decisively, and achieve decisive results faster and more accurately than ever before.

This oft-repeated theory has a few problems. The first one is, of course, that it does not appear likely that units above the brigade level will be able to network well due to the equipment variations described above. But an equally important challenge lies in the use of the new tools to collect data and distribute it. Even if we presume a force that is at least "virtually uniform," that is, had general electronic compatibility, then the likely result is an information overflow, bombarding the receiver with a flood of data he can neither assimilate nor use. The data need to be processed into usable information and distributed in useful forms so that it actually produces situational awareness and not merely more data. For example, one serious drawback of a more efficient sensor-to-shooter cycle is that it can lead to "friendly fire" incidents by increasing the chances to communicate the wrong target coordinates. It is not always easy to locate targets and, having located them, to be sure to distinguish enemy targets from friendly units, vehicles, and so forth. Allowing time for a human to double-check the position of friendly forces tends to defeat the advantage gained.

Colonel Winn Noyes, former chief of Digital Force Coordination at Fort Hood, describes the problem this way:

> Imagine driving down the highway with many things on your mind. Suddenly, you notice that you are approaching an intersection in which the traffic light is yellow. You must make a decision, and an improper one could cost lives. Technology can supply you with huge amounts of data, such as your speed, the distance to the intersection, the temperature of the road surface and the mechanical state of your car. Even if you could read all the data, you would not have time to use them. Yet, if that data were converted to a couple of simple displays, your complex decision would become a simple, rapid and almost intuitive response. If the displays are right, you can quickly understand the situation and act with more precision and accuracy than ever before.

As the example illustrates, the various data provide situation awareness. But the "couple of simple displays" Colonel Noyes describes do not exist and are not in sight. Instead, a large headquarters like CENTCOM or III Corps has hundreds of computer screens and dozens of different types of displays, many of them not at all simple. What the user needs is to truly understand the situation portrayed by all these inputs. The missing element is analysis, and that has to be performed by human beings. The military uses dozens, perhaps hundreds, of computer-driven analytical tools (nobody really knows how many, and some tools are variations of others). The example above is interesting because it reflects much of the current thinking about applying automated tools to combat. It leaves out the enemy. The true critical variable missing from the example is the other drivers on the road. The only reason the question of the yellow light is important is the possibility of a collision with another vehicle. If there are no other vehicles, then there is no problem. The other solution, of course, is to adopt a simple rule such as "always stop for yellow lights." But the whole point of information-saturated networking is to avoid the inaccuracy, inefficiencies, and redundancy produced by simple rules.

Sensors and Intelligence[5]

So far, we have seen that situational awareness begins with data collection by a variety of sensors ranging from reconnaissance satellites to individual soldiers. In conventional, somewhat digitalized operations (circa 2006) all this information is very loosely integrated by a variety of often incompatible means. The new modular force (the Schoomaker reorganization) adds more reconnaissance assets at the lowest levels and seeks to integrate these assets with existing sensors into responsive networks that will reduce the fog of war, allow commanders to make better decisions, and put informed U.S. forces inside potential adversaries' decision cycles—that is information dominance again, the critical ingredient of Rapid Decisive Operations. Future Force concepts add many more sensors and many more platforms (ground robots, unmanned aerial vehicles, etc.). But, like so much else about transformation, it is harder than it looks in PowerPoint slides.

Hide and Seek

This kind of information dominance is important to the modular force, but vital to the Future Force. The entire Future Force from corps down to squads is expected to significantly enhance its performance through situational awareness. In fact, it is expected to substitute information and responsiveness for armor and firepower, a tall order and a very different thing from merely improved performance. It also requires a Future Force that the enemy cannot detect in time to take effective measures. The whole idea of trying to hide a brigade, much less a division or a corps, is a bit of a stretch, but some planners think it can be done, at least to the extent necessary. In large part this depends on "low observables" (i.e., providing few signatures that can be detected) to prevent them from being found and fired on. Notional drawings of Future Combat Systems (FCS) usually give them curved surfaces, presumably to defeat radar. Since the development of the U.S. Air Force's F-117A fighter in the early 1980s, there has been great interest in stealth technology, not only for aircraft but also for tanks, ships, and other mobile warfighting systems. Stealth technology is actually a combination of techniques and materials that reduce the chances of being detected, primarily by enemy radar. The U.S. F-117A fighter, for example, is coated with radar-absorbing material, uses radar-opaque composites instead of metals, and features a low profile with no surfaces that reflect radar directly back. But the F-117 (and the B-2 stealth bomber) is neither silent nor invisible. It merely presents a reduced radar and infrared signature that makes it harder to target.

The Army plan to field a stealthy aircraft died when the RAH-66 Comanche helicopter was canceled after years of hostile Congressional scrutiny. While it was questionable how stealthy the Comanche would have actually been (helicopter rotor blades create problems for signature reduction), it would have been more so than current helicopters, which try to remain safe by flying behind concealment such as trees. Eventually Congress, Donald Rumsfeld, and Schoomaker all agreed that the improvement was not worth the price tag. The billions would be better spent on upgrades to the existing helicopter fleet. While the use of stealth methods for aircraft has been well established, its application to sea- and ground-based systems is less so. The use of stealth methods to conceal such systems as tanks and artillery may be even more difficult. These methods need to defeat not only radar and infrared sensors but also optical, magnetic, radio frequency, and acoustic ones. Most importantly they need to defeat or at least confuse human observers that need not observe them directly but can locate them through anomalies in the environment. Artillery pieces and tank main guns, for example, emit a detectable electrical impulse in addition to noise and flash when fired. In principle, at least, this means they can be remotely detected and targeted.

Because so much of the Army concept for Future Combat Systems depends on being hard to find, the subject is worth consideration. Proven stealth methods have several possible drawbacks when applied to any future Army force that places a premium on reducing the size, weight, and support requirements for its vehicles. Stealthy vehicles, for example, may weigh more from the addition of external radar-absorbent coatings, from engines that are insulated and buried inside the structure to reduce the heat and noise they generate, and from exotic and sophisticated engine exhaust nozzles that also help reduce heat generation. Additionally, the projected future battlefield with its myriad of sensors will probably require survivable vehicles to carry countermeasures. All of these add weight and volume that equate to penalties in speed, range, performance, and, of course, deployability.

Also, the materials currently used in stealth aircraft may not be robust enough for ground combat. Most of the radar resistant coatings for aircraft require more maintenance than is practical under battlefield conditions. A stealthy vehicle with nicks and gouges from enemy fire (or rough use) or covered with mud and dust may not be very stealthy after all.

Another problem with incorporating stealth technology into vehicles is that the technology requires vehicle shapes that may not prove optimum. Low radar cross-section antenna, for example, may not be optimum for ground combat applications. Because range is reduced by many of stealth's physical constraints, stealth vehicles may need to be larger than desired in order to carry defensive measures and sufficient fuel. These vehicles probably cannot be equipped with external fuel tanks because doing so would increase their radar reflectivity. All external protrusions, such as the edges of hatches, must be perfectly matched to prevent radar energy from being reflected. Because of this, the detail work entailed in the design and construction of a stealth vehicle is likely to be much more exacting than in current systems. Even the smallest oversight in panel matching can make a stealth vehicle vulnerable to radar. Such exacting requirements increase engineering, manufacturing, and maintenance costs. All of these factors apply to stealth aircraft, making them several times as expensive and difficult to maintain as conventional aircraft. It is hard to see why the same would not be true for stealthy ground vehicles.

Finally, the heavily networked, "information dominant" Future Force will be a literal beacon of electromagnetic activity as the various systems use wireless links to continuously pass high volumes of information. While reduced power output, improved signal detection, directional antennas, and frequency hopping can help reduce the vulnerability of any single vehicle, it seems inevitable that the general location of the force will quickly be known with sufficient certainty to steer sensor carrying vehicles such as unmanned aerial vehicles (UAVs) to pinpoint its various elements. Failing that, the enemy might choose to simply flood the battlefield with small, expendable teams carrying antitank rocket launchers. Since every component of the Future Force is vital to the functioning of the whole, losses will be correspondingly serious. It should also be mentioned that such a networked force could easily be much harder to build and operate than it is to detect and destroy.

No Place to Hide

The real fight is a close-in sensor fight.
—Vice Admiral (ret.) Arthur Cebrowski, Director of Force Transformation, 2003

It is not enough for Future Forces to hide successfully; they must also overcome enemy attempts to do likewise. The flip side of stealth is sensor development. Sensors are also key to the evolution of practical precision weapons, and interest in sensors is high, particularly those that can penetrate foliage and adverse weather and can see through clouds, fog, haze, and smoke. Sensors fall in three broad physical categories: electromagnetic (e.g., electro-optical, radio frequency, and low frequency), mechanical (acoustic, seismic, and inertial), and chemical/biological. Fusing passive and active sensors into working architectures is a complex business involving space-based systems, standoff airborne systems [such as Joint Surveillance Target Attack Radar Systems (JSTARS)], unmanned air vehicles, unattended ground sensors, ground and airborne command and control systems, aircraft, and other precision weapon carriers.[6]

The problem of hiding military hardware is increased by the rapid advances in sensors, some (such as low frequency radar) designed specifically to defeat "stealth" measures. Improvements in stealth inevitably will give birth to improvements in detection. As a result, the demand for platforms and equipment that provide persistent intelligence, surveillance, and reconnaissance (ISR) will increase. A glimpse of this capability was shown in Operation Iraqi Freedom, which demonstrated at least the potential of shared awareness and speed as a result of high-speed networking and ISR capabilities.[7]

The III Corps was the test-bed for these systems and carried them to Iraq for the second Gulf War. As the first "digitized" corps, it could call on a vast array of joint and service collection systems in space, in the air, at sea, and on the ground, to detect and track enemy forces. One of their first lessons was that increased capability did not somehow equate to a decreased need for soldiers. Having reduced its overall troop level in anticipation of improved "digital" effectiveness, the corps quickly found that not only did all the traditional soldier tasks still need to be performed, but increased digitalization meant more maintenance and a full complement of contractors to perform it.

In theory these systems can provide actionable targets, but in practice this has not always worked out well. The absolute number of such systems is often quite small and the lag time from detecting a possible target, understanding that it is a suitable target, and actually firing on it can be unacceptably long. Nevertheless, tactical targeting has greatly improved over the past few years. Three sensors in particular make this possible: UAVs, Guardrail Common Sensor aircraft, and JSTARS aircraft. These sensors are linked to the corps artillery's own advanced data processing system through the all-source analysis system in the corps' ACE (Analysis and Control Element). Note, however, that UAVs and JSTARS are available only in very small numbers. During the second Iraq war no more than four Hunter UAVs were ever up at once in the entire theater. JSTARS is similarly limited. Furthermore, both JSTARS and Guardrail depend on nearly total air domination by friendly forces. Even a fairly feeble air threat can be very dangerous to these slow-moving, unarmed systems.

The combination of enhanced sensors and information networked targeting systems is expected to provide targets for artillery, strike aircraft, helicopters, or smart missiles and defeat threats all across the spectrum of conflict. Even light infantry forces generate a variety of detectable signatures—visual, chemical, infrared, electromagnetic, radar, and acoustic—that make them vulnerable to active sensor systems (such as synthetic aperture, moving target indicator, and foliage penetrating radars) and passive (and air-deployed ground-based) sensors (such as low light level TV, thermal imagers, multispectral analyzers, engine electrical ignition, and magnetic field detectors). These signatures can betray the location, strength, and activities of enemy forces, enabling targeting systems to direct attacks against them. A scenario by the RAND Corporation illustrates how they envision using these systems against guerrillas moving heavy weapons by vehicle:[8]

> The JSTARS crew is directed to look for vehicle traffic along several roads. During its mission, the JSTARS' Moving Target Indicator radar detects suspicious vehicle traffic in the area of concern. This information is used to cue a UAV [Unmanned Air Vehicle] equipped with a FolPen [foliage-penetrating] radar and EO/IR [electro-optical/infrared] sensors. The UAV—using its thermal imager—detects and follows several trucks that appear to be carrying weapons. The trucks disappear into a wooded area. The UAV then uses its FolPen radar to follow the vehicles down the hidden road to an assembly area. Ground sensors are then dropped. Using acoustic and thermal imagers, remote operators are able to identify the personnel and vehicles as hostile. Tactical air (TACAIR) is called in to destroy the site.[9]

This scenario omits a couple of salient points. First of all, it assumes that guerrilla trucks can somehow be distinguished from other trucks despite whatever pains the guerrillas take to avoid this. Second, it presumes that it can somehow be determined remotely that these trucks are carrying weapons. Neither of these is trivial, and it is hard to see how they can be reliably accomplished. In Bosnia, Serbia/Kosovo, Afghanistan, and both Iraq wars the problem was not so much finding possible targets as discriminating among them. Even friendly and enemy convoys have been mistaken for each other. In Iraq and Afghanistan it has proven impossible to tell a vehicle full of radical gunmen from one carrying a family home from the market. Ground forces are required in significant numbers to man roadblocks and carry out the old-fashioned, inelegant, and very dangerous method of searching vehicles by hand.

The example also presumes an enemy of very limited resources. Since JSTAR and similar systems exist in very small numbers, it may be simpler, cheaper, and more efficient for a resourceful enemy to eschew elaborate deception measures and simply attack the aircraft on the ground or in the air or attack the crew.

Nevertheless, the capabilities of new detection systems are remarkable by the standards of any previous conflict. One countersniper ballistic analyzer, the Lifeguard sniper location system developed by the Lawrence Livermore National Laboratories, detects a sniper's bullet after the round has been fired, analyzes its flight path, and then establishes the bullet track back to its point of origin with an error of no more than two feet.[10]

So far, however, capabilities like the Lifeguard are closer to technology demonstrations than to deployable systems. Furthermore, the likelihood of having the required number of networked analyzers available at the critical spot is vanishingly small. Even if it proves possible to so equip nearly every vehicle and every squad, enemy snipers may simply avoid frontline combat units and attack more vulnerable support and logistic units. Ironically, the dispersed, fluid battlefield envisioned by FCS may make this more possible since small, hidden enemy teams of a few men each may be missed and left to attack the vulnerable rear.

Once again, it must be emphasized that these systems have limitations that are often omitted in glowing descriptions of their potential. For example, reports from Iraq suggest that the new generation of thermal imaging (i.e., infrared detection) equipment has performed well, especially at night. But it still has problems. Although designed to detect targets out to 1,500 meters and beyond to take advantage of the range of the M1 main gun, solar heat reflecting from the sand and captured by hot dust in the air is said to noticeably degrade the performance of these systems. Under the worst conditions of heat and dust (e.g., daytime convoy movement) the range of these sights was supposedly reduced to about 300 meters with average visibility no better than 700–800 meters during stops. Additionally, some sources report that a significant number of thermal sights and other electronics simply broke down, disabled by fine crystalline sand particles.[11]

The days of paper maps, acetate, and alcohol pens are not over yet, but they seem to be numbered. Maneuver control system workstations now project digital maps in corps and division command posts. Because of the Blue Force Tracker and improved reconnaissance (both made possible by the Global Positioning System) these maps are intended to provide current locations of friendly and enemy units, as well as near real-time displays from sensor networks. For example, UAV video, JSTARS moving target indicator displays, weather satellite imagery, and an air picture are all routinely shown on flat panel displays around the digital map in the corps analysis and control element (also called the all-source intelligence system).

In practice, however, the major improvement has been the ability to track friendly forces. Enemy information in the Iraq war was often sketchy or inaccurate since the systems were designed to look for conventional forces with identifiable signatures. At the tactical level most units found the enemy by the simple process of advancing to contact. However, the ability to have accurate positioning for one's own forces is an often misunderstood advantage. In real life it can be very difficult for a commander operating by conventional reporting over radios to have a good idea of where his units really are at a given time. With the Global Positioning System and Blue Force Tracker (BFT) friendly force positions can be known with accuracy. During the first Gulf War reconnaissance assets were sometimes used to give friendly commanders a good picture of what their own forces were actually doing. This information is important in obvious ways like avoiding fratricide, but also unexpected ones. For example, resupply convoys can reliably hook up with the units they are supporting. This is absolutely essential for high-tempo operations but in the past was a serious problem and not always successful. BFT is one of the true electronic success stories of the second Gulf War. As a measure of its success, the USMC initiated a priority program to incorporate BFT in its own operations.

Some enthusiasts have created the impression that information superiority will reveal every militarily relevant fact about an area of operations. If recent experience is any guide, that goal is distant, and perhaps unachievable. The best information collection tool remains the human soldier, and it is hard to see how an automated system can replace him. The relatively small force deployed for the second Iraq war was provided with a large slice of the available reconnaissance assets of the entire Department of Defense. Even then its information was far from perfect or even complete. The even smaller force sought for the Future Force is likely to have even more difficulty thanks to its greater reliance on reconnaissance.

Deception, camouflage, concealment, and uncertainty still exist in warfare, and sensors still have limitations based on range, resolution, weather, and simple availability. Furthermore, we are incapable of processing, analyzing, and assimilating all of the data we currently collect. For the foreseeable future, commanders will need to prioritize their information requirements with an inevitable loss of resolution.

Of course, greatly increased amounts of information can become overwhelming. Sensors can collect so much information that soldiers become bogged down trying to process it, or they may delay action waiting for the final bit of information that provides a perfect picture. Worse yet, sensor displays can produce a false sense of omniscience. Automated data processing systems provide a technical means to manage and sort large volumes of data, but systems operators still must analyze that data, just as they evaluate any other traditional source of information. Further, those data are not always obvious or easy to analyze.

Kris Alexander, a military intelligence officer at U.S. Central Command Headquarters in Qatar during Operation Iraqi Freedom described his experience this way:

> . . .a vast amount of information was available to us, but there was no simple way to find and use the data efficiently. For instance, our search engine was an outdated version of AltaVista. (We've got Google now, a step in the right direction.) And while there were hundreds of people throughout the world reading the same materials, there was no easy way to learn what they thought. Somebody had answers to my questions, I knew, but

how were we ever to connect? The scary truth is that most of the time analysts are flying half blind.[12]

Plans for the Future Force call for it to assimilate information, prepare plans, and execute them on very compressed timetables. A rapid influx of complex data makes this task harder, not easier. Major Don Vandergriff, an Army analyst, argues that battlefield commanders have become so laden with meetings, teleconferences, e-mail requests for information, and taskings from senior leadership that a top-heavy organizational structure newly enabled by network connectivity "has diminished their operational effectiveness."[13] Likewise, members of the Stryker Brigade at Fort Lewis reported that the new information systems resulted in a ceaseless demand for "reports about everything, all the time."[14]

This means that traditional staff skills are at least as important as the ability to operate complex sensing and processing technologies. Commanders have more intelligence collection and analytical capabilities than ever before, and in the future they will have even more. Commanders and staffs must learn to drive the intelligence process, massing capabilities in real time the same way they mass fires. Operations (activities of friendly forces) and Intelligence (activities of enemy forces) may have to become one discipline instead of separate activities. But officers still must receive priority intelligence requirements from their commanders, refine them into detailed collection plans, and synchronize collectors, processors, and dissemination networks to support the commander's concept of the operation so that the right information is quickly identified and flows rapidly to where it is needed. The objective is to focus on the enemy and how it fights in real time. This is really a big job and a staff function. But, too often commanders prefer to gush over systems while ignoring the necessary work that tasks the system in the first place and makes the results useful in the second. In the information driven Army, the critical center for all of this is the corps' Analysis and Control Element.

The ACE is intended as the fusion point for national, joint, and service collection platforms, and it develops targets according to the commander's priorities. Within the ACE, sensor networks are able to feed an all-source analysis system, a powerful processing system capable of fusing data collected by multiple sensors. Unfortunately, this system exists in name only and is actually a collection of computer applications rather than an integrated system. It is unfortunate because this should be the source of the long sought, real-time common operational picture that is distributed through digital networks allowing simultaneous, near real-time distribution of relevant reports to multiple consumers. The ACE is a real system and provides data that is light-years ahead of older methods. It is not the all-knowing source of all knowledge.[15]

At the point of the information spear feeding the ACE are individual sensors of all kinds, including live soldiers. Many of these, however, do not belong directly to the corps and are in the service of subordinate units that have their own pressing needs. Individual sensors can be effective in monitoring individual targets, once located. But one important goal of transformation is to create networks of sensors to replace human reconnaissance elements. Networks will allow cross-cuing among sensors, optimizing their strengths and minimizing their weaknesses. Networks also permit redundant coverage of commanders' most critical intelligence requirements and thus ensure they are answered on time. Despite claims to the contrary, it is hard to produce integrated sensor networks that are somehow expected to break down the traditional "stovepipes" separating intelligence disciplines. These networks will be characterized by precision collectors, linked to near real-time communications systems, powerful visual displays, and processors connecting sensors with shooters. This sophisticated, resilient networked structure will let the intelligence organization focus on the enemy in real time. In this vision, intelligence systems are no longer tied to planning assumptions and are able to shift focus as the fight. The key term, however, is "emerging." The kind of dense, robust, deployable sensor network pictured is very much a developmental concept and has yet to be demonstrated. In practice, sensors tend to be numbered in single digits, not the hundreds pictured above.

Furthermore, what this vision describes is less about intelligence than it is reconnaissance—the provision of immediate operational information about the close enemy (close means different things at the brigade, division, and corps levels). In most descriptions of future battlefields the process degenerates further into target identification, finding targets and directing the shooters. Intelligence is an analytic process that considers information from all sources and processes it to yield knowledge. The emphasis on "targetable" information and the sensor-shooter loop tends to work against actual intelligence analysis.

This vision also does little to solve the bureaucratic and institutional barriers among the various intelligence disciplines at higher levels, such as encouraging the famously secretive CIA and National Security Agency to share information in a timely manner and respond quickly to requests from the field. Instead of the straightforward information sharing function pictured by visionaries, intelligence community "sharing" is a wilderness of passwords, permissions, certificates, competing protocols, and incompatible systems. This is exacerbated by swarms of defense industry and IT hucksters ever anxious to peddle their latest, ever more complex hardware and computer applications.

Communications

As shown by the experience of units in Iraq that outran their communications, the array of systems, applications, sensors, and so forth are useless if they cannot communicate. Military battlefield intelligence increasingly relies on broadcast dissemination networks such as the Global Broadcast System or the tactical reconnaissance intelligence exchange system to simultaneously share video, graphic, or textual data with multiple consumers over secure circuits. Data communications within the digitized III Corps travel on a state-of-the-art, secure tactical local area network capable of carrying 256 kilobytes of data between nodes. Within larger command posts, the network's capacity increases up to 768 kilobytes. This is more than 25 times faster than the Internet access time of an average home computer.[16] Unfortunately, expanded capacity leads to demands for more elaborate reporting, overtaxing the system.

Data are sorted, correlated, fused, and passed to shooters using a variety of powerful processors. The all-source analysis system is the central piece of this processing network because of its links to the other components of the Army tactical command and control system. The III Corps' analysis and control element also employs a wide variety of other processors to display and sort data, to focus effects, and thus to enable operation-centric warfare.

However, the experience in Iraq showed that coordinating and synchronizing these not-always-compatible systems remains a serious issue. For the most part, software applications and data systems (as well as sensors) are developed in isolation rather than as part of a grand overarching scheme. None of these complex and expensive systems are of much use without trained personnel to operate them and soldiers who understand how to use the data produced. Equally important, they are high maintenance items that need well-trained, computer savvy technicians to keep them running. Furthermore, they are of little use without communications, what technicians like to call connectivity. And the means envisioned for connectivity in the digitized Army increasingly depends on orbiting satellites.

The U.S. military needs every bit of its available SATCOM capability. Since 1991, the satellite communications required to support an increment of 5,000 deployed soldiers has increased from 1 Mbps (million bits per second) during Operation Desert Storm to an initial assessment of about 51 Mbps during Operation Iraqi Freedom, and it continues to increase. With the arrival of the massively networked information systems in the digitized Army that rate of increase can only become greater.[17] In conflicts from Kosovo to the war in Iraq, the constraints imposed by limited bandwidth are both real and immediate.

U.S. Central Command's (CENTCOM's) use of commercial SATCOM grew from less than 100 Mbps in August 2001 to more than 2 billion bits per second (2 Gbps) in the winter of 2003.[18] Before Operation Enduring Freedom (OEF), the greatest demand CENTCOM experienced for information transfer using SATCOM was about 500 Mbps. Its average use was about 100 Mbps. Once Operation Enduring Freedom got underway the command found that 500 Mbps was the absolute minimum it needed, and use sometimes went past 1 Gbps.[19]

The U.S. Department of Defense tries to meet this demand with its own constellation of five communications satellites called Milstar, completed in 2003. The first Milstar satellite was launched in 1994 and is at the end of its projected life span. However, at $800 million a copy for the satellites and $461 million each for the Lockheed Martin Titan 4B rocket that launches them these satellites are altogether a very expensive proposition, without even considering all the earthbound hardware required for the system.[20] As a result, the U.S. military has increasingly come to rely on commercial satellite providers such as INTELSAT, INMARSAT, PanAmSat, and Eutelsat to meet its needs. This solution has its own difficulties. Commercial SATCOM system coverage is designed to serve fixed coverage areas with the strongest customer base. Typically, the U.S. military must respond to contingencies and conflicts outside those areas. There is no assurance that commercial SATCOM coverage will increase at the rate need by military users. Furthermore, most tactical Army and Air Force units have no organic terminal equipment compatible with the C, Ku, and Ka commercial satellite communications bands.[21]

Digits at the Two-Star UEx[22]

Under the Modular Army reorganization a two-star UEx (division) will have four or five brigades, each somewhat larger and more self-contained, having picked up support assets that previously were part of the division structure. The brigade UAs have taken over the role of the division as the lowest, completely self-contained tactical units. However, the maneuver elements of each brigade are reduced from that of a conventional pre-reorganization brigade. Despite the changes, brigades will still depend on a coordinating headquarters provided by the Unit of Employment, aka division headquarters. Both the new brigades and the streamlined division will depend heavily on assets from the corps, the three-star UEx. The two-star Unit of Employment's focus is almost entirely tactical. It is also the highest-level unit that is most directly concerned with the day-to-day business of actual fighting. The 4th Infantry Division (Mechanized) experimented for years with the concept of integrating technology with weapons systems and applying the effects of that combination over a mechanized division's battlespace. Both in training and in the second Iraq war, it has found that digitized systems can enhance situational awareness, lethality, and survivability, but there are some drawbacks.

Divisions and brigades in Iraq developed doctrine on the fly, learning to use sensors to kill, protect the force, and select the time and place for effective maneuver. The Air Force operated JSTARS is the sensor of choice for wide-area battlefield surveillance. It is the initial sensor to note the enemy's entrance into the division's battlespace. Moving target indicators (MTIs) from the JSTARS are broadcast to about seven different command posts [Unit of Employment (division) main, the UE tactical command post, and the five BCTUAs]. They provide indications and warnings of enemy activity as well as targeting information, but their primary use is cuing optical sensors such as UAVs and manned Apache and OH-58D Kiowa helicopters. For coordination, divisions and some brigades in OEF were equipped with the Defense Collaborative Tool Set, a system that enabled virtual meetings with video whiteboard.

The common ground station (CGS) receives the MTI and other information from the JSTARS aircraft. Using JSTARS in combination with other sensors, enemy positions and organizations are confirmed. Ideally, the time from target acquisition by the UAV analyst to the call for fire at the firing unit is less than 60 seconds. Before UAVs and digital systems like All Source Analysis System (ASAS), target nominations were passed over radio nets and manually plotted on maps to validate targeting criteria, fire control measures, and friendly unit locations. At a minimum, the process took several minutes to complete. By then the target may have moved too far to be affected by the indirect fire mission, or friendly forces may have entered the danger zone. In principle, the digital process is so much more efficient that numerous targets can be nominated and prosecuted in the same period as a single mission under the old analog system.

In theory, the analyst at the CGS could request fire either directly from the division or brigade artillery or other attack assets such as close air support. This would establish the kind of sensor-to-shooter link envisioned for future combat. The future sensor of choice for targeting will probably be a less expensive version of current UAVs. Its cameras will yield accurate target locations as well as types and numbers. Using current UAVs, an analyst can place the camera crosshairs on a target and freeze the image. The analyst then generates a report that contains the target location and description. This report is routed to an ASAS-RWS (Remote Workstation) at levels below the division where the operator has previously created alert filters based on the high payoff target list and an attack guidance matrix. If the report matches the alert criteria, an alarm is generated and a target intelligence message is routed to the system that will actually conduct the attack.

The goal is to be able to classify and destroy or at least weaken targets deep in the corps UE's battlespace before they ever come within direct fire range of the division's frontline trace. The example of the direct UAV, Longbow Apache, OH-58D, artillery, or air support sensor-to-shooter links shows how using digitization can influence the close fight. The ability to engage and destroy more targets in the same time period than were destroyed under the analog system reduces the number of enemy forces that must be faced directly. This kind of attrition by deep attack is nothing novel and certainly attainable. However, the ability to consistently reduce the enemy to the point that it cannot bring effective force to bear is far more difficult and probably not possible against a modern conventional force. It also calls for near-perfect knowledge of friendly dispositions and a great deal of faith in the system. Against terrorists and insurgents the ability is irrelevant since they do not present that kind of target in the first place.

Force XXI battle command brigade and below (FBCB2) is the command information system intended to provide on-the-move, near real-time command and control information on locations of friendly forces down to the level of the soldier or individual platform (e.g., tank or helicopter). The near real-time information on friendly locations relative to enemy locations is supposed to allow friendly forces to operate inside of the enemy's decision loop. This is a form of information dominance.

The information provided from the sensors discussed above and FBCB2 should allow commanders to better visualize the battlefield. Here again, integrating information age technology with sensors battlefield surveillance and targeting is expected to provide commanders in the digitized division with the information needed to visualize the battlefield and make decisions based upon real-time command and control information. Enhanced situational awareness provided by information age technology increases the speed and accuracy of logistic operations. Shared situational awareness allows logisticians instant access to precise resupply requirements compiled by the supported unit, resulting in more accurate and efficient combat service support.

Brigade Combat Teams (UA) can move farther apart because they can see each other "virtually." This enables each BCTUA to cover more territory than a conventional brigade. However, dispersion is not all a good thing. For one thing, it gives enemies an opportunity to exploit the gaps between units. This once more points up the need for not merely good intelligence and reconnaissance, but near-perfect coverage of the battle area so that no such enemy tactic can succeed. Furthermore, even near-perfect knowledge is not enough if the friendly units cannot react fast enough.

The speed of ground movement is an important limitation and works against the goal of "speed and agility." The UEx (division) must detect opportunity and crisis early, but if the commander decided to integrate ground forces into his response, he would be limited by their movement time. Under the BCTUA system, given highly successful reconnaissance of the kind predicted (or more accurately, hoped for), the commander may not even maintain a ground reserve. With larger areas of responsibility and fewer maneuver elements the BCTUA may not be able to hold back a reserve. Also, if BCTUAs indeed cover significantly larger areas of responsibility, the distance a reserve needs to travel to exploit a situation may make it irrelevant. Additionally, even with the increased logistical knowledge, the supplies still have to be delivered, and they, too, are limited by the speed of ground transportation. These considerations limit the commander's freedom of action.

Another issue is that BCTUA operations enormously increase the value of its intelligence gathering and fire assets to the point at which they are vital to the survival of the BCTUAs and their controlling UE. However, these high-value assets (HVAs) are vulnerable to ground attack by small and light forces. In exercises where friendly forces maneuver on a dispersed battlefield, HVAs found themselves under constant threat of enemy attack. This forced brigade commanders to keep combat forces off the frontlines in order to protect these assets. As a result, the BCTUA, with its reduced combat strength, will be hard-pressed to both fight and protect itself. As the nature of the division UE becomes better defined, this tension between HVA, security, and combat maneuver forces will be an important issue.

The Stryker Brigade in the Modular Army[23]

Under current plans the new Stryker Brigades will fight as part of a UEx (division or corps). According to the U.S. Army Training and Doctrine Command, the new units are crafted as "a capable, effective and welcome partner [for Force XXI divisions] if and when we have to execute major theater war requirements." Planners recognize that such participation would definitely require outside augmentation. This prospect is not entirely pleasing to corps and division planners who complain that their resources are already stretched to support their newly assigned fourth and fifth brigades, with whom the corps or division has trained and who understand the way the larger unit operates.[24]

Another critical problem is the dismounted infantry's vulnerability to artillery fire. The current solution is that the Stryker brigade, when deployed, will be the primary focus of the joint task force (JTF) commander and have first priority on all of the JTF's fire support assets. Obviously this is not welcomed by commanders of other fighting units who have their own needs for firepower support. In reality it probably is not a tenable solution.

So far, the requirement that BCTUAs deploy under a division or corps head-quarters has allowed planners to sidestep the lack-of-organic-support issue that has so bedeviled the Army's light formations. The result, at least for planning purposes, is a greatly reduced logistics footprint. An example is the lean brigade support battal-ion planned for the Brigade Combat Teams. Despite the alleged "expeditionary" nature of the new units, the structure reflects the assumption of a secure air base for the brigade force—at least for the tactical assembly area—and a resulting reliance on air resupply. Another belief supporting the new structure is that by not "topping off" all brigade vehicles every night, there will be less fuel consumption and fewer fuel truck requirements. Perhaps, but the practice works against the rule that units should be fully prepared at all times. Other areas under exploration include re-examination of allocation rules, the possibility of prepositioning some supplies, and the elimination of vehicle maintenance while the unit is on the move. One identified brigade self-reliance target specifies "three days of fighting supplies and six to seven days of operational capability."[25]

As the logistical problem shows, creating new doctrine is always hard. Still, if all goes as planned, information age technologies will enable the Force XXI Army to make two significant leaps—from platform-centric to network-centric engagements and from plan-centric to operation-centric warfare if the service develops the means to execute it. The doctrinal and organizational changes required to execute these leaps is as important as developing the technology. The reorganization to create the BCTUA's was rapid and perhaps hasty, and doctrine lagged behind. Conventional armies have operated according to a battle plan drawn on a paper map. Staff officers laboriously create plans, each plan with multiple branches and sequels in an attempt to anticipate the course of the battle. In concept, information technology allows every platform and tactical operation center to display both the plan and the reality. Commanders can compare what was planned with what is actually happening.

Not only commanders but also each of their subordinates will need a similar set of displays on their computer screens. This means that modifications, adjustments, and in-stride changes should be anticipated, articulated, and executed with a level of speed, accuracy, and precision never before possible. Soldiers achieve a level of common understanding that lets them fight the enemy as he actually is, not as the planners hoped he would be. This, of course, brings us back to the reconnaissance problem. The entire concept is based on the assumption that the information-enabled headquarters knows with considerable accuracy where both the friendly forces are and what they are doing as well as where the enemy is and what it is doing.

Given this very large assumption, simplifying and synchronizing otherwise com-plex aspects of battle becomes quicker and more precise. Soldiers focus on informa-tion that is rapidly provided, not on trying to get the information. A tactical example is the AH-64 Apache attack helicopter. During the second Iraq war, Apaches attacked as a unit. But helicopters tended to fight as individuals or, at best, small teams. Each helicopter must individually unmask, search for, and acquire a target reference point before searching for the targets, which may have moved since the unit finalized and rehearsed its operations plan. With digital enhancements, the helicopters should fight as networks of systems. Upon reaching the attack position, only the flight leaders need unmask. After sweeping with their radar, they watch their computer displays for the location of friends and enemies. Then they can quickly sort, assign, and designate specific targets for all the aircraft in their network and send that information with a data burst transmission. Each aircraft can then slew its weapons to the target cues provided while remaining behind cover. Now, when the whole unit unmasks, the targets are in their sights. They simply pull the trigger. By rapidly slewing from one assigned target to another, this lethal network of sensors and shooters can in theory destroy its targets in about a third of the time a group of Apaches acting individually could, with less chance of two helicopters attacking the same target. Using advanced, non-line-of-sight precision guided munitions (PGM) with a pop-up capability (when they become available), the helicopters could avoid having to unmask at all.

Likewise, given the projected systems, when a tank battalion commander is rolling onto his objective, he is supposed to be able to see where the enemy is and make adjustments. As a brigade commander rolls onto his first objective with his lead battalion, he can rapidly assess his combat power, logistical status, and enemy situation to take advantage of situational developments unforeseen during planning and rehearsal. Division and corps commanders can quickly see and understand shifting priorities across a wide front and adjust the concentration of combat power effects throughout the battlespace. It is a fine picture, but there is nothing radically new in it. Further, it fails to anticipate some of the problems likely to arise.

First of all, it assumes that the battalion commander has superior battlefield knowledge since he knows everything his subordinates know. In the past this was true to the extent that the commander had a better grasp of the overall situation but not the details of each subordinate unit's particular situation. With the new systems, he would have all the details and the obligation to react to them. This invites micromanagement and leaves the subordinate units as maneuver elements and information sources but with little real discretion of their own. Given the habits of higher commanders (in the first Gulf War General Norman Schwarzkopf tried to oversee the actions of all the forward battalions), this is a real issue. It is bad since it deprives the subordinate elements of the ability to react immediately to local opportunities and dangers. Improved capability at the bottom implies the discretion to use it without waiting for higher headquarters.

Rapid Deployment Revisited[26]

As noted earlier, part of the solution to the problem of creating light, rapid deployment forces is to make them smaller. This means fewer vehicles and soldiers, reducing both the demand for shipping space and the units' logistic support requirement. This was the solution that led to the creation of the Light Infantry Divisions in the 1980s. But now the task is to combine lightness with increased lethality and survivability. The Army expects to accomplish this by having more capable vehicles, but fewer of them, using the same vehicle for a variety functions. It seems clear that tanks and artillery, for example, are both required because they perform different functions, direct fire versus indirect fire. But if combat vehicles such as tanks and self-propelled artillery are viewed as launching systems for munitions and if one vehicle could fire both kinds of ammunition with comparable performance, it should be able to perform the function of both direct and indirect fires, assuming, of course, that it can perform both roles nearly simultaneously in separate locations. This is not impossible, since the idea is to mass fires on both types of targets from a remote location.

However, this kind of multiple use poses a daunting coordination challenge, not to mention questions of priority and enemy countermeasures. The simpler requirement to sort targets and assign each target to a different firing system becomes enormous when there are only a limited number of firing systems each with a very limited supply of ammunition. As envisioned, the PGM enabled BCTUA cannot afford to waste ammunition. Nor can it afford to allow targets to approach within direct fire range. This creates a demanding set of priorities.

Multimode/Multiple Target Warheads are a possible means for a single gun platform to accomplish different roles. "Multimode" means that the same basic projectile can be used to carry various specialized warheads. Current planning by Defense Advanced Research Projects Agency sees four different types of warhead: antitank, antipersonnel, antihelicopter, as well as one specialized to attack vehicles whose armor is lighter than that of a tank, such as infantry fighting vehicles. The multiple target part comes from the plan for each of these warheads to carry more than one submunition. The antitank model would carry perhaps five independently self-guiding missiles designed to attack from above where the tank's armor is weakest. In theory at least, each missile/submunition would proceed to seek out a separate target, making it possible to attack five tanks simultaneously with a single round of ammunition. The antihelicopter version might operate more like a shotgun shell, firing a pattern of "dumb" (unguided) submunitions, proximity fused to explode when close to a helicopter.[27]

Smaller ammunition helps too. Smaller rounds mean that more can be carried per aircraft for deployment and more can be carried on each tactical vehicle in combat, making each aircraft that much more efficient and each vehicle that much more effective. The Army's state-of-the-art antitank weapon is the Line-Of-Sight-Antitank missile (LOSAT), a 1989 design fielded in limited numbers beginning in 2003. LOSAT is very effective, but it is good for only one thing, killing main battle tanks. As the name implies, the launcher has to have a direct line-of-sight on the enemy vehicle, making it vulnerable to countermeasures (e.g., being shot at). Furthermore, the rounds are 6.4 inches in diameter, are almost 10 feet long, and weigh about 175 pounds.

The problem with new PGMs, like so many other future systems, is that they sometimes remain stubbornly in the future. The Army has long theorized about the advantages of bringing precision fires down to the battalion and company level. But the development contract for the Precision Guided Mortar Munition to accomplish this was not awarded until December 2004 to ATK Ordnance and Ground Systems of Plymouth, Massachusetts. Company commanders probably will not have their own precision fire support anytime soon.

CHAPTER 11

THE REAL ARMY AFTER NEXT

A New Strategic Focus[1]

The wars in Afghanistan and Iraq added a high-priced dose of reality to ideas of "transformation" as hard as those realities might be resisted. Those conflicts conform reasonably well to the sort of unconventional or asymmetric military engagement that analysts have been predicting for years. But despite a decade and more of rhetoric about the changing nature of military conflict, the U.S. Department of Defense (DoD), like that of most advanced nations, resolutely prepared for business as usual, conventional war against conventional nation states.

The Defense Department issued its Strategic Guidance for the years 2006–2011 in March 2004 marking the formal abandonment of the "strategic pause," the predicted decade of relative peace that would allow time for risk in military transformation. Instead, the country was deeply involved in Afghanistan, in Iraq, and in a worldwide war on terrorism with no prospect of an early end to any of them.

The new Guidance began positively enough, recognizing a changed environment where the most likely form of conflict would be "irregular" challenges (e.g., terrorism, insurgency, or civil war). Second came less likely but "catastrophic" attacks with chemical, biological, nuclear, or radiological weapons. Third was the possibility that an adversary might gain a decisive advantage through some breakthrough technology (biological weapons, directed energy, nanotechnology, or cyber methods).[2]

It sounded like a welcome reappraisal, but when the fiscal year 2005 National Defense Authorization Act was signed on October 28, the impact was hardly noticeable. The biggest single expenditure, $10 billion, was reserved for missile defense. But the bill funded almost $3 billion for research and development for the Future Combat System (FCS), and more than $900 million for the sixth and final Stryker Brigade Combat Team. The Act also allotted $292 million for enhancements to 67 M1A2 Abrams main battle tanks and $51.5 million to enhance the Bradley fighting vehicle. The only nod to the most likely threats identified in the Strategic Guidance was an increase of about 900 soldiers for Army Special Forces. Despite the continuing vagueness of the concept, technological uncertainties, and doubts about its application to the current conflicts, the Army continued to put its bets on the FCS.

President George W. Bush also declared his continuing faith in transformation when he announced what the White House described as the most comprehensive restructuring of U.S. military forces overseas since the end of the Korean War. By 2015, the President's plan would close hundreds of U.S. facilities overseas and bring home about 60,000 to 70,000 uniformed personnel. Heavy forces would be returned from Europe (and presumably the Mideast) and replaced with "advanced, deployable capabilities and airborne units."[3]

The announcement was another step in the move from a forward deployed military to a U.S.-based one, the change in U.S. strategic posture that necessitated a rapid-deployment Army in the first place. Warfighting would be very difficult without the capabilities of a transformed force.[4]

"Over the coming decade," the President promised, "we will deploy a more agile and more flexible force, which means that more of our troops will be stationed and deployed from here at home. We will move some of our troops and capabilities to new locations, so they can surge quickly to deal with unexpected threats. We'll take advantage of 21st century military technologies to rapidly deploy increased combat power. The new plan will help us fight and win these wars of the 21st century."[5]

Once more, he emphasized a focus on "capabilities instead of numbers. Leveraging US advantages in speed, reach, precision, knowledge, and combat power is now the defining concept for military action...We learned that small, highly trained and networked units, platforms, and even individual warriors can have an effect on the battlefield that was previously reserved for much larger formations."[6]

The Quadrennial Defense Review of 2005

When Donald Rumsfeld's handcrafted QDR was finally released in February 2006, the 2005 Quadrennial Defense Review sounded very much like the 2001 version. The first 25 pages or so recounted the DoD's various successes under the Secretary of Defense. Most of the rest was a strong reiteration of the Rumsfeld transformation philosophy invoking the words "transform," "transformation," or "transformational" at least 57 times in 113 pages. As in 2001 the combat systems emphasized in the report focused on mobility, information dominance, and avoiding engagement, important tenets of transformation.[7]

The document articulated three priorities: defeating terrorist networks, defending the homeland, and "shaping the choices of countries at strategic crossroads" (apparently a euphemism for diplomacy and economic assistance, neither of which is the responsibility of the Defense Department).[8] The major emphasis was on efficiency, partnerships outside of the armed forces, intelligence, networks, and irregular warfare.[9]

These priorities would be accomplished by changes in management, business approaches, collaboration, and networks rather than anything that involved actually engaging an irregular enemy. The continuing demands of the campaigns in Afghanistan and Iraq were apparently too difficult to think about—the "lessons learned" were generalities and should have been learned long before the war on terrorism: "being organized to work with and through others...take early preventive measures ...increase freedom of action...minimize costs in lives and treasure." [10] These were ordinary tenets of national strategy and one, "being organized to work with and through others" was a basic part of Effects Based Operations.

It then described "defeating terrorist networks" with various high-tech capabilities that are not only technologically challenging but largely unfunded. [11]

Along with promising that the DoD would do just about everything, it reiterated the "1-4-2-1" policy while it conspicuously avoided recognizing that the United States simply did not have the force structure to match the announced intentions. But, according to the report, the current size of the force is just right, and net increases can be avoided by reprogramming existing positions. [12] Because of transformation capabilities, only restructuring is needed. The F-22 program was preserved but stretched out, extending the time to purchase aircraft without increasing their numbers. FCS received a bare mention.

It sounded very much as if the military future of the United States was being staked to transformation. The administration and the DoD in particular seemed to ignore the fact that thousands of infantrymen were searching the mountains of Afghanistan and hundreds of tanks and armored vehicles patrolled the streets of Iraq. It was as though the wars in Afghanistan and Iraq had never happened.

Future Enemies

The QDR made no convincing attempt to relate capabilities to threats. But, the question of whom the Future Force might fight is not trivial, and simply invoking "full-spectrum dominance" will not suffice. Here again the Army After Next (AAN) example is instructional.

After the conventional enemies discussed earlier, the AAN war gaming focused on two other types of opponents: one was a major military competitor that cannot or does not emulate the digitized American military. In this view, such an enemy would offset its relative technological inferiority with one version of asymmetric warfare, in this case countering the high-tech Americans by attacking their vulnerabilities rather than their strengths. Instead of trying to match expensive main battle tanks (much less gold-plated Future Force vehicles), the competitor would concrete on cheap counters such as land and sea mines, distributed air defense, coastal seacraft, submarines, inexpensive cruise and ballistic missiles, and unsophisticated weapons of mass destruction. In principle, the AAN would counter these methods with superior operational and decision-making capabilities, strategic mobility, and battlefield awareness. [13] This is all fine, but awfully vague. Given a numerically superior enemy well-equipped with large numbers of reasonably effective weapons and willing to fight, exactly how would these qualities be applied? Air-centric Rapid Decisive

Operations may have a real problem if that enemy manages even a minimal air defense. EBO is a fine concept but hard to apply below the strategic level.

RDO and EBO have even less application to the second "enemy"—a transnational business complex conducting legal and illegal activities, backing an insurgency. This was a corporation with a global C2 system supported by financial, information, and media coordination offices, allowing it to exploit advanced information technology. It included a number of smaller businesses ranging from private security forces to shipping (land, air, and sea), piracy, drugs, and arms sales—all of these viewed as ways to make money. Because of what the corporation considered unacceptable interference in its affairs, it planned to take control of the country where its corporate headquarters was located. The device for this was an insurgency called the New Nationalist Movement. The complexity and resilience of such an organization means that any opponent must be prepared for a long conflict.

The corporation had a diffused, web-like structure that was difficult to attack. The real, central piece of the organization's effort was an attempt to manipulate public perceptions of the opposing force. The global nature of the organization's structure (in particular its information systems) led the United States to attempt worldwide "decapitation" operations. When several of the corporation's satellite communications and information personnel were captured, it sued the U.S. and host nation governments, claiming that the arrest was illegal and simply an attempt to punish people for their political beliefs.[14]

AAN defeated the first sort of foe despite difficulties, but success against the second sort was far more problematic. The insurgency was a special problem since nothing in the array of high-tech had very much application to other-than-conventional-war challenges, especially a conflict that was as much political as military. It also had a distinct similarity to the current struggle against Al-Qaeda. As with Al-Qaeda, the challenges were as much informational, psychological, and legal as military. Given the generally marginal role of military psychological warfare in recent conflicts, including Gulf War II, all the military services may face grave difficulties in these realms. The QDR's grudging increase in Civil Affairs soldiers and psychological operations is a hopeful sign, but the real problem has been the usually late, thoroughly secondary, and often inept use of these units. Scattering millions of leaflets over a combat zone will not serve.[15]

Concerns with the Future Force

Critics of the Modular Army and the Future Force see a similarity to the disastrous Pentomic Army scheme of the 1950s. Then as now the Army leadership confronted an uncertain strategic situation and new technological advances. The answer was the Pentomic design of dispersed, semi-independent units and flattened organizational structures. Like the Modular Army and the Future Force it attempted to shave support and increase capability by means of technology that did not exist. The organization that resulted might have been survivable on the nuclear battlefield (at least temporarily) but was too specialized for survival to accomplish much else. By analogy, the Future Force is so oriented on one capability—rapid deployment—that it may be capable of little else.[16]

Others object that behind the technological bells and whistles future concepts are really predicated on old models of conventional combat against a symmetrical enemy, another conventional force. As one cynic remarked—"FCS is really just a tank with a radio." This approach is not likely to be effective against the complex concepts and technologies that can be brought to bear in the midterm future (2015–2020). Moreover, if the U.S. Army operates under the assumption that a small force can carry out a military strategy by being well trained and having high-technology weapons, that the force will have information dominance, and that war will be relatively bloodless, then it runs the risk of relearning the lessons of Vietnam, Afghanistan, Somalia, and postwar Iraq. It may also be that, given the nature of the possible corporate enemy discussed earlier, the military may be the wrong sphere for many future conflicts.

In other words, the problem with the Future Force is that it is an army. It is based on familiar ideas and supports existing service cultures, tankers, aviators, and so forth. It also does not help that the Future Force is, like most of the Modular Army, designed to combat opposing armed forces that are at least similar in concept. Its central method of attack, massing of precision fires from a distance, has little application outside conventional war. It is simply not intended to cope with the real world of insurgencies, terrorists, and messy battlefields occupied by civilians as well as military forces. It is even less suited to occupation duties of the sort the Army carried out in Iraq where local knowledge is not merely interesting or important, it is vital. Furthermore, these concepts do not necessarily support the idea of a force projection Army, primarily based in the continental United States.

The Stryker Brigades and the Future Force try to grapple with this problem by creating a lighter, more deployable force—but even if they succeed the whole idea of conventional deployment may be under threat. The rapid proliferation of satellite reconnaissance and long-range missile technology, not to mention cyberwar methods, all place deployment ports and airfields at risk. Sea transport (still needed for any reasonable Future Force) is especially vulnerable since it depends on large, well-known ports, it is relatively slow moving, and it is difficult to hide. Furthermore, it often has to move through predictable choke points such as the Straits of Hormuz or Gibraltar.

Since the Modular Army and the Future Force (in whatever form) will depend very heavily on air support, the Air Force is faced with the unappetizing choice of either trying to fly combat missions from the United States or basing tactical aircraft at vulnerable overseas locations. The basing problems encountered during the war in Afghanistan provide a graphic example of this dilemma. Against a more capable enemy, it would have been even more acute and perhaps insoluble.

Critics also maintain that the Army focuses too heavily on space-based command, control, and communications assets for the post-2010 force structure. It necessarily will rely on space-based communications, but satellite connections and capability may not always be available in the volume needed. It is dangerous to bank so heavily on space-based assets and ignore more traditional, terrestrial-based communications systems.

One of the primary means to lighten the FCS is the use of the network to achieve information dominance. But more importantly, FCS depends entirely on the assumption of not merely information superiority but near-perfect information. Douglas MacGregor, a long-time critic of the Future Force concept, analyzed the idea of substituting "situational awareness" for armor, firepower, and, to some degree, mobility:

> Less obviously, it also implies that this information will enable us to understand the enemy's intentions and anticipate his actions. In order for this to occur, everyone, at all levels, must have the same information and interpret it in the same ways resulting in the fabled common operational picture. The technological capacity to accomplish is attainable in principle but the actual accomplishment is far away. For example, the Blueforce tracking system that enables commanders to monitor their own forces is not interoperable with FBCB2 and neither of these systems is interoperable with FCS.[17]

It is entirely possible to use improved sensors and reconnaissance to get inside the enemy's decision cycle. It is not possible to have such complete information that an enemy force can consistently be defeated before it ever comes within direct fire range. But this is what the lightly armored Future Force expects to accomplish. The highly trained, lavishly equipped forces envisioned for the Future Force are open to defeat by flooding the battlefield with large numbers of soldiers carrying inexpensive rocket launchers, mines, cheap expendable jammers, and man-packed antiaircraft missiles. What happens when an FCS vehicle loaded with a small number of very accurate PGMs meets a swarm of less capable but far more numerous enemy armored vehicles? Use of these techniques means that an enemy must be willing to lose large numbers of indifferently trained soldiers, but enemies have shown that willingness. It will require the adversary to sacrifice, but sacrifice has a special power.

Any Future Force also runs a serious risk that an adversary may be able to disable its computers and electronic systems. The obvious way to accomplish this is by using nuclear weapons to create electromagnetic pulse effects. The result would be widespread damage to electronic systems but a relatively small number of human casualties. A sufficiently capable foe could detonate a nuclear device at high altitude and avoid casualties altogether while trashing American reconnaissance-strike and battlefield situational awareness systems.[18] A cheaper, simpler alternative might be small unmanned aerial vehicles (UAVs) carrying crude jammers. Some components of sensors and communications systems can be protected from wide-area electromagnetic effects, but it will be expensive and the step has yet to be taken. Other components, e.g., antennas, are far more difficult to protect.

Here, the obvious counter is that any force sophisticated enough to use nuclear weapons will be just as adversely affected. Not so if that force is organized for ground combat without relying on information networking for its survival. After a nuclear airburst, the Future Force might have trouble coping with an industrial-age formation that communicated by means of flares and signal flags. Or, more likely, old-fashioned radios.

A more mundane objection is that ordinary wear and tear and enemy action may well mean that a high-tech force will eventually become a low-tech one. Advanced weapon systems could easily be expended faster than they can be replaced. Because high-tech weapon system components need extensive maintenance, demand for them can quickly outpace maintenance capabilities. Heavy, continuous use of weapons systems increases the failure rate of high-tech subsystems. The use of these degraded systems increases their breakdown rate. After several weeks or months of combat, the maintenance posture and reduction of theater stocks may compel a high-tech force to fight with partially functioning systems in a fairly low-tech manner.[19]

In fact, the entire rationale for strategic speed (deployment) as the overriding necessity is questionable. This idea is fed by the belief, promulgated by the Air Force and Marine Corps, that rapid response is required when contingencies arise and gave rise to Air Force emphasis on "halt-phase" strategy. However, most of these contingencies do not call for heavy forces or their equivalent and can be handled by existing organizations. As Colonel MacGregor points out, what the Army does after it arrives is much more important than how fast it gets there. The reorganized brigades fielded under the Modular Army plan can deploy quickly enough and arrive with sufficient force to be decisive. It is hard to conceive of a situation in which a Brigade Combat Team could be rapidly defeated. If one should arise, it is hard to believe that an FCS brigade would fare better.[20]

Logistic Impact

The need to reduce logistic support is one of the primary reasons for the smaller, uniform design of the Future Force brigades. The Modular brigades lack this advantage and are unlikely to greatly relieve the logistic burden. FCS brigades will be smaller, and, in principle, a smaller organization requires less of everything from beans to bullets, from fuel to batteries. By fielding an entire Army composed of identical multifunctional units, it should be possible to eliminate the present hugely complicated inventory of necessary spare parts. It is also presumed that advanced technology will produce systems that are less prone to breakdown and thus require less maintenance and fewer replacements. This is all fine if it proves to be true, but technology goes only so far. Any unit in combat will require considerable logistic support for routine replenishment of everything expended. More importantly, the enemy purposely sets out to interrupt this process and to do damage and nearly always succeeds. The wounded, friendly and enemy, must be evacuated, prisoners guarded, and replacements provided for U.S. casualties. Vehicles must be repaired or replaced, troops fed, mail delivered, and so forth.

The Stryker Brigade Combat Teams addressed this shortfall by creating 205-person combat service support companies increasing the original 392-person brigade

support battalions by about 50 percent each. These companies are primarily transportation, maintenance, and supply augmentation and represent the Army coming
to grips with the physics of logistics. As yet there is no clear idea how this will be
accomplished for the newly reorganized Brigade Combat Teams and even less idea
how it will be done for the Future Force brigades.

If the solution turns out to be Stryker-style combat support companies, that will
undoubtedly help at the unit level. But they still need to receive support from outside
the Brigade Combat Team Units of Action (BCTUA). Unless the plan is to ship
spare parts directly from the United States or Europe to each brigade (a dubious
proposition), some infrastructure is still required in theater. As analyzed by Colonel
(ret.) MacGregor,

> Because no thorough plan to fundamentally restructure how the Army supports fighting
> forces was developed in parallel, the more numerous two-battalion brigades actually
> result in a personnel requirement for more support troops. Organizationally, the concept
> increases dependency on external support from Army division and corps echelons, as
> well as the larger joint force and defeats the very idea of independence.[21]

It was not until 2005 that the Army finished a Modular Force Structure Analysis
to figure out the support requirements for the anticipated 43 new Brigade Combat
Teams (BCT). It developed that an additional 56,000 soldiers would be needed to
support the BCTs, at a cost of about $13.5 billion per year over and above previous
budget forecasts. Naturally this did not include any additional forces to conduct the
newly discovered priority for stabilization and reconstruction.[22]

The Problem with Maps

The seemingly routine issue of maps and similar products provides an instructive
example of the more general problem in providing the sort of intelligence needed to
enable any Future Force. Terrain is uniquely important to ground combat. It conditions the character of both attack and defense. For this reason, ground elements like
the FCS are obsessively concerned with information about terrain, usually in the
form of maps and map-like products.

Observing Operation Iraqi Freedom, it would seem as if the mapping problem
was solved. During that war the 101st Airborne (and other units) were able to print
maps in the field, complete with customized graphics. In some cases revised maps
were provided all the way down to platoon level. But the secret was that these were
standard maps loaded well before the war into the FalconView map system, and then
overlain with appropriate unit symbols, phase lines, and the like. At scales of
1:100,000 or 1:50,000 they were more than sufficient for conventional operations.
Unfortunately, the FCS will require mapping of much greater accuracy and near real
time currency.

The importance of geographic intelligence was vividly demonstrated in the air war
against Kosovo. A U.S. missile strike landed with perfect accuracy at the programmed coordinates, but instead of a building used by Serbian intelligence, the

target turned out to be the Chinese Embassy. The targeteers had used an outdated map.

The United States has the world's largest geospatial information establishment, the largest part of which is the National Geospatial Agency (NGA, formerly the National Imagery and Mapping Agency). NGA's business is called geospatial intelligence, which the agency defines as "the exploitation and analysis of imagery and geospatial information to describe, access, and visually depict physical features and geographically referenced activities." In other words, they make maps and take photos.

Why is this especially important to the Future Force? Future Force units will deploy with significantly less ammunition than current forces and, because of its stripped-down supporting structure, less ammunition will be available when that runs out. This tenuous situation is hopefully survivable by the use of precision guided munitions. After all, if every shell or bomb strikes its target and each target is precisely the right one for the situation, then relatively few bombs or shells are needed. This degree of accuracy and situational awareness depends in large part on very accurate understanding of local terrain, weather, and so forth. Furthermore, the Force plans to avoid enemy PGMs, first by never allowing them to come within range and second by denying the enemy exact knowledge of the Force's location. This demands not only precise knowledge of the enemy and friendly locations but also of the intervening terrain. Once again this brings us back to the need for accurate, on-the-spot, geospatial intelligence. Now, as shown in Afghanistan and Iraq, when the enemy gets a vote, this plan has immediate difficulties. The enemy has shown great ingenuity in the use of decoys, ruses, misinformation, detailed knowledge of local terrain, and concealment. Friendly units will move through unfriendly terrain populated by at least some civilians who are more than happy to relay information on the Force's whereabouts.

But even presuming that the enemy is exceptionally stupid, suicidal, or just inept, geographic detail in the specificity and timeliness required simply is not there. Most NGA military maps are clearly labeled, "not for targeting." Obviously high-precision mapping products exist, a laser system called LIDAR (Light Detection and Ranging) can provide mapping data with a resolution of about 4 inches, but like all optical systems is sensitive to dust and smoke. Plus, the maps produced with such systems cover only limited areas and are significantly more difficult to produce than those required for conventional operations. This accounts for the preference for using human "eyes on target" when expending PGMs.[23]

With the exception of the most populous areas and a few more of special interest, the world is not well mapped. Some parts are hardly mapped at all. This is only somewhat of a problem for conventional air and artillery fire since they depend on forward observers who relay the strike of the round and make corrections. Future Force, however, does not have the rounds to waste adjusting fire. Neither does an aircraft that may have flown halfway around the world.

Why can this not be overcome? Future Force seeks to overcome it with swarms of networked sensors. The problem is that the sensors do not exist, and it is questionable whether they can be produced and distributed across the battlefield in the manner required. For the foreseeable future the United States can provide only a finite number of collection platforms, and each of those platforms can perform only a limited number of functions. Each has a limited field of view and limited persistence in the target area. At the tactical level "even though much progress has been made...organic collection assets remain limited."[24] NGA is very frank about these limits, as pointed out in their *Geospatial Intelligence Basic Doctrine*.

> Poor weather, unfavorable lighting and hostile activity can limit collection...For example, IR imaging, LIDAR [and other collection systems] are ineffective during periods of cloud cover. Electro-optical [imaging] is only feasible during daylight conditions.[25]

This is less of a problem for conventional forces since they can afford errors and do not require persistent surveillance and near-perfect information.

But even if imagery collection can somehow be made universal, production capacity is also limited. Precision intelligence is not an automatic result of collection and distribution—it requires analysis. That requires trained analysts to process and analyze the data, but the number of trained analysts and analytic workstations is limited. As was also shown in recent conflicts, the ability to disseminate intelligence is constrained by available communications. The number of transmitters and receivers is limited, as is the amount of available bandwidth. Methods of data compression and other techniques to squeeze more use out of available bandwidths continue to be developed, but the amount and complexity of data have increased along with them. As NGA puts it, "While digital technology has streamlined this process in many ways, it has exacerbated it in others, by permitting the collection of larger, high-resolution data sets."[26] And, as one analyst put it, "FCS needs the mother of all data sets."

Then there is the issue of latency. In places like Baghdad, GPS navigation was limited simply by the lack of up-to-date street maps. Collection and exploitation systems have made enormous progress in supporting near-real time exploitation of remote sensing data, but they cannot eliminate latency. Initial collection of information does not yield immediate, useful knowledge. It can take hours, days, or even weeks of additional collection and analysis before a problem is completely understood.

FCS and Future Force advocates will reply that advanced tools not yet available will enable huge improvements in collection, analysis, and dissemination. Although advances in intelligence collection, analysis, and dissemination have gone a long way toward reducing uncertainty and providing an information advantage, they cannot eliminate uncertainty, nor is it likely they can reduce it a sufficient level. This applies to all forms of intelligence and operational information, not just maps.

The Network Again

If we don't have the network the whole program will sink.[27]

In February 2004, the Army announced another exercise in renaming. The service's internet would henceforth be known as the LandWarNet, the Army part of DoD's Global Information Grid (GIG). The new label includes all Army networks —from military bases in the United States to forward deployed forces. When fielded, the Warfighter Information Network–Tactical, Joint Tactical Radio System, Transformational Communications System, GIG-Bandwidth Expansion, and Network Centric Enterprise Services will all be integral parts of LandWarNet.

> What we want to do is move from what we've just conducted (Operation Iraqi Freedom) to something even more devastating to any adversary: the ability to conduct not only simultaneous operations but distributed throughout the battlespace, completely on the non-linear basis, based largely on information and intelligence that we have to have. If we do not have the information—the situational understanding—if we do not have the intelligence, this will not work.[28]

For the FCS or any Future Force to operate systems like these requires a significant increase in the number of supporting elements, particularly relay/retransmission vehicles used to establish and maintain the tactical internet. The relay/retransmission and additional satellite systems are absolutely critical to digital communications within deployed divisions, brigades, and below. But they are normally mounted on soft-skinned vehicles devoid of self-protection. Because of their vulnerability and very high value, commanders will be forced to divert resources to protecting them. Also because of their criticality, it is worth considerable effort on the part of the enemy to destroy even a few of these vehicles.[29]

As was seen in Iraq, the current tactical network is complex, is very maintenance intensive, and is built around static, line-of-sight nodes that must go off-line during movement. This was enough of a problem in the relatively flat desert. Managing the node locations over complex urban, mountain, or jungle terrain becomes extremely challenging. The new Modular units and the Future Force place great emphasis on agility, the ability to continually execute fluid maneuvers. But the network is optimized for operations in open areas and has difficulty supporting operations in complex urban terrain such as Baghdad. Relying on exposed nodes that require protection and depend on reliable power, the network's physical structure is extremely vulnerable. Electronic interference, power surges, nuances of terrain, and system crashes of individual, complex computers all contribute to the network's vulnerability.[30]

Training Still Matters

The roots of the division's successful attack to Baghdad are found on the training fields of Fort Stewart, Fort Irwin, and Kuwait. The division crossed the line of departure with a mature and trained group of staff officers, commanders, and soldiers...National Training Center (NTC) rotations produced a seasoned fighting force that was trained and ready to fight and win.[31]

—After Action Report, Third Infantry Division (Mechanized), Operation Iraqi Freedom, July 2003

One of the serious but less widely addressed problems of the new technology is that it creates important training issues as illustrated in the previous chapters.

The new systems are more effective but also at least an order of magnitude more complex.[32]

The training maneuvers needed for current combat units are complicated enough, requiring hundreds of people and millions of dollars to put each brigade-sized unit through a training cycle. But the advanced systems now being fielded, and the ones planned for FCS and the Future Force, add a huge training challenge. When the "digitized" 4th Infantry Division (Mechanized) went to Iraq, it carried along a staff of about 60 civilian contractors to maintain its command and control systems. There were no military personnel trained for the job.

The problem applies not only to information systems but also to the digitized versions of industrial age equipment. The latest upgrade to the Bradley fighting vehicle, the M2A3 version, requires that the crew learn about 85 separate tasks in order to operate the vehicle. Army researchers found that 37 (44 percent) were new tasks and another 18 (21 percent) were significantly modified from earlier versions of the vehicle. "Additionally, the A3 equipment is more complex, though not beyond the capabilities of well-trained operators, especially those with at least a moderate degree of computer familiarity." In fact, researchers found that the M2A3 differs more from the M2A2 "than the original Bradley did from the M113 armored personnel carrier."[33] These are skills that not only must be acquired, but also maintained through continuous training. The training problem is further complicated by the reality that the Army cannot afford to upgrade all its Bradleys and still build the Future Force. This means that at least three variants will remain operational for some time, each with a different set of training demands. Add Stryker and/or FCS to the mix, and the problem goes from serious to nightmare.

Early predictions that automation would reduce complexity have not come true. In fact, troubleshooting is much more difficult than ever because as complexity increases the number of possible causes of each problem increases almost exponentially.

As was shown in the case of the BCTUAs, the digital expertise to effectively support advanced systems is currently provided by civilian contractors, not uniformed soldiers. This is important because, in the words of an Army research report, "the most central component of a digital system is its computer software, whose operations soldiers must master before the system can be used effectively." Contrary to the optimistic predictions, a forthcoming "Nintendo" generation of digitally savvy soldiers has not appeared in great numbers. In the most recent survey (2001), covering soldiers of all ranks, 86–96 percent used computers either at home or at work. This sounds encouraging, but about 80 percent used them mostly or entirely for e-mail, games, and the Internet. Only about 20 percent used computer applications such as graphics programs. Furthermore, contrary to popular legend, junior enlisted soldiers (the youngest and most numerous) were the least likely to have real computer skills.[34]

Experience in playing video games does not yield experience in design, maintenance, repair, or programming. At least to the Army's satisfaction, the answer to this is embedded training. This is "a function hosted in hardware and/or software, integrated into the overall equipment configuration." In other words, the equipment includes programming to train the operator. This saves time and expense and works well enough with simple applications, but it is questionable how well it will work with complex systems. Furthermore, many of the required skills are still manual ones. Learning to replace a vehicle track, for example, is not something that can be effectively taught without actual hands-on experience. Even if embedded training were the whole answer, it would not by any means eliminate the training burden. Instead, it simply shifts it to the user level.[35] Furthermore, most of the soldiers in a Future Force unit will still be infantrymen, an often neglected specialty that has also become more complex.

> . . . there is a notion by some that everyone is an Infantryman in the future force—as if anyone can just do it like taking out the garbage or something. Infantry skills are complex and take a lot of quick reflex and physical training to survive. Everyone must be a Warrior—not an Infantryman.
>
> —LTC Steven D. Russell, 1st Bn, 22d ID

Then there is the matter of training for levels above the basic line soldier.

> Today the toughest job in the Army is Stryker rifle company commander. This officer currently maneuvers nine rifle squads, three weapons squads, snipers, mortars, 14 combat vehicles and soon a mobile gun. It takes training time and multiple repetitions to get good at maneuvering this force.[36]

It should be added that the job of a company commander in the projected Future Force will be even more complex as UAVs, robotic platforms, and other advanced gadgets are added.

Often neglected are the unglamorous staff officers needed to manage the complexities of the Modular Army and the Future Force. Their task becomes more complex, too. Training for most unit staff positions occurs only after staffers have been in the positions for some time, if it happens at all. The solution to date has been to expect staffs to train themselves assisted by instructional materials on CD. This is a limited solution though, since most units do not have the time to conduct staff training in addition to their other duties and responsibilities. As a result, the responsibility is too often passed off to the already overtasked individual staff members.

Indeed, all members of Future Force units will need to train together instead of at several different locations. This is an absolute requirement in order to be sure all systems within a unit are trained to interoperate properly. It will also produce an important increase in unit cohesion. These facts are clearly recognized by General Kevin P. Byrnes, commander of all Army training:

> We've got a very complex training challenge with the technology that is going to be in our systems. When you've got to have all 19 [FCS] systems working together to get the full benefit, I can't just train unmanned aerial vehicle operators in one place; train mortar operators at another place; and train communications guys in another place. To get the value, I've got to train them together before they go to the field, before they're deployable. They've got to be able to work together.[37]

Unfortunately, the Army is not even remotely set up to train this way. The closest is the National Training Centers at Fort Irwin, California, but even this large multibillion dollar installation is not currently capable of conducting that degree of integrated training. Building and maintaining necessary skill levels for FCS as currently pictured is an important obstacle and will probably be advanced as another argument for a smaller, more selective force.

An Alternate Approach

FCS—Special Operations Version

With the ground mobility vehicle (GMV) and building on experience in Afghanistan and Iraq, very quietly and with minimal fanfare, the special operations community (chiefly Army Special Forces) managed to develop its own form of air mechanization and something like FCS on a shoestring budget. It lacked most of the futuristic technology expected, but it was adapted to the actual environment of conflict, not some hypothetical future war with a near peer fighting on a conventional battlefield.

Special operators had for years experimented with a variety of motorcycles and light, dune-buggy-type machines that were fun to drive but seldom rugged enough for the demands placed on them. The need was finally brought into sharp focus by Desert Storm. British SAS and U.S. Special Forces tried patrolling and surveillance on foot, but the distances were too great and the terrain often too open. Too often they found themselves on the run from ragtag forces whose only advantage was ordinary motor transport.

The Scud hunt made the need acute because the distances to be traversed across the rocky western desert were immense. Locally modified HMMWVs and small commercial trucks were the quick solution but not a long-term one. So, after 1991 special operators focused the efforts on various light civilian trucks and small all-terrain vehicles originally designed for cross-country work. Beginning in the spring of 1998, U.S. Army Special Operations Command (USASOC) and Letterkenny Army Depot worked to develop the Special Operations Forces (SOF)-specific GMV. Rather than begin from the ground up, they started with the standard HMMWV and developed a modification kit that added additional weapons points, radio racks, antenna connections, and provision for additional water, ammunition, armor, and fuel. A full set of camouflage nets to conceal the vehicle was also provided. The GMV could be lifted in by helicopter over short ranges and air landed by C-130s for deep penetration.

It is perhaps the closest existing example of an FCS-like capacity and was employed in western Iraq in the kind of wide-ranging, dispersed, semi-independent operations envisioned for the Future Force. The "vanilla" unmodified HMMWV weighs only 9,800 pounds, well below the 19–20 ton limit imposed for the FCS vehicle.. The SOF GMV fully loaded with weapons, food, minimal armor, ammunition, fuel, and everything else needed weighed closer to 13,000 pounds. Capable as they are, they have nothing like the capacity that will be needed to make FCS work, and it took intensive maintenance to keep them running. But what the SOF vehicle really lacks is the bandwidth intensive, highly networked FCS-type system. Instead, it has the basic "asymmetric tool kit" of SOF developed computer applications (usually in a laptop computer) plus the minimum amount of navigation and communications gear necessary to the mission. Furthermore, it is equipped with multifunction racks that make it easy (or at least easier) to switch out electronics as required for various missions. More important, it works, is affordable, is available now, and has been shown to be effective. It would not survive on the kind of high intensity battlefield FCS would fight on, but that battlefield seems a remote possibility for the foreseeable future.

By the time of Afghanistan it was standard practice for special operations units in some environments to be fully motorized, and the GMV was distributed to the 5th, 3rd, 2/19th, and 1/10th Special Forces Groups.

For operations in Iraq, some Army SF units created their own "war pigs," standard 2.5 ton and 5 ton trucks cut down and modified. The resulting vehicles gave the units rapid, long-range mobility at minimum cost, allowing them to carry a full supply of communications and targeting gear while remaining capable of self-defense. Most importantly, they could carry a large amount of ammunition, water, and other supplies that gave them true long-range mobility with no supporting structure. Acting as "mother ships," they would refuel and rearm the GMVs, extending their range and duration. Armed with heavy machine guns and rapid-fire grenade launchers, as well as portable antitank and antiaircraft missiles, they ranged across the "Scud box" of western Iraq preempting enemy missile launches, calling in air strikes, and generally creating havoc.[38]

Simultaneously, the intelligence sergeants at USASOC and U.S. Special Operations Command came up with their own analytical support automation based on the rugged Panasonic "Toughbook" laptop.[39] The waterproof, shock-mounted computer is widely used in the military, and the special operators developed their own suite of software to go with it. The resulting package weighs about 12 pounds (mostly the weight of batteries and the case), but it provides wireless downloads as well as maps and data handling tools. At $5,000 each the systems are a comparative bargain. Based on the experiences in Afghanistan, modified versions of the GMV added better Global Positioning System navigation, a DC power supply, roll bars, and side rails, as well as increased and improved capacity to mount various arms including antitank weapons. When required, an auxiliary fuel tank and additional crew seating could be added. The vehicle was so successful that it now is produced in four basic models: GMV-S (Special Forces), GMV-R (Ranger), GMV-N (SEALs), and GMV-ST (Special Tactics) for the Air Force. Further, the benefit was not limited to the SOF world. The new fifth brigade (BCTUA) of the 101st Airborne Division is to be equipped with another version of the GMV (the Air Assault GMV) optimized for movement by helicopter. If it is not air-mech, it is something darn close to it.[40]

Looked at another way, it was a fighting network, a distributed system conducting nonlinear operations. In a period of less than three years the SOF community had developed and fielded an FCS-like capability with a far lower price tag.

"Who Are You Going To Believe, Me or Your Own Eyes?"

—Groucho Marx

That is not true. Hell no, we're not doing that.[41]

—An Army spokesman reacts to speculation that FCS might have to be delayed by several years

Most programs for "transformation" have ulterior motives—preserving existing command slots, papering over branch inefficiencies, deflecting serious questions about real reform, and maintaining as much of the organizational and institutional status quo as possible.[42]

By late 2005, patience with both Stryker and FCS finally began to run out. It was now obvious that the two vital parts of the Future Combat System were in trouble, the Future Combat Vehicle and the network. Both were still in development, and costs were spiraling out of sight. Meanwhile, in Iraq, Stryker crews were strapping sandbags on their vehicles to soak up the fragments thrown off the slat armor.

Doubts had begun to crystallize, not only in Congress but within the Army as well.[43] So far, Congress had supported the Army's commitment to FCS as its overall estimated cost rose from about $90 billion in 1999 to $115 billion–$127 billion to cover 17 (or 18, possibly 19) systems and a command-and-control network. Then, in March 2005, Army spokesmen somewhat sheepishly revealed that the estimated cost to equip 15 Modular brigades of roughly 3,000 soldiers (about one-third of the planned force) was now $145 billion over 20 years, not including a projected $25 billion for the communications network needed to connect the Future Force.

This was not welcome news in Congress where an increasing number of members were beginning to feel the entire project was futile and the costs out of control.[44] When confronted with the revised timeline, Congressman Ike Skelton (D-MO), ranking Democrat on the House Armed Services Committee, responded, "I don't think the troops can wait 10 or 15 years for a new armored vehicle to be developed."[45] It was all too much. Senator John McCain (R-AZ), chairman of the powerful Senate Armed Services Airland Subcommittee called for hearings into the handling of the FCS program.[46] The Army response was to offer another program reconstruction.

According to Bloomberg News, the Army began diverting FCS money to purchase and maintain prosaic equipment needed for Iraq and Afghanistan. Of the roughly $3 billion scheduled for FCS in 2005–2006, "about $886 million would be used to buy tactical radios," the news service said. The Stryker armored vehicles would receive an extra $672 million. Another $579 million was earmarked to buy training ammunition. Future funding for FCS had reportedly been moved around as well. Bloomberg noted that "the biggest portion of the shifted Future Combat Systems money, about $1.3 billion, will be allocated through 2011 for 'tactical vehicles,' including upgrades and repairs of General Dynamics M1A2 tanks and United Defense Industries Inc.'s Bradley Fighting Vehicles damaged in Iraq."[47] Despite at least five years of effort, most of FCS was still no more than digits on a hard drive. The final design of the gun vehicle was still unclear, and the advanced armor systems were still in the research phase. Although no one said so out loud, FCS was slipping further and further into the future. In a stinging editorial, the *New York Times* dubbed it "The Science Fiction Army" saying, "The Army needs more armor, not less. Greater mobility and highly advanced radio networks are fine, but not at the cost of leaving American soldiers more exposed to lethal dangers."

Stryker again came in for its share of the drubbing. So far the Stryker debate had been largely confined to the defense press and occasionally the back pages of the *Washington Post.* But on March 31, 2005, the *Post* featured a front page headline reading "Study Faults Army Vehicle." The story included extensive quotes from a "classified Army study" that featured a long list of complaints about the Stryker's performance, including "design flaws, inoperable gear and maintenance problems that were getting worse, not better." Titled "Initial Operations Report—Operations in Mosul, Iraq," it claimed that the anti-RPG (rocket propelled grenade) slat armor was so heavy that tires and wheel assemblies were failing at the rate of about 9–11 daily in the 300 vehicle fleet. Worse yet, as many as 50 percent of the RPGs fired at Strykers were exploding on the slat armor, spraying shrapnel on the exposed gunners and vehicle commanders. The report also held negative implications for the Future Combat System.

The heart of FCS was to be the networked computer system. But, according to the report, the version in Stryker simply did not work. The commander's displays were poorly designed, and none of the 100 displays in Iraq were working because of "design and functionality shortcomings." When they did work, the computers were too slow and tended to freeze up at critical moments. Similarly, the remote-controlled weapons station could not hit targets while moving. Finally, the top-heavy design and poor interior arrangements "contributed to the deaths of three soldiers in rollover accidents."

The Army counterpunched by making available Stryker Brigade soldiers in Iraq who swore by the vehicle, saying that, maintenance and computer problems aside, its overall performance was superior. Surely this was all true, but it missed the point. Stryker was not supposed to be a better-than-average armored truck. The Stryker Brigade Combat Teams were intended as exemplars of the FCS and the centerpiece of Transformation, an information-enabled, low-maintenance, logistically austere, rapidly deployable force, and it was not any of those things.[48]

In the wake of the March 2005 embarrassment over spiraling costs, Secretary of the Army Dr. Francis J. Harvey had announced a restructuring of the business aspects of the Future Combat Systems program. This made it doubly unfortunate when, in September, the Government Accountability Office (GAO) released a report critical of the costs of the Modular Army. In 2004, the service had estimated that modularity would cost about $28 billion dollars through 2011. In March 2005 the estimate went up to $48 billion, a 71 percent increase in one year without even a single brigade having been fully modularized. Furthermore, GAO pointed out, the $48 billion covered only equipment, not the $27.5 billion in associated personnel and construction costs. Furthermore, Modularity and FCS together would cost at least $200 billion over 20 years to equip perhaps one-third of the Army. Worse yet, the report concluded, the Army did not even have a real system for figuring out how much the program actually cost.[49] The House and Senate Armed Services Committees both accused the Pentagon of hiding even more cost overruns by shifting the baselines from which estimates were made. It looked as if it might not be possible to afford either modularity or FCS, but certainly not both.[50]

The Army made a desperate attempt that same month to preserve FCS as a coherent program rather than what it was devolving into—a set of incremental developments to be grafted piecemeal onto the Modular Army. It was a valiant attempt. A prototype Manned Ground Vehicle (MGV) whizzed about, a rotary wing UAV buzzed around, and computer animations showed how a networked force might work, but much of it remained little more than concepts on PowerPoint slides. Furthermore, the MGV did not meet stipulated weight limits, and the design of the Mobile Gun System was under revision yet again. The UAV was an old design, not an innovation. The Future Combat System, declared Secretary Harvey, "is becoming a reality." Perhaps, but whatever it was becoming it was doing so too slowly and too expensively.[51] Even the most basic changes seemed nearly impossible. After three years and billions of dollars, the Boeing-led effort to get all soldiers on a common radio faced massive restructuring.

On September 30, the Army Public Affairs Office issued a brief statement announcing that the Modular Army designations of UA, Units of Employment–X's (UEx's), and so forth were being discarded and units were reverted to their old designations. The Units of Employment–Y would be called an Army, the three-star UEx a corps, and the two-star UEx a division. Brigade Combat Team Units of Action would simply be called Brigade Combat Teams. The announcement did not mention that to date no unit had completed the transition to modular organization. It was a tacit admission that some new structures expected under the Modular Army (streamlined divisions and so forth) were not workable and the old division-corps-Army structure would remain.[52] In the words of Steve Daskal, a veteran operations analyst:

> As the saying goes, "I was born at night, but not LAST night," and I recognize the stuff and nonsense in the [briefing] for what it is—an admission that the force restructuring schemes that have flitted about since the departure of General Reimer as CSA are dead, with the FCS mega-system-of-systems not far behind.[53]

FCS received another blow from Andy Marshall on October 5. In the summer, the Office of the Secretary of Defense had asked Marshall for concise recommendations on military procurement, based on current and expected strategic conditions. On

October 5, Marshall's "Red Team" delivered its recommendations—prominent among them was "Delay the Army's Future Combat Systems."[54]

On October 14, 2005, the Future Combat System received the closest thing to an obituary notice that it was ever likely to receive. In a memorandum for the chairman of the Joint Chiefs of Staff, General Peter J. Schoomaker listed his top three priorities for the Army:

1. Win the Long War While Sustaining the All-Volunteer Force.
2. Accelerate the Future Combat Strategy.
3. Accelerate Business Transformation and Process Improvements.

The key was the second item, explained as "Resource and execute modular force conversions as rapidly as possible, enable early spinout of Future Combat System technologies and execute the global re-stationing plan of the Total Army." The important code words were "enable early spinout of Future Combat System technologies."[55] FCS would be used to spin off useful technologies that could be grafted onto the Modular Army. It was recognition that the original far-reaching goals for FCS were much too optimistic about the effectiveness, value, and affordability of a force structure and system of systems dependent upon near-perfect real-time situational awareness and seamless, nearly unlimited bandwidth vertical and horizontal network communications.

Interviewed shortly afterwards by *Defense News,* the general amplified his priorities with regard to FCS:

> We'll still have the M1 tank, Bradley and Stryker out to 2025 and 2030—they're not going away. We're spiraling FCS technologies onto them. If we can lighten the M1 by putting the lightweight tank gun on it, and lighten its ammunition load and increase its survivability through active protection, you're working the current modular force into the future, and the future into the current. That's what we're trying to do.[56]

Steve Daskal decoded the general's statements:

> What I'm sensing here is a complete abandonment of the original extreme and unrealistic goals set for Future Combat Systems. This is at least an implicit recognition that "the future ain't all it's cracked up to be:"—Survivability cannot be largely or totally dependent upon situational awareness—it must come from a mix of armor, active protection systems, tactics, and superior situational awareness.[57]

At least for the next 25 years, the tank of the future turns out to be the veteran M1 Abrams, upgraded with whatever technology can be gleaned from the FCS program.[58] The real Army After Next turns out to be much like its predecessors—an improved version of what came before. But that is not the end for FCS and the Future Force—it is too large, is too vested, and has too many interested parties for that. In April 2006, the Future Combat System was honored as one of the Pentagon's most expensive weapons systems, an overall increase of well over 50 percent above its initial estimate.[59] By September the Army was so stretched by the demands of war and transformation, it actually had trouble meeting its payroll. But the needed funds were "reprogrammed" from equipment repair and training, not transformation.[60] Like the mythical hydra, the Future Force had too many heads to be killed altogether.

Conclusion: Lessons Unlearned

On the ground in Iraq and Afghanistan, the armed forces are conducting the long predicted nonlinear, noncontiguous operations. And, they finally face the future enemy—the textbook example of a poorly defined but highly motivated foe, unconstrained in its methods and with access to the technology of the developed world. The fedayeen and Al-Qaeda and their brethren do not need to develop a highly capable, reasonably secure worldwide communications system. They can have one for the price of a cell phone. As with the enemy, U.S. forces have been quick to see the application of well-understood and available existing technology. Lacking futuristic mil-spec individual radios, soldiers in Iraq purchased ordinary, cheap handheld ones. They were not spectacular, but they were good enough, they were affordable, and they were available with a phone call and a credit card. When the vaunted "information network" hiccoughed in Iraq, commercial iridium satellite phones, some of them personally purchased by soldiers, filled the gap. Underneath the radar, a different form of transformation was taking place thanks to the initiative of individual soldiers and small units.

The war in Afghanistan was initially successful. A stunning military victory was achieved in large part because of the use of new technologies. But the United States (aided by the international community) has been slow to secure the victory through reconstruction. The result has been a guerrilla war with a resurgent Taliban. In Iraq looting progressed to insurgency to civil war. By the spring of 2006 the United States, intent on keeping Iraq together, had spent more blood and treasure there than any country ever had spent on another in the history of the world. Three years after U.S. and British forces invaded Iraq the contrast between what was expected and what actually happened was stark. A study by the Center for Strategic and International Studies stated that not only had reconstruction been stymied but conditions in the country had actually deteriorated.[61]

Because of inexcusably poor planning prompted by the desire to demonstrate the success of transition concepts, the initial military achievements of the invasion and the march to Baghdad have been thoroughly eclipsed. The most serious problems facing Iraq and its American occupiers—endemic violence, a shattered state, a nonfunctioning economy, and a decimated society—were almost inevitable consequences that flowed from the breakage of the Iraqi state.[62] But they were exacerbated by the application and misapplication of doctrine that tried to reduce warfare to a targeting drill while loudly proclaiming the opposite. Effects Based Operations (EBO) as a concept claims to link military means to larger objectives and correct an allegedly shallow view of war as a purely military enterprise. Military force must be used to accomplish political goals. But that did not happen. The war plan was not directed toward the most important issue, the postconflict state of Iraq and Afghanistan.

Difficult as it may be for Army transformation and air power enthusiasts to swallow, at least ten lessons have been driven home by the wars in Iraq and Afghanistan. All mitigate against the exclusive use of a small, lightweight, one-size-fits-all medium force conducting rapid dominance operations supported by air power.

1. Fight the war you are in. Many of the problems in both Iraq and Afghanistan arose from the DoD's implacable desire to implement transformation concepts whether they were appropriate or not. The Defense Secretary famously said, "You have to go to war with the Army you have, not the Army you want."[63] It is equally true that you also have to fight the war you have, not the one you want. The wars in Afghanistan and Iraq were emphatically not the one desired by Rumsfeld-style futurists. They are wars dominated by political factors, where cultural knowledge, the language, history, and nature of the lands and peoples, is an important part of information dominance. It is not a form of knowledge that can be readily gathered by UAVs and quickly displayed as part of the common operational picture.

2. Doctrine should drive technology, not the other way around. Rapid Dominance and allied concepts are very effective applications of high technology against conventional foes. They are not effective against an enemy that either offers few suitable targets or simply refuses to quit. Rapid Decisive Operations (RDO) are likewise effective in warfighting but contain a large element of wishful thinking in seeking to avoid responsibility for postwar activities including reconstruction and security. There is still no coherent concept to orchestrate the requirements of RDO, EBO, and postconflict stabilization. Effects Based Operations are a good idea but far too difficult to implement below the strategic level. In practice it really means coordination among various entities that often have incompatible motives, methods, agendas, and widely varying capabilities.

3. Air power is a valuable adjunct, but it cannot carry the day by itself. Afghanistan and Iraq are both instances where air power was unable to solve the military problem. It is a very expensive substitute for old-fashioned tube artillery and has yet to prove it can do the same job. The favorite of defense policy makers for over a decade, air power lost some of its luster in favor of ground forces, especially special operations units. Loren Thompson agrees that there has been a "decided bias in favor of air power among senior policymakers" but that bias "has begun to shift in the direction of ground forces."[64] Air power is a valuable support element that went a long way toward making success possible in Afghanistan and Iraq, but in neither case could it have succeeded alone.

4. Thinly manned forces have not demonstrated that they can be effective. To operate independently during Operation Iraqi Freedom, 3rd Infantry Division Brigades were expanded to more than 5,000 soldiers, and Marine Regiments were expanded to more than 6,000. Forces levels in Iraq have remained much higher than anticipated. Those in Afghanistan continued to rise for three years. In August 2006 an additional 25,000 soldiers and marines were alerted for deployment to Iraq.[65]

5. The idea of a "full-spectrum," one-size-fits-all Army of uniform organizations is a chimera. Afghanistan is a motorized war depending on helicopters and light vehicles. Iraq is an armored vehicle's war. Without large numbers of armored vehicles there U.S. and Coalition operations would have been impossible. More armor was needed, not less. In Afghanistan, reconstruction teams, civic action, and medical teams help restore confidence in government and undermine an insurgency. The Army continues to treat

"irregular" operations as lesser included cases of conventional war and makes only minor changes in organizations, equipment, or training for it. The Army, and the other armed forces, must effectively engage and win both conventional, high tempo wars of firepower and maneuver and unconventional, long endurance wars against irregulars. One size emphatically does not fit all.

6. The intelligence problem is very much improved but does not even approximate the kind of all-knowing "situational awareness" anticipated for the Modular Army, much less the Future Force. If there is a single, overriding, critical failure in both Iraq and Afghanistan, it is the lack of useful intelligence. This enabled Iraqi exiles to pass off large quantities of self-serving moonshine as intelligence. But an important reason that so much faith was placed in such dubious sources was that so little else was available. Useful intelligence, especially at the strategic and operational levels, is the product of analysis by human beings. They may be aided by technology, and the information may be collected through technology, but in the end it is a human product. Much of the "intelligence" discussed in connection with the Modular Army and Future Forces is actually tactical reconnaissance and surveillance. In part, this is because it is easier to accomplish and its value is easier to appreciate. Another part is the unrelenting desire to substitute technology for human beings. Successful analysis is not only the product of compiled information—it requires experience, education, and judgment.

7. Enemies adapt. Opponents are often quick to shift tactics and techniques to counter a rival's advantages. After the fighting in Afghanistan, Usama bin Laden himself appeared in a video tape (aired by Al-Jazeera, the Arab language news station) instructing viewers on the best ways to deal with U.S. air-centric operations through deception and conceal-ment.[66] Al-Adel, a jihadist Web publication, distributed practical advice to Iraqis and foreign jihadis on using guerrilla tactics against American and British troops. "Turn the mujahideen military force into small units with good administrative capabilities," it sug-gested; this "will spare us big losses. Large military units pose management problems," Al-Adel further explained. "They occupy large areas which are difficult to conceal from air reconnaissance and air attack."[67]

8. Nothing in "digitization" is likely to change these things. The light, multitalented, fully networked, highly survivable vehicles do not exist and are not on the drawing boards, and the technology to produce them is barely in sight. Nor is it clear they would be very useful in the kinds of war being waged. Digitization was not critical to success in either Afghanistan or Iraq. New technology (e.g., miniaturization) has been very helpful. But both wars demonstrate convincingly that technology is not an all purpose solution. In the "long war" against terrorism, the most useful tools turn out to be low-tech and manpower intensive. Instead of Joint Surveillance Target Attack Radar Systems and satellites, intel-ligence comes from raids, patrols, and patient, often frustrating work with local villagers. Instead of computer produced analysis, patient intelligence work capitalizes on this information, poring over captured documents and hundreds of detainee interviews. Fur-thermore, new technology cannot solve fundamental issues in legitimacy, governance, or policing techniques.

9. Securing the victory is almost as important as achieving it. Stability forces and psycho-logical operations are not a sideshow; in conflicts like Iraq and Afghanistan they are cru-cial. Tactical psyops were often well used, but the larger arena of national psyops was poorly handled and treated as an afterthought. Failure to seize and maintain dominance in

security and public information in Iraq materially contributed to the growth and prolonging of the insurgency there and the gradual slide toward civil war. Insurgency, the
glacial pace of reconstruction, rampant criminal violence, and difficulties in creating an
indigenous security force became reality in Iraq. The United States clearly had the ability
to mitigate these problems through well-planned psychological operations and public
information but was hesitant and late in recognizing the need. The prospects for a
democratic revolution followed by a triumphant U.S. withdrawal appear slim.

10. The entire U.S. defense establishment claims loudly, frequently, and fervently that they
    believe in the American soldier (presumably including airmen, sailors, and Marines). But
    they do not believe in them sufficiently to want very many or spend very much on them.
    Only after the Army and Marine Corps were stretched to the breaking point did the DoD
    reluctantly agree to increase the size of the services. But there was no hesitation to commit
    $117 billion on the chance that a radically more capable, information-enabled Objective
    Force/Future Force can be produced in the short term. This reflects a degree of pro-
    technology bias that is almost staggering.

The example of transformation illustrates what happens when people fall in love
with an idea, and as an idea transformation is terrific. In a time of uncertainty and
doubt it was more than just welcome; it was the solution to all problems. Followed
assiduously it would produce a strategically responsive Army capable of quickly
and successfully conducting any operation from humanitarian assistance to full-
scale war with far fewer casualties and all at a lower cost. Who could resist such an
appealing prospect?

Information dominance is another fine concept. It is always better to know more
than the enemy. Being smart is good, but it is not enough to win wars. Tactical
mobility (agility), sustainability, lethality, and the will to win are needed. All the networked information systems in the world are of little use if the enemy has the tactical
initiative, superior mass, and a willingness to sacrifice lives. Information dominance
depends on networks that are completely reliable; an information dependent force
that has anything less is an invitation to disaster. Furthermore, the bandwidth-
intensive wireless networks must be protected from both unintentional interference
and hostile jamming. That kind of reliability is still far out of reach, even for secure,
fiber optic cables in the United States. Better and more sustainable equipment is a
plus, but it will not make up for inadequate numbers of trained, motivated, well-
led troops armed with the most effective possible equipment, not industry-inspired
blue sky projects that are neither sustainable nor relevant to the grim realities of waging complex operations in demanding environments.[68]

Transformation was a triumph of desperate optimism on the part of the Defense
Secretary and Army leaders, heavily influenced by salesmanship on the part of the
defense industry. The technological leap of the original Army Transformation Plan
was aimed at an enemy that more closely resembled the USSR of the Cold War era
than the enemies faced in the real world. Even had its development gone as hoped,
its application to threats like terrorism and insurgency is doubtful. Transformation
focused on "a fashionable but arbitrary mixture of space systems, information

networks and unmanned vehicles that equated new with better," as phrased by Loren Thompson of the Lexington Institute. "Congress...gave it the benefit of the doubt."[69]

The success of transformation depends on cooperative enemies that play to the strengths of high-tech forces. In the real world, few opponents will offer targets for the sort of short, sharp push-button, computer wars beloved of military futurists. If Afghanistan, Iraq, and the "global war on terrorism" are any example, old-fashioned conventional units are not as disposable as once thought. This fact, combined with the realities of limited defense funding, makes it probable that "digitized" versions of current armored and mechanized land formations will remain in business for some time to come. As demonstrated in Iraq and Afghanistan, infantry and heavy armor are the only existing ways to seize and hold ground against determined opposition.

On February 8, 2006, Secretary Rumsfeld delivered a short, bland, and little noticed pronouncement about something called "transformation." "The word transformation," he said, "has attracted a lot of attention but in many ways it is more accurate to see this process of continuous analysis and change as a shift in emphasis, or weight, from the practices and assumptions of the past."[70] Gone were the promised fundamental changes, replaced by a "shift in emphasis."

Nothing in it indicated that the secretary was announcing the end of an effort that had cost many billions of dollars over seven years. Transformation had been introduced as a revolution, but over $100 billion later it had turned into business as usual.

> ...you may fly over a land forever; you may bomb it, atomize it, pulverize it and wipe it clean of life—but if you desire to defend it, protect it and keep it for civilization, you must do this on the ground the way the Roman legions did, by putting your young men into the mud.
>
> —T. R. Fehrenbach, *This Kind of War*

Pre-reorganization Structure of the U.S. Army

For those unfamiliar with the conventional (pre-reorganization) structure of the U.S. Army, the following is a quick guide.[1]

As configured in 2004 the basic maneuver element of the U.S. Army was the battalion, usually composed of four (sometimes five) companies of 100–150 personnel each. A battalion has a total of about 600 persons assigned. Battalions are usually "pure" formations. That is, all companies in a battalion are of the same kind, e.g., infantry, armor, engineer, intelligence, transportation, etc. For reasons of history and tradition, artillery and air defense companies are called batteries, and cavalry (reconnaissance) battalions are called squadrons. Companies are commanded by captains and battalions by lieutenant colonels. Special Forces companies are commanded by majors.

Three battalions usually constitute a brigade, which has a total of about 1500 personnel. Brigades, like battalions are normally pure. They are usually commanded by colonels. Regiments (i.e., the Ranger Regiment) and Special Forces Groups are somewhat smaller than brigades and are commanded by colonels. In wartime some brigades may be commanded by a Brigadier General.

Before Modular reorganization, the active Army consisted of four corps headquarters and ten divisions. Divisions are referred to as heavy and light. Heavy divisions consist of both mechanized infantry and armored/cavalry divisions. Light divisions include infantry, airborne infantry, and air assault infantry.

There were seven different division and regimental designs including a planned medium division:

- Armored (heavy);

- Mechanized Infantry (heavy);
- Cavalry (heavy);
- Light Infantry (light);
- Airborne Infantry (light);
- Air Assault Infantry (light); and
- Medium (composite of Stryker brigades and other types of brigades).[2]

In addition, the active Army had two separate infantry brigades and two cavalry regiments. In total, the active Army had 34 combat brigades.

Divisions normally have three brigades, either one armored and two mechanized infantry or two armored and one mechanized infantry (infantry that is carried in armored personnel carriers). They also include an aviation brigade, engineer brigade, and a brigade of artillery. There are a large number of logistics and support assets including transportation, air defense, medical, intelligence, signal, military police, and chemical. Division strength is hard to gauge since it can vary widely. The Army gives 16,000 as the typical strength of a heavy division and 13,000 as that of a light division. However, divisions in combat are normally organized as division task forces, making them considerably larger. The 101st Airborne Division, considered a light division, numbered about 17,000 when configured for combat in Iraq (2004). When the 3rd Infantry Division (Mechanized) led the invasion of Iraq, it was at least twice the peacetime size of the division.[3]

Two or more divisions are normally organized as a corps. The corps is usually the senior tactical headquarters of the Army in the field. In addition to at least two divisions, a corps includes a wide variety of brigade-sized support assets including artillery, aviation, and so forth. Corps are tailored for the theater and mission for which they are deployed. Once tailored, however, they contain all the combat, combat support, and combat service support capabilities required to sustain operations for a considerable period. The exception is the XVIII Airborne Corps, which has a world-wide contingency mission. Specialized units such as psychological operations battalions and civil affairs units may be assigned to corps when required. Corps are commanded by lieutenant generals.

Still larger formations such as a Field Army (two corps or the equivalent) and an Army Group have been created in the past when the size of fighting forces demanded it. The Third Army was deployed in early 2003 as the command headquarters for U.S. Army forces in Operation Iraqi Freedom.

New Designations Under the Modular Army

In 2003, the new Chief of Staff of the Army, General Peter Schoomaker, announced that the Army's Modular reorganization would be reflected with new designations for units. Brigades would be called Units of Action, divisions and corps would be called Units of Employment–X, and higher echelons would be called Units of Employment–Y. This proved confusing so Units of Employment–X, formerly

THE ARMY RE-INVENTS ITSELF 1994-2006

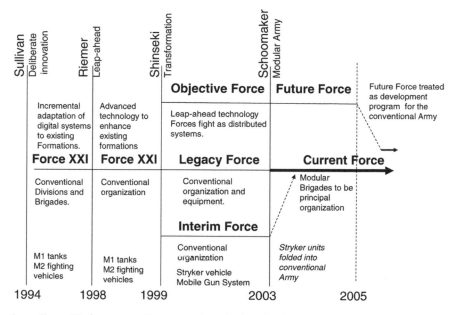

Army Force Modernization Programs described in this book.

divisions, were termed two-star UEx's and Units of Employment–X, formerly corps, were called three-star UEx's.

This also proved pointless and unworkable. As of September 21, 2005, the terms Unit of Action (UA), Unit of Employment–X (UEx), and Unit of Employment–Y (UEy) are no longer used. According to the Department of the Army directive of that date:

- The UEys now all have Army designations as follows: TRMCOM is 1st Army; ARCENT is 3rd Army; ARNORTH is 5th Army; ARSOUTH is 6th Army; USAREUR is 7th Army; 8th Army remains 8th Army until Korea stands down, then USARPAC will become 8th Army.

- FORSCOM, TRADOC, and AMC names will not change.

- The three-star UEx's remain as corps (I Corps, III Corps, and XVIII Corps).

- The two-star UEx's retain their current designations as divisions (3rd ID, 1st Cav Div, 82nd Abn, etc.).

- The Units of Action (UA) become Brigade Combat Teams (BCT).

- Maneuver Enhancement Brigades (ME) become Combat Support Brigades (ME) CSB (ME), Multi Functional Aviation Brigades (MFAB) become Combat Aviation Brigades (CAB).

This essentially restores the pre-reorganization structure from division level up. The remaining difference is that each division will now have four and eventually five reduced size brigade combat teams in place of three brigades.

U.S. Army Organizations (Major Units, 2006)

Heavy Divisions

1st Armored Division, Wiesbaden Germany
1st Cavalry Division, Fort Hood, Texas
1st Infantry Division, Wurzburg, Germany
2nd Infantry Division, Camp Red Cloud, Korea
3rd Infantry Division, Fort Stewart, Georgia
4th Infantry Division, Fort Hood, Texas

Light Divisions

10th Mountain Division, Fort Drum, New York
25th Infantry Division, Schofield Barracks, Hawaii

Airborne (Parachute)/Air Assault (Helicopter)

82nd Airborne Division, Fort Bragg, North Carolina
101st Airborne Division, Fort Campbell, Kentucky

Integrated Divisions (Active-duty Headquarters w/Reserve Component Units)

7th Infantry Division, Fort Carson, Colorado
24th Infantry Division, Fort Riley, Kansas

Army Special Operations Command (USASOC)

Headquarters, Fort Bragg, North Carolina

U.S. Army Special Forces Command (Airborne)

1st Special Forces Group (Airborne)
3rd Special Forces Group (Airborne)
5th Special Forces Group (Airborne)
7th Special Forces Group (Airborne)
10th Special Forces Group (Airborne)
19th Special Forces Group (Airborne), ARNG
20th Special Forces Group (Airborne), ARNG
1st Special Warfare Training Group

U.S. Army Civil Affairs and Psychological Operations Command (Airborne)

96th Civil Affairs Battalion (Airborne)
4th Psychological Operations Group (Airborne)
Includes 6 Psychological Operations Bns

U.S. Army Special Operations Support Command (Airborne)

528th Special Operations Support Battalion (Airborne)
112th Special Operations Signal Battalion (Airborne)

75th Ranger Regiment (Headquarters)

1st Ranger Bn
2nd Ranger Bn
3rd Ranger Bn

160th Special Operations Aviation Regiment

(Actually an independent brigade of helicopters specially trained and equipped to support Special Operations Forces)

The Army National Guard

The Army National Guard consisted of the following:

* 15 Enhanced Separate Brigades (mechanized infantry, armor, armored cavalry regiments);
* 19 Divisional Brigades (light and mechanized infantry and armor);
* 1 Separate Brigade; and
* 1 Scout Group.

Deployed Units

As of March 30, 2006, the Army reported that it had approximately 209,000 Active, Reserve, and National Guard soldiers deployed on the following operations:[4]

Operation/Location Approximate Number of Soldiers

Operation Iraqi Freedom (OIF)—Iraq 136,000
South Korea 31,600
Operation Noble Eagle—United States 16,000
Operation Enduring Freedom (OEF)—Afghanistan 18,000
Other Operations/Exercises 4,000
KFOR (Kosovo)/SFOR (Bosnia) 1,700
Joint Task Force (JTF)—Guantanamo Bay, Cuba 1,700
JTF Bravo—Honduras 1,100
Multinational Force Observers (MFO)—Sinai 680
OEF—Philippines 100

NOTES

Chapter 1

1. John M. Collins traces the idea that land power is decisive and that the ultimate object of battle is the destruction of the enemy army to Clausewitz and contrasts it with the belief that naval power is actually supreme. *Grand Strategy: Principles and Practices* (Annapolis: U.S. Naval Institute, 1973), 16.

2. DA, *Field Manual 3-0 Operations* (Washington, D.C.: Department of the Army, June 14, 2001), 1–11.

3. The Project on Defense Alternatives provides an "RMA Debate" Web page with extensive material on the issues surrounding the "revolution" at http://www.comw.org/ram (accessed August 25, 2006).

4. George W. Bush, Republican candidate for President of the United States, speaking before the Corps of Cadets at South Carolina's Citadel military college on September 23, 1999. Quoted in Nicholas Lemann, "Dreaming about War," *The New Yorker,* July 16, 2001, at http://www.comw.org/qdr/lemannNYM.html (accessed March 10, 2006).

5. Michele Flournoy, Project Director, *Report of the National Defense University Quadrennial Defense Review 2001 Working Group* (Washington: National Defense University, Institute for National Strategic Studies, November 2000), 14. See also *Report of the Defense Science Board Task Force on DOD Warfighting Transformation* (Washington: Office of the Under Secretary of Defense for Acquisition and Technology, August 1999), 5–6.

6. Quote is from Stuart Johnson, Center for Technology and National Security Policy at National Defense University, Washington, D.C., found in David Talbot, "How Technology Failed in Iraq," *MIT Technology Review* (October 2004): 5.

7. Quoted in *The Economist,* November 18, 2000, 30.

8. USAF, "Global Power, Global Reach," U.S. Air Force White Paper, June 1990.

9. "The Shape of the Battle Ahead," *The Economist,* November 18, 2000, 29–33. On the other hand, mobilized populations have shown great staying power as witness the populations of England, Germany, and Japan during World War II.

10. U.S. DoD, *Transformation Trends,* February 10, 2006, U.S. DoD Office of Force Transformation, 1, courtesy of the Office of Force Transformation, Arlington, VA.

11. The acronym FCS is used interchangeably to refer to both Future Combat System (singular) and Future Combat Systems (plural) with no obvious distinction. Since FCS (singular) is a collective or "system of systems," the acronym is used here to indicate the singular, collective form. The plural is simply confusing and serves no useful purpose.

12. Dennis Steele, "The Army Magazine Hooah Guide to Army Transformation," *Army,* February 2001, 22.

13. Professor Gaddis expands on this idea in his excellent *Surprise, Security and the American Experience* (Cambridge, MA: Harvard University Press, 2004).

14. David Wood, "Surprise at Saddam's Tactics May Be Rooted in US Myopia," Newhouse News Service, March 28, 2003, Newhouse.com (accessed May 20, 2003).A precision weapon is one capable of delivering guided conventional munitions with a 50- to 60-percent probability of destroying a target with a first-round hit. Precision munitions have a guidance or homing element including a target acquisition and tracking subsystem and a missile or projectile guidance subsystem. The era of precision weapons can be dated to May 12, 1943, when a Royal Air Force Liberator patrol bomber dropped a Mk 24 acoustic homing torpedo that subsequently seriously damaged the U-456, driving it to the surface where it was subsequently sunk by convoy escort vessels. On September 9, 1943, a German Fritz-X radio-guided glide bomb dropped from a Dornier Do 217 bomber sank the Italian battleship Roma as it steamed towards Gibraltar. By war's end, Germany and the United States had employed various proto-smart weapons in combat, including radio, radar, and television-guided bombs and missiles, against targets ranging from industrial sites to bridges and enemy shipping. Richard P. Hallion, "Precision Guided Munitions and the New Era of Warfare," APSC Paper Number 53, Air Power Studies Center RAAF Base Fairbairn Act 2600, Australia, 1995.

15. It must be pointed out that "Army After Next" as used by U.S. military planners was a program or process. It is not the name of a future organization, and certain military persons become apoplectic when it is used that way. Nevertheless, it is a useful and evocative way to refer to the Army that will exist after 2025 or so, and for that reason it is so used here.

16. U.S. Army, "US Army White Paper: Concepts for the Objective Force," Department of the Army, 2001, courtesy of The Objective Task Force, Department of the Army, 2531 Jefferson Davis Highway, Arlington, VA.

17. Donald Rumsfeld, "After Action Report—Lessons Learned," unclassified briefing, undated, probably late 2003.

18. George F. Will, "The Hour of Air Power," *Newsweek,* March 31, 2003, 66.

19. Paul J. Kern (Lieutenant General USA), DoD News Briefing, November 17, 2000. Transcript prepared by the Federal News Service, Inc., Washington, D.C. Federal News Service is a private company.

20. Fredrick W. Kagan, "War and Aftermath" *Policy Review Online,* August/September 2003, http://www.policyreview.org/aug03/kagan.html (accessed September 12, 2003).

21. Maneuver warfare of the sort currently favored by conventional armed forces is considered "3rd generation." None of these terms are rigidly defined. William Lind, the originator of the term "4th generation warfare" applies it to terrorist-like groups but also to conventional military operations characterized by small, agile high-tech forces focused on flexible missions. See Lind, "The Changing Face of Warfare: Into the 4th Generation," *Marine Corps Gazette,* October 1989, 21–30.

22. For a discussion of the September 2001 attacks as a form of asymmetric or 4th generation warfare, see William S. Lind, "Fourth Generation Warfare's First Blow," *Marine Corps Gazette,* November 2001, 11–15. Lind believes that the appropriate response would have been to promptly devastate Afghanistan and devise a plan to destroy Islamic culture.

23. Lind, "The Changing Face of Warfare."

24. William S. Cohen, Secretary of Defense, United States, *Annual Report To the President and Congress, 1998,* April 1998, http://www.dtic.mil/execsec/adr98/index.html. See also section 167 of Title 10, U.S. Code ("Unified combatant command for special operations forces").

25. Roger Guillemette, "Titan 4B to Launch Classified Payload from California," *Florida Today,* September 29, 2001, http://www.space.com/missionlaunches/fl_titan4_preview_010930.html (accessed December 17, 2004).

26. *The Economist.*

27. Ibid.

28. DARPA, Future Combat System, www.darpa.mil/tto/Programs/fcs (accessed May 26, 2003).

29. Stephen Trimble, "2008 Deployment Still Set for Objective Force, White Says," *Aerospace Daily,* October 22, 2002, 1.

30. Quoted in Jason Sherman, "Coming Attraction: At Play in the Fields of the Future With the Army's Objective Force," *Armed Forces Journal International* (July 2000): 40–44.

Chapter 2

1. Andrew Bracevich, "New Rules: Modern War and Military Professionalism," *Parameters,* December 1990, 14.

2. Michael Roberts, "The Military Revolution, 1560–1660," in *The Military Revolution Debate,* ed. Clifford J. Rogers (Boulder, CO: Westview Press, 1995).

3. Lester W. Grau (Lieutenant Colonel U.S. Army, Ret.), interview via telephone, October 11, 2004. See also Lester W. Grau, "Continuity and Change: A Soviet General Staff View of Future Theater War," *Military Review* (December 1991): 11–24; David M. Glantz, *The Non-linear Nature of Future War: A Soviet/Commonwealth View* (Fort Leavenworth, KS: Foreign Military Studies Office, 1992).

4. William S. Lind et al., "The Changing Face of War: Unto the Fourth Generation," *Military Review* (October 1989): 2–11.

5. William Eldard, Office of Net Assessment, Office of the Undersecretary of Defense (Procurement), personal correspondence of the author, September 18, 1998.

6. See, for example, the comments of retired Army General Fred M. Franks, in Harlan K. Ullman and James P. Wade, *Shock and Awe: Achieving Rapid Dominance* (Washington, D.C.: National Defense University, 1996), Appendix C, 57.

7. Martin Van Creveld et al., "The Revolution in Strategy," in *Command in War* (Cambridge, MA: Harvard University Press, 1987), 17–102, especially 61. See also Robert M. Epstein, ed., "The Transformation of Warfare," in *Napoleon's Last Victory: 1809 and the Emergence of Modern War* (Lawrence, KS: University of Kansas Press, 1994), 15–60 and Andrew N. Liaropoulos, "Revolutions in Warfare: Theoretical Paradigms and Historical Evidence—The Napoleonic and First World War Revolutions in Military Affairs," *Journal of Military History* 70, no. (2006): 363–384.

8. Robert J. Bunker, review of *Strategy and the Revolution in Military Affairs: From Theory to Policy,* by Steven Metz and James Kievit, *Air Chronicles* (Maxwell Air Force Base, AL: Air University, 1996).

9. Nicholas Lemann, "Dreaming about War," *The New Yorker,* July 16, 2001, http://www.comw.org/qdr/lemannNYM.html.

10. For an overview of the RMA debate, see MacGregor Knox and Williamson Murray, eds., *The Dynamics of Military Revolution 1300–2050* (Cambridge, UK: Cambridge University Press, 2001), especially Chaps. 1 and 9. Also Clifford J. Rogers, *The Military Revolution Debate* (Boulder, CO: Westview Press, 1995).

11. Carl Builder, *The Masks of War* (New York: Macmillan Publishing Co., Inc., 1989), 132.

12. For an examination of the underlying assumptions of U.S. war fighting, see Russell F. Weigley, *The American Way of War* (Bloomington, IA: Indiana University Press, 1973), and F.G. Hoffman, *Decisive Force: The New American Way of War* (Westport, CT: Praeger, 1996), especially 1–18, 99–133.

13. This list is taken from Stephen J. Blank, "The War That Dare Not Speak Its Name," *Journal of International Security Affairs* (Spring 2005).

14. The fighting on the Syrian front did not formally end until a cease-fire agreement in May 1974.

15. U.S. Army, *The Army of Desert Storm* (Washington, D.C.: Center for Military History, 1995).

16. U.S. Army Field Manual (FM) 100-5, *Operations,* editions of 1976 and 1982. The 1986 version of FM 100-5 retained the basic AirLand Battle tenets, as did the 1993 revision, which expanded the doctrine to include "full-dimensional operations" for a new strategic era. See also William R. Richardson (General USA), "FM 100-5: The AirLand Battle in 1986," *Military Review,* originally written in 1986, republished in the issue January-February 1997: 46–51.

17. U.S. Department of the Army, "Force Modernization, Army 86/90," *Commander's Call* (Washington, D.C.: Department of the Army, 1982), 2–40. See also John A. Wickham (General U.S. Army, Army Chief of Staff 1983–1987), "White Paper" reprinted by the *Army Times,* May 7, 1984, 10–12.

18. DoD, *SD-2—Buying Commercial & Nondevelopmental Items: A Handbook,* DoD Defense Standardization Program, Appendix 1, April 1, 1996

19. U.S. Army FM 6-60. *Tactics, Techniques, and Procedures for Multiple Launch Rocket System (Mlrs) Operations* (Washington, D.C.: Department of the Army, April 23, 1996).

20. "Closely Held USAF White Paper Warned Lack of Vision Could Cost Service," *Inside the Air Force,* May 17, 1991, 13–14.

21. Years later Warden stated that his explicit purpose had been to create a new vision of warfare that would take full advantage of air capabilities and alter the view of the relationship between the Army and the Air Force. Harold R. Winton, "Partnership and Tension: The Army and the Air Force between Vietnam and Desert Shield," *Parameters* (Spring 1996): 100–119.

22. Jane's "Blowback," *Jane's Intelligence Review,* July 26, 2001, 12–23.

23. Except as otherwise noted, information on Islamist terrorism and related organizations was derived from materials and information provided by the Higgins Foundation, Counterterrorism Research Center, Arlington, VA, with special thanks to Peter M. Leitner and Brian P. Fairchild.

24. CRS, "Al Qaeda Profile and Threat Assessment," Report RS22049, Congressional Research Service, Library of Congress, Washington, DC, February 10, 2005, 1–2.

25. The bulk of Saudi regular forces, especially their armor, were deployed well away from the border with Iraq.

26. Tom Clancy, *Marine: A Guided Tour of a Marine Expeditionary Unit* (New York: HarperCollins, 1997), 311.

27. USAF, "Reaching Globally, Reaching Powerfully: The United States Air Force in the Gulf War" (Washington, D.C.: Secretary's Staff Group, Department of the Air Force, September 1991), 41.

28. Mark Choate (Captain, USA), "Knowing is Half the Battle," *INSCOM Journal,* Almanac 2003 issue (December 2003): 8–9.

29. Ibid., 8–9.

30. Dennis Drew (Colonel (Ret.) USAF), "Desert Storm as a Symbol," *Air Power Journal* (Fall 1992): 6, 13.

31. Steven A. Hildreth, "Evaluation of U.S. Army Assessment of Patriot Antitactical Missile Effectiveness in the War Against Iraq," Congressional Research Service, prepared for the House Government Operations Subcommittee on Legislation and National Security, April 7, 1992. For the debate over the effectiveness of the Patriot missile system, see Stephen Budiansky, "Playing Patriot Games," *U.S. News and World Report,* November 22. 1993, 16; Seymour Hersh, "Missile Wars," *The New Yorker,* September 26, 1994, 86–98; and Jock Friedly, "MIT Torn by Bitter Dispute over Missile," *Science,* February 23, 1996, 1050–52.

32. Thomas A. Keaney and Eliot A. Cohen, "Was Desert Storm a Revolution in Warfare?" in *Gulf War Air Power Survey Summary Report,* Washington, 1993. The GWAPS Summary Report examines the alleged revolutionary nature of the conduct of the Persian Gulf War.

33. U.S. Government, Department of Defense, *Conduct of the Persian Gulf War, Final Report to Congress* (Washington, D.C.: GPO, 1992), 164.

34. Secretary of Defense Dick Cheney, interview by Harry Smith, *Meet the Press,* CBS-TV, April 14, 1991.

35. James Blackwell, Michael J. Mazarr, and Don M. Snider, *The Gulf War: Military Lessons Learned* (Washington: CSIS, July 1991), 21.

36. Robert S. Dudney, "McPeak on the War," Air Force, May 1991, http://www.afa.org/magazine/perspectives/desert_storm/0591watch_print.html (accessed June 6, 2003).

37. Vernon Loeb, "Bursts of Brilliance," *Washington Post Magazine,* December 15, 2002, W06. See also Dudney, "McPeak on the War."

38. U.S. Government, Department of the Air Force, *Basic Air Force Doctrine,* 1997, 1.

39. These ideas are developed at length in Brian G. Watson's thoughtful study, "Reshaping the Expeditionary Army to Win Decisively" (Carlisle, PA: Strategic Studies Institute, U.S. Amy War College, August 2005), especially 3–4.

40. Ibid.

41. Colin Powell (General, USA and Chairman, JCS), *National Military Strategy of the United States* (Washington, D.C.: U.S. Government Printing Office, 1992), 19.

42. See General Accounting Office, "Operation Desert Storm: Evaluation of the Air Campaign," Report GAO/NSIAD-97-134 (June 1997): 32–36.

43. These difficulties should not have come as much of a surprise. An exercise named "Touted Gleem" had been conducted in late 1990 to discern the problems of SCUD hunting. An MAZ-543 TEL was deployed at night in terrain similar to Iraq. F-15E, F-111F, and F-16 aircraft equipped with state-of-the-art night-capable systems tried to find the launcher after

being given the precise coordinates. They discovered the MAZ-543 was impossible to find even when its coordinates were known. See William C. Story, Jr., "Ballistic Missiles, Cruise Missiles, and Land-Based Air Power," School Of Advanced Airpower Studies, Air University, Maxwell Air Force Base, AL, June 1994, 25

44. Interview with General Vuono, March 24, 1993, United States Army Center for Military History (CMH), Washington, D.C., quoted in Glen R. Hawkins and James Jay Carafano, *Prelude to Army XXI* (Washington, D.C.: CMH, 1997), 24.

45. Ibid. Sullivan quote appears in Richard M. Swain, *Lucky War: The Third Army in the Desert* (Fort Levenworth, KS: USCGSC Press, 1997), xv.

46. Fred Franks and Tom Clancy (General, USA, Commander VII Corps in the Gulf War), *Into the Storm: A Study in Command* (Berkley: Berkley Publishing Group, 1998), 91.

47. Eliot A. Cohen, "American Views of the Revolution in Military Affairs," in *Advanced Technology and Future Warfare*, Mideast Security and Policy Studies No. 28 (Ramat Gan, Israel: Begin-Sadat Center For Strategic Studies, 1998).

48. Franks and Clancy, *Into the Storm*, 559.

49. Richard Cheney, *Annual Report to the President and Congress* (Washington, D.C.: U.S. Government Printing Office, 1992), 131.

50. Richard Cheney, *Annual Report to the President and Congress* (Washington, D.C.: U.S. Government Printing Office, 1993), 3.

51. Anthony Lake, "From Containment to Enlargement" (Remarks of Anthony Lake, Assistant to the President for National Security Affairs, Johns Hopkins University School of Advanced International Studies, Washington, D.C. September 21, 1993).

52. Gaddis Smith quote is taken from John D. Steinbrenner, "Statement to the House Committee on National Security" (John D. Steinbrenner Director, Foreign Policy Studies, The Brookings Institution, Hearings on United States Security Interests in the Post-Cold War World. U.S. Senate, Washington, D.C., June 6, 1996).

53. Charles Knight, "U.S. Military Policy—Expanding to Fill the post-Soviet Vacuum," The Project on Defense Alternatives, Cambridge, MA, June 2000, http://www.comw.org/pda/0006vacuum.html (accessed August 25, 2000).

54. Anthony Lake, *A Strategy of Enlargement and the Developing World* (Washington, D.C.: U.S. Department of State, October 25, 1993), 1. For a history of the development of the idea of "democratization" in U.S. policy, see Ernest R. May, *American Cold War Strategy; Interpreting NSC-68* (New York: Bedford Books of St. Martin's Press, 1993), especially 30.

55. Andrew J. Bacevich and Eliot A. Cohen, eds., *War Over Kosovo* (New York: Columbia University Press, 2001); see also Stephen T. Hosmer, *Why Milosevic Decided to Settle When He Did* (Santa Monica: RAND, 2001).

56. Information on missile accuracy is taken from Global Security Org. "Cruise Missile Strike—26 June 1993, Operation Southern Watch," http://www.globalsecurity.org/military/ops/strike_930626.htm (accessed October 2, 2004).

57. TRADOC Pam 525-5, *Force XXI Operations* (Fort Monroe, VA: United States Army Training and Doctrine Command, August 1, 1994), Sec. 2-3, Future Battle.

58. John T. Correll, "On Course for Global Engagement," *Air Force,* published by the U.S. Air Force Association, January 1999, 1.

59. U.S. Army Field Manual (FM) 100-5, *Operations* (Washington, D.C.: U.S. GPO, 1993).

60. Richard H. Estes (Lieutenant Colonel USAF), "Giulio Douhet: More on Target Than He Knew," *Air Chronicles* Web site, http://www.airpower.maxwell.af.mil/airchronicles

(accessed April 13, 2000). Also, Tony Mason (Air Vice-Marshal, Royal Air Force, UK), *Airpower: A Centennial Appraisal* (Indianapolis, IN: Macmillan Publishing Co., 1994).

61. Mason, *Airpower: A Centennial Appraisal.*

62. Quote is from Major General Charles D. Link, Assistant Deputy Chief of Staff for Plans and Operations, Headquarters U.S. Air Force (Remarks delivered at the fall meeting of the National Capitol Flight, Bolling Air Force Base, Washington, D.C., October 10, 1995). Giulio Douhet (General, Italian Air Corps, WWI) wrote *The Command of the Air,* trans. Dino Ferrari (Italian publication, 1921; new imprint, Washington, D.C.: Office of Air Force History, 1983); Alexander P. De Seversky (Major, Russian Air Corps, WWI; later aeronautical designer and theorist) wrote *Victory Through Air Power* (New York: Simon and Schuster, 1942). These books are the conceptual basis for much contemporary thinking about the role and potential of military aviation. They have the status of canonical literature among many air power enthusiasts.

Chapter 3

1. Paul Davis, "Protecting the Great Transition," in *New Challenges for Defense Planning: Rethinking How Much is Enough* (Santa Monica: RAND, 1994), 140.

2. William L. Bond (Brigadier General, USA), "The United States Army Battlefield Digitalization Process" briefing, April 20, 1998, 7.

3. U.S. DA, *Army Digitization Master Plan,* Department of the Army, 1995.

4. William W. Hartzog (General USA), "The Army XXI Heavy Division," briefing text courtesy of Headquarters, U.S. Army Training and Doctrine Command, Fort Monroe, VA, 1998. General Hartzog was the TRADOC commander.

5. U.S. Army Field Manual 100-5, *Operations* (Washington, D.C.: U.S. GPO, 1993), quote appears on p. 6-23.

6. Per U.S. doctrine, LIC is a political-military confrontation between contending states or groups below conventional war and above the routine, peaceful competition among states. It frequently involves protracted struggles of competing principles and ideologies. Low-intensity conflict ranges from subversion to the use of the armed forces. It is waged by a combination of means, employing political, economic, informational, and military instruments. Low-intensity conflicts are often localized, generally in the Third World, but contain regional and global security implications. DA Field Manual 100-5, *Operations,* G-9, 14.

7. DA, *On Point: the United States Army in Operation Iraqi Freedom* (Fort Leavenworth, KS: Army Center for Lessons Learned, December 22, 2004).

8. Rick Machamer (Lieutenant Colonel U.S. Army), "Force XXI: Welcome to the 21st Century Soldiers" (Washington D.C.: Department of the Army, April 1995), 16–18.

9. NATO, "Operation Deliberate Force," fact sheet, Regional Headquarters, Allied Forces Southern Europe, December 16, 2002.

10. Statistics on NATO weapon usage is from a briefing by Lieutenant General Michael Ryan, USAF, the commander of Allied Air Force Southern Europe (presented to the February 1996 Corona South meeting, Orlando, FL). Copy in the files of the Air Force Historical Support Office, Bolling AFB, D.C.

11. Ralph E. Eberhart (Lieutenant General, USAF), "Airpower: An Airman's Perspective," briefing paper prepared by AF/X0, April 1996, slide 129. Copy in the files of the Air Force Historical Support Office, Bolling AFB, D.C.

12. U.S. Air Force, "Example Bosnia," slide 10, Air and Space Power Course, U.S. Air War College, Maxwell Air Force Base, Alabama, undated. Obtained 2005.

13. Transcript of statement by Richard Holbrooke to Elizabeth Farnsworth, *The News Hour with Jim Lehrer,* PBS television, February 21, 1996.

14. USAF, *U.S. Air Force Key Issues Book* (Washington, D.C.: Department of the Air Force, 1997).

15. BG Leslie Keene (USAF), "The Affordable Solution-JSF." BG Keene was Director, Joint Strike Fighter Office (undated briefing, probably 1997).

16. U.S. Government, *Army Posture Statement FY00* (presented to the Committees and Subcommittees of The United States Senate and The House of Representatives First Session 106th Congress, Department of the Army, Washington, D.C., February 1999, p. 57).

17. This section based on "Force XXI/EXFOR/Experimental Division, 1993–1997" from CSI "Sixty Years of Reorganizing for Combat: A Historical Trend Analysis" Combat Studies Institute, U.S. Army Command and General Staff College, Fort Leavenworth, KS, January 2000, unpaged copy; and DA, *Army Digitization Master Plan 1996* (Washington, D.C.: Army Digitization Office, Department of the Army, 1996), http://www.globalsecurity.org/military/library/report/1996/army_digit_m-plan96-00exec.htm (accessed February 16, 2005).

18. CSI, "Force XXI/EXFOR/Experimental Division, 1993–1997."

19. Interview with Usama Bin Ladin, published in the 15th issue of *Nida'ul Islam* magazine, October–November 1996, found on Federation of American Scientists Web site, http://www.fas.org/irp/world/para/docs/LADIN.htm (accessed August 2003). See also U.S. Government, *Final Report of the National Commission on Terrorist Attacks Upon the United States* (Washington, D.C.: U.S. Government Printing Office, July 2004), 273.

20. Laurie Mylroie, "Who is Ramzi Yousef? And Why It Matters," *The National Interest* (Winter 1995/96): 21–27.

21. Federal Bureau of Investigation, "Fact Sheet: The Charges Against International Terrorist Usama Bin Laden," Department of Justice, Washington D.C., 1998.

22. The 9/11 Commission Report, *Final Report of the National Commission on Terrorist Attacks Upon the United States* (New York: W.W. Norton & Company, 2004), 109, hereafter referred to as the "9/11 Commission Report." See also Andrea Mitchell, "CIA Insider Says US Fighting Wrong War," *NBC News,* June 23, 2004.

23. 9/11 Commission Report, 111–114.

24. JCS, *Joint Vision 2010* (Washington, D.C.: U.S. Department of Defense, July 1996).

25. It might be objected that diverting a logistics package tailored for one unit to a different unit might not be an efficient or effective process.

26. For example, Douglas C. Lovelace, Jr., *The Evolution In Military Affairs: Shaping The Future US Armed Forces* (Carlisle, PA: Strategic Studies Institute, U.S. Army War College, June 16, 1997); and Bradley Graham, "Pentagon's Plan for Future Draws Heavily from Cold War Past," *Washington Post,* May 11, 1997, 19.

27. "Project 2025 Final Report to the Chief of Staff, US Air Force," Department of the Air Force, Washington, D.C., June 17, 1996. The report was prepared by the Air University at Maxwell AFB, AL.

28. James Riggins and David E. Snodgrass, "Halt Phase Plus Strategic Preclusion: Joint Solution for a Joint Problem," *Parameters* (Autumn 1999): 70.

29. Ronald R. Fogleman (General and Chief of Staff, U.S. Air Force) (remarks at the Orlando Air Force Association Symposium, Orlando, FL, February 15, 1996. Courtesy of the Aerospace Education Foundation, Arlington, VA.)

30. Quoted in John A. Tirpak, "Future Engagement," *Air Force, Journal of the Air Force Association* (January 1997), http://www.afa.org/magazine/Jan1997/0197engagement.asp.

31. Ronald R. Fogleman (General and Chief of Staff, U.S. Air Force), Statement before the House National Security Committee, U.S. Congress, May 22, 1997.

32. Michael E. O'Hanlon, "Beware the RMA'nia!" (paper presented at the National Defense University, September 9, 1998).

33. U.S. Congress, "U.S. Military Operations in Somalia," Hearings before the U.S. Senate Committee on Armed Services, Senate Hearing 103-846, May 12, 1994, 41.

34. Harlan K. Ullman and James P. Wade, with L.A. "Bud" Edney, Fred M. Franks, Charles A. Horner, Jonathan T. Howe, and Keith Brendley, *Shock and Awe: Achieving Rapid Dominance* (Washington, D.C.: National Defense University Press, 1996), http://www.shockandawe.com/index1.htm (accessed January 21, 2003).

35. Scott Peterson, "U.S. Mulls Air Strategies in Iraq," *Christian Science Monitor,* January 30, 2003, 1.

36. Ullman, Wade, et al., *Shock and Awe,* 6.

37. Ibid., 5.

38. Ibid., 3.

39. Ibid.

40. David Drehle, "Looking Past Iraq," *The Washington Post Magazine,* 12–19, 24–20, quoted material appears on p. 26.

41. Phillip Gold, "Defense Gets Back To Basics," *Washington Times,* November 19, 2001, 17.

42. William S. Cohen, (U.S. Secretary of Defense), *Report of the Quadrennial Defense Review* (Washington, D.C.: Office of the Secretary of Defense, May 1997), 13.

43. Data on the F-22 program are from GAO Letter Report "Tactical Aircraft: Restructuring of the Air Force F-22 Fighter Program," Letter Report, 06/04/97, GAO/NSIAD-97-156.

44. U.S. Government, "Army Public Affairs Guidance on Media Contacts Regarding QDR" (Washington, D.C.: Department of the Army). Originally published in *Inside the Pentagon,* June 5, 1997.

45. James Riggins and David E. Snodgrass, "Halt Phase Plus Strategic Preclusion: Joint Solution for a Joint Problem," *Parameters* (Autumn 1999): 70–85.

46. U.S. Government, *Report of the Quadrennial Review* (Washington, D.C.: U.S. Department of Defense, May 1997).

47. U.S. Government, "Assessment of the May 1997 Quadrennial Defense Review" (Washington, D.C.: The National Defense Panel, 1998). Also published in *Joint Force Quarterly* (Summer 1998).

48. Ibid.

49. John T. Correll, "They Call it Transformation," *Air Force, Journal of the Air Force Association* (February 1998): 5.

50. DoD, *Report of the Defense Science Board Task Force on DoD Warfighting Transformation,* Office of the Undersecretary of Defense for Acquisition and Technology, U.S. DoD, August 1999.

51. Department of the Army, "United States Army Posture Statement," February 1998, 27–33.

52. Quoted in Daniel Verton, "Benefits of Army Digitization Program Uncertain," *Federal Computer Week,* August 2, 1999, http://www.anu.edu.au/mail-archives/link/link9908/0046.html (accessed October 7, 2005).

53. U.S. Army, "Army Modernization and Digitization Overview," Army Digitization Office at Legacy Force Web page, https://ibct.army.mil/library/LegacyForce.xml (accessed November 2, 2002); also John J. Twohig et al., "Structuring Division XXI," *Military Review* 78 (May–June 1998), 2–6.

54. Twohig et al., "Structuring Division XXI."

55. At that time (1998) the ARNG had 15 enhanced Separate Brigades (eSB), some of which are heavy while others are light. These are conventional combat formations. The heavy eSBs, for example, are organized around tanks and infantry fighting vehicles supported by artillery and attack helicopters. The eSBs are specifically tasked to "provide an important hedge against adverse circumstances—such as the use of weapons of mass destruction—in major theater wars by augmenting or reinforcing active combat units." Each enhanced Brigade is prepared to deploy within 90 days of its mobilization. William S. Cohen, *Report of the Quadrennial Defense Review* (Washington, D.C.: U.S. DoD, May 1997), 32. See also *United States Army Posture Statement FY2001* (Washington, D.C.: Department of the Army, February 2000), http://www.army.mil/aps/aps_ch3_1.htm (accessed November 3, 2000).

56. CNN Washington Bureau Report, "Army Plans Changes to Streamline Combat Structure," June 9, 1998, 4:23 A.M. EDT.

57. Douglas Macgregor (Colonel, USA), "The Macgregor Briefings," The Project on Defense Alternatives, The Commonwealth Institute, Cambridge, MA, http://www.comw.org/pda/macgregor/index.html (accessed August 11, 2000).

58. *Joint Forces Quarterly* (Summer 1998): 47–54.

Chapter 4

1. Quote taken from Mark Gubrund, "Nanotechnology and International Security" (College Park, MD: University of Maryland, 1997).

2. Dana Priest, "Army's Apache Helicopter Rendered Impotent in Kosovo," *Washington Post,* December 29, 1999, A01.

3. "Predator over the Balkans," *Worldwide Defence Review* (UK), 2002, http://www.global-defence.com (accessed May 6, 2003).

4. U.S. DoD, "Joint Statement on the Kosovo After Action Report" (presented by Secretary of Defense William S. Cohen and Gen.eral Henry H. Shelton, Chairman of the Joint Chiefs of Staff, before the Senate Armed Services Committee, October 14, 1999).

5. Ibid.

6. IISS, "Air Power Over Kosovo: A Historic Victory," *Strategic Comments,* International Institute of Strategic Studies, September 28, 1999, 1.

7. Associated Press, "NATO Missiles Hit Chinese Embassy," *Associated Press Wire,* May 7, 1999, http://search.washingtonpost.com/wp-srv/WAPO/19990507/V000016-050799-idx.html (accessed June 7, 2002).

8. Federation of American Scientists, "Operation Allied Force, Operation Noble Anvil," http: // www. fas.org/man/dod-101/ops/allied_force.htm (accessed June 15, 2002).

9. This explanation is adapted from Kurt A. Klausner (Lieutenant Colonel, USAF), "Will Bandwidth be the Major Limiting Factor of Future Air Operations?" *Air Power Review* (UK) (Summer 2003): 91–102.

10. Alan D. Campen, *The First Information War* (Fairfax, VA: AFCEA International Press, 1992), 122; also Charles E. Croom, Jr. (Brigadier General, USAF), "A United States European Command J6 Communications Perspective of the Kosovo Crisis," n.d., Headquarters, ECJ6-O U.S. European Command, Stuttgart, Germany.

11. David R. Oliver and Arthur L. Money, "Unmanned Aerial Vehicles Roadmap 2000–2025," Office of the Secretary of Defense, April 6, 2001, 13, at http://www.acq.osd.mil/usd/road.doc (accessed December 10, 2003).

12. Charles E. Croom (Brigadier General, USAF) "A United States European Command J6 Communications Perspective of the Kosovo Crisis," n.d., HQ USEUCOM, 40, in Klausner, "Will Bandwidth be the Major Limiting Factor of Future Air Operations?" 94.

13. For a concise summary of these and similar arguments, see Stephen Biddle, "The New Way of War?" *Foreign Affairs* (May/June 2002).

14. See, for example, Stephen T. Hosmer, *Why Milosevic Decided to Settle When He Did* (Santa Monica: RAND Corp., 2001).

15. Mark Thompson, "Warfighting 101," *Time Magazine,* June 14, 1999, 23.

16. Benjamin S. Lambeth, *The Transformation at American Airpower* (Ithaca, NY: Cornell University Press, 2000). See also Wesley K. Clark, *Waging Modern War* (New York: Public Affairs, 2002), especially 424–438.

17. Giulio Douhet (General, Italian Air Corps, WWI), *The Command of the Air,* trans. Dino Ferrari (Italian publication, 1921; new imprint, Washington, D.C.: Office of Air Force History, 1983), 30.

18. Merrill A. McPeak (General (Ret.), USAF), "The Kosovo Result: The Facts Speak for Themselves," *Armed Forces Journal International* (September 1999): 64.The Joint Direct Attack Munition (JDAM) is an ordinary aerial bomb with satellite-guided tail fins attached. This allows aircraft at any altitude to drop it on target through clouds, smoke, or darkness. At about $20,000 each, it is far cheaper than the $1 million cruise missile that was the preferred PGM during the 1990s.

19. U.S. Government, Steve Michael (Major, USAF), "Air Force Leaders Discuss Allied Force Lessons Learned," press release, Air Force Doctrine Center, Department of Defense, December 22, 1999, http://www.defense-aerospace.com/, listed as "US Air Force Discuss Kosovo Ops (Dec. 22)" (accessed August 26, 2006).

20. Stephen Biddle, "The New Way of War?" *Foreign Affairs* (May/June 2002).

21. Merrill A. McPeak (General (Ret.), USAF), "The Kosovo Result," *Armed Forces Journal* (September 1999): 62, 64.

22. Joseph Nusbaum and Kevin A. O'Brien, "Intelligence Collection for asymmetric threats—Part II," *Jane's Intelligence Review,* November 1, 2000, courtesy of Joseph Nusbaum.

23. *Time Magazine,* June 14, 1999, 21–23.

24. Mike Tharp and Kevin Whitelaw, "Why Did It Take So Long to Send the Apaches?" *U.S. News OnLine* May 3, 1999, http://www.usnews.com/usnews/issue/990503/3leb2.htm (accessed April 10, 2000).

25. One senior White House official recalls Pentagon officials saying that the Apache deployment could result in casualties as high as "50 percent within days." "Their assessment was so bleak," the official said, "It was almost a no-brainer." Priest, "Army's Apache Helicopter Rendered Impotent in Kosovo."

26. Priest, "Army's Apache Helicopter Rendered Impotent in Kosovo."

27. DA, *On Point: The United States Army in Operation Iraqi Freedom* (Fort Leavenworth, KS: Center for Lessons Learned, December 22, 2004), 24.

28. Al-Quds Al-Arabi, February 23, 1998, quoted in Federal Bureau of Investigation, "Fact Sheet: The Charges Against International Terrorist Usama Bin Laden," Department of Justice, Washington, D.C., 1998. Although Bin Laden was not a recognized religious leader entitled to

issue fatwas, he was usually careful to have his pronouncements supported by Islamic leaders faithful to his cause.

29. Madeleine K. Albright (U.S. Secretary of State), "Remarks on Report of the Accountability Review Boards on the Embassy Bombings in Nairobi and Dar es Salaam," Washington, D.C., January 8, 1999, as released by the Office of the Spokesman, U.S. Department of State, Washington, D.C., 1999.

30. Federal Bureau of Investigation, "Bombings of the Embassies of the United States of America at Nairobi, Kenya, and Dar Es Salaam, Tanzania, August 7, 1998," U.S. Department of Justice, Washington, D.C. 20535, November 18, 1998. [Note: this information is drawn from the declassified executive summary of the report, the full report remains classified.]

31. USIS, "Clinton Announces Anti-Terrorist Strikes" (transcript), United States Information Service, Washington, D.C., August 20, 1998.

32. CNN, "Pakistan Lodges Protest over U.S. Missile Strikes," August 21, 1998, http://www.cnn.com/US/9808/21/air.strikes.02/ (accessed October 3, 2004); also B. Raman, "U.S. Bombing of Terrorist Camps in Afghanistan," *Times of India,* November 3, 1998, unpaged copy.

33. CNN, "Pakistan Lodges Protest over U.S. Missile Strikes."

34. Eqbal Ahmad, "The Limits of Infinite Reach," *Al Ahram* (Cairo, Egypt), September 10–16, 1998, http://weekly.ahram.org.eg/1998/394/foc2.htm (accessed October 3, 2004).

35. Reuters, "US Commandos Set to Seize Bin Laden," *Reuters Limited,* April 13, 1999.

36. Andrea Koppel, "Taliban's U.S. Headquarters Decries U.N. Sanctions," *CNN,* November 15, 1999, http://www.cnn.com/US/9911/15/taliban.ny/ (accessed September 15, 2004).

37. Global Security, "Afghanistan—Militia Facilities," http://www.globalsecurity.org/military/world/afghanistan/militia-fac.htm (accessed October 8, 2003).

38. CINC, short for "Commander-in-Chief." As used here, it refers to the four-star generals who actually command fighting forces.

39. Elaine M. Grossman, "The Halt Phase Hits a Bump," *Air Force* (published by U.S. Air Force Association) (April 2001): 17.

40. U.S. Joint Forces Command, "A Concept for Rapid Decisive Operations" (J9 Joint Futures Lab), first circulated in 1999, formally issued in 2002. Courtesy of U.S. Joint Forces Command.

41. Ibid.

42. Elaine M. Grossman, "Airpower Gains in the Doctrine Wars," *Air Force* (March 2000): 3.

43. Grossman, "The Halt Phase Hits a Bump."

44. U.S. Joint Forces Command, "A Concept for Rapid Decisive Operations," B-2.

45. Grossman, "The Halt Phase Hits a Bump."

46. United States, *National Military Strategy of the United States,* 1997, quoted in Stephen Blank, "The War That Dare Not Speak Its Name," *Journal of International Security Affairs* (Spring 2005), http://www.securityaffairs.org/issues/2005/08/blank.php (accessed March 23, 2006).

47. Andrew W. Marshall, with Zalmay Khalilzad and John P. White, *Strategic Appraisal: The Changing Role of Information in Warfare* (Santa Monica: RAND Corp., 1999), Foreword, 3.

48. USJFCOM (U.S. Joint Force Command), *Rapid Decisive Operations,* October 22, 1999.

49. JFCOM (U.S. Joint Forces Command), *Rapid Decisive Operations (RDO) White Paper,* Coordinating Draft (Version 2.0), August 9, 2001.

50. William Bunch, "US Plan for Saddam: Shock and Awe," *Philadelphia Daily News,* February 26, 2003, 4.

51. Robert A. Pape, *Bombing to Win: Air Power and Coercion in War* (New York: Cornell University Press, 1996). Quotes are taken from Scott Peterson, "US Mulls Air Strategies In Iraq," *Christian Science Monitor,* January 30, 2003, 1.

52. Ibid.

53. Jim Katzaman, "Short Path to the Future," Air Force News Service, September 13, 1996.

54. U.S. Government, *Joint Vision 2020* (Washington, D.C.: Office of the Chairman of the Joint Chiefs of Staff, 2000); see also Dennis J. Reimer, *Army Vision 2010* (Washington, D.C.: Office of the Chief of Staff of the Army, undated, released November 1996).

55. U.S. Government, JCS, *Joint Vision 2020.* To a large degree, *Joint Vision 2020* is restatement and reemphasis of the earlier *Joint Vision 2010,* released in July 1996.

56. For example, David A. Deptula (Brigadier General, USAF), "Effects Based Operations: Change in the Nature of Warfare," Aerospace Education Foundation, Arlington, VA, 2001.

57. Paul K. Davis, *Effects Based Operations* (Santa Monica, CA: RAND Corp., 2001).

58. USJFCOM, "Rapid Decisive Operations," briefing, U.S. Joint Forces Command, dated June 1, 2001.

59. DoD, "Rapid Decisive Operations Briefing," U.S. Department of Defense, dated October 20, 2000.

60. Allen W. Batschelet (Lieutenant Colonel, USA), "Effects-Based Operations for Joint Warfighters," U.S. Army Professional Writing Collection, 2003, http://www.army.mil/prof_writing/ olumes/volume1/june_2003/6_03_3.html (accessed March 18, 2006).

61. Bruce Wong (Colonel, USAF), "Preparing for QDR 2001," U.S. Air Force, http://www.mors.org/QDR2001/WGBriefings/af_MORSBrief/tsld027.htm (accessed 25 August 2000).

62. Chris Hellman, "What Next for the 'Army After Next'?" *Weekly Defense Monitor,* Center for Defense Information, 1779 Massachusetts Avenue, NW, Washington, D.C., September 9, 1999, http://www.cdi.org/weekly/1999/issue35.html#1 (accessed December 14, 2000).

63. Ibid.

64. General Eric K. Shinseki, "Address to the Eisenhower Luncheon, 45th Annual meeting of the Association of the Untied States Army" October 12, 1999, courtesy of the Office of the Chief of Staff, United States Army, Washington, D.C.

65. Department of the Army, "Army Transition," in *Army Vision* (Washington, D.C.: Department of the Army, http://www.army.mil/armyvision/default.htm (accessed November 3, 2000).

66. Lewis Bernstein, "Army Experimental Formations and Their Possible Influence on the Establishment of the Force XXI Experimental Force" monograph, CAC History Branch, Research Division, Center for Army Lessons Learned, TRADOC History Conference/Workshop, October 23, 1996, 1. For accounts of two nineteenth century instances, Bernstein suggests Odie B. Faulk, *The US Camel Corps: An Army Experiment* (New York: Oxford University Press, 1976); Charles M. Dollar, "Putting the Army on Wheels: The Story of the Twenty-Fifth Infantry Bicycle Corps," *Prologue* 17.1 (Spring 1985): 7–23; and Marvin E. Fletcher, "The Black Bicycle Corps," *Arizona and the West* 16.3 (Autumn 1974): 219–232.

For further information on the military use of bicycles, see Stephen T. Tate, "Human Powered Vehicles in Support of Light Infantry Operations" (master's thesis, U.S. Army Command and General Staff College, Fort Leavenworth, KS, 1989).

67. Ibid., 29

68. Matthew Cox, "Off Track? Plan for Medium-Weight Force Has Skeptics Among Tankers," *Army Times,* November 8, 1999; "Helo Supporters Concerned About Aviation's Role in the 'New Army,'" *Inside the Army,* October 25, 1999, 5; Daniel Dupont, "Observers Surprised by Army's Decision to Kill ATACMS Block IIA," *Inside the Army,* January 6, 2000, 7.

69. Stephen P. Aubin, "Stumbling Toward Transformation: How the Services Stack Up," *Strategic Review* (Spring 2000): 39–47.

70. Hunter Keeter, "Commandant Seeks Inter-Service Discussion Over Expeditionary Roles, Missions," *Defense Daily,* October 31, 2000, 1.

71. David L. Grange, Huba Wass De Czege, et al., *Air Mechanization* (Nashville: Turner Publishing, 2000).

72. Ibid.

73. U.S. Army, "U.S. Army Posture Statement Fiscal Year 2001," Department of the Army, Washington DC, 1.

74. U.S. General Accounting Office, "Army National Guard: Combat Brigades' Ability to be Ready for War in 90 Days is Uncertain" (Washington, D.C.: GAO, June 1995), 3.

75. "Army Posture FY 01," 15-16.

76. Ibid., 17.

77. U.S. Government, "DARPA and Army Select Contractors for Future Combat Systems Programs," Press release No. 236-00, Office of the Assistant Secretary of Defense (Public Affairs), Washington, D.C., May 9, 2000.

78. This effort is also integrated with Joint Forces Command's program for warfighting concept development. The 10th Mountain Division (Light Infantry) participated in a Joint Contingency Force–Advanced Warfighter Experiment (JCF-AWE) in September 2000, to test ways of improving light forces and contingency force capabilities.

79. Loren B. Thompson, "Heavy Armor," *Defense Daily Network,* August, 1999, http://www.defensedaily.com/reports/harmor.htm (accessed December 15, 2000).

80. Trainor suggests that Schwartzkopf's feelings about SOF were a result of his experience with them during the invasion of Grenada. Personal correspondence with the author, January 1997.

81. Message, *Saudi Arabia Situation Report 026-90, Scud attack,* MAC Intelligence, Scott Air Force Base, IL, January 19, 1991.

82. Department of the Army, *Certain Victory: The United States Army in the Gulf War* (Washington, D.C.: GPO, 1993), 182–183; Douglas C. Waller, *The Commandos* (New York: Simon and Schuster, 1994), 341–342.

83. Michael R. Gordon and Bernard E. Trainor (General ret., USMC), *The General's War* (Boston: Little, 1995), 245; Waller, *The Commandos,* 344–345.

84. Waller, *The Commandos,* 349–350.

Chapter 5

1. AUSA, "Future Combat Systems: Tough Challenge," *AUSA News* (Association of the U.S. Army) (September 2000): 25.

2. Information in this section not otherwise identified is from materials kindly provided by the Public Affairs Office of the Infantry Center, Fort Benning, GA, and Chief of Staff of the Army, CSA Planning Directive No. 1, "Medium Weight Force, Initiative Brigade Combat Teams," courtesy of the Office of the Chief of Staff, Washington, D.C., undated, received January 2000.

3. Ibid.

4. The case of the M1 (and later the Stryker) illustrates the difficulty in estimating airlift for combat vehicles. Although the "official" estimate allows for two M1s per C-5 flight, some sources maintain that if the M1 is "full-up," that is, combat loaded with fuel, ammunition, and so forth, the C-5 can carry only one over intercontinental ranges.

5. David Talbot, "How Technology Failed in Iraq," *MIT Technology Review,* October 2004, 5.

6. Sally Shutt, Press release, Office of Public Affairs, The Infantry Center, Fort Benning, GA, May 2000.

7. To be C-130 transportable, MAV must enter and exit the aircraft capable of immediate combat operations and not exceed 13,000 pounds maximum axle weight on the treadways of C-130 aircraft, and its combat capable deployment weight must not exceed 38,000 pounds GVW (19 stons) to allow C-130 transport of 1,000 nautical miles without requiring a USAF waiver for maximum aircraft weight on a fixed runway. C-130 with MAV must be capable of assault strip landing with a waiver for maximum aircraft weight.

8. Initial Operating Capability has various definitions; in this case, it means able to conduct most operations with a mix of IAVs and legacy equipment. It does not mean fully capable or ready for combat.

9. Ali Bettencourt, "Army Tests Lightweight Armored Vehicles at Knox," U.S. Army press release, January 3, 2000.

10. LAV stands for Land Attack Vehicle. Designation of these vehicles can quickly become confusing. The LAV III would normally be described as an APC (Armored Personnel Carrier) but the U.S. Army used both Interim Combat Vehicle and Infantry Carrier Vehicle to describe the Stryker version of the LAV. Such vehicles are often referred to as IFVs (Infantry Fighting Vehicles) or, in the past, MICVs (Mechanised Infantry Combat Vehicles).

11. Piranha III information sheet, courtesy of MOWAG AG, Unterseestrasse 65, 8280 Kreuzlingen, Switzerland, undated.

12. "Lewis Readies for Brigade Training," Public Affairs Office, I Corps and Fort Lewis, Washington, December 1999.

13. Training and Doctrine Command (TRADOC), Press Briefing Transcript "Status of Brigade Combat Team Development at Fort Lewis and the Planned Performance Demonstration at Fort Knox," December 16, 1999, Department of the Army, Washington, D.C., http://www.fas.org/man/dod-101/army/unit/docs/991216-briefing_tradoc_press.htm (accessed August 3, 2000).

14. Stacy Wamble, "Brigade Combat Team Under Construction at Fort Knox," Press Release Fort Knox Public Affairs Office, Fort Knox, Kentucky, January 5, 2000. Courtesy of U.S. Army News Service, Washington, D.C.

15. Lockheed Martin, "HIMARS," http://www.army-technology.com/projects/himars/index.html (accessed August 3, 2000).

16. Department of the Army, "Army Officially Begins Transformation To Initial Brigade Combat Teams," Press release No. 00-023, Department of the Army, Washington, D.C., April 13, 2000.

17. U.S. Army AMSTA-LC-CLD Solicitation DAAE07-00-R-M032, U.S. Army Tank-automotive and Armaments Command (TACOM), Warren, MI, December 30, 1999. This Executive Summary for the Brigade Combat Team (BCT) effort provides an overview of the specific acquisition and the BCT program. Courtesy of Ms. LeRuth Shepard, Contracts Officer, TACOM.

18. Dennis Steele, "The Interim Armored Vehicle," *Army,* January 2001, 29–32.

19. U.S. Army, "Operational Requirements Document for a Family of Medium Armored Vehicles (MAV)," U.S. Army Tank-Automotive and Armaments Command (TACOM), Warren, MI, January 31, 2000. Courtesy of Ms. LeRuth Shepard, Contracts Officer, TACOM.

20. Dennis Steele, "The Interim Armored Vehicle."

21. Richard J. Newman, "The Army Ponders Its Future," *Air Force Magazine,* November 2000, at http://www.afa.org/magazine/Nov2000/1100army.html (accessed December 7, 2000. Richard J. Newman was senior editor and Pentagon correspondent for *U.S. News and World Report.*

22. Quoted in Newman, ibid.

23. Lutz Unterseher, "Wheels or Tracks? On the 'Lightness' of Military Expeditions," Commonwealth Institute, July 2000, http://www.comw.org/pda/0007wheels.html (accessed August 25, 2000).

24. Jeffery R. Barnett, "Funding Two Armies," *Armed Forces Journal International* (May 2000): 14–15.

25. Ibid.

26. For example, John W. Handy (Major General, USAF), Secretary of the Air Force, Air Force Policy Directive 38-1, Department of the Air Force, June 1, 1996 (directs simplification of USAF structure).

27. Department of the Air Force, *Air Force Posture Statement,* Washington, D.C., 1998, 40–42. Also Department of the Air Force, *Air Force Posture Statement,* Washington, D.C., 2000, 32–38.

28. John T. Correll (Editor in Chief), *Air Force* (January 1999): 1.

29. This article, titled "Precision Decision," was coauthored by LTC Antulio J. Echevarria II, USA.

30. John Barry and Evan Thomas, "The Kosovo Cover-up," *Newsweek,* August 27, 2000.

31. Nicholas Lemann, "Dreaming About War," *The New Yorker,* July 16, 2001.

32. Ibid.

33. Condoleezza Rice, "Promoting The National Interest," *Foreign Affairs,* no. 1 (2000): 52–54.

34. Kim Burger, "Army Officials Object to Aspect of GAO's Transformation Report," *Inside the Army,* March 5, 2001, 1.

35. Robert Nolin, "New Army to Be Faster, More Mobile, Chief of Staff Tells Broward Convention," *Fort Lauderdale Sun-Sentinel,* March 2, 2001, 1. Chris Strohm, "Shinseki Says More Money Will Be Added for Transformation," *Inside the Army,* March 5, 2001, 13.

36. Loren B. Thompson, "Saved By Reality: The Army Finds A Future," *Defense Week,* October 9, 2001, 1.

37. Ibid.

38. George I. Seffers, "The Voice Of Combat," *Federal Computer Week,* August 6, 2001, 17.

39. Kevin J. Dwyer, "4th ID Puts Readiness for Digital War to the Test" *Killeen Daily Herald* (Texas), October 9, 2001, 1.

40. Gina Cavallaro, "Digital Division," *Army Times,* March 3, 2003, 28.

Chapter 6

1. George W. Bush, "A Period Of Consequences" (speech delivered at The Citadel, Charleston, South Carolina, September 23, 1999). All George W. Bush quotes in this section are taken from the Citadel speech unless otherwise indicated.

2. Nicholas Lemann, "Dreaming About War," *New Yorker,* July 16, 2001. Admiral (Ret.) Crowe is former chairman of the Joint Chiefs of Staff.

3. Ibid.

4. Linda D. Kozaryn and Jim Garamone, "Bush, Rumsfeld Pledge Support to Military," U.S. DoD Press release, American Forces Press Service, January 26, 2001.

5. Jim Garamone, "Bush Addresses NATO, US Military Transformation" U.S. DoD Press release, American Forces Press Service, February 13, 2001.

6. President George W. Bush (speech at Norfolk Naval Air Station, February 13, 2001), http://www.whitehouse.gov/news/releases/20010213.html (accessed August 26, 2006).

7. Peter Huessy, "General's Assessment Of War," *Washington Times,* October 8, 2004, 19.

8. Stan Crock, "An Arms Industry Too Big for the Task at Hand," *Washington Post,* August 31, 2003, B1–B2.

9. Christopher J. Dorobek, "Pentagon OKs New Info Grid," *Federal Computer Week,* September 3, 2001. See also DoD Directive 5000.1, 2001.

10. Timothy Noah, "The Rumsfeld Death Watch," *Slate* (on-line), posted Tuesday, August 7, 2001.

11. Ibid.

12. John M. Donnelly, "Rumsfeld Makes War," *Chicago Tribune,* October 22, 2001, 1. Also, Bernard Weinraub with Thom Shanker, "Rumsfeld's Design for War Criticized on the Battlefield," *New York Times,* April 1, 2003, 1.

13. George W. Bush, "Statement by the President in His Address to the Nation," Office of the Press Secretary, White House, Washington, D.C., September 7, 2003, http://www.whitehouse.gov/news/releases/2001/09/20010911-16.html.

14. U.S. polling data are summarized at the *PollingReport.com* Web site, http://www.pollingreport.com.

15. Michael Kinsley, "Bipartisan Etiquette," *Washington Post,* October 26, 2001, 35.

16. Michelle Ciarrocca, "Post-9/11 Economic Windfalls for Arms Manufacturers," *Foreign Policy in Focus,* September 2002, http://www.fpif.org/briefs/vol7/v7n10arms_body.html (accessed February 12, 2005).

17. Bob Woodward and Dan Balz, "Bush Awaits History's Judgment," *Washington Post,* February 3, 2002, 1.

18. Office of the Secretary of Defense, *Quadrennial Defense Review 2001* (Washington, D.C.: September 30, 2001). The QDR and other related analyses can be found on the *QDR Page,* http://www.comw.org/qdr.

19. Elaine M. Grossman, "Key Review Offers Scant Guidance," *Inside The Pentagon,* October 4, 2001, 1.

20. David A. Fulghum, "QDR Became 'Pabulum' as Decisions Slid," *Aviation Week & Space Technology,* October 8, 2001, 21–22.

21. Lisa Troshinsky, "Analysts: Navy Needs To Be Better at Selling Transformation," *Navy News & Undersea Technology,* October 9, 2001, 1.

22. Adam J. Hebert, "Air Force Lacks Basing Options for Airstrikes on Afghanistan," *Inside The Air Force,* October 12, 2001, 1.

23. Daniel Goure, "Strategic Reality Requires New Force Structure," *Defense News,* November 12–18, 2001, 21.

24. Loren B. Thompson, "Saved By Reality: The Army Finds A Future," *Defense Week,* October 9, 2001, 1.

25. Ibid.

26. Ibid.

27. Army Secretary Thomas White, interview, *Defense Week,* December 17, 2001, 2.

28. Ibid.

29. Robert Woodward, *Bush's War* (New York: Simon & Schuster, 2002), 17.

30. For a vivid picture of life under the Taliban, see Khaled Hosseini, *The Kite Runner* (Riverhead), 2003.

31. Woodward, *Bush's War,* 5.

32. Patrick E. Tyler and Elaine Sciolino, "Bush Advisers Split on Scope of Retaliation," *New York Times,* September 20, 2001, 1. Also BBC, "Wolfowitz: Key US Hawk," September 26, 2001, http://news.bbc.co.uk/1/hi/world/americas/1564448.stm (accessed June 9, 2003). U.S. DoD, "Deputy Secretary Wolfowitz Interview with Associated Press," (Interview with Thelma LeBrecht, Associated Press), U.S. DoD Press release, September 10, 2002. Also, "Wolfowitz: Saddam off the Hook," *NewsMax.com,* January 8, 2002, http://www.newsmax.com/archives/articles/2002/1/8/65355.shtml (accessed June 9, 2003).

33. Woodward, *Bush's War,* especially 39–40.

34. Rowan Scarborough, "Special Operations Assigned Major Role," *Washington Times,* September 25, 2001, 1.

35. Rowan Scarborough, *Rumsfeld's War* (Washington DC: Regency, 2004), 3–4.

36. Woodward, *Bush's War,* 88.

37. William D. O'Malley, *Persian Gulf Security: Possible Airfield Deployment Options* (Santa Monica, CA: RAND Corporation, September, 2001); Adam J. Hebert, "Air Force Lacks Basing Options for Airstrikes on Afghanistan," *Inside The Air Force,* October 12, 2001, 1.

38. Ibid.

39. David Fastabend, "EBO and the Classical Elements of Operational Design," briefing U.S. Army Futures Center, Arlington, VA, January 31, 2006, especially slides 13 and 14.

40. Woodward, *Bush's War,* 174.

41. Woodward, *Bush's War,* 192–193.

42. See Robin Moore, *The Hunt for Bin Laden* (New York: Random House, 2003), for a detailed description of the special operations mission.

43. Defense Dialog, "The Buildup of US Military Force around Afghanistan Continues," *Federal News Service,* Summary of Broadcasts of Monday, October 1, 2001.

44. See Eric Micheletti, *Special Forces: War on Terrorism in Afghanistan,* trans. Cyril Lombardini (Paris: Histoire & Collections, 2004).

45. DOD Briefing by Secretary Rumsfeld and General Myers, October 8, 2001.

46. U.S. Army, Psychological Operations leaflet, courtesy of U.S. Army Special Operations Command, 2001.

47. Statement of Osama bin Laden and spokesman, aired on Al-Jazeera TV, October 7, 2001, found at Mid-East Web, http://www.mideastweb.org/osamabinladen3.htm (accessed October 14, 2003).

48. Woodward, *Bush's War,* 211.

49. USASOC, *Weapon of Choice: ARSOF in Afghanistan* (Fort Leavenworth, KS: Combat Studies Institute), written by U.S. Army Special Operations Command, Fort Bragg, NC, 82–84 and 96.

50. The USASOC official history (ibid.) refers to the raid on Omar's compound only obliquely; e.g., page 112 mentions refueling "helicopters supporting another combat operation in the area."

51. Seymour M. Hersh, "Escape and Evasion," *New Yorker,* November 5, 2001.

52. It is difficult to know how seriously to take this since Delta never reveals casualties. It was only following an inadvertent remark by a retired Delta trooper that it was revealed that Delta commandos may have been killed in the 1980 Iranian rescue debacle.

53. Romesh Ratnesar, "The Ground War: Into The Fray," *Time,* October 29, 2001, 42–43.

54. The anti-Taliban resistance forces were based chiefly on the remnants of the pre-Taliban national army and part-time militia mustered by various local warlords (some of whom were no better than thugs and drug lords). The full title of the force was the United and National Front for the Salvation of Afghanistan. See www.afghaninfo.com for info on the c. 2001 anti-Taliban forces (accessed May 20, 2003).

55. USASOC, *Weapon of Choice,* 126–127.

56. Secretary Rumsfeld was interviewed on CNN's *Late Edition* and ABC's *This Week,* among others. See *Radio TV Defense Dialog* (Broadcasts of Friday–Sunday, October 26–28, 2001), Federal News Service, October 29, 2001.

57. Woodward, *Bush's War,* 272.

58. Stephen Biddle, "Afghanistan and the Future of Warfare," *Foreign Affairs,* March–April 2003, 31–46.

59. Thomas E. Ricks and Bob Woodward, "Marines in Afghanistan," *Washington Post,* November 26, 2001, 1.

60. Biddle, "Afghanistan and the Future of Warfare," 36, 41–42.

61. The account of the battle for Tora Bora is compiled from press reports, chiefly Philip Smucker, "How Bin Laden Got Away," *Christian Science Monitor,* March 4, 2002, 1, 15–17; Philip Smucker, "After Tora Bora," *Christian Science Monitor,* January 28, 2002, 1; Matthew Forney, "Inside the Tora Bora Caves," *Time* (on-line edition), December 11, 2001, http://www.time.com (accessed November 21, 2003); and Barton Gellman and Thomas E. Ricks, "US Concludes Bin Laden Escaped at Tora Bora Fight," *Washington Post,* April 17, 2002, 1, and Peter Huessy, "General's Assessment Of War," *Washington Times,* October 8, 2004, 19.

62. Global Security, "Afghanistan Militias, Camps," http://www.globalsecurity.org/military/world/afghanistan/darunta.htm (accessed October 5, 2004).

63. Rowan Scarborough, "Defense, CIA Vie for Power," *Washington Times,* November 30, 2004, 7. Also Associated Press, "Detainee Helped Bin-Laden Flee," *Washington Post,* March 23, 2005, 2.

64. Quote from Matthew Forney, "Inside the Tora Bora Caves," *Time* (on-line edition), December 11, 2001, http://www.time.com (accessed November 21, 2003).

65. Bin Laden's escape from Tora Bora is probably one of the most commented on single events since the 9/11 attacks. It even became an issue in the 2004 U.S. presidential campaign.

See, for example, Associated Press, "Detainee Helped Bin Laden Flee, Document Says," *Washington Post,* March 23, 2005, 2.

66. U.S. Department of Defense, "Talking Points—October 26, 2004—Bin Laden and Tora Bora," U.S. DoD Office of Public Affairs.

67. Douglas Frantz, "Hundreds of Qaeda Fighters Slip Into Pakistan," *The New York Times,* December 19, 2001, 1. See also Seymour M. Hersh, "The Getaway," *The New Yorker,* January 28, 2002, 36–40.

68. Quoted material from Smucker, "How Bin Laden Got Away" 1, 15–17. See also Philip Smucker, "Tora Bora falls, but no bin Laden," *Christian Science Monitor,* December 17, 2001, http://www.csmonitor.com/2001/1217/p1s1-wosc.html (accessed February 4, 2005).

69. Smucker, "How Bin Laden Got Away."

70. Ibid.

71. In a 2004 newspaper interview Franks called attention to the presence of U.S. troops other than special operators at the battle, including elements of the 10th Mountain and 101st Airborne Divisions as well as troops from a USMC Expeditionary Unit. The fact remains that Afghan forces were expected to carry the brunt of the fighting, however many U.S. JADMs and Spectre Gunships may have supported them. See Peter Huessy, "General's Assessment Of War," *Washington Times,* October 8, 2004, 19.

72. Sean D. Naylor, "Not a Good Day to Die," *Armed Forces Journal* (March 2005): 30–35, quoted material appears on page 35.

73. DA, *On Point,* Chap. 2, p. 36; and Mark Choate (Captain, USA), "Knowing is Half the Battle," *INSCOM Journal, Almanac* 2003 issue (December 2003): 8–9.

74. Interview with Major General Franklin L. Hagenbeck, Commanding General, Coalition Joint Task Force Mountain in Afghanistan and Commanding General, 10th Mountain Division (Light), Fort Drum, New York. Robert H. McElroy with Patricia Slayden Hollis [Editor *Field Artillery* (Fort Sill, OK)], "Fire Support For Operation Anaconda," September–October 2002, 5.

75. Naylor, "Not a Good Day to Die."

76. Ibid.

77. This description is taken from Biddle, "Afghanistan and the Future of Warfare," 37, 39–40.

78. Ibid., 44–45.

79. John Barry and Evan Thomas, "Boots, Bytes and Bombs," *Newsweek,* February 17, 2003, 12.

80. *Inside the Pentagon,* October 3, 2002, 1; and November 21, 2002, 1.

81. Elaine M. Grossman, "Army Eyes 'Joint Fire Control Teams' To 'Enable' Lighter Ground Troops," *Inside The Pentagon,* January 29, 2004, 1.

82. ITP, "Breakdown in Army Air Force Communications in Afghanistan," *Inside The Pentagon,* February 27, 2003, 1. See also "Air Leaders: A-10 Upgrades May Be Cut But Retirement Not Accelerated," June 5, 2003, 1.

83. Vago Muradian, "Afghan Campaign Serves as 'Lower-Risk' Proving Ground for Systems, Concepts," *Defense Daily International,* January 11, 2002, 1.

84. Harry D. Raduege, Jr. (Lieutenant General, USAF), director, Defense Information Systems Agency, letter quoted in Kurt A. Klausner, "Will Bandwidth be the Major Limiting Factor of Future Air Operations?" *Air Power Review* (UK) (Summer 2003): 94. See also John M. Donnelly, "Panel Probes Military's Fight for Radio Waves," *Defense Week,* April 22, 2002, 3.

85. For example, interview with Army Secretary Thomas E. White, "Afghanistan Validates Army Way, Secretary Says," *Defense Week,* December 17, 2001, 2.

86. Based on the author's conversations with members of the special operations community. For a depiction of the tension and occasional hostility among and between special operations forces and the CIA, see Robin Moore's *The Hunt for Bin Laden* (New York: Random House, 2003).

87. Biddle, "Afghanistan and the Future of Warfare," 41–43.

88. "'Afghanistan Validates Army Way,' Secretary Says," *Defense Week,* December 17, 2001, 2.

89. DA, "Army Announces Name for Interim Armored Vehicle," Press release No. R-02-009, February 27, 2002, Department of the Army, Washington, D.C.

90. Frank Tiboni, "Shinseki's Term Was a Quiet Storm," *Army Times,* June 16, 2003, 10. Crusader was well positioned to secure Congressional support since it involved a number of manufacturers in a number of Congressional Districts: United Defense, Limited Partnership (UDLP) (Minneapolis, MN) was the prime contractor. General Dynamics Land Systems (Muskegon, MI, and Sterling Heights, MI) and General Dynamics Armament Systems (Burlington, VT) were major subcontractors for mobility and resupply. Honeywell, Raytheon, and General Dynamics were the major software subcontractors.

91. U.S. DoD, "Termination Papers For Crusader Signed," News Release No. 408-02, August 6, 2002, U.S. Department of Defense, Washington, D.C.

92. The account of Mountain Sweep was compiled from open sources, chiefly Colin Soloway, "An Unnerving Report from the Afghan Front," *Newsweek,* September 30, 2002, ctstudies.com (accessed June 14, 2004); CNN, "Operation Mountain Sweep Nets Taliban, Weapons," August 26, 2002, CNN.com (accessed June 13, 2004); PRNewswire, "Witnesses Say Operation Mountain Sweep Was a Disaster," October 1, 2002, rense.com (accessed June 14, 2002); Ananova, "Mountain Sweep Fails to Find Al-Qaeda Fighters," undated, ananova.com (accessed June 14, 2004).

93. Quote is from Soloway, "An Unnerving Report from the Afghan Front."

94. Tim McGirk and Michael Ware, "Losing Control," *Time,* November 18, 2002, 56–59.

95. For example, "Afghanistan: Provincial Leaders To Send Revenues To Capital Every 15 Days," Kabul Radio Afghanistan (in Pashto) 1500 GMT 21 May 03, Foreign Broadcast Information Service, IAP20030521000161. Also "Afghan Government Introduces Administrative, Financial Reforms," Mashhad Voice Of The Islamic Republic Of Iran External Service (in Dari) 0330 GMT 22 May 03, Foreign Broadcast Information Service, IAP20030522000028.

96. Atiq Sarwari and Robert Crews, "Afghanistan Hangs on a Thread," *Los Angeles Times,* May 15, 2003, 1.

97. U.S. Department of Defense, "Fact Sheet—Provincial Reconstruction Teams," September 27, 2004; and Donna Miles, "Terrorists Can't Compete with Provincial Reconstruction Teams," American Forces Press Service, Washington, D.C., April 21, 2004.

98. Miles, "Terrorists Can't Compete with Provincial Reconstruction Teams." For NGO and United Nations criticism of PRT operations, see Charlotte Watkins, *Provincial Reconstruction Teams (PRTs)* (Oxford, UK: Oxford Brookes University, September 30, 2003), especially Chap. 4.

99. John Barry, "The Army Cleans House." *Newsweek,* August 11, 2003, 8.

100. Marcia Triggs, "Stryker Gets New Armor," Army News Service, March 9, 2002.

101. Scott R. Gourley, "Stryker's Mobile Gun System," *Army Magazine* (U.S. Department of the Army), May 2003, 35.

102. Ibid.

103. Roxana Tiron, "Stryker Not Up To Speed in Some Areas, Soldiers Claim," *National Defense,* October 2002, 18.

104. Sean D. Naylor, "It's Stryker Against M113A3—Again," *Army Times,* September 23, 2002, 13.

105. Ibid.

106. Associated Press, "Army's New Stryker Brigades Sit Out Iraq War, Train in California," April 2, 2003.

107. Megan Scully, "JFCOM Chief: Stryker Interim Armored Vehicle A 'Work In Progress,'" *Inside The Army,* September 23, 2002, 1.

108. Jon Dougherty, "Critics Pan Army's 'Stryker,'" WorldNetDaily.com, June 4, 2003 (accessed June 21, 2004).

109. Christopher J. Toomey, "Army Digitization: Making it Ready for Prime Time," *Parameters* (Winter 2003–2004): 40–53.

110. Vago Muradian and Sean Naylor, "Pentagon Considers End to Stryker," *Army Times,* August 23, 2002, 14.

111. Ibid.

112. Erin Q. Winograd, "Gingrich Tells Top DOD Officials Army's Stryker Shouldn't Be Fielded," *Inside The Army,* September 30, 2002, 1.

113. T.M. Shultz, "On the Fast Track to Iraq?" *Yuma (AZ) Sun,* September 8, 2002, 1; Mike Barber, "Bin Laden Target of Urban Warfare Training at Fort Lewis," *Seattle Post-Intelligencer,* October 10, 2002, 23.

114. Neil Baumgardner, "Army Fighting OSD Proposal To Cut Three Stryker Brigades," *Defense Daily,* October 11, 2002, 3.

115. Erin Q. Winograd, "Army Executes PR Gambit To Bolster Stryker Against Critics," *Inside The Army,* October 21, 2002, 1. Pat Towell, "Rumsfeld Defense Plan on Track as Senate Clears Spending Bill," *Congressional Quarterly Weekly,* October 19, 2002, 2756.

116. Stephen Trimble, "2008 Deployment Still Set for Objective Force, White Says," *Aerospace Daily,* October 22, 2002, 1.

117. Neil Baumgardner, "Shinseki Rails Against Stryker Critics," *Defense Daily,* October 23, 2002, 8.

118. Erin Q. Winograd, "Army, OSD Agree on Six Stryker BCTs; Last Two Will Be More Capable," *Inside The Army,* November 25, 2002, 1.

119. Ibid.

120. Michelle Ciarrocca, "Post-9/11 Economic Windfalls for Arms Manufacturers," *Foreign Policy in Focus,* September 2002, http://www.fpif.org/briefs /vol7/v7n10arms_body.html (accessed February 12, 2005).

121. Frank Tiboni, "US Army Study: Stryker Outpaces M113," *DefenseNews.com,* January 31, 2003 (accessed February 1, 2003).

Chapter 7

1. See, for example, Judith Miller, "Inquiry Faults U.N.'s Oil-for-Aid Program," *New York Times,* February 3, 2005, http://www.nytimes.com/2005/02/03/international/middleeast/03food.html.

2. George Friedman, "The Problem with the CIA," *The STRATFOR Weekly,* July 13, 2004, 1.

3. William M. Arkin, *Code Names* (Hanover, NH: Steerforth Press, 2005), 421. The "slam dunk" comment by CIA director George Tenet was widely reported; see, for example, CNN, April 19, 2004, http://edition.cnn.com/2004/ALLPOLITICS/04/18/woodward.book/ (accessed February 20, 2005).

4. Ibid. For an example of how U.S. intelligence was misled, see John Diamond, "A Desert Mirage: How U.S. Misjudged Iraq's Arsenal," *USA Today,* February 3, 2004, http://www.usa-today.com/news/world/iraq/2004-02-03-iraq-misjudge-usat_x.htm (accessed June 1, 2004).

5. In an interview with National Public Radio aired on September 15, 2004, Christopher Dickey, *Newsweek's* long-time correspondent in the Middle East, stated that even though the secular Hussein disliked and distrusted radical Islamists his government was willing to support and encourage them when it suited Iraq's purposes.

6. Suzann Chapman, "DOD Announces Shift in Tactics," AeroSpace World section, *Air Force* (October 2002): 14.

7. DA, *On Point,* Chap. 2, p. 31.

8. Timothy Rider, "Web of Integrated Command," *Army Communicator* (Fall 2003): 6–10.

9. U.S. Army CENTCOM Lessons Learned, Number 21745-32627 (02232).

10. Gerald F. Seib, "Tough Words on Iraq War Faced Scorn But Ring True," *Wall Street Journal,* July 16, 2003, A21.

11. Rowan Scarborough, "US Rushed Post-Saddam Planning," *Washington Times,* September 3, 2003, 1.

12. Chris Mackey and Greg Miller, *The Interrogators* (New York: Little, Brown and Co., 2004), 301.

13. Suzann Chapman, "CENTCOM is not moving," AeroSpace World section, *Air Force* (October 2002): 14.

14. Ibid.

15. DoD, "Backgrounder On Exercise Internal Look," Department of Defense briefing, Wednesday, December 4, 2002, courtesy of Federal News Service Inc., Washington, D.C., 2.

16. Keith Epstein, "War Game Preps US For Iraq," *Tampa Tribune,* December 4, 2002.

17. Mark Hosenball, "Terrorism Nabbing Nashiri," *Newsweek,* December 2, 2002, 4. The Houston Chronicle, "US Spy Plane Strikes al-Qaeda," November 5, 2002, A1. American officials believed that the persons accompanying al-Harethi were also al-Qaeda operatives. See James Risen, "Threats and Responses: Hunt for Suspects; C.I.A. is Reported to Kill a Leader of Qaeda in Yemen," *New York Times,* November 5, 2002, A1; see also "CIA 'Killed al-Qaida Suspects' in Yemen," *BBC News World Edition,* November 5, 2002, http://news.bbc.co.uk/2/hi/middle_east/2402479.stm (accessed September 28, 2003). Al-Harethi's remains were identified by a mark on his leg, which was found near the blast. "U.S. Kills Cole Suspect," CNN.com, November 5, 2002, http://www.cnn.com/2002/WORLD/meast/11/04/yemen.blast/ (accessed January 19, 2004).

18. For example, CNN and the cover of *Newsweek* magazine. See *Newsweek,* March 31, 2003; also CNN, "Shock and Awe Phase of Iraq War Put on Hold," CNN Washington Bureau, March 20, 2003, http://www.cnn.com/2003/US/03/20/sprj.irq.pentagon/ (accessed March 30, 2003).

19. William Bunch, "US Plan for Saddam: Shock and Awe," *Philadelphia Daily News,* February 26, 2003, 4.

20. David Wood, "Surprise at Saddam's Tactics May Be Rooted in US Myopia," Newhouse News Service, March 28, 2003, Newhouse.com (accessed May 20, 2003).

21. Ibid.

22. DA, *On Point,* Chap. 2, p. 15.

23. John Barry and Evan Thomas, "Boots, Bytes and, Bombs," *Newsweek* February 17, 2003, 12. See also Michael Duffy and Mark Thompson, "Secretary of War," *Time,* December 29, 2003, 83–96.

24. Evan Thomas and Daniel Klaidman, "The Battle Within," *Newsweek,* September 15, 2003, 17.

25. Fred Kaplan, "Rumsfeld's New Man," *Slate.msn.com,* June 10, 2003 (accessed June 17, 2003.

26. Peter J. Boyer, "The New War Machine," *The New Yorker,* June 30, 2003, 55–71.

27. Thomas E. Ricks, "Desert Caution," *Washington Post,* January 28, 2003, C01.

28. Statement by Douglas J. Feith, Under Secretary of Defense for Policy, Senate Committee on Foreign Relations, February 11, 2003. See also Jay Garner (Lieutenant General (ret.)), interview transcript, *Frontline,* October 9, 2003, Public Broadcasting System, http://www.pbs.org/wgbh/pages/frontline/shows/truth/ interviews/garner.html (accessed June 21, 2004).

29. Christian Lowe, "Secret Mission Revealed," *Army Times,* September 15, 2003, 22.

30. Heike Hasenhauer, "Preparing for War," *Soldier* (a Department of the Army publication, April 2003), 4–5.

31. David Talbot, "How Technology Failed in Iraq," *MIT Technology Review,* November 2004, 36–44.

32. Oliver Burkeman, "Shock Tactics," *The Guardian* (UK), March 25, 2003, http://www.guardian.co.uk/Iraq/Story/0,2763,921286,00.html (accessed February 7, 2004).

33. Vernon Loeb and Jonathan Weisman, "Quick Collapse of Iraqi Military Is 'Very Real Likelihood,'" *Washington Post,* March 19, 2003, A18.

34. Tommy Franks (General, USA), *American Soldier* (New York: HarperCollins, 2004), 448–49. Quoted material appears in Steven Collins (Lieutenant Colonel, UK), "Mind Games," *NATO Review, 2003,* http://www.iwar.org.uk/psyops/resources/iraq/mind-games.htm.

35. Collins, "Mind Games."

36. Faye Bowers, "Behind The Lines, An Unseen War," *Christian Science Monitor,* April 4, 2003, 4.

37. Jack Kelley and Kevin Johnson, "Commando Force Poised To Track and Kill Saddam," *USA Today,* March 19, 2003, 1.

38. Bowers, "Behind The Lines."

39. Sandra I. Erwin, "Army 'Transformation' Plans Could Be Revisited After War," *National Defense Magazine,* May 2003, 3.

40. Ibid.

41. Larry D. Welch et al., *Report of the Independent Assessment Panel for the Future Combat System* (Alexandria, VA: Institute for Defense Analyses, 2003).

42. CDI, "US Forces in the Middle East," Center for Defense Information Web site, December 12, 2002, http://www.cdi.org/terrorism/forcesinthemideast5.cfm (accessed June 7, 2004).

43. Robert Woodward, *Plan of Attack* (New York: Simon & Schuster, 2004), 351–56, 373–75.

44. CIA, "Testimony of Acting Director of Central Intelligence John E. McLaughlin before the Senate Armed Services Committee on 9-11 Commission Findings," 17 August 2004 (as prepared for delivery). Courtesy Central Intelligence Agency.

45. Woodward, *Plan of Attack,* 194–199.

46. Kelley and Johnson, "Commando Force Poised To Track and Kill Saddam," 1

47. Quoted material is from Kelly and Johnson, ibid.

48. Space Today, Web site at spacetoday.org, dated 2003 (accessed October 24, 2005).

49. Linda Burgess, "Iraq War: Special Forces Followed up on Afghanistan Success," *Stars and Stripes,* "Freedom in Iraq" special section, Tuesday, May 27, 2003.

50. Bowers, "Behind The Lines," 4.

51. Sapa-AP, "Expect a Powerful Thrust to BAGHAD—Experts," *Independent Online,* February 18, 2003, http://www.iol.co.za/index.php (accessed September 30, 2004).

52. Burkeman, "Shock Tactics."

53. James Kitfield, "The Army's Gamble," *National Journal,* March 29, 2003, 6–8.

54. Rumsfeld, Pentagon press briefing, March 30, 2003.

55. For humanitarian disaster predictions see "Excerpts From Debate on Senate Floor on Use of Force Against Iraq," *New York Times,* October 8, 2002, Section A-14; also "International Study Team Report," January 30, 2003, http://www.ippnw.de/frieden/irak/summary.htm. Immanuel Wallerstein, "Iraq War: The Coming Disaster," *Los Angeles Times,* April 14, 2002, A-24; Kathryn Westcott, "'Humanitarian Disaster' Looms in Iraq," *BBC News,* October 3, 2002, http://news.bbc.co.uk/2/hi/middle_east/2295589.stm (accessed May 3, 2003); Ed Vulliamy et al., "Aid Groups Warn of Disaster in Iraq," "Special Report: Iraq," *London Observer,* December 22, 2002, http://www.observer.co.uk/iraq/story/0,12239,864412,00.html (accessed May 3, 2003).

56. William Bunch, "US Plan for Saddam: Shock and Awe," *Philadelphia Daily News,* February 26, 2003, 4.

57. Bowers, "Behind The Lines," 4.

58. The story of the attack on Dora farm is detailed in Woodward, *Plan of Attack,* 380–399.

59. After Action Report, Operation Iraqi Freedom, Third Infantry Division (Mechanized), July 2003, 3–5. See also Emily Hsu, "3rd ID: 'Antiquated' Communications Strained Troops in Iraqi Freedom," *Inside The Army,* August 11, 2003, 1.

60. David Talbot, "How Technology Failed in Iraq," *MIT Technology Review,* November 2004, 36–44.

61. DA, *On Point,* Chap. 5, p. 8.

62. Ibid.

63. After Action Report, Operation Iraqi Freedom, Third Infantry Division (Mechanized), July 2003, 197–98.

64. Joshua Davis, "If We Run Out of Batteries, This War is Screwed," *Wired Magazine,* June 2003, http://www.wired.com/wired/archive/11.06/ (accessed May 27, 2003).

65. Ibid.

66. Ibid.

67. U.S. Army After Action Review, Fort Benning, GA, September 12–14, 2003, quoted material from S. Thorne Harper, "Lessons Learned In Battle," *Columbus Ledger-Enquirer* (GA), September 14, 2003.

68. For examples of troop ingenuity in adapting digital systems under difficult conditions, see John A. Rutt, (Lieutenant Colonel, USA), "From Tactical to Installational, the 63rd Signal Battalion in OEF," *Army Communicator* (Fall 2003): 10–14.

69. Rowan Scarborough, "US Forces Outran Water, MREs in Rush to Baghdad," *The Washington Times,* April 25, 2003, 12.

70. James Kitfield, "The Army's Gamble," *National Journal,* March 29, 2003, 6–8.

71. The Army version of the war in *On Point* includes several references to the use of the 82d and 101st to secure lines of communication; see, for example, Chap. 5, p. 3.

72. Bernard Gwertzman, "Interview with Retired Marine Corps General Bernard Trainor," Council on Foreign Relations, March 24, 2003, http://www.cfr.org/ publication.php?id=5751 (accessed October 10, 2004).

73. Talbot, "How Technology Failed in Iraq."

74. Thomas W. Collins (Lieutenant Colonel, USA), "The 173rd Airborne Brigade in Iraq," courtesy of Public Affairs Office, U.S. Army Southern European Task Force (Airborne), June 2003. A version of this material was published under the same title in *Army* magazine for June 2003, 42–46. Note: the official Army version of this operation in DA, *On Point,* Chap. 4, 74–90, does not mention the early arrival of the armor; however, the map on p. 74 seems to support Collins's account.

75. Peter Fitzgerald (Sergeant, USA), "509th Operations in Northern Iraq," *Army Communicator* (Fall 2003): 3–4.

76. Mark Choate (Captain, USA), "Knowing Is Half the Battle," *INSCOM Journal,* Almanac 2003 issue (December 2003): 8–9.

77. Davis, "If We Run Out of Batteries, This War is Screwed."

78. Choate, "Knowing is Half the Battle," 21; also DA, *On Point,* Chap. 4, 32.

79. USAF, *United States Air Force Posture Statement 2004,* Department of the Air Force, 2004, 15.

80. Arkin, *Code Names,* 380.

81. Talbot, "How Technology Failed in Iraq," 5.

82. William Branigin, "A Brief, Bitter War For Iraq's Military Officers," *Washington Post,* April 27, 2003, 25.

83. Associated Press, "Homicide Bomber Kills Four US Troops in Najaf," March 30, 2003.

84. David A. Fulghum, "Fast Forward," *New York Times,* April 28, 2003, 34.

85. Ibid.

86. Branigin, "A Brief, Bitter War For Iraq's Military Officers."

87. Fulghum, "Fast Forward."

88. John Keegan, *The Iraq War* (New York: Alfred A. Knopf, 2004).

89. Ibid.

90. The figure of 5 and one-third divisions comes from Richard A. Cody, "General Richard Cody Army Vice Chief of Staff, General Richard Cody Delivers Remarks on Army Transformation," Washington Transcript Service, September 17, 2004.

91. Gina Cavallaro, "Digital Division," *Army Times,* March 3, 2003, 28.

92. Dionne Searcey, "Thousands from 4th Division Deployed to Gulf," *Killeen Herald* (Texas), March 28, 2003, 1.

93. Rowan Scarborough, "Bush Deploys 'Iron Horse' of Army to Gulf," *Washington Times,* January 21, 2003, 1.

94. Dionne Searcey, "4th Infantry Members Yet to See Battle," *Killeen Daily Herald* (Texas), April 13, 2003, 1.

95. Ibid.

96. David Rising, "4th Infantry Sees First Combat Action since Vietnam," *Killeen Daily Herald* (Texas), April 16, 2003, 1.

97. CBS, "Special Operations Imperative to War Efforts," *Evening News with Dan Rather*, April 7, 2003.

98. DA, *On Point*, Chap. 4, 75.

99. Defense Today, "Developed by Lab, New Gun Trucks Fielded in Iraq," *Defense Today*, May 6, 2005, via email.

Chapter 8

1. Transcript of President Bush's May 1, 2003, speech from the deck of the *USS Abraham Lincoln*, http://www.abcnews.go.com/sections/world/Primetime/iraq_bushtranscript030501. html (accessed May 12, 2003).

2. Ibid.

3. Tom Bowman, "Rumsfeld Taunting But Naysayers Persist," *Baltimore Sun*, May 18, 2003, 17.

4. CNN, "The War in Iraq" Web page, http://www.cnn.com/SPECIALS/2003/iraq/war. tracker/05.01.index.html (accessed October 7, 2004).

5. Anthony H. Cordesman, "The Critical Role of Iraqi Military, Security, and Police Forces: Necessity, Problems, and Progress," Fourth Revised Draft: October 7, 2004, Office of External Relations • Center for Strategic and International Studies. Text can be found at http://www.csis.org/features/iraq_ MilitarySecrPoliceForce.pdf. Prisoner estimates from DA, *On Point: the United States Army in Operation Iraqi Freedom* (Fort Leavenworth, KS: Army Center for Lessons Learned, December 22, 2004). Chap. 2, 39.

6. DA, *On Point*, Chap. 5, p. 4.

7. John Keegan, *The Iraq War* (New York: Alfred A. Knopf, 2004), 200.

8. Tom Bowman, "US Misjudged Power Vacuum, Critics Claim," *Baltimore Sun*, April 25, 2003, A-1.

9. Sean Loughlin, "Rumsfeld on Looting in Iraq: Stuff Happens" broadcast, CNN, April 12, 2003, courtesy of CNN Washington Bureau.

10. Jay Garner (Lieutenant General (ret.)), interview transcript, *Frontline*, October 9, 2003, Public Broadcasting System, http://www.pbs.org/wgbh/pages/frontline/shows/truth/ interviews/garner.html (accessed June 21, 2004).

11. Keegan, *The Iraq War*, 206.

12. Hans Binnendijik and Stuart E. Johnson, *Transforming for Stabilization and Reconstruction Operations* (Washington, D.C.: National Defense University Press, 2004), 15–17.

13. Franks interview, "General's Assessment Of War." The Bush administration maintained stoutly that it was actually acting to enforce the UN sanctions imposed after 1991 but almost no one in the international community accepted that reasoning.

14. Steven Collins (Lieutenant Colonel, UK), "Mind Games," *NATO Review*, 2003, http://www.iwar.org.uk/psyops/resources/iraq/mind-games.htm

15. Karen DeYoung, "US Sped Bremer to Iraq," *Washington Post*, May 24, 2003, A1.

16. Ibid.

17. Donald H. Rumsfeld, Secretary of Defense, and General Richard B. Myers, chairman, Joint Chiefs of Staff, "DoD News Briefing—Secretary Rumsfeld and Gen. Myers," News Transcript, United States Department of Defense, June 30, 2003.

18. Garner, interview transcript, *Frontline*.

19. Steve Chapman, "The Spoils of Victory Are Really Spoiled," *Chicago Tribune,* May 15, 2003, 1.

20. Garner, interview transcript, *Frontline.*

21. Christopher J. Castelli, Daniel G. Dupont, and Amy Butler, "Air Force Secretary Eyed for Top Army Job," *InsideDefense.com,* May 1, 2003.

22. Thomas E. Ricks, "Air Force's Roche Picked To Head Army," *Washington Post,* May 2, 2003, 1. Also Castelli, Dupont, and Butler, "Air Force Secretary Eyed For Top Army Job."

23. Frank Tiboni, "US Army To Get Top-Down Review To Achieve Objective Force by 2010," *DefenseNews.com,* July 10, 2003.

24. Ibid.

25. Quote appears in "Picking The Right Man," *Defense News,* May 5, 2003, 28; See also Castelli, Dupont, and Butler, "Air Force Secretary Eyed For Top Army Job."

26. Robert Burns, "A Shift Takes Shape in Army," *Boston Globe,* April 27, 2003, 5.

27. "Picking The Right Man," *Defense News.*

28. Robert Burns, "Army Shake-Up Has Rumsfeld in Power Position," Associated Press, April 26, 2003.

29. Michael Elliott, "So, What Went Wrong?" *Time,* October 6, 2003, 30.

30. Ibid.

31. Gerry J. Gilmore, "Rumsfeld: No US Troop Increase Foreseen for Iraq," American Forces Press Service, August 21, 2003.

32. Dana Milbank and Bradley Graham, "Bush Revises Views on 'Combat' in Iraq," *Washington Post,* August 19, 2003, A15.

33. "A Change Of Heart," *Economist,* London, September 6–12, 2003, 32.

34. Gerry J. Gilmore, "Rumsfeld: No US Troop Increase Foreseen for Iraq," American Forces Press Service, August 31, 2003. See also "Rumsfeld: Troop Level in Iraq up to Cent-Com," CNN.com, http://www.cnn.com/2003/WORLD/meast/08/25/sprj.irq.main/ (accessed July 23, 2004).

35. Gilmore, "Rumsfeld: No US Troop Increase Foreseen for Iraq."

36. Glen Kessler and Mike Allen, "Bush to Seek $60 Billion or More for Iraq," *Washington Post,* 1, 13.

37. Rowan Scarborough, "US Rushed Post-Saddam Planning," *Washington Times,* September 3, 2003, 1.

38. Ibid.

39. Jonathan Turley, "US Soldiers Lack Best Protective Gear," *USA Today,* http://www.usa-today.com/news/opinion/editorials/2003-12-17-turley_x.htm.

40. Interview with Representative Duncan Hunter (R-CA), CNN TV, 6:00 P.M., December 12, 2003, transcript courtesy of CNN.

41. Douglas Macgregor (Colonel (ret.), USA), Testimony before the House Armed Services Committee on July 15, 2004 .

42. *Meet The Press,* NBC TV, 10:30 A.M. June 13, 2004, and *CNN Late Edition,* 12:00 P.M., June 13, 2004, transcripts courtesy of Federal News Service (U.S. Government), June 14th, 2004.

43. Donald H. Rumsfeld and Tommy R. Franks, "Summary of Lessons Learned, Prepared Testimony, Senate Armed Services Committee," July 9, 2003, unpaged.

44. Scarborough, "US Rushed Post-Saddam Planning," 27. See also Christian Lowe, "Secret Mission Revealed," *Army Times,* September 15, 2003, 22.

45. Vice Admiral Arthur K. Cebrowski (ret.) (Director, US DoD Office of Force Transformation), "Emerging Global Threats Require New Methods of Operation," *Aerospace Daily,* May 14, 2003, 1.

46. Walter Pincus and Dan Morgan, "Congress Supports Doubling Special Operations Funding," *Washington Post,* June 5, 2003, 31. See also Jeff Hollendonner, "Saxton Meets with Special Ops Troops Back from Iraq, Afghanistan," press release, Office of Congressman James Saxton (member, House Armed Services Committee), September 23, 2003.

47. Quoted material from Pincus and Morgan, "Congress Supports Doubling Special Operations Funding."

48. Ann Scott Tyson, "Boots on Ground, Now Also the Eyes Special Operations Forces Are Doing More Intelligence Gathering in Terror War," *Christian Science Monitor,* March 11, 2004, http://www.csmonitor.com/2004/0311/p01s02-usmi.html.

49. Pincus and Morgan, "Congress Supports Doubling Special Operations Funding."

50. William Matthews, "Stryker Critics in US House Lose Battle To Withhold Funds," *DefenseNews.com,* May 13, 2003 (accessed May 14, 2003).

51. General Accounting Office, "Military Transformation: Realistic Deployment Timelines Needed for Army Stryker Brigades," Report GAO-03-801, 2.

52. Kim Burger, "Testing Time for the Mobile Gun System," *Jane's Defence Weekly,* June 4, 2003, 1.

53. Nick Jonson, "First Stryker Brigade To Achieve IOC This Month, Army Says," *Aerospace Daily,* May 21, 2003, 1.

54. Erin Q. Winograd, "Rep. Saxton Continues To Question Army Plans for Stryker Vehicles," *Inside The Army,* March 24, 2003, 1.

55. Tom Squitieri, "Doubts Linger on Whether Stryker Is up to Job in Iraq," *USA Today,* September 30, 2003, 17.

56. Ibid.

57. Richard Sisk, "Army Chief Exits," *Daily News,* June 12, 2003, http://www.nydailynews.com/news/wn_report/story/91619p-83265c.html (accessed June 12, 2003).

58. John Barry, "The Army Cleans House," *Newsweek,* August 11, 2003, 8.

59. Donald Devine, "Counteroffensive…and Fallout," *Washington Times,* October 14, 2003, washingtontimes.com (accessed October 15, 2003).

60. Jeffrey Fleishman, "Iraqi Shiite Cleric Is Buried; Followers Lack a Successor," *Los Angeles Times,* September 3, 2003, 1. Also, Dexter Filkins and Richard A. Oppel, Jr., "Huge Suicide Blast Demolishes U.N. Headquarters in Baghdad," *New York Times,* August 20, 2003, 1.

61. George W. Bush, "President Addresses the Nation," Office of the Press Secretary, White House, Washington, D.C., September 7, 2003, http://www.whitehouse.gov/news/releases/2003/09/20030907-1.html. See also Elisabeth Bumiller, "Bush Seeks $87 Billion and U.N. Aid For War Effort," *New York Times,* September 8, 2003, 1. Also, "Bush to Double Iraq Spending," *Washington Post,* September 8, 2003, 1–17.

62. Vernon Loeb and Steve Vogel, "Reserve Tours Are Extended," *Washington Post,* September 9, 2003, 1.

63. Cordesman, "The Critical Role of Iraqi Military, Security, and Police Forces: Necessity, Problems, and Progress."

64. Ibid.

65. Ibid.

66. Ellen Knickmeyer, "Under US Design Iraq's New Army Looks a Good Deal Like the Old One," *Washington Post,* November 21, 2005, 1, 11.

67. The story of the Stryker's problems with add-on armor was originally provided by a military blog site; the same information can be found at http://www.globalsecurity.org/military/systems/ground/iav.htm (accessed November 04, 2004). Note: In photos of Stryker vehicles in Iraq it appears that the slat armor adds at least twice as much as the estimated 18 inches.

68. Personal correspondence of the author.

69. Joe Burlas, "First Stryker Brigade Proving Its Worth in Iraq," Army News Service, April 6, 2004. James Dunnigan, "How Stryker Survives in Iraq," *Strategy Page,* April 15, 2004, http://www.strategypage.com/dls/articles/2004415.asp (accessed July 25, 2004); Task Force Olympia, which is the Stryker Brigade's official Web page at http://www.strykernews.com/; and Jeremy Heckler (Sergeant, U.S. Army), "Stryker Brigade Encounters First Combat in Iraq," U.S. Army News Service, December 17, 2003. See also Toby Harnden, "I Got My Kills ...I Just Love My Job," *London Daily Telegraph,* November 9, 2004, 1, which describes combat by non-Stryker units, also without exotic reconnaissance assets.

70. Burlas, "First Stryker Brigade Proving Its Worth in Iraq." A photo of a Stryker on patrol in Samarra appears on p. 8 of *Soldier* magazine for September 2004. See also "Stryker Vehicle Destroyed," *KOMO-TV News,* December 13, 2003, http://www.komotv.com/stories/28783.htm (accessed September 12, 2004).

71. Quoted material from Dunnigan, "How Stryker Survives in Iraq."

72. Personal correspondence of the author received October 8, 2004.

73. Matthew Cox, "Stryker Wins Praise from Skeptical Troops," *Army Times,* November 1, 2004, S10, 12.

74. Quote credited to *Jane's Defense Weekly,* http://www.gdlscanada.com/news/releases/20-10-2004.asp (accessed December 18, 2004). The same quote appears in promotional material for the Stryker.

75. Arieth O'Sullivan, "Stryker APC Deal Tabled for Two Years," *Jerusalem Post,* July 20, 2004, 4.

76. Stephen Priestley, "All in the Family—Canada's LAV III ISC and the US Army's Stryker ICV," Canadian Forces Vehicles Web site, http://www.sfu.ca/casr/101-veherp3.htm (accessed March 12, 2005).

77. Talbot, "How Technology Failed in Iraq," 36–44, quote appears on p. 36.

78. Ibid., 44.

79. Richard Hooker (Colonel, USA), former special assistant in the office of the Secretary of the Army quoted in Macgregor, 2.

80. Talbot, "How Technology Failed in Iraq," 36–44.

81. Ibid.

82. Ibid., 44. The Army's rather different official account of the counterattack can be found in Chap. 5, pp. 56–57, in DA, *On Point.*

83. Ibid.

84. DA, *On Point,* Chap. 5, p. 16.

85. "Country Report Iraq," Main Report, *The Economist,* March 2003. See also Branigin, "A Brief, Bitter War For Iraq's Military Officers," 25–26.

86. Stephen Larrabee et al., *The Changing Global Security Environment: New Opportunities and Challenges* (Santa Monica, CA: RAND Corp., June 2003), 202–4. Quoted material is from DA, *On Point,* Chap. 2, p. 2.

87. Talbot, "How Technology Failed in Iraq," 36–44; also personal correspondence of the author.

88. "The Janus-Faced War," *Economist,* April 26–May 2, 2003, 36–37.

89. Talbot, "How Technology Failed in Iraq," 42.

90. Talbot, "How Technology Failed in Iraq," 44.

Chapter 9

1. The U.S. Department of Defense (DoD) 2004 *Military Strategy of the United States* calls for transformation "in-stride," meaning the gradual incorporation of new technologies while actively pursuing the war on terrorism; see, for example, p. iii.

2. Ibid., 2,3.

3. Tom Infield, "War Leaves Little in Reserve for Military," *Philadelphia Inquirer,* April 3, 2003, 1. See also "Force Development FAQ," USAF/DCSP, www.dp.hq.af.mil, dated December 1, 2002 and December 27, 2002 (accessed December 14, 2003).

4. Sean D. Naylor, "Overhauling the US Army," *Defense News,* September 29, 2003, 1.

5. U.S. DoD 2004 *Military Strategy of the United States,* 9.

6. U.S. Department of Defense, "How Might We Think About Stress on the Force?" Briefing by Under Secretary of Defense David Chu, dated February 11, 2004.

7. Rowan Scarborough, "Major Overhaul Eyed For Army," *The Washington Times,* February 3, 2004, 1.

8. Michael O'Hanlon, "The Need to Increase the Size of the Deployable Army," *Parameters* (Autumn 2004): 4–17. See also Michael O'Hanlon, "Rebuilding Iraq and Rebuilding the US Army," *Saban Center Middle East Memo #3,* June 4, 2004, http://www.brook.edu/views/op-ed/ohanlon/20040604.htm (accessed October 1, 2004).

9. Elaine M. Grossman, "Army Eyes 'Joint Fire Control Teams' To 'Enable' Lighter Ground Troops," *Inside The Pentagon,* January 29, 2004, 1.

10. Sean D. Naylor, "Overhauling the US Army," *Defense News,* September 29, 2003, 14.

11. Naylor, "Overhauling the US Army," 3.

12. U.S. Army, "Future Force Structure," fact sheet, U.S. Army Training and Doctrine Command, February 2004, http://www-tradoc.army.mil.

13. Naylor, "Overhauling the US Army," 14.

14. David Fastabend, "An Appraisal of the New Brigade-Based Army," *Parameters* (Autumn 1997): 73–81.

15. DoD, "How Might We Think About Stress on the Force?" briefing as presented by O'Hanlon, "The Need to Increase the Size of the Deployable Army," 4–17.

16. Department of the Army, "The Army Campaign Plan," undated, slides 11–14; see also Elaine M. Grossman, "Revised Army Approach To Readiness Meets Kudos—And Obstacles," *Inside The Pentagon,* July 15, 2004, 1.

17. See Department of the Army Field Manual 7-30, *The Infantry Brigade,* Section 1-4 "Separate Infantry Brigades" (Washington, D.C.: GPO, October 1995, updated October 2000).

18. Note: some versions of the proposed UAs include an aviation (helicopter) bn, but others do not. See, for example, http://www-tradoc.army.mil/pao/Web_specials/Leadership_of_Futures/UAUE.htm

19. See, for example, "Army Modular Force," briefing, U.S. Army Training and Doctrine Command, February 25, 2005.

20. Raytheon Company, "Excaliber Precison Guided, Extended Range Artillery Round," http://www.raytheon.com/products/excalibur/ (accessed May 7, 2004).

21. See, for example, Third Infantry Division, "1/3 ADA Inactivation-5/7 Cavalry Activation Ceremony Tomorrow," Release No. PR04-201, July 20, 2004. Courtesy of Public Affairs Office, Third Infantry Division, Fort Stewart, GA.

22. Scarborough, "Major Overhaul Eyed For Army," 1.

23. See, for example, John R. Brinkerhoff (Colonel, USA), "The Brigade-Based New Army" *Parameters* (Autumn 1997): 60–72; and Dennis Steele, "Countdown to the Next Century," *Army,* November 1996, 16–22.

24. Peter Schoomaker (General, Chief of Staff, USA), testimony before the House Armed Services Committee, July 21, 2004, as reported by the Armed Forces Press Service, U.S. Department of Defense, July 29, 2004.

25. James Jay Carafano, "Welcome Back, Soldier, to Active Duty," *Journal Sentinal* (Milwaukee, WI), July 10, 2004, http://www.jsonline.com/news/editorials/jul04/242796.asp.

26. For example, Brinkerhoff , "The Brigade-Based New Army"; and Fastabend, "An Appraisal of the New Brigade-Based Army," 60–81.

27. Fastabend, "An Appraisal of the New Brigade-Based Army," 73–81.

28. Quoted in David A. Fulghum and Robert Wall, "Internet War," *Aviation Week & Space Technology,* July 12, 2004, 24.

29. Ibid.

30. Fastabend, "An Appraisal of the New Brigade-Based Army." The writer is now (2006) a major general and chief of staff at the Army Futures Center, Fort Monroe, VA.

31. GAO Report No. GAO-04-635T, Statement of Paul L. Francis, Director, Acquisition and Sourcing Management, GAO. Testimony Before the Army's Future Combat Systems' Features, Risks, and Alternatives, Subcommittee on Tactical Air and Land Forces, Committee on Armed Services, House of Representatives, U.S. Congress, April 1, 2004, 1.

32. Ibid., 22.

33. Noah Shachtman, "GAO Says Army on Road to Ruin," *Wired,* April 5, 2004, http://www.wired.com/news/technology/0,1282,62931,00.html (accessed October 30, 2004).

34. Estimates from GAO Report No. GAO-04-635T, Statement of Paul L. Francis, 1.

35. Frank Tiboni, "Army Speeds Up Some Future Combat Technology," *FCW.com,* August 2, 2004, http://www.fcw.com/fcw/articles/2004/0802/tec-fcs-08-02 (accessed September 21, 2004).

36. Anne Plummer, "Army's New Plan for FCS Supported By Retired Gen. Welch, Adm. Cebrowsk," *Inside The Army,* August 9, 2004, 1. See also Tiboni, Army Speeds Up Some Future Combat Technology."

37. C. Todd Lopez (Staff Sergeant, USAF), "New Pamphlet explains Transformation," news release, Air Force Print News, August 5, 2003.

38. Department of the Air Force, *United States Air Force Posture Statement 2004,* 3, 31–32.

39. Chidanand Rajghatta, "Aging IAF Shoots Down USAF Top Guns," http://www.freerepublic.com/focus/f-news/1157246/posts, *The Times of India,* http://www.freerepublic.com/, http://timesofindia.indiatimes.com/cms.dll/html/uncomp/articleshow/745557.cms, June 18, 2004, 1; and Nick Childs, "War Games in India 'Show up US,'" http://www.freerepublic.com/focus/f-news/1159444/posts, news.bbc.co.uk June 24, 2004 (accessed September 7, 2004).

40. Rajghatta, "Aging IAF Shoots Down USAF Top Guns," *The Times of India,.*

41. R. Jeffery Smith, "Air Force Faulted on 50-Plane Purchase," *Washington Post,* July 24, 2004, A1, A12.

42. "Lockheed Martin Awarded $2B Air Force Contract for 22 F/A-22s," *Aerospace Daily & Defense Report,* July 2, 2004, newsletter published by *Aviation Week.*

43. Laura A. Colarusso, "Air Force of the Future," *Armed Force Journal* (September 2004): 24–29.

44. Aircraft data courtesy of U.S. Air Force Air Combat Command, Office of Public Affairs, Langley AFB, VA, April 2003, verified September 2004.

45. Colarusso, "Air Force of the Future," 25.

46. "USAF to Buy Hundreds of STOVL JSFs, CSAF Says," *Aerospace Daily & Defense Report,* September 14, 2004, 1.

47. Christopher Bolkcom, "Air Force FB-22 Bomber Concept," RS21848, Congressional Research Service, Library of Congress, May 26, 2004.

48. General Dynamics, "US Army Orders Vehicles for Fourth Stryker Brigade from GD," press release, General Dynamics Land Systems division of General Dynamics, March 10, 2004.

49. Dave Ahearn, "Senators Assail Stryker Overweight Problems," *Defense Today,* August 18, 2004, 1.

50. Ibid.

51. Ibid.

52. Ann Roosevelt, "All Stryker Variants Now in Production," *Defense Daily,* October 19, 2004, 3. The ten Stryker vehicle variants are the infantry carrier, fire support vehicle, engineer squad vehicle, command vehicle, medical evacuation vehicle, antitank guided missile vehicle, the MGS, NBCRV, Mortar Carrier, and Mobile Gun System.

53. Matthew Cox, "Standing Up New Brigade Units of Action," *Army Times,* August 2, 2004, 18. Also Associated Press, "Reorganization Plan Brings New Soldiers to US Army Bases," Associated Press News Service, July 23, 2004.

54. Sean B. Naylor, "Ranger Regiment to Get 16 Strykers," *Army Times,* 18.

55. Matthew Cox, "No Mobile Gun System for Stryker—for Now," *Army Times,* June 9, 2005, 19, http://www.armytimes.com/print.php?f=0292925904303.php (accessed June 17, 2005).

56. ISAF Public Information Office, September 24, 2004. Headquarters ISAF-Kabul (AFG) Darmstadt, Germany.

57. http://www.cnn.com/SPECIALS/2003/iraq/forces/casualties/ (accessed October 7, 2004).

58. Jim Garamone, "Deploying Unit Shows Differences Between Active, Reserve," press release, American Forces Press Service, February 14, 2004.

59. Associated Press, "Pentagon: About 200 Hurt in Iraq Last Week," October 5, 2004, http://www.ap.org.

60. In the early 1970s, military leaders had deliberately structured the armed forces to ensure that no large-scale conflict could be fought without a reserve call-up. This was done to ensure that no war could be fought in isolation by the new all-volunteer military.

61. Jane McHugh and Sean Taylor, "Guard Recruiting Mission Falls Short of Goal," *Army Times,* October 4, 2004, 23

62. Vince Crawley, "GAO Report Says Reserve Well Running Dry," *Army Times,* October 4, 2004, 24–25.

63. Ibid.

64. Associated Press, "Army Won't Shorten Combat Tours," October 27, 2004.

65. Christopher J. Toomey, "Army Digitization: Making it Ready for Prime Time," *Parameters* (Winter 2003–2004): 40–53.

66. Ibid.

67. U.S. DoD, Transcript, DoD News Briefing—Secretary Rumsfeld and General Myers, Chairman, Joint Chiefs of Staff, January 7, 2003, Federal News Service Inc., Washington, D.C.

68. Ibid.

69. Mark Mazzetti, "So, Who's In Charge Here?" *Newsweek,* December 22, 2003, online (accessed September 24, 2004).

70. U.S. DoD, News Briefing, January 7, 2003. See also U.S. DoD, "US Special Operations Forces Given Larger Role in War on Terrorism," Defense Department Report, January 7, 2003.

71. U.S. DoD, "US Special Operations Forces Given Larger Role in War on Terrorism"; Ann Scott Tyson, "Boots On Ground, Now Also the Eyes, Special Operations Forces Are Doing More Intelligence Gathering in Terror War," *Christian Science Monitor,* March 11, 2004, http://www.csmonitor.com/2004/0311/p01s02-usmi.html.

72. Ibid. The USMC has always sought to benefit from opportunities in the special ops community (including funding) but has resisted placing any significant forces under the continuing jurisdiction of USSOCOM.

73. Quote is from Tyson, "Boots On Ground, Now Also the Eyes."

74. Rowan Scarborough, "Green Berets Take On Spy Duties," *Washington Times,* February 19, 2004, http://www.washtimes.com/national/20040219-123000-1473r.htm.

75. USG, *The 9/11 Commission Report,* Final Report of the National Commission on Terrorist Attacks Upon the United States (New York: W. W. Norton and Co., 2004), 415–16.

76. Richard A. Best, Jr. and Andrew Feickert, "Special Operations Forces (SOF) and CIA Paramilitary Operations: Issues for Congress," Congressional Research Service, Report No. RS22017, January 4, 2005, 2.

77. Ibid.

78. Johnathan Weismna and Renae Merle, "Pentagon Scales Back Arms Plans," *Washington Post,* January 5, 2005, 1.

79. "US Military Prepares for '05 QDR," *Defense News,* July 12, 2004, 36.

80. Amy Klamper, "Army Seeks $12 Billion Annually for Transformation," *Congress Daily,* February 10, 2005, GovExec.Com, http://www.govexec.com/dailyfed/0205/021005cdam2.htm (accessed February 12, 2005).

81. CARE, "Afghanistan at the crossroads," June 23, 2003; "Not a Dress Rehearsal," *The Economist,* August 16, 2003, 41–43; and International Rescue Committee, "Afghanistan: A Call for Security," June 17, 2003. Cited in Charlotte Watkins, "Provincial Reconstruction Teams (PRTs)" (MSc thesis, Oxford Brookes University, UK, September 30, 2003).

82. U.S. Department of Defense, "Fact Sheet—Provincial Reconstruction Teams," September 27, 2004.

83. Personal correspondence of the author with members of the 450th Civil Affairs Battalion (ARNG); see also Chris Stump (Specialist USA), "Civil Affairs Teams Work for Afghanistan's Future," American Forces Press Service, December 12, 2004.

84. William Cole, "Hawai'i Units in Afghanistan Drive," *Honolulu Advertiser,* January 4, 2004, 1.

85. Associated Press, "Tours for 6,500 Troops Extended," October 31, 2004.

86. Gerry J. Gilmore, "Rumsfeld: Troop Reductions Not Likely until Iraqis Stronger," American Forces Press Service, October 10, 2004.

87. Stabilization is generally taken to mean creation of a secure and stable environment and the provision of basic human needs (food, water, shelter, medical care, etc.), while reconstruction suggests the establishment of stable long-term institutions (rule of law, economic activity, etc.). Stabilization creates the conditions for reconstruction. Per Defense Directive 3000.cc, "Defense Capabilities to Transition to and from Hostilities."

88. In response, the Army began to revive its moribund Foreign Area Officer program, previously a career dead end for any officer unwise enough to be involved. Now suddenly foreign cultures were important, and plans were made to train hundreds of officers in Arabic language and culture. To be effective, such training would require years, not months, but that did not dampen plans to assign one such officer to every deployed combat brigade in Afghanistan and Iraq. Even if fully trained, that number was woefully inadequate for any serious application, but something was, admittedly, better than nothing, and late was better than never.

89. U.S. DoS, "Iraqi Elections," report, published by U.S. Department of State's Bureau of International Information Programs, February 2005. The report may be found at http://usinfo.state.gov/products/ pubs/iraqelect/.

90. Jonathan Weisman, "Army Repair Posts Scramble to Keep the Troops Equipped," *Washington Post,* December 13, 2004, 1.

91. BBC, "Iraq Election Log: 4 February 2005," British Broadcasting Company Web site, http://news.bbc.co.uk/2/hi/in_depth/middle_east/2004/iraq_log/default.stm (accessed February 12, 2005).

92. Bradley Graham, "General Says Army Reserve is Becoming a Broken Force," *Washington Post,* January 6, 2005, 1.

93. Daniel Cooney (Associated Press), "Afghan Insurgency Likely To Intensify, U.S. Warns," *Philadelphia Inquirer* (Web site), April 4, 2006, http://www.philly.com/mld/inquirer/news/nation/14256069.htm; and "U.S. Military Deployments," *Army Times,* April 3, 2006.

Chapter 10

1. Quoted in Chris Hellman, "What Next for the 'Army After Next?'" *Weekly Defense Monitor,* Center for Defense Information, Washington, D.C., September 9,1999, 1.

2. Except as otherwise noted, this section is based on Leon J. LaPorte (Lieutenant General, Army) and Winn Noyes (Colonel, Army), "Operation-Centric Warfare," *Army Magazine,* August 2000, 16–20. At the time of writing, General LaPorte was the commander, III Corps, and Colonel Noyes was his chief of Digital Coordination at Fort Hood.

3. For an examination of one possible support arrangement, see Jeremy D. Smith (Captain, USA), "Proposed Unit of Action/Unit of Employment, X Doctrinal Concept of Support," *Quartermaster Professional Bulletin,* Autumn 2004, http://www.quartermaster.army.mil/oqmg/Professional_Bulletin/2004/Autumn04/Proposed_Unit_of_Action_Unit_of_Employment X Doctrinal_Concept_of_Support.htm (accessed November 10, 2004).

4. General Kevin P. Byrnes (USA), commanding general of Training and Doctrine Command (TRADOC), "Future force structure" section of "Leadership of Futures" briefing, news release, TRADOC Public Affairs, Fort Monroe, VA, undated, received September 2004. Can also be found at the TRADOC Web site, http://www-tradoc.army.mil/pao/.

5. Except as otherwise noted, this section is based on Charles J. Green, (Colonel, USA) and James D. Edwards, (Major, USA), "III Corps Expands the Knowledge Base for Employing Sensors," *Army Magazine,* 25–28. At the time of writing, Colonel Green was the assistant chief of staff, G-2 (intelligence), III Corps. Major Edwards was the chief, plans and exercises, G-2, III Corps.

6. For a discussion of future sensor development, see Scientific Advisory Board, *Sensors,* a volume in the *New World Vistas: Air and Space Power for the 21st Century* series, HQ USAF/ SAB, Washington, D.C., 1996.

7. Arthur Cebrowski (Vice Admiral (ret.), USN) (Director, U.S. DoD Office of Force Transformation), "Emerging Global Threats Require New Methods of Operation," *Aerospace Daily,* May 14, 2003, 1.

8. Alan Vick et al., *Enhancing Air Power's Contribution Against Light Infantry Targets* (Santa Monica, CA: RAND Corp., 1996). Also Richard G. Davis, *Strategic Air Power in Desert Storm* (Washington D.C.: Air Force History and Museums Program, 1995), 36.

9. Vick et al., *Enhancing Air Power's Contribution Against Light Infantry Targets,* 9–28, quote from p. 28.

10. Ibid., 54–57.

11. Iraq.ru, "War in Iraq—A Week of War," March 30, 2003, www.iraqwar.ru (accessed January 7, 2004). Note: the Iraq.ru site claims to be a group of "Russian journalists and military experts providing accurate and up-to-date news and analysis of the war against Iraq." Nearly all of their coverage is highly critical of the US-led coalition. See also Raytheon Company, "Raytheon Delivers Improved Second Generation Thermal Sights," news release, Raytheon Company Media Relations, August 19, 2003.

12. Kris Alexander (Captain, USAR), "Blogs for Spies?" *Wired Magazine,* March 2005, http://www.wired.com/wired/archive/13.03/view.html?pg=2?tw=wn_story_top5 (accessed April 1, 2005).

13. Grossman, "Revised Army Approach To Readiness Meets Kudos—And Obstacles."

14. Interview, Stryker Brigade NCOs, March 6, 2005.

15. U.S. DA, FM34-25-3, *All-Source Analysis System and the Analysis and Control Element* (Washington, D.C., Department of The Army, October 3, 1995), Chap. 2 "Analysis and Control Element."

16. US DoD, "Global Command and Control System, Tactical Information Broadcast System (TIBS)," Global Command and Control System (GCCS), Defense Information Systems Agency, July 8, 2002. See also USMC, "Global Broadcast System—(GBS)," MARCOR-SYSCOM PGD Web site, http://www.marcorsyscom.usmc.mil/sites/pmcomm/GBS.asp, dated March 9, 2005 (accessed June 15, 2005).

17. USAF, "Milstar Fact Sheet," Air Force Space Command, Public Affairs Office, Peterson AFB, CO, February 2003. See also Karl A. Klausner (Lieutenant Colonel, USAF), "Will Bandwidth be the Major Limiting Factor in Future Air Operations?" *Air Power Review* (UK), Summer 2003, 91–102.

18. Lieutenant Colonel Thomas Mahoney, STRATCOM J6S Office, "RE: Follow-up Question on Commercial SATCOM," e-mail message to Lieutenant Colonel Patrick Rayermann, February 20, 2003; Robert Hart, Regional SATCOM Support in Rayerman, 60.

19. Patrick Rayermann (Colonel, USA), "Exploiting Commercial SATCOM: A Better Way," *Parameters* (Winter 2003–2004), 54–66. At the time of writing, Colonel Rayermann was chief operations officer of the Army Space and Missile Defense Command.

20. Justin Ray, "Last Milstar Successfully Soars to Orbital Perch," *Spaceflight Now,* April 8, 2003, http://spaceflightnow.com/titan/b35/ (accessed October 18, 2004).

21. Ibid.

22. Based on work by Benjamin S. Griffin (Major General, USA) and Archie Davis (Lieutenant Colonel, USA), "Operation-Centric Warfare Setting the Conditions for Success at Brigade and Battalion," *Army Magazine,* August 2000, 27–30. At the time this was written, Major General Griffin was the commanding general, 4th Infantry Division (Mechanized) and Lieutenant Colonel Davis was the public affairs officer of the 4th Infantry Division.

23. Except as otherwise noted, the material in this section is based on an interview with Colonel Mike Mehaffey, USA.

24. Scott R. Gourley, "New Brigade Structure Begins To Emerge," *Army,* February 2000, http://www.ausa.org/transformation/article_newbrigade.html (accessed August 12, 2002). See also TRADOC, "The Hooah Guide to Army Transformation," U.S. Army Training and Doctrine Command, 2000.

25. Ibid.

26. Information on the BAT and the LOCAAS is taken from Glenn Goodman, Jr., "Tank Eradicators," *Armed Forces Journal* (August 2000): 38–41.

27. Material on the ECT program is taken from Ingo May, "Future Combat Systems Technologies" briefing, U.S. Army Research Laboratory, January 11, 2000.

Chapter 11

1. For an overview of the Army After Next as originally conceived, see U.S. Army, "Transcript of a Brief on the Army After Next, U.S. Army News Release 97a-77, July 10, 1997. Also, Dennis J. Reimer (General, U.S. Army), "The Army After Next: Knowledge, Speed and Power," *Military Review,* May–June 1999, 10–14. General Reimer was at that time Chief of Staff of the Army. A concise explanation is provided by Greg de Somer (Lieutenant Colonel, Australian Army), "The Implications of the United States Army's Army-After-Next Concepts for the Australian Army," Land Warfare Studies Centre Working Paper No. 104, June 1999.

2. Jason Sherman, "Facing a New Reality," *Armed Forces Journal* (December 2004), 20–25.

3. White House, "Making America More Secure by Transforming Our Military," Fact Sheet, Office of the Press Secretary, August 16, 2004, http://www.whitehouse.gov/news/releases/2004/08/20040816-5.html.

4. Ibid.

5. President George W. Bush, direct quote from his address of August 16, 2004, appears in White House, "Making America More Secure by Transforming Our Military."

6. White House, "Making America More Secure by Transforming Our Military."

7. DoD, Quadrennial Defense Review, U.S. Department of Defense, Washington, D.C., February 6, 2006, vi–vii.

8. Ibid., 3, 36–39.

9. Ibid., 1–2.

10. Ibid., 17–18.

11. Ibid., 23–24.

12. George Cahlink, "Magnus Calls Proposed Force Cuts 'Very, Very Bad,'" *Defense Daily,* April 7, 2006, 1.

13. Arthur Cebrowski (Vice Admiral (ret.) USN) (Director, U.S. DoD Office of Force Transformation), "Emerging Global Threats Require New Methods Of Operation," *Aerospace Daily,* May 14, 2003, 1.

14. The description of the "enemy corporation" is adapted from John M. House (Colonel, USA), "The Enemy After Next," *Military Review,* March–April 1998, 22–27.

15. This kind of enemy may be better dealt with by police and special operations units.

16. Glen R. Hawkins and James Jay Carafano, *Prelude to Army XXI,* (Washington, D.C.: Center for Military History, 1997), "Prelude to Army XXI," Section 2.

17. Douglas Macgregor (Colonel (ret), USA), "Army Transformation: Implications for the Future," statement before the House Armed Services Committee, U.S. Congress, July 15, 2004.

18. Peter A. Wilson, "Asymmetric Threats," in *Strategic Assessment 1998 Engaging Power for Peace,* ed. Hans Binnendijk (Washington: National Defense University Press, 1998), 171–72.

19. Lester W. Grau (Lieutenant Colonel, U.S. Army (ret.)), "Bashing the Laser Range Finder With a Rock," *Military Review,* May/June 1997, 42–53.

20. Wilson, "Asymmetric Threats."

21. Macgregor, "Army Transformation: Implications for the Future."

22. Ibid.

23. For information on LIDAR mapping, see http://aolab.phys.dal.ca/pages/LidarBasics and http://coastal.er.usgs.gov/lidar/.

24. NGA, *Geospatial Intelligence Basic Doctrine* (Washington, D.C.: National Geospatial Intelligence Agency, 2004), 32.

25. Ibid.

26. Ibid.

27. Albert Puzzuoli, "Advanced Planning Briefing to Industry," U.S. DoD, PEO Ground Combat Systems, October 31, 2003, unpaged, courtesy of Soldier PEO Systems, Fort Belvoir, VA.

28. USA, "LandWarNet is New Name for Army Network," news release, U.S. Army Public Affairs, Washington, D.C., February 26, 2004.

29. Puzzuoli, "Advanced Planning Briefing to Industry."

30. Christopher J. Toomey, "Army Digitization: Making it Ready for Prime Time," *Parameters* (Winter 2003–2004): 43.

31. After Action Report, Third Infantry Division (Mechanized), Operation IRAQI FREEDOM, July 2003, unpaged copy.

32. Louis Sahagun, "The 11th Cav to Iraq," *Army Times,* October 18, 2004, http://steve-gilliard.blogspot.com/2004/10/11th-cav-to-iraq.html.

33. USA, "Project Train Mod," Special Report 57, U.S. Army Research Institute, Alexandria, VA, June 2003, 5.

34. Cited in USA, "Evaluating the Design of Computer Based Training (CBT) for Digital Systems," U.S. Army Research Institute, Alexandria, VA, June 2003, 24. Quoted material appears on p. 27.

35. Toomey, "Army Digitization: Making it Ready for Prime Time," 44.

36. Jeffery R. Sanderson (Lieutenant Colonel, USA), "Transformation: A Commander's Perspective," *Armor, Journal of the US Army Armor School* (January–February 2005): 7–13. Quoted material appears on p. 12.

37. General Kevin P. Byrnes, commanding general of Training and Doctrine Command (TRADOC), "Future Force Structure" section of "Leadership of Futures" briefing, news

release, TRADOC Public Affairs, Fort Monroe, VA, undated, received September 2004, also at the TRADOC Web site, http://www-tradoc.army.mil/pao/.

38. Linda Robinson, *Masters of Chaos* (New York: Public Affairs, 2004), 194–96.

39. Information on the "Toughbook" can be found at http://www.panasonic.com/business/toughbook/federal.asp.

40. Information on the GMV provided courtesy of Kim Russell, Protocol Office, Letterkenny Army Depot.

41. Sean D. Naylor, "Overhauling the US Army," *Defense News,* September 29, 2003, 3.

42. Douglas Macgregor (Colonel (ret.), USA), *Presentation to Members of the House Armed Services Committee, 21 April 2005,* courtesy of Glenside Analysis Inc.

43. Kevin P. Byrnes (General, USA), "Gen. Kevin P. Byrnes' remarks at The Association of the United States Army's Industry Day, Hampton, Va. April 14, 2004," Transcript courtesy U.S. Army Training and Doctrine Command.

44. Tim Weiner, "An Army Program to Build a High-Tech Force Hits Cost Snags," *New York Times,* March 28, 2005, http://www.nytimes.com/2005/03/28/politics/28weapons.html?th&emc=th. See also "Army 'Future' Diverted to Iraq," http://www.defensetech.org/archives/001186.html (accessed March 31, 2005).

45. John Diamond and Steven Komarow, "Humvee Vulnerabilities Raise Doubts on Future," *USA Today,* June 21, 2005, 1.

46. Renae Merle, "McCain, Auditors Question Army Modernization Effort," *Washington Post,* March 17, 2005, 2. See also Megan Scully, "Misstatement Could Extend McCain Probe of FCS Deal," *The Hill* (newspaper, Washington, D.C.), http://www.hillnews.com/thehill/export/TheHill/Business/032305.html (accessed April 1, 2005).

47. DefenseTech, "Army Future Diverted to Iraq," quoted on the DefenseTech.org Web site, http://www.defensetech.org/archives/001186.html (accessed April, 2005).

48. For soldier comments on Stryker, see Steve Fainabu, "Soldiers Defend Faulted Strykers," *Washington Post,* April 3, 2005, A21.

49. Governmental Accountability Office, "Force Structure: Actions Needed to Improve Estimates and Oversight of Costs for Transforming Army to a Modular Force," Report No. GAO-05-92, September 2005.

50. Charles R. Babcock, "Weapons Are Far Over Budget," *Washington Post,* April 8, 2006, A9.

51. Greg Grant, "Rolling FCS into Reality," *Army Times,* October 3, 2005, 22.

52. U.S. Army, "Army Announces Unit Designations in the Modular Army," news release, September 30, 2005, Army Public Affairs, Washington, D.C. See also U.S. Army, "New Army Unit Designations in the Modular Army: Talking Points and Answers to Key Questions," undated, unattributed, received October 5, 2005.

53. Personal correspondence of the author, October 6, 2005. Steven Daskal is a retired intelligence officer and defense systems analyst who has worked threat and operational testing issues for 25 years.

54. Vago Muradian and Gopal Ratnam, "U.S. Services Brace For Cuts," *Defense News,* October 17, 2005, 1.

55. Peter J. Schoomaker (General, USA), "The Army's Top Three Priorities," Memorandum for Chairman of the Joint Chiefs of Staff, October 14, 2005.

56. Peter Schoomaker, U.S. Army Chief of Staff, Interview, *Defense News,* October 18, 2005, 1.

57. Personal correspondence of the author, October 25, 2005.

58. Major General Terry Tucker (USA, Chief of Armor), quoted in Sean Taylor, "Abrams Upgrades," *Army Times,* March 14, 2005, 8–9.

59. Babcock, "Weapons Are Far Over Budget."

60. William Matthews, "Taking a Crisis to the Polls," *Army Times,* August 7, 2006, 10.

61. Shibley Telhami, "Challenge Bigger than Iraq," *The Baltimore Sun,* March 26, 2006, 22. Dr. Telhami is a Nonresident Senior Fellow at the Saban Center for Middle East Policy, Brookings Institution, Washington, D.C. Fredrick D. Barton and Bathsheba N. Crocker, *Capturing Iraqi Voices,* Center for Strategic and International Studies, Washington, D.C., 2004.

62. David E. Hendrickson and Robert W. Tucker, *Revisions in Need of Revising: What Went Wrong in the Iraq War*, Strategic Studies Institute, U.S. Army War College, December 2005, vi.

63. CNN, "Troops Put Thorny Questions to Rumsfeld," Cable News Network Web site, http://www.cnn.com/2004/WORLD/meast/12/08/rumsfeld.troops/index.html, December 9, 2004 (accessed March 14, 2005).

64. Ibid.

65. Matthew Cox, "US Raises Troop Levels as Baghdad Violence Mounts," *Army Times,* August 7, 2006, 15.

66. Bin Laden tape transcript dated February 11, 2003, courtesy of the British Broadcasting Corporation, Press Office. Translation by the BBC.

67. Ben Venzke and Aimee Ibrahim, *al-Qaeda's Advice for Mujahideen in Iraq: Lessons Learned in Afghanistan, v 1.0,* IntelCenter, Alexandria VA (private firm) April 14, 2003, and "Al Qaeda Organization Addresses a Message to Iraqi, Islamic Peoples (Internet) www.alfjr. com in Arabic," March 5, 2003. Found in Bruce Hoffman, *Al Qaeda, Trends in Terrorism, and Future Potentialities: An Assessment* (Washington, D.C.: RAND Corporation, 2003), 7.

68. This paragraph is based on various e-mail exchanges with military analyst Steven Daskal during late 2004 and early 2005.

69. Quoted in William Matthews, "Transforming Transformation," *Armed Forces Journal* (July 2004): 12–14.

70. U.S. DoD, *Transformation Trends,* February 10, 2006, U.S. DoD Office of Force Transformation, 1, courtesy of the Office of Force Transformation, Arlington, VA.

Appendix

1. TRADOC, U.S. Army Training and Doctrine Command, http://srp.army.mil/public/lm/contact.jsp (accessed December 20, 2004). Comments added by the author.

2. Andrew Feickert, *U.S. Army's Modular Redesign: Issues for Congress* (Washington, D.C.: Congressional Research Service, January 6, 2005).

3. For the reorganized structure of the 3rd Division, see http://www.stewart.army.mil/.

4. Compiled from Feickert, *U.S. Army's Modular Redesign* and U.S. Army as reported by the *Army Times,* April 10, 2006, 7.

GLOSSARY

AAN — Army After Next

AGS — Armored Gun System

AQ — Al-Qaeda (literally "the base," terrorist network)

AWACS — airborne warning and control system (aircraft)

AWE — Advanced Warfighting Exercise (U.S. Army)

BCT — Brigade Combat Team

BUR — Bottom Up Review

C2 — Command and Control

C4ISR — Command, Control, Communications, Computers, Intelligence, Surveillance, and Reconnaissance

CENTCOM — U.S. Central Command (also USCENTCOM)

CINC — Commander-in-Chief, by doctrine refers only to the President of the United States. Informally used in reference to regional Combatant Commanders, aka "Theater CINCs," or "war fighting CINCs."

Combatant Command — The armed forces of the United States are organized into ten unified combat commands with broad, continuing missions that require the participation of significant elements of two or more services. Reserve Affairs and Worldwide Support Command, U.S. Strategic Command, U.S. Transportation Command, and U.S. Joint Forces Command are organized around functional responsibilities, while U.S. Central Command, U.S. European Command, U.S. Northern Command, U.S. Pacific Command, and U.S. Southern Command have geographic areas of responsibility. Generally speaking, commands with geographic responsibilities are known as "unified commands," or informally as "warfighting commands," which means that they are the ones that actually conduct hostilities in most instances. U.S. Special Operations Command is a special case in that it has both functional and warfighting responsibilities, but its geographic respon-sibilities are worldwide. Based on U.S. Department of Defense, Joint Pub 3-0, *Doctrine for Joint Operations* (Washington: DoD, September 10, 2001), Chapter II. Updated by the author.

DARPA — Defense Advanced Research Projects Agency (U.S. DoD)

Digitization — the process of upgrading existing equipment by adding computers

DoD — Department of Defense (U.S.)

EIS — Enhanced Imaging System (imaging system in satellites)

FBCB2 — Force XXI Battle Command Brigade and Below (communications system)

FCS — Future Combat System(s)

FM — Field Manual (U.S. Army)

GAO — formerly Government Accounting Office, now Governmental Accountability Office

GMV — Ground Mobility Vehicle (heavily modified HMMWV)

HMMWV — High-Mobility Multipurpose Wheeled Vehicle

GPS — Global Positioning System

INSCOM — Intelligence and Security Command (U.S. Army)

IBCT — Interim/Initial Brigade Combat Teams (two terms for the same organization)

JDAM — Joint Direct Attack Munition (laser guided bomb)

JSR — Joint Strategy Review

JSTARS — Joint Surveillance Target Attack Radar Systems

LAM — Land Attack Missile (usually refers to cruise missiles)

LAV — Light Armored Vehicle, also Land Attack Vehicle (two terms for the same type of vehicle)

LID — Light Infantry Division

MEF — Expeditionary Force (a division task force, USMC)

Milstar — U.S. DoD satellite-based communications system

MGS — Mobile Gun System

MRC — Major Regional Contingency

MTW — Major Theater War

NATO — North Atlantic Treaty Organization

NDP — National Defense Panel

NTC — National Training Center (U.S. Army, Fort Irwin, California)

OAF — Operation Allied Force (NATO campaign in former Yugoslavia—1999)

OEF — Operation Enduring Freedom, U.S. Coalition campaign in Afghanistan (2001–)

ONA — Office of Net Assessment

Operation Deliberate Force — NATO air operation against the Bosnian Serb Army—1995

Operation Joint Endeavor — NATO peacekeeping mission to former Yugoslavia—1995

OSD — Office of the Secretary of Defense—Civilian leadership of the Pentagon, the Defense Secretary, and his staff.

PGM — Precision Guided Munition(s) (smart bomb)

POMCUS — Prepositioned Organizational Materiel Configured to Unit Sets

QDR — Quadrennial Defense Review

RISTA — Reconnaissance, Intelligence, Surveillance and Target Acquisition (inclusive term for reconnaissance functions)

RMA — Revolution in Military Affairs

SATCOM — Communication via orbiting satellites

SBCT — Stryker Brigade Combat Teams

SEALS — U.S. Navy commandos

SecDef — Secretary of Defense (U.S.)

SF — U.S. Army Special Forces

SINCGARS — Single Channel Ground and Airborne Radio System (secure radio system)

SIPRNet — Secure Internet Protocol Router Network (U.S. Government secure version of the Internet)

SOF — Special Operations Forces

Taliban — Jihadist movement that seized control of Afghanistan 1996–2001 (literally "seekers")

TI — Tactical Internet

TOC — Tactical Operations Center

TOW — M-220 Tube-launched, optically tracked, wire-guided antitank missile. Standard heavy antitank missile of the U.S. armed forces

TRADOC — Training and Doctrine Command (U.S. Army)

UAV — Unmanned Aerial Vehicle

UBL — Usama bin Laden, leader of Al-Qaeda (alternative spelling—Osama)

UCAV — Unmanned Combat Aerial Vehicle (an armed UAV)

Selected Bibliography

3rd Infantry Division (Mechanized). *After Action Report.* Operation Iraqi Freedom, Fort Stewart, GA: Third Infantry Division, July 2003.
————. "1/3 ADA Inactivation-5/7 Cavalry Activation Ceremony Tomorrow." Release No. PR04-201. Fort Stewart, GA: Public Affairs Office, Third Infantry Division, July 20, 2004.
9/11 Commission. *The 9/11 Commission Report, Final Report of the National Commission on Terrorist Attacks Upon the United States.* New York: W.W. Norton & Company, 2004.
Ahearn, Dave. "Senators Assail Stryker Overweight Problems." *Defense Today,* August 18, 2004, 1.
Ahmad, Eqbal. "The Limits of Infinite Reach." *Al Ahram* (Cairo, Egypt), September 10–16, 1998. http://weekly.ahram.org.eg/1998/394/foc2.htm (accessed October 3, 2004).
Albright, Madeleine K. (U.S. Secretary of State 1997–2001). "Remarks on Report of the Accountability Review Boards on the Embassy Bombings in Nairobi and Dar es Salaam," as released by the Office of the Spokesman U.S. Department of State, Washington, D.C., January 8, 1999.
Al-Qaeda. "Al Qaeda Organization Addresses a Message to Iraqi, Islamic Peoples (Internet) www.alfjr.com in Arabic," March 5, 2003. Cited by Bruce Hoffman in testimony before the House Armed Services Committee, February 16, 2006, as reported in RAND Report No. CT-255, February 2006.
————. "Army's New Stryker Brigades Sit Out Iraq War, Train In California," Associated Press wire service, April 2, 2003.
————. "Army Won't Shorten Combat Tours," Associated Press wire service, October 27, 2004.
Arkin, William M. *Code Names.* Hanover, NH: Steerforth Press, 2005.
Association of the U.S. Army. "Future Combat Systems: Tough Challenge." *AUSA News,* September 2000, 25–26.
Aubin, Stephen P. "Stumbling Toward Transformation: How the Services Stack Up." *Strategic Review,* Spring 2000, 39–47.

Babcock, Charles R. "Weapons Are Far Over Budget." *Washington Post,* April 8, 2006, A9.

Barber, Mike. "Bin Laden Target of Urban Warfare Training at Fort Lewis." *Seattle Post-Intelligencer,* October 10, 2002, 23.

Barnett, Jeffery R. "Funding Two Armies." *Armed Forces Journal International,* May 2000, 14–15.

Barry, John. "The Army Cleans House." *Newsweek,* August 11, 2003, 8.

Barry, John, and Evan Thomas. "The Kosovo Cover-up." *Newsweek,* August 2, 2000, 15–16.

Barton, Fredrick D., and Bathsheba N. Crocker. *Capturing Iraqi Voices.* Washington D.C.: Center for Strategic and International Studies, 2004.

Batschelet, Allen W. (Lieutenant Colonel USA). "Effects-Based Operations for Joint Warfighters." U.S. Army Professional Writing Collection, 2003. http://www.army.mil/prof_writing/volumes/volume1/june_2003/6_03_3.html (accessed March 18, 2006).

Baumgardner, Neil. "Shinseki Rails Against Stryker Critics." *Defense Daily,* October 23, 2002, 8.

———. "Army Fighting OSD Proposal To Cut Three Stryker Brigades." *Defense Daily,* October 11, 2002, 3.

Bernstein, Lewis. "Army Experimental Formations and Their Possible Influence on the Establishment of the Force XXI Experimental Force" monograph, CAC History Branch, Research Division, Center for Army Lessons Learned, TRADOC History Conference/Workshop, October 23, 1996.

Best, Richard A., Jr., and Andrew Feickert. "Special Operations Forces (SOF) and CIA Paramilitary Operations: Issues for Congress." Congressional Research Service Report No. RS22017, January 4, 2005.

Bettencourt, Ali. "Army Tests Lightweight Armored Vehicles at Knox." U.S. Army press release, January 3, 2000.

Biddle, Stephen. "The New Way of War?" *Foreign Affairs,* May/June 2002.

———. "Afghanistan and the Future of Warfare." *Foreign Affairs,* March/April 2003, 31–46.

Bin Laden, Osama (leader, Al-Qaeda terrorist organization, c. 1989–). Statement of Osama bin Laden and spokesman, aired on Al-Jazeera TV, October 7, 2001.

———. Tape transcript dated February 11, 2003, British Broadcasting Corporation, Press Office.

———. Interview, *Nida'ul Islam,* no. 15 (http://www.islam.org.au), October–November 1996, found on Federation of American Scientists Web site, http://www.fas.org/irp/world/para/docs/LADIN.htm (accessed August 2003).

Binnendijik, Hans, and Stuart E. Johnson, *Transforming for Stabilization and Reconstruction Operations.* Washington, D.C.: National Defense University Press, 15–17.

Blackwell, James, Michael J. Mazarr, and Don M. Snider. *The Gulf War: Military Lessons Learned.* Washington: CSIS, July 1991.

Blank, Stephen. "The War That Dare Not Speak Its Name." *Journal of International Security Affairs,* Spring 2005. http://www.securityaffairs.org/issues/2005/08/blank.php (accessed March 23, 2006).

Bolkcom, Christopher. "Air Force FB-22 Bomber Concept." Congressional Research Service Report No. RS21848, Library of Congress, May 26, 2004.

Bond, William L. (Brigadier General USA). "The United States Army Battlefield Digitalization Process" briefing dated April 20, 1998.

Bowers, Faye. "Behind the Lines, an Unseen War." *Christian Science Monitor,* April 4, 2003, 4.

Boyer, Peter J. "The New War Machine." *The New Yorker,* June 30, 2003, 55–71.

Bracevich, Andrew. "New Rules: Modern War and Military Professionalism." *Parameters,* December 1990, 12–16.

Bracevich, Andrew, and Eliot A. Cohen, eds. *War Over Kosovo.* New York: Columbia University Press, 2001.

Brinkerhoff, John R. "The Brigade-Based New Army."*Parameters,* Autumn 1997, 60–72.

Budiansky, Stephen. "Playing Patriot Games." *US News and World Report,* November 22, 1993, 16.

Builder, Carl. *The Masks of War.* New York: Macmillan Publishing Co., Inc., 1989.

Bumiller, Elisabeth. "Bush Seeks $87 Billion and U.N. Aid For War Effort." *New York Times,* September 8, 2003, 1.

Bunch, William. "US Plan for Saddam: Shock and Awe." *Philadelphia Daily News,* February 26, 2003, 4.

Bunker, Robert J. Review of *Strategy and the Revolution in Military Affairs: From Theory to Policy,* by Steven Metz and James Kievit. Carlisle Barracks, PA: Strategic Studies Institute, U.S. Army War College, 1995. Appears in *Air Chronicles,* Air University, Maxwell Air Force Base, Alabama, 1996.

Burger, Kim. "Army Officials Object to Aspect of GAO's Transformation Report." *Inside the Army,* March 5, 2001, 1.

Burgess, Linda. "Iraq War: Special Forces Followed Up on Afghanistan Success." *Stars and Stripes,* "Freedom in Iraq" special section, May 27, 2003.

Burlas, Joe. "First Stryker Brigade Proving Its Worth in Iraq." Army News Service, April 6, 2004.

Burns, Robert. "A Shift Takes Shape in Army." *Boston Globe,* April 27, 2003, 5.

———. "Army Shake-Up Has Rumsfeld in Power Position." Associated Press wire service, April 26, 2003.

———. "Testing Time for the Mobile Gun System." *Jane's Defence Weekly* (UK), June 4, 2003, 1.

Bush, George W. (U.S. President 2001–2008). "A Period Of Consequences." Speech delivered at The Citadel, Charleston, South Carolina, September 23, 1999. http://citadel.edu/pao/addresses/pres_bush.html (accessed July 21, 2006).

———. Speech at Norfolk Naval Air Station, February 13, 2001. http://frwebgate6.access.gpo.gov (accessed June 23, 2003).

———. Speech from the deck of the *USS Abraham Lincoln,* May 1, 2003. http://www.abcnews.go.com/sections/world/Primetime/iraq_bushtranscript030501.html (accessed May 12, 2003).

———. "President Addresses the Nation." Office of the Press Secretary, White House, Washington D.C., September 7, 2003.

———. "Statement by the President in His Address to the Nation." Office of the Press Secretary, White House, Washington D.C., September 7, 2003.

Byrnes Kevin P. (General USA), commanding general of U.S. ArmyTraining and Doctrine Command (TRADOC). "Future Force Structure" section of "Leadership of Futures" briefing, news release, TRADOC Public Affairs, Fort Monroe, VA, undated, received September 2004.

————. "Gen. Kevin P. Byrnes' remarks at The Association of the United States Army's Industry Day, Hampton, Va. April 14, 2004," news release, Training and Doctrine Command Public Affairs, Fort Monroe, VA, 2004.

Cahlink, George. "Magnus Calls Proposed Force Cuts 'Very, Very Bad.'" *Defense Daily,* April 7, 2006, 1.

Campen, Alan D. *The First Information War.* Fairfax, VA: AFCEA International Press, 1992.

Castelli, Christopher, J. Daniel G. Dupont, and Amy Butler. "Air Force Secretary Eyed for Top Army Job." *InsideDefense.com,* May 1, 2003.

Cavallaro, Gina. "Digital Division." *Army Times,* March 3, 2003, 28.

Cebrowski, Arthur K. (Vice Admiral ret. USN, Director, U.S. DoD Office of Force Transformation). "Emerging Global Threats Require New Methods of Operation." *Aerospace Daily,* May 14, 2003, 1.

CENTCOM Lessons Learned, Number 21745-32627 (02232), U.S. Army Central Command, Tampa, FL, 2004.

Chapman, Suzann. "DOD Announces Shift in Tactics." AeroSpace World section, *Air Force,* October 2002, 14.

Cheney, Richard (U.S. Secretary of Defense 1989–1983; U.S. Vice-President 2001–2008). *Annual Report to the President and Congress.* Washington, D.C.: U.S. Government Printing Office, 1992.

————. *Annual Report to the President and Congress.* Washington, D.C.: U.S. Government Printing Office, 1993.

Choate, Mark (Captain USA). "Knowing Is Half the Battle." *INSCOM Journal,* Almanac 2003 issue, December 2003, 8–9, 21.

Clark, Wesley K. *Waging Modern War.* New York: Public Affairs, 2002, especially 424–438.

CNN. "Army Plans Changes to Streamline Combat Structure." Cable News Network, Washington Bureau Report, June 9, 1998.

————. "Shock and Awe Phase of Iraq War Put on Hold." Cable News Network, Washington Bureau, March 20, 2003. http://www.cnn.com/2003/US/03/20/sprj.irq.pentagon/ (accessed March 30, 2003).

————. "Troops Put Thorny Questions to Rumsfeld." Cable New Network Web site, December 9, 2004, http://www.cnn.com/2004/WORLD/meast/12/08/rumsfeld.troops/ index.html (accessed March 14, 2005).

Cody, Richard A. "Army Vice Chief of Staff General Richard Cody Delivers Remarks on Army Transformation." Washington Transcript Service, September 17, 2004.

Cohen, Eliot A. "American Views of the Revolution in Military Affairs." In *Advanced Technology and Future Warfare.* Mideast Security and Policy Studies No. 28. Ramat Gan, Israel: Begin-Sadat Center For Strategic Studies, 1998.

Cohen, William S. (U.S. Secretary of Defense, 1997–2001). *Report of the Quadrennial Defense Review.* Washington, D.C.: Office of the Secretary of Defense, 1997.

————. *Annual Report To the President and Congress, 1998.* Washington, D.C.: Office of the Secretary of Defense, April 1998.

Colarusso, Laura A. "Air Force of the Future." *Armed Forces Journal,* September 2004, 24–29.

Cordesman Anthony H. "The Critical Role of Iraqi Military, Security, and Police Forces: Necessity, Problems, and Progress." Office of External Relations, Center for Strategic and International Studies, Fourth Revised Draft, October 7, 2004.

Correll, John T. "On Course for Global Engagement." *Air Force,* published by the U.S. Air Force Association, January 1999, 4–8.

―――. "They Call it Transformation." *Air Force,* February 1998, 5.

Cox, Matthew. "Off Track? Plan for Medium-Weight Force Has Skeptics Among Tankers." *Army Times,* November 8, 1999, 7.

―――. "Stryker Wins Praise from Skeptical Troops." *Army Times,* November 1, 2004, S10, 12.

―――. "Standing Up New Brigade Units of Action." *Army Times,* August 2, 2004, 18.

―――. "No Mobile Gun System for Stryker—for Now" *Army Times,* June 9, 2005, 19.

Crock, Stan. "An Arms Industry Too Big for the Task at Hand." *Washington Post,* August 31, 2003, B1–B2.

Croom, Charles E. (Brigadier General USAF). "A United States European Command J6 Communications Perspective of the Kosovo Crisis." n.d. HQ USEUCOM ECJ6-O, Stuttgart, Germany, 40.

CRS. "Al Qaeda Profile and Threat Assessment." Congressional Research Service Report No. RS22049, Library of Congress, Washington, D.C., February 10, 2005.

CSA Planning Directive No. 1. "Medium Weight Force, Initiative Brigade Combat Teams." Office of the Chief of Staff, Department of the Army, Washington D.C., undated, received January 2000.

CSI. *Sixty Years of Reorganizing for Combat: A Historical Trend Analysis.* Fort Leavenworth, KS: Combat Studies Institute, U.S. Army Command and General Staff College, January 2000.

DA Field Manual (FM) 100-5. *Operations.* Editions of 1976, 1982, 1986, and 1993. Washington, D.C.: Department of the Army.

―――. "Force Modernization, Army 86/90." *Commander's Call.* Washington, D.C.: Department of the Army, 1982.

―――. *Army Digitization Master Plan.* Washington, D.C.: Department of the Army, 1995.

―――. Field Manual 7-30. *The Infantry Brigade.* Washington, D.C.: Department of the Army, October 1995, updated October 2000.

―――. Field Manual 34-25-3. *All-Source Analysis System and the Analysis and Control Element.* Washington, D.C.: Department of the Army, October 1995.

―――. *Army Digitization Master Plan 1996.* Washington, D.C.: Army Digitization Office, Department of the Army, 1996.

―――. "Army Public Affairs Guidance on Media Contacts Regarding QDR." Washington, D.C.: Department of the Army. As published in *Inside the Pentagon,* June 5, 1997.

―――. "Transcript of A Brief on The Army After Next." U.S. Army News Release 97a-77, July 10, 1997.

―――. *United States Army Posture Statement FY 1999.* Washington, D.C.: Department of the Army, February 1998.

―――. *United States Army Posture Statement FY 2000.* Washington, D.C.: Department of the Army, February 1999.

―――. "The Army Campaign Plan" briefing. 1st ed. Washington, D.C.: Department of the Army, n.d., probably 1999, since revised.

―――. "Lewis Readies for Brigade Training." Fort Lewis, WA: Public Affairs Office, I Corps and Fort Lewis, December 1999.

―――. *United States Army Posture Statement FY2001.* Washington, D.C.: Department of the Army, February 2000.

————. "Army Officially Begins Transformation to Initial Brigade Combat Teams." Press Release No. 00 023. Washington, D.C.: Department of the Army, April 13, 2000.

————. *US Army White Paper: Concepts for the Objective Force.* Arlington, VA: Objective Task Force, Department of the Army, 2001.

————. *Field Manual 3-0 Operations.* Washington, D.C.: Department of the Army, June 14, 2001.

————. "Army Announces Name for Interim Armored Vehicle." Press Release No. R-02-009. Washington, D.C.: Department of the Army, February 27, 2002.

————. "Army Modernization and Digitization Overview." Army Digitization Office at Legacy Force. https://ibct.army.mil/library/LegacyForce.xml (accessed July 21, 2006).

————. "Evaluating the Design of Computer Based Training (CBT) for Digital Systems." Alexandria, VA: U.S. Army Research Institute, Department of the Army, June 2003.

————. "Project Train Mod." U.S. Army Research Institute Special Report 57. Alexandria, VA: Department of the Army, June 2003.

————. *After Action Review, Operation Iraqi Freedom.* Fort Benning, GA: The Infantry Center, September 2003.

————. *On Point: The United States Army in Operation Iraqi Freedom.* Fort Leavenworth, KS: Army Center for Lessons Learned, December 22, 2004.

————. "Army Announces Unit Designations in the Modular Army." News Release. Washington, D.C.: Army Public Affairs, September 30, 2005.

————. "New Army Unit Designations in the Modular Army: Talking Points and Answers to Key Questions." Washington, D.C.: Department of the Army, n.d., received October 5, 2005.

Davis, Paul K. "Protecting the Great Transition." In *New Challenges for Defense Planning: Rethinking How Much is Enough.* Santa Monica, CA: RAND Corporation, 1994.

————. *Effects Based Operations.* Santa Monica, CA: RAND Corporation, 2001.

Davis, Richard G. *Strategic Air Power in Desert Storm.* Washington D.C.: Air Force History and Museums Program, Department of the Air Force, 1995.

Defense Dialog. "The Buildup of US Military Force around Afghanistan Continues." Federal News Service, Summary of Broadcasts of Monday, October 1, 2001.

Defense News. "US Military Prepares for '05 QDR." *Defense News,* July 12, 2004, 36.

DefenseTech. "Army Future Diverted to Iraq." DefenseTech.org Web site, http://www.defensetech.org/archives/001186.html (accessed April 2005).

Defense Week. "Afghanistan Validates Army Way, Secretary Says." Interview with Army Secretary Thomas E. White. *Defense Week,* December 17, 2001, 2.

Deptula, David A. (Brigadier General USAF). "Effects Based Operations: Change in the Nature of Warfare." Arlington, VA: Aerospace Education Foundation, 2001.

de Seversky, Alexander P. (Major, Russian Air Corps, WWI; later aeronautical designer and theorist) *Victory Through Air Power.* New York: Simon and Schuster, 1942.

de Somer, Greg (Lieutenant Colonel, Australian Army). "The Implications of the United States Army's Army-After-Next Concepts for the Australian Army." Land Warfare Studies Centre Working Paper No. 104, June 1999.

DeYoung, Karen. "US Sped Bremer to Iraq." *Washington Post,* May 24, 2003, A1.

DoD. *Conduct of the Persian Gulf War, Final Report to Congress.* Washington, D.C.: Department of Defense, 1992.

————. *SD-2 - Buying Commercial & Nondevelopmental Items: A Handbook.* Washington, D.C.: Defense Standardization Program, Department of Defense, April 1, 1996.

———. *Joint Vision 2010*. Washington, D.C.: Joint Chiefs of Staff, U.S. Department of Defense, July 1996.

———. *Report of the Quadrennial Review*. Washington, D.C.: U.S. Department of Defense, May 1997.

———. *Report of the Defense Science Board Task Force on DoD Warfighting Transformation*. Washington, D.C.: Office of the Undersecretary of Defense for Acquisition and Technology, Department of Defense, August 1999.

———. "Joint Statement on the Kosovo After Action Report." Presented by Secretary of Defense William S. Cohen and General Henry H. Shelton, Chairman of the Joint Chiefs of Staff, before the Senate Armed Services Committee, October 14, 1999.

———. "DARPA and Army Select Contractors for Future Combat Systems Programs." Press Release No. 236-00. Washington, D.C.: Office of the Assistant Secretary of Defense (Public Affairs), May 9, 2000.

———. "Rapid Decisive Operations Briefing." Washington, D.C.: Department of Defense, October 20, 2000.

———. *Quadrennial Defense Review 2001*. Washington, D.C.: Office of the Secretary of Defense, September 30, 2001.

———. "Global Command and Control System, Tactical Information Broadcast System (TIBS)." Alexandria, VA: Global Command and Control System (GCCS), Defense Information Systems Agency, U.S. Department of Defense, July 8, 2002.

———. "Termination Papers for Crusader Signed." News Release No. 408-02. Washington, D.C.: Department of Defense, August 6, 2002.

———. "Backgrounder on Exercise Internal Look." Department of Defense briefing. Washington, D.C.: Federal News Service Inc., December 4, 2002.

———. *Military Strategy of the United States*. Washington, D.C.: U.S. Department of Defense, 2004.

———. "How Might We Think About Stress on the Force?" Briefing by Under Secretary of Defense David Chu, Washington, D.C.: U.S. Department of Defense, February 11, 2004.

———. "Fact Sheet—Provincial Reconstruction Teams." Washington, D.C.: Department of Defense, September 27, 2004.

———. "Talking Points—October 26, 2004—Bin Laden and Tora Bora." Washington, D.C.: Office of Public Affairs, Department of Defense, 2004.

———. *Transformation Trends*. Washington, D.C., Arlington. VA: Office of Force Transformation, Department of Defense, February 10, 2006.

Donnelly, John M. "Rumsfeld Makes War." *Chicago Tribune,* October 22, 2001, 1.

Donnelly, John M. "Panel Probes Military's Fight for Radio Waves." *Defense Week,* April 22, 2002, 3.

Dorobek, Christopher J. "Pentagon OKs New Info Grid." Federal Computer Week, September 3, 2001.

Douhet, Giulio (General, Italian Air Corps, WWI). *The Command of the Air.* Translated by Dino Ferrari. Italian publication, 1921; new imprint, Washington, D.C.: Office of Air Force History, 1983.

Drew, Dennis (Colonel (Ret.) USAF). "Desert Storm as a Symbol." *Air Power Journal* (Fall 1992): 6, 13.

Dudney, Robert S. "McPeak on the War." *Air Force*, May 1991, http://www.afa.org/magazine/perspectives/desert_storm/0591watch_print.html (accessed June 6, 2003).

Eberhart, Ralph E. (Lieutenant General USAF). "Airpower: An Airman's Perspective." Briefing paper. Washington, D.C.: Air Force Historical Support Office, Bolling AFB, April 1996.

Epstein, Robert M., ed. *Napoleon's Last Victory: 1809 and the Emergence of Modern War.* Lawrence, KS: University of Kansas Press, 1994.

Erwin, Sandra I. "Army 'Transformation' Plans Could Be Revisited After War." *National Defense Magazine,* May 2003, 3.

Estes, Richard H. (Lieutenant Colonel USAF). "Giulio Douhet: More on Target than He Knew." *Air Chronicles* Web site, http://www.airpower.maxwell.af.mil/airchronicles (accessed April 13, 2000).

FAS. "Operation Allied Force, Operation Noble Anvil." Federation of American Scientists, http://www.fas.org/man/dod-101/ops/allied_force.htm (accessed June 15, 2002).

Fastabend, David. "An Appraisal of the Brigade-Based New Army." *Parameters* (Autumn 1997): 60–81.

———. "EBO and the Classical Elements of Operational Design." Briefing. Arlington, VA: U.S. Army Futures Center, January 31, 2006.

FBI. "Fact Sheet: The Charges Against International Terrorist Usama Bin Laden." Washington, D.C.: Federal Bureau of Investigation, Department of Justice, 1998.

———. "Bombings of the Embassies of the United States of America at Nairobi, Kenya, and Dar Es Salaam, Tanzania, August 7, 1998." Washington, D.C.: Federal Bureau of Investigation, Department of Justice, November 18, 1998. (Declassified executive summary; the full report remains classified.)

FBIS. "Afghan Government Introduces Administrative, Financial Reforms" (IAP20030522000028). Mashhad Voice of The Islamic Republic of Iran External Service (In Dari), 0330 GMT, May 22, 2003. Translated by Foreign Broadcast Information Service, Washington, D.C.

Filkins, Dexter, and Richard A. Oppel, Jr. "Huge Suicide Blast Demolishes U.N. Headquarters In Baghdad." *New York Times,* August 20, 2003, 1.

Fitzgerald, Peter (Sergeant USA). "509th Operations in Northern Iraq." *Army Communicator* (Fall 2003): 3–4.

Flournoy, Michele, Project Director. *Report of the National Defense University Quadrennial Defense Review 2001 Working Group.* Fort McNair, Washington, D.C.: National Defense University, Institute for National Strategic Studies, November 2000.

Fogleman, Ronald R. (General USAF, and Chief of Staff, U.S. Air Force 1994–1997). Remarks at the Orlando Air Force Association Symposium, Orlando, FL, February 15, 1996. Courtesy of the Aerospace Education Foundation, Arlington, VA.

———. "Information Technology's Role in 21st Century Air Power." *Aviation Week & Space Technology* (February 17, 1997): 74.

———. Statement before the House National Security Committee, U.S. Congress, May 22, 1997.

Forney, Matthew. "Inside the Tora Bora Caves." *Time* (on-line edition), December 11, 2001, http://www.time.com (accessed November 21, 2003).

Franks, Fred, and Tom Clancy (Franks was General USA, commander VII Corps in the Gulf War). *Into the Storm: A Study in Command.* Berkley: Berkley Publishing Group, 1998, 91.

Franks, Tommy (General USA, and Commander, U.S. Central Command 2000–2003). *American Soldier.* New York: HarperCollins, 2004.

Fulghum, David A. "QDR Became 'Pabulum' As Decisions Slid." *Aviation Week & Space Technology* (October 8, 2001): 21–22.

————. "Fast Forward." *New York Times,* April 28, 2003, 34.

GAO. "Tactical Aircraft: Restructuring of the Air Force F-22 Fighter Program." Letter Report, June 4, 1997, GAO/NSIAD-97-156. Washington, D.C.: General Accounting Office, 1997. Note: In July 2004, GAO was renamed the Government Accountability Office under the GAO Human Capital Reform Act (Public Law 108-271, July 7, 2004).

————. "Operation Desert Storm: Evaluation of the Air Campaign." General Accounting Office, Report GAO/NSIAD-97-134. June 1997.

————. "Military Transformation: Realistic Deployment Timelines Needed for Army Stryker Brigades." Governmental Accountability Office Report GAO-03-801, June 2003.

————. "Statement of Paul L. Francis, Director, Acquisition and Sourcing Management, GAO." Testimony on "The Army's Future Combat Systems' Features, Risks, and Alternatives." Governmental Accountability Office Report GAO-04-635T, before the Subcommittee on Tactical Air and Land Forces, Committee on Armed Services, House of Representatives, U.S. Congress, April 1, 2004.

————. "Force Structure: Actions Needed to Improve Estimates and Oversight of Costs for Transforming Army to a Modular Force." Governmental Accountability Office Report GAO-05-92, September 2005.

Gaddis, John Lewis. *Surprise, Security and the American Experience.* Cambridge, MA: Harvard University Press, 2004.

Garner, Jay, (Lieutenant General (Ret.) USA). Interview transcript. *Frontline,* October 9, 2003, Public Broadcasting System, http://www.pbs.org/wgbh/pages/frontline/shows/truth/interviews/garner.html (accessed June 21, 2004).

Gellman, Barton, and Thomas E. Ricks. "US Concludes Bin Laden Escaped at Tora Bora Fight." *Washington Post,* April 17, 2002, 1.

General Dynamics. "US Army Orders Vehicles for Fourth Stryker Brigade from GD." Press Release, General Dynamics Land Systems division of General Dynamics, Falls Church, VA, March 10, 2004.

Gilmore, Gerry J. "Rumsfeld: No US Troop Increase Foreseen for Iraq." American Forces Press Service, August 21, 2003.

————. "Rumsfeld: Troop Reductions Not Likely Until Iraqis Stronger." American Forces Press Service, October 10, 2004.

Glantz, David M. *The Non-linear Nature of Future War: A Soviet/Commonwealth View.* Fort Leavenworth, KS: Foreign Military Studies Office, 1992.

Global Security, "Afghanistan—Militia Facilities," http://www.globalsecurity.org/military/world/afghanistan/militia-fac.htm (accessed October 8, 2003).

————. "Cruise Missile Strike—26 June 1993, Operation Southern Watch," http://www.globalsecurity.org/military/ops/strike_930626.htm (accessed October 2, 2004).

Gold, Phillip. "Defense Gets Back To Basics." *Washington Times,* November 19, 2001, 17.

Goure, Daniel. "Strategic Reality Requires New Force Structure." *Defense News,* November 12–18, 2001, 21.

Gourley, Scott R. "New Brigade Structure Begins To Emerge." *Army,* February 2000, http://www.ausa.org/transformation/article_newbrigade.html (accessed August 12, 2002).

————. "Stryker's Mobile Gun System." *Army Magazine* (U.S. Department of the Army), May 2003, 35.

Graham, Bradley. "Pentagon's Plan for Future Draws Heavily from Cold War Past." *Washington Post,* May 11, 1997, 19.

Grange, David L., and Huba Wass De Czege et al. *Air Mechanization.* Nashville: Turner Publishing, 2000.

Grant, Greg. "Rolling FCS into Reality." *Army Times,* October 3, 2005, 22.

Grau, Lester W., Lieutenant Colonel U.S. Army (Ret.). Interview via telephone, October 11, 2004.

———. "Continuity and Change: A Soviet General Staff View of Future Theater War." *Military Review,* December 1991, 11-24.

Griffin, Benjamin S. (Major General USA), and Archie Davis (Lieutenant Colonel USA). "Operation-Centric Warfare Setting the Conditions for Success at Brigade and Battalion." *Army Magazine,* August 2000, 27–30.

Grossman, Elaine M. "Airpower Gains in the Doctrine Wars." *Air Force,* March 2000, 3.

———. "The Halt Phase Hits a Bump" *Air Force* (published by U.S. Air Force Association), April 2001, 17.

———. "Key Review Offers Scant Guidance." *Inside The Pentagon,* October 4, 2001, 1.

Gwertzman, Bernard. "Interview with Retired Marine Corps General Bernard Trainor." Council on Foreign Relations, Washington, D.C., March 24, 2003, http://www.cfr.org/publication.php?id=5751 (accessed October 10, 2004).

Hallion, Richard P. "Precision Guided Munitions and the New Era of Warfare." APSC Paper No. 53. Air Power Studies Center, Australia, 1995.

Handy, John W. (Major General USAF). Air Force Policy Directive 38-1. Washington, D.C.: Department of the Air Force, June 1, 1996.

Hartzog, William W. (General USA). "The Army XXI Heavy Division." Briefing. Fort Monroe, VA: Headquarters, U.S. Army Training and Doctrine Command, 1998.

Hasenhauer, Heike. "Preparing for War." *Soldier* (a Department of the Army publication), April 2003, 4–5.

Hawkins, Glen R., and James Jay Carafano. *Prelude to Army XXI.* Washington, D.C.: United States Army Center for Military History, 1997, 24.

Hebert, Adam J. "Air Force Lacks Basing Options for Airstrikes on Afghanistan." *Inside The Air Force,* October 12, 2001, 1.

Heckler, Jeremy (Sergeant U.S. Army). "Stryker Brigade Encounters First Combat In Iraq." Press Release, U.S. Army New Service, December 17, 2003.

Hellman, Chris. "What Next for the 'Army After Next'?" *Weekly Defense Monitor,* Center for Defense Information, Washington, D.C., September 9, 1999, 1.

Hendrickson, David E., and Robert W. Tucker. *Revisions in Need of Revising: What Went Wrong in the Iraq War.* Strategic Studies Institute, U.S. Army War College, December 2005, vi.

Hoffman, F.G. *Decisive Force: The New American Way of War.* Westport, CT: Praeger, 1996.

Hollendonner, Jeff. "Saxton Meets with Special Ops Troops Back from Iraq, Afghanistan." Press Release, Office of Congressman James Saxton (member, House Armed Services Committee), Washington, D.C., September 23, 2003.

Hosmer, Stephen T. *Why Milosevic Decided to Settle When He Did.* Santa Monica, CA: RAND Corp., 2001.

Hosseini, Khaled. *The Kite Runner.* New York: Riverhead Books, 2003.

House, John M. (Colonel USA). "The Enemy After Next." *Military Review,* March–April 1998, 22–27.

Hsu, Emily. "3rd ID: 'Antiquated' Communications Strained Troops in Iraqi Freedom." *Inside The Army,* August 11, 2003, 1.

IISS-US. "Air Power Over Kosovo: A Historic Victory." *Strategic Comments*. Washington, D.C.: International Institute of Strategic Studies, September 28, 1999.

Infield, Tom. "War Leaves Little in Reserve for Military." *Philadelphia Inquirer,* April 3, 2003, 1.

Inside the Air Force. "Closely Held USAF White Paper Warned Lack of Vision Could Cost Service." *Inside the Air Force* (newsletter), May 17, 1991, 13–14.

ITP. "Breakdown in Army Air Force Communications in Afghanistan." *Inside the Pentagon,* February 27, 2003, 1.

Jane's "Blowback." *Jane's Intelligence Review,* July 26, 2001, 12–23.

JCS. *Joint Vision 2010*. Washington, D.C.: Office of the Chairman of the Joint Chiefs of Staff, U.S. Department of Defense, July 1996.

JCS. *Joint Vision 2020*. Washington, D.C.: Office of the Chairman of the Joint Chiefs of Staff, U.S. Department of Defense, 2000.

JFCOM. *Rapid Decisive Operations*. Norfolk, VA: U.S. Joint Force Command, October 22, 1999.

———. "Rapid Decisive Operations." Briefing. Norfolk, VA: U.S. Joint Forces Command, June 1, 2001.

———. *A Concept for Rapid Decisive Operations*. Norfolk, VA: U.S. Joint Forces Command (J9 Joint Futures Lab), first circulated in 1999, formally issued in 2002.

———. *Rapid Decisive Operations (RDO) White Paper*. Coordinating Draft (Version 2.0). Norfolk, VA: United States Joint Forces Command, August 9, 2001.

Jonson, Nick. "First Stryker Brigade To Achieve IOC This Month, Army Says." *Aerospace Daily,* May 21, 2003, 1.

Kagan, Fredrick W. "War and Aftermath." *Policy Review Online,* August/September 2003, http://www.policyreview.org/aug03/kagan.html (accessed September 12, 2003).

Keaney, Thomas A., and Eliot A. Cohen. "Was Desert Storm a Revolution in Warfare?" In *Gulf War Air Power Survey Summary Report*. Washington: U.S. Government Printing Office, 1993.

Keegan, John. *The Iraq War*. New York: Alfred A. Knopf, 2004.

Kelley, Jack, and Kevin Johnson. "Commando Force Poised To Track and Kill Saddam." *USA Today,* March 19, 2003, 1.

Kern, Paul J. (Lieutenant General USA). DoD News Briefing, November 17, 2000. Transcript prepared by the Federal News Service, Inc., Washington, D.C. Federal News Service is a private company.

Kessler, Glen, and Mike Allen. "Bush to Seek $60 Billion or More for Iraq." *Washington Post,* September 4, 2003, 1, 13.

Kinsley, Michael. "Bipartisan Etiquette." *Washington Post,* October 26, 2001, 35.

Kitfield, James. "The Army's Gamble." *National Journal,* March 29, 2003, 6–8.

Klamper, Amy. "Army Seeks $12 Billion Annually for Transformation." *Congress Daily,* February 10, 2005, found at GovExec.Com, http://www.govexec.com/dailyfed/0205/021005cdam2.htm (accessed February 12, 2005).

Klausner, Karl A. (Lieutenant Colonel USAF). "Will Bandwidth be the Major Limiting Factor in Future Air Operations?" *Air Power Review* (UK), Summer 2003, 91–102.

Knickmeyer, Ellen. "Under US Design Iraq's New Army Looks a Good Deal Like the Old One." *Washington Post,* November 21, 2005, 1, 11.

Knight, Charles. "US Military Policy—Expanding to Fill the post-Soviet Vacuum." The Project on Defense Alternatives, Cambridge, MA, June 2000, at http://www.comw.org/pda/0006vacuum.html (accessed August 25, 2000).

Knox, MacGregor, and Williamson Murray, eds. *The Dynamics of Military Revolution 1300–2050.* Cambridge, UK: Cambridge University Press, 2001.

Lake, Anthony. "From Containment to Enlargement." Remarks of Anthony Lake, Assistant to the President for National Security Affairs, Johns Hopkins University School of Advanced International Studies, Washington, D.C., September 21, 1993

Lambeth, Benjamin S. *A Strategy of Enlargement and the Developing World.* Washington, D.C.: U.S. Department of State, October 25, 1993.

———. "Control of The Air: The Future of Air Dominance and Offensive Strike." Conference paper. Santa Monica, CA: RAND Corporation, November 1999.

LaPorte, Leon J. (Lieutenant General USA), and Winn Noyes (Colonel USA). "Operation-Centric Warfare." *Army Magazine,* August 2000, 16–20.

Larrabee, Stephen, et al. *The Changing Global Security Environment: New Opportunities and Challenges.*Santa Monica, CA: RAND Corporation, June 2003.

Lemann, Nicholas. "Dreaming about War." *The New Yorker,* July 16, 2001, at http://www.comw.org/qdr/lemannNYM.html (accessed March 10, 2006).

Liaropoulos, Andrew N. "Revolutions in Warfare: Theoretical Paradigms and Historical Evidence—The Napoleonic and First World War Revolutions in Military Affairs." *Journal of Military History,* no. 2 (2006): 363–384.

Lind, William S., et al. "The Changing Face of War: Unto the Fourth Generation." *Military Review,* October 1989, 2–11.

———. "Fourth Generation Warfare's First Blow." *Marine Corps Gazette,* November 2001, 11–15.

Link, Charles D. (Major General USAF). Assistant Deputy Chief of Staff for Plans and Operations, Headquarters U.S. Air Force. Remarks delivered at the fall meeting of the National Capitol Flight, Bolling Air Force Base, Washington D.C., October 10, 1995.

Loeb, Vernon. "Bursts of Brilliance." *Washington Post,* December 15, 2002, W06.

Loeb, Vernon, and Steve Vogel. "Reserve Tours Are Extended." *Washington Post,* September 9, 2003, 1.

Loeb, Vernon, and Jonathan Weisman. "Quick Collapse of Iraqi Military Is 'Very Real Likelihood.'" *Washington Post,* March 19, 2003, A18.

Lopez, C. Todd (Staff Sergeant USAF). "New Pamphlet Explains Transformation." News Release, Air Force Print News, August 5, 2003.

Loughlin, Sean. "Rumsfeld on Looting in Iraq: Stuff Happens" broadcast. CNN, Cable News Network, Washington Bureau, April 12, 2003.

Lovelace, Douglas C., Jr. *The Evolution In Military Affairs: Shaping The Future US Armed Forces.* Carlisle, PA: Strategic Studies Institute, U.S. Army War College, June 16, 1997.

Lowe, Christian. "Secret Mission Revealed." *Army Times,* September 15, 2003, 22.

MacGregor, Douglas (Colonel USA). "The MacGregor Briefings." The Project on Defense Alternatives. Cambridge, MA: The Commonwealth Institute, 2000.

———. "Army Transformation: Implications for the Future." Testimony before the House Armed Services Committee on July 15, 2004. Ashburn, VA: Glenside Analysis Inc.

———. *Presentation to Members of the House Armed Services Committee, 21 April 2005.* Ashburn, VA: Glenside Analysis Inc.

Machamer, Rick (Lieutenant Colonel U.S. Army). "Force XXI: Welcome to the 21st Century." *Soldiers.* Washington, D.C.: Department of the Army, April 1995, 16–18.

Mackey, Chris, and Greg Miller. *The Interrogators.* New York: Little, Brown and Co., 2004.

Marshall, Andrew W., with Zalmay Khalilzad and John P. White. *Strategic Appraisal: The Changing Role of Information in Warfare.* Santa Monica, CA: RAND Corporation, 1999.

Mason, Tony (Air Vice-Marshal, Royal Air Force, UK). *Airpower: A Centennial Appraisal.* Indianapolis, IN: Macmillan Publishing Co., 1994.

Matthews, William. "Stryker Critics in US House Lose Battle to Withhold Funds." DefenseNews.com, May 13, 2003 (accessed May 14, 2003).

———. "Transforming Transformation." *Armed Forces Journal,* July 2004, 12–14.

May, Ernest R. *American Cold War Strategy; Interpreting NSC-68.* New York: Bedford Books of St. Martin's Press, 1993.

May, Ingo. "Future Combat Systems Technologies." Briefing. U.S. Army Research Laboratory, Department of the Army, Adelphi, MD, January 2000.

McGirk, Tim, and Michael Ware, "Losing Control." *Time,* November 18, 2002, 56–59.

McElroy, Robert H., with Patricia Slayden Hollis, ed. "Fire Support for Operation Anaconda." *Field Artillery,* Fort Sill, OK, September–October 2002, 5–7.

McLaughlin, John E. "Testimony of Acting Director of Central Intelligence John E. McLaughlin before the Senate Armed Services Committee on 9-11 Commission Findings," August 17, 2004 (as prepared for delivery). Washington, D.C.: Central Intelligence Agency.

Michael, Steve (Major USAF), "Air Force Leaders Discuss Allied Force Lessons Learned." Press Release. Air Force Doctrine Center, Department of the Air Force, Washington, D. C., December 21, 1999, at http://www.defense-aerospace.com/data/communiques/archives/1999Dec/data/1999Dec1344.

Micheletti, Eric. *Special Forces: War on Terrorism in Afghanistan.* Translated by Cyril Lombardini. Paris: Histoire & Collections, 2004.

Milbank, Dana, and Bradley Graham. "Bush Revises Views on 'Combat' in Iraq." *Washington Post,* August 19, 2003, A15.

Miles, Donna. "Terrorists Can't Compete With Provincial Reconstruction Teams." American Forces Press Service, Washington, D.C., April 21, 2004.

Moore, Robin. *The Hunt for Bin Laden.* New York: Random House, 2003.

MOWAG. "Piranha III Information Sheet." MOWAG AG, Unterseestrasse 65, 8280 Kreuzlingen, Switzerland, undated, received 2005.

Muradian, Vago, and Ratnam Gopal. "U.S. Services Brace For Cuts." *Defense News,* October 17, 2005, 1.

Muradian, Vago, and Sean Naylor. "Pentagon Considers End to Stryker." *Army Times,* August 23, 2002, 14.

Mylroie, Laurie. "Who is Ramzi Yousef? And Why It Matters." *The National Interest,* Winter 1995/1996, 21–27.

NATO. "Operation Deliberate Force." Fact sheet. Regional Headquarters, Allied Forces Southern Europe, December 16, 2002.

Naylor, Sean D. "It's Stryker Against M113A3—Again." *Army Times,* September 23, 2002, 13.

———. "Overhauling the US Army," *Defense News,* September 29, 2003, 14.

———. "Not a Good Day to Die." *Armed Forces Journal,* March 2005, 30–35.

NDP. "Assessment of the May 1997 Quadrennial Defense Review." Washington, D.C.: The National Defense Panel, 1998. Also published in *Joint Force Quarterly,* Summer 1998.

Newman, Richard J. "The Army Ponders Its Future." *Air Force Magazine,* November 2000, http://www.afa.org/magazine/Nov2000/1100army.html (accessed December 7, 2000).

NGA. *Geospatial Intelligence Basic Doctrine.* Bethesda, MD: National Geospatial Intelligence Agency, 2004.

Noah, Timothy. "The Rumsfeld Death Watch." *Slate* (online) posted August 7, 2001.

Nolin, Robert. "New Army to Be Faster, More Mobile, Chief of Staff Tells Broward Convention." *Fort Lauderdale Sun-Sentinel,* March 2, 2001, 1.

O'Hanlon, Michael E. "Beware the RMA'nia!" Paper presented at the National Defense University, September 9, 1998.

———. "The Need to Increase the Size of the Deployable Army." *Parameters,* Autumn 2004, 4–17.

Oliver, David R., and Arthur L. Money. Unmanned Aerial Vehicles Roadmap 2000–2025, Office of the Secretary of Defense, Washington, D.C., April 6, 2001.

O'Malley, Stephen. "Persian Gulf Security: Possible Airfield Deployment Options." Santa Monica, CA: RAND Corporation, September 2001.

O'Rourke, Ronald. "Defense Transformation: Background and Oversight Issues for Congress." Congressional Research Service Report No. RL32238, Library of Congress, February 17, 2006.

O'Sullivan, Arieth. "Stryker APC Deal Tabled for Two Years." *Jerusalem Post,* July 20, 2004, 4.

Pape, Robert A. *Bombing to Win: Air Power and Coercion in War.* Ithaca, NY: Cornell University Press, 1996.

Peterson, Scott. "US Mulls Air Strategies In Iraq." *Christian Science Monitor,* January 30, 2003, 1.

Pincus, Walter, and Dan Morgan. "Congress Supports Doubling Special Operations Funding." *Washington Post,* June 5, 2003, 31.

Plummer, Anne. "Army's New Plan for FCS Supported by Retired Gen. Welch, Adm. Cebrowsk." *Inside The Army,* August 9, 2004, 1.

Powell, Colin (General USA and Chairman JCS 1989–1993). *National Military Strategy of the United States.* Washington, D.C.: U.S. Government Printing Office, 1992, 19.

Priest, Dana. "Army's Apache Helicopter Rendered Impotent in Kosovo." *Washington Post,* December 29, 1999, A01.

Priestley, Stephen. "'All In the Family'—Canada's LAV III ISC and the US Army's Stryker ICV." Canadian Forces Vehicles Web site, http://www.sfu.ca/casr/101-veherp3.htm (accessed March 12, 2005).

Puzzuoli, Albert. "Advanced Planning Briefing to Industry." U.S. DoD, PEO Ground Combat Systems, Soldier PEO Systems, Fort Belvoir, VA, October 31, 2003.

Ratnesar, Romesh. "The Ground War: Into The Fray." *Time,* October 29, 2001, 42–43.

Rayermann, Patrick (Colonel USA). "Exploiting Commercial SATCOM: A Better Way." *Parameters,* Winter 2003–2004, 54–66.

Reimer, Dennis J. (General USA; US Army Chief of Staff, 1995–1999). *Army Vision 2010.* Washington, D.C.: Office of the Chief of Staff of the Army, undated, released November 1996.

———. "The Army After Next: Knowledge, Speed and Power." *Military Review,* May–June 1999, 10–14.

Reuters. "US Commandos Set to Seize Bin Laden." *Reuters Limited,* April 13, 1999.

Rice, Condoleezza (U.S. National Security Advisor, 2001–2005; Secretary of State, 2005–2008). "Promoting the National Interest." *Foreign Affairs,* January/February 2000, 52–54.

Richardson, William R. (General USA) "FM 100-5: The AirLand Battle in 1986." *Military Review,* originally written in 1986, republished in the issue of January–February 1997, 46–51.

Ricks, Thomas E. "Desert Caution." *Washington Post,* January 28, 2003, C01.

———. "Air Force's Roche Picked To Head Army." *Washington Post,* May 2, 2003, 1.

Rider, Timothy. "Web of Integrated Command." *Army Communicator,* Fall 2003, 6–10.

Riggins, James, and David E. Snodgrass. "Halt Phase Plus Strategic Preclusion: Joint Solution for a Joint Problem." *Parameters,* Autumn 1999, 70–85.

Risen, James. "Threats and Responses: Hunt for Suspects; C.I.A. is Reported to Kill A Leader of Qaeda in Yemen." *New York Times,* November 5, 2002, 1.

Rising, David. "4th Infantry Sees First Combat Action since Vietnam." *Killeen Daily Herald* (Killeen, Texas), April 16, 2003.

Robinson, Linda. *Masters of Chaos.* New York: Public Affairs, 2004, 194–96.

Rogers, Clifford J., ed. *The Military Revolution Debate.* Boulder, CO: Westview Press, 1995.

Rumsfeld, Donald H. (White House Chief of Staff, 1974–1975; Secretary of Defense, 1975–1977 and 2001–2008), and Tommy R. Franks. "Summary of Lessons Learned." Prepared Testimony. Senate Armed Services Committee, July 9, 2003.

Rumsfeld, Donald H., and General Richard B. Myers, USAF, chairman, Joint Chiefs of Staff. "DoD News Briefing—Secretary Rumsfeld and Gen. Myers." News Transcript. Washington, D.C.: U.S. Department of Defense, June 30, 2003.

———. "After Action Report—Lessons Learned." Unclassified Briefing, undated, probably late 2003.

Rutt, John A. (Lieutenant Colonel USA). "From Tactical to Installational, the 63rd Signal Battalion in OEF." *Army Communicator,* Fall 2003, 10–14.

Ryan, Michael (Lieutenant General USAF), commander Allied Air Force Southern Europe. Briefing presented to the February 1996 Corona South meeting, Orlando, FL.

Sanderson, Jeffery R. (Lieutenant Colonel USA). "Transformation: A Commander's Perspective." *Armor,* Journal of the U.S. Army Armor School, January–February 2005.

Sapa-AP. "Expect a powerful thrust to Baghad—experts." *Independent Online,* February 18, 2003, http://www.iol.co.za/index.php (accessed September 30, 2004).

Scarborough, Rowan. "Special Operations Assigned Major Role." *Washington Times,* September 25, 2001, 1.

———. "US Forces Outran Water, MREs In Rush To Baghdad." *Washington Times,* April 25, 2003, 12.

———. "US Rushed Post-Saddam Planning." *Washington Times,* September 3, 2003, 1.

———. *Rumsfeld's War.* Washington, D.C.: Regency, 2004.

———. "Major Overhaul Eyed For Army." *Washington Times,* February 3, 2004, 1.

Schoomaker, Peter (General, Chief of Staff, U.S. Army 2003–2007). Testimony before the House Armed Services Committee, July 21, 2004, as reported by the Armed Forces Press Service, U.S. Department of Defense, July 29, 2004.

———. "The Army's Top Three Priorities." Memorandum for Chairman of the Joint Chiefs of Staff, October 14, 2005.

———. Interview. *Defense News,* October 18, 2005, 1.

Scully, Megan. "JFCOM Chief: Stryker Interim Armored Vehicle a 'Work In Progress.'" *Inside the Army,* September 23, 2002, 1.

———. "Misstatement Could Extend McCain Probe of FCS Deal." *The Hill* (Washington, D.C.), http://www.hillnews.com/thehill/export/TheHill/Business/032305.html (accessed April 1, 2005).

Searcey, Dionne. "Thousands from 4th Division Deployed to Gulf." *Killeen Daily Herald* (Killeen, Texas), March 28, 2003, 1.

———. "4th Infantry Members Yet to See Battle." *Killeen Daily Herald* (Killeen, Texas), April 13, 2003, 1.

Seib, Gerald F. "Tough Words On Iraq War Faced Scorn But Ring True." *Wall Street Journal,* July 16, 2003, A21.

Shachtman, Noah. "GAO Says Army on Road to Ruin," *Wired,* April 5, 2004, http://www.wired.com/news/technology/0,1282,62931,00.html (accessed October 30, 2004).

Sherman, Jason. "Coming Attraction: At Play in the Fields of the Future with the Army's Objective Force." *Armed Forces Journal International,* July 2000, 40–44.

Sherman, Jason. "Facing a New Reality." *Armed Forces Journal,* December 2004, 20–25.

Shinseki, Eric K. (General USA and Chief of Staff U.S. Army 1999–2003). "Address to the Eisenhower Luncheon, 45th Annual meeting of the Association of the Untied States Army," October 12, 1999.

Smith, Jeremy D. (Captain USA). "Proposed Unit of Action/Unit of Employment, X Doctrinal Concept of Support." *Quartermaster Professional Bulletin,* Autumn 2004.

Smucker, Philip. "How Bin Laden Got Away." *Christian Science Monitor,* March 4, 2002, 1, 15–17.

Squitieri, Tom. "Doubts Linger On Whether Stryker Is Up To Job In Iraq." *USA Today,* September 30, 2003, 17.

Steele, Dennis. "Countdown to the Next Century." *Army,* November 1996, 16–22.

———. "The Interim Armored Vehicle." *Army,* January 2001, 29–32.

Steinbrenner, John D. "Statement To The House Committee On National Security." Washington, D.C.: Foreign Policy Studies, The Brookings Institution, June 6, 1996.

Story, William C., Jr. "Ballistic Missiles, Cruise Missiles, and Land-Based Air Power." School of Advanced Airpower Studies, Air University, Maxwell Air Force Base, AL, June 1994.

Strohm, Chris. "Shinseki Says More Money Will Be Added for Transformation." *Inside the Army,* March 5, 2001, 13.

Stump, Chris (Specialist USA). "Civil Affairs Teams Work for Afghanistan's Future." American Forces Press Service, December 12, 2004.

Swain, Richard M. (Colonel ret. USA). *Lucky War: The Third Army in the Desert.* Fort Leavenworth, KS: USCGSC Press, 1997.

TACOM AMSTA-LC-CLD Solicitation DAAE07-00-R-M032. U.S. Army Tank-Automotive and Armaments Command, Warren, MI, December 30, 1999.

Talbot, David. "How Technology Failed in Iraq." *MIT Technology Review,* November 2004, 5, 36–44.

Taylor, Sean. "Abrams Upgrades." *Army Times,* March 14, 2005, 8–9.

Tiboni, Frank. "U.S. Army Study: Stryker Outpaces M113." *DefenseNews.com,* January 31, 2003 (accessed February 1, 2003.

———. "US Army To Get Top-Down Review To Achieve Objective Force By 2010." *Defense News,* July 10, 2003, 1.

———. "Army Speeds Up Some Future Combat Technology." *FCW.com,* August 2, 2004, http://www.fcw.com/fcw/articles/2004/0802/tec-fcs-08-02 (accessed September 21, 2004).

Tiron, Roxana. "Stryker Not Up To Speed in Some Areas, Soldiers Claim." *National Defense,* October 2002, 18.

Toomey, Christopher J. "Army Digitization: Making it Ready for Prime Time." *Parameters,* Winter 2003–2004, 40–53.

Towell, Pat. "Rumsfeld Defense Plan on Track as Senate Clears Spending Bill." *Congressional Quarterly Weekly,* October 19, 2002, 2756.

TRADOC Pam 525-5. *Force XXI Operations.* Fort Monroe, VA: U.S. Army Training and Doctrine Command, August 1994.

———. "Future Force Structure." Fact Sheet. Fort Monroe, VA: U.S. Army Training and Doctrine Command, February 2004.

———. "Army Modular Force." Briefing. Fort Monroe, VA: U.S. Army Training and Doctrine Command, February 25, 2005.

TRADOC Pam 525-3-0. *The Army Future Force Capstone Concept 2015–2024,* April 2005.

Triggs, Marcia. "Stryker Gets New Armor." Army News Service, March 9, 2002.

Trimble, Stephen. "2008 Deployment Still Set For Objective Force, White Says." *Aerospace Daily,* October 22, 2002, 1.

Twohig, John J., et al. "Structuring Division XXI." *Military Review,* May–June 1998, 2–6.

Ullman, Harlan K., and James P. Wade et al. *Shock and Awe: Achieving Rapid Dominance.* Washington, D.C.: National Defense University Press, 1996.

Unterseher, Lutz. "Wheels or Tracks? On the 'Lightness' of Military Expeditions." Commonwealth Institute, July 2000, http://www.comw.org/pda/0007wheels.html (accessed August 25, 2000).

USAF. *Global Power, Global Reach.* U.S. Air Force White Paper. Washington, D.C.: Department of the Air Force, June 1990.

———. *Reaching Globally, Reaching Powerfully: The United States Air Force in the Gulf War.* Washington, D.C.: Secretary's Staff Group, Department of the Air Force, September 1991.

———. "Project 2025 Final Report to the Chief of Staff, US Air Force." Washington, D.C.: Department of the Air Force, June 17, 1996. The report was prepared by the Air University at Maxwell AFB, AL.

———. *Basic Air Force Doctrine.* Washington, D.C.: Department of the Air Force, 1997, 1.

———. *US Air Force Key Issues Book.* Washington, D.C.: Department of the Air Force, 1997.

———. *United States Air Force Posture Statement FY 1998.* Washington, D.C.: Department of the Air Force, 1998.

———. *United States Air Force Posture Statement FY 2001.* Washington, D.C.: Department of the Air Force, 2000.

———. *United States Air Force Posture Statement 2005.* Washington, D.C.: Department of the Air Force, 2004.

———. Briefing, Air and Space Power Course, U.S. Air War College, Maxwell Air Force Base, AL, undated, obtained 2005.

U.S. Congress. "US Military Operations in Somalia." Hearings before the U.S. Senate Committee on Armed Services, Senate Hearing 103-846, May 12, 1994.

USASOC. *Weapon of Choice: ARSOF in Afghanistan.* Fort Leavenworth, KS: Combat Studies Institute, written by U.S. Army Special Operations Command, Fort Bragg, NC, 2005.

USIS. "Clinton Announces Anti-Terrorist Strikes" (transcript). Washington, D.C.: United States Information Service, August 20, 1998.

Van Creveld, Martin, et al. *Command in War.* Cambridge: Harvard University Press, 1987.

Venzke, Ben, and Aimee Ibrahim. *al-Qaeda's Advice for Mujahideen in Iraq: Lessons Learned in Afghanistan.* Vol. 1.0. Alexandria VA: IntelCenter (private firm), April 14, 2003.

Verton, Daniel. "Benefits of Army Digitization Program Uncertain." *Federal Computer Week,* August 2, 1999, http://www.anu.edu.au/mail-archives/link/link9908/0046.html (accessed May 21, 2003).

Vick, Alan, et al. *Enhancing Air Power's Contribution Against Light Infantry Targets.* Santa Monica, CA: RAND Corp., 1996.

Wamble, Stacy. "Brigade Combat Team Under Construction at Fort Knox." Press Release. Fort Knox, KY: Fort Knox Public Affairs Office, January 5, 2000.

Watkins, Charlotte. *Provincial Reconstruction Teams (PRTs).* Oxford Brookes University (UK), September 30, 2003.

Watson, Brian G. *Reshaping the Expeditionary Army to Win Decisively.* Carlisle, PA: Strategic Studies Institute, U.S. Amy War College, August 2005.

Weigley, Russell F. *The American Way of War.* Bloomington, IN: Indiana University Press, 1973.

Weiner, Tim. "An Army Program to Build a High-Tech Force Hits Cost Snags." *New York Times,* March 28, 2005, http://www.nytimes.com/2005/03/28/politics/28weapons.html?th&emc=th (accessed April 21, 2005).

Weinraub, Bernard, with Thom Shanker. "Rumsfeld's Design for War Criticized on the Battle-field." *New York Times,* April 1, 2003, 1.

Welch, Larry D., et al. *Report of the Independent Assessment Panel for the Future Combat System.* Alexandria, VA: Institute for Defense Analyses, 2003.

White House. "Making America More Secure by Transforming Our Military." Fact Sheet. Washington, D.C.: Office of the Press Secretary, August 16, 2004.

Wickham, John A. (General USA, Army Chief of Staff 1983–1987). "White Paper." *Army Times,* May 7, 1984, 10–12.

Will, George F. "The Hour of Air Power." *Newsweek,* March 31, 2003, 66.

Williams, Daniel. "NATO Missiles Hit Chinese Embassy." *Washington Post,* May 8, 1999, 1.

Winograd, Erin Q. "Gingrich Tells Top DOD Officials Army's Stryker Shouldn't Be Fielded." *Inside The Army,* September 30, 2002, 1.

———. "Army Executes PR Gambit to Bolster Stryker Against Critics." *Inside The Army,* October 21, 2002, 1.

———. "Army, OSD Agree On Six Stryker BCTs; Last Two Will Be More Capable." *Inside The Army,* November 25, 2002, 1.

———. "Rep. Saxton Continues To Question Army Plans for Stryker Vehicles." *Inside The Army,* March 24, 2003, 1.

Winton, Harold R. "Partnership and Tension: The Army and the Air Force between Vietnam and Desert Shield." *Parameters,* Spring 1996, 100–119.

Wong, Bruce (Colonel USAF). "Preparing for QDR 2001." U.S. Air Force, http://www.mors.org/QDR2001/WGBriefings/af_MORSBrief/tsld027.htm (accessed August 25, 2000).

Wood, David. "Surprise at Saddam's Tactics May Be Rooted in US Myopia." Newhouse News Service, March 28, 2003, Newhouse.com (accessed May 20, 2003).

Woodward, Bob, and Dan Balz. "Bush Awaits History's Judgment." *Washington Post,* February 3, 2002, 1.

Woodward, Robert. *Bush's War.* New York: Simon & Schuster, 2002.

Woodward, Robert. *Plan of Attack.* New York: Simon & Schuster, 2004.

INDEX

ABOUT THE AUTHOR

THOMAS K. ADAMS is a national security consultant based in the Washington, D.C. area. He is the author of US Special Operations: The Challenge of Unconventional Warfare (1998) and numerous articles dealing with military and national security subjects. He is a veteran of thirty-four years military service, principally in intelligence and special operations at tactical, operational, and strategic levels from Vietnam to Bosnia. Later, as a civilian, he assisted and supported counterterrorist investigations worldwide.